Progressivism in America

Progressivism in America

Past, Present, and Future

Edited By

DAVID B. WOOLNER

and

JOHN M. THOMPSON

OXFORD
UNIVERSITY PRESS

OXFORD
UNIVERSITY PRESS

Oxford University Press is a department of the University of
Oxford. It furthers the University's objective of excellence in research,
scholarship, and education by publishing worldwide.

Oxford   New York
Auckland   Cape Town   Dar es Salaam   Hong Kong   Karachi
Kuala Lumpur   Madrid   Melbourne   Mexico City   Nairobi
New Delhi   Shanghai   Taipei   Toronto

With offices in
Argentina   Austria   Brazil   Chile   Czech Republic   France   Greece
Guatemala   Hungary   Italy   Japan   Poland   Portugal   Singapore
South Korea   Switzerland   Thailand   Turkey   Ukraine   Vietnam

Oxford is a registered trademark of Oxford University Press
in the UK and certain other countries.

Published in the United States of America by
Oxford University Press
198 Madison Avenue, New York, NY 10016

Library of Congress Cataloging-in-Publication Data
Progressivism in America : past, present and future / edited by David B. Woolner and John M. Thompson.
pages cm
Includes bibliographical references and index.
ISBN 978–0–19–023141–5 (alk. paper)
1. Progressivism (United States politics)   2. Liberalism—United States—History.   3. United
States—Politics and government—History.   I. Woolner, David B., 1955–   II. Thompson, John M., 1977–
JK271.P76 2016
320.51'30973—dc23
2015016948

1 3 5 7 9 8 6 4 2
Printed in the United States of America
on acid-free paper

CONTENTS

Preface and Acknowledgments   vii

Contributors   xi

Introduction   xvii
   DAVID B. WOOLNER AND JOHN M. THOMPSON

PART ONE   ANTECEDENTS

1. TR, Wilson, and the Origins of the Progressive Tradition   3
   CHARLES POSTEL

2. Franklin Roosevelt and the Progressive Tradition   17
   ALAN BRINKLEY AND DAVID B. WOOLNER

3. From the Politics of Hope to the Politics of Frustration: FDR's Legacy
   and the Quandaries of Postwar Liberalism   31
   KEVIN MATTSON

4. Progressive Politics and the Rise of the Modern Right   47
   JOHN M. THOMPSON

PART TWO   PROGRESSIVE POLITICS TODAY

5. Progressivism and Government: Building the Case for
   a Dignified and Decent Life for All   65
   JEFF MADRICK

6. Financial Reform after the 2008 Crisis   81
   MICHAEL KONCZAL

7. Reopening the American Political System   95
   MARK SCHMITT

8. Insecurity, Austerity, and the American Social Contract   109
   JACOB S. HACKER

9. Labor, Race, Gender, and Poverty in America   129
   DORIAN T. WARREN

10. Crafting a Progressive Foreign Policy in Today's World   141
    ROSA BROOKS

11. The Progressive Tradition and the Problem of Global Warming   165
    MARK LYTLE

12. Bringing Human Rights and Women's Rights Home:
    From the Roosevelt Era to the Present   179
    ELLEN CHESLER

PART THREE   CRITIQUES

13. Barack Obama: Progressive?   199
    JONATHAN ALTER

14. Really Existing Progressivism: Its Strengths and Weaknesses
    in America   209
    CHRISTOPHER CALDWELL

PART FOUR   THE FUTURE OF PROGRESSIVE POLITICS

15. A Progressive Agenda for the Twenty-first Century   215
    JOSEPH E. STIGLITZ

16. The Way Forward: Progressive Problems, Progressive Hopes   233
    E. J. DIONNE JR. AND ELIZABETH THOM

Index   245

PREFACE AND ACKNOWLEDGMENTS

The historic election of Barack Obama in 2008, at the height of the world economic crisis that plunged the United States into what we now call the Great Recession, and the clear socioeconomic parallels with the election of Franklin Roosevelt at the peak of the Great Depression in 1932, have raised a number of fundamental questions about America's past, present, and future. This is especially true among progressives, many of whom see the parallels between the events of the 1920s and 1930s and the collapse of the global economic system in 2008 as confirmation that the United States is in dire need of serious structural reform. Is it time for the United States to turn away from the free market/antigovernment sentiment that has held the upper hand in political debates since the early 1980s? Was the election that swept President Obama and the Democrats into power in 2008 the harbinger of a shift toward a more expansive view of government among the American public? Or, as the rise of the Tea Party and the midterm elections of 2010 and 2014 seem to indicate, were the events of 2008 simply an aberration—a short-term reaction to the economic collapse that occurred in the final months of the Bush administration? What policies should be put in place to help us return to an era of prosperity? And how should we meet the many other challenges we face—such as climate change—both at home and abroad?

In an effort to answer these questions, the Franklin and Eleanor Roosevelt Institute joined forces with the Clinton Institute for American Studies at University College Dublin to host a major international conference that would bring together a distinguished group of historians, economists, political scientists, policy makers, and journalists. Moreover, given the parallels between the socioeconomic factors that gave rise to the onset of the Great Depression and Great Recession—including that vast disparity in wealth evident in both crises—the organizers of the conference were especially interested in exploring how best to fashion a progressive response to the current crisis.

The conference, which shares the same title as this book, took place over a fascinating two days at the Clinton Institute in November 2013. Public intellectuals such as the Nobel Prize–winning economist, Joseph Stiglitz, and leading political commentators such as Jonathan Alter and E. J. Dionne spoke at the proceedings. In addition, thanks to the conference's association with the Center for Civic Engagement at Bard College, a number of distinguished international observers and participants traveled from as far away as Palestine and Kyrgyzstan in order to contribute. All agreed that the important work that went into the conference should be expanded upon, refined, and shared with the broader public. The result is this unique publication, which not only explores how current policy makers might formulate a progressive response to the onset of the Great Recession but also tries to place the current crisis in context by looking not only at the past but also the future.

The organization of an undertaking such as this could not have taken place without the steadfast support of a number of individuals and organizations. Much of the inspiration for the conference and the resulting book stems from the initiative of two colleagues at the Roosevelt Institute, Senior Fellows Mark Schmitt (now Director of Political Reform at the New America Foundation), and Ellen Chesler, the Director of the Roosevelt Institute's Women and Girls Rising Initiative. Their early support and interest helped keep this idea alive at its earliest stages. Inspiration—and a good deal of practical advice—also came from numerous conversations with Bard College professors Richard Aldous and Mark Lytle, whose friendship, astute analysis, and on-the-ground experience at University College Dublin proved invaluable. And none of this would have been possible without the critical support of Liam Kennedy, the Director of the Clinton Institute, who first proposed the idea of a joint Roosevelt-Clinton endeavor at a chance meeting with one of the editors of this volume some years ago, and enthusiastically embraced the conference when it was first proposed in the summer of 2012. The editors owe an equally important debt of gratitude to Felicia Wong, the president of the Roosevelt Institute, who threw the full weight of the institute and its Four Freedoms Center behind the project. Another critical early endorsement came from Roosevelt Institute Board Chair Anna Eleanor Roosevelt, who was delighted to see her grandparents' legacy brought forward in this fashion, as well as President William Jefferson Clinton, who endorsed our efforts and agreed to open the event with a thoughtful video talk that inspired considerable discussion and contemplation over the course of the proceedings.

Our sincere and heartfelt thanks also go out all of the participants in the conference and book, who graciously accepted our invitation to share their expertise and whose biographies are listed in the "Contributors" section below, as well as to the many commentators and chairs, who added an important intellectual underpinning to the proceedings in Dublin. Here, we wish to extend special thanks to Daniel Geary of Trinity College Dublin, Roosevelt Institute Fellow Sabeel Rahman, and the well-known Irish radio personality, Áine Lawlor, whose penetrating questions for the *Washington Post*'s E. J. Dionne and the *Weekly Standard*'s Christopher Caldwell about the future of progressive and conservative politics in the United States brought the conference to a fitting close. We also wish to thank Jonathan Becker, director of the Center for Civic Engagement at Bard College. His support, among other things, facilitated the expansion of the conference to include an international dimension through the participation of Munther Dajani, professor of political science and area studies at Al Quds University in Jerusalem; Alexander Kubyshkin and Valery Monakhov, professor of American studies and dean of the Smolny School of Arts and Sciences in St. Petersburg, respectively; and Begaiym Esenkulova, assistant professor of law at American University in Central Asia. Dr. Becker was skillfully assisted in this effort by the Center for Civic Engagement's Lisa Whalen.

In keeping with the deep literary and intellectual traditions of the people of Ireland, we are most grateful to Fintan O'Toole, literary editor of the *Irish Times* and visiting lecturer in Irish letters at Princeton University, for providing the conference with his incisive and often witty observations about the impact of the 2008 economic crisis on Ireland and the implications for Europe and the wider world.

For the vital logistical and other support that went into organizing the Dublin conference we wish to thanks the staff of the Clinton Institute, especially the manager, Catherine Carey; for the support of UCD's School of History and Archives we wish to thank Associate Professor Maurice Bric; and for their support of the initiatives of the Roosevelt Institute's Four Freedoms Center we would like to thank David Douglas and the Wallace Genetic Foundation. For the much needed administrative assistance that went into the publication of this book we wish to thank Andrew Dominello and Stefano Imbert at Oxford University Press; and last but certainly not least, the editors wish to thank Dana Bliss, senior editor of social work at Oxford, whose support, editorial advice, and patience are most sincerely appreciated.

David Woolner & John Thompson
Hyde Park & Dublin

CONTRIBUTORS

Jonathan Alter is an award-winning author, reporter, columnist, and television analyst. Since 2011 Alter has written for *Bloomberg View*, a worldwide commentary site under the aegis of Bloomberg News. He spent twenty-eight years at *Newsweek*, where he was a longtime senior editor and columnist. He has also written for the *New York Times*, the *Washington Post*, the *Washington Monthly*, the *Atlantic*, *Vanity Fair*, the *New Republic*, and other publications. He is the author of *The Promise: President Obama, Year One*, (New York: Simon & Schuster, 2010) and *The Defining Moment: FDR's Hundred Days and the Triumph of Hope* (New York: Simon & Schuster, 2006).

Alan Brinkley is Allan Nevins Professor of History at Columbia University. A specialist in the history of twentieth-century America, his publications include *Franklin Delano Roosevelt* (New York: Oxford University Press 2009), *Liberalism and Its Discontents* (New York: Harvard University Press, 1998), and *The End of Reform: New Deal Liberalism in Recession and War* (New York: Vintage Books, 1995).

Rosa Brooks is a professor at the Georgetown University Law Center where she teaches courses on international law, national security, and constitutional law. She is a columnist and contributing editor for *Foreign Policy* and serves as a senior fellow at the New America Foundation. From 2009–2011 she served as counselor to Under Secretary of Defense for Policy Michele Flournoy. During her tenure at the Department of Defense, Brooks founded the Office for Rule of Law and International Humanitarian Policy. She has also served as a senior advisor at the US Department of State, a consultant for Human Rights Watch, a fellow at the Carr Center at Harvard's Kennedy School of Government, and as a board member of Amnesty International USA. She is the coauthor of *Can Might Make Rights? The Rule of Law After Military Interventions* (New York: Cambridge University Press, 2006) and has written numerous scholarly articles on international law, failed states, postconflict reconstruction, human rights, terrorism, and the law of war.

Christopher Caldwell is a senior editor at the *Weekly Standard* and the author of *Reflections on the Revolution in Europe* (New York: Doubleday, 2009). His essays and reviews appear in many US and European publications.

Ellen Chesler is a senior fellow at the Roosevelt Institute, where she directs the Women and Girls Rising program. She is author of *Woman of Valor: Margaret Sanger and the Birth Control Movement in America* (New York: Simon & Schuster, 1992), which remains in print in a new paperback edition released in 2007. She is coeditor with Wendy Chavkin, MD, MPH of *Where Human Rights Begin* (New Brunswick: Rutgers Univesity Press, 2009), a volume of essays that emerged from a fellowship program they directed for the Open Society Foundation. Chesler has also written extensively for academic and public policy anthologies, journals, newspapers, magazines, and blogs. Over her forty-year career, she has held positions in government (chief of staff to New York City Council President Carol Bellamy, 1978–1984); philanthropy (Open Society Foundation, 1997–2006, and the Twentieth Century Fund, 1992–1997); and academia (Hunter College of the City University of New York, 2007–2010, and Barnard College, 1988–1989, 1992–1993) and is widely respected for both the intellectual and practical perspectives she brings to her work. She is currently a member of the advisory committee of the Women's Rights Division of Human Rights Watch and served for many years on the board of the Planned Parenthood Federation of America and as chair of the board of the International Women's Health Coalition. She has twice been a member of the US delegation to the UN Commission on the Status of Women. She holds a BA from Vassar College and a PhD with distinction in history from Columbia University.

E. J. Dionne Jr., is a senior fellow at the Brookings Institution, a syndicated columnist for the *Washington Post*, and university professor in the Foundations of Democracy and Culture program at Georgetown University. A nationally known and respected commentator on politics, Dionne appears weekly on National Public Radio and regularly on MSNBC. He has also appeared on *News Hour with Jim Lehrer* and other PBS programs. He is chair of the editorial committee of the journal *Democracy* and is the author of the award-winning *Why Americans Hate Politics* (New York: Touchstone Books, 1991). He is the author and editor or coeditor of several other books and volumes, including *They Only Look Dead: Why Progressives Will Dominate the Next Political Era* (New York: Touchstone, 1996) and *Our Divided Political Heart: The Battle for the American Idea in an Age of Discontent* (New York: Bloomsbury, 2012).

Jacob S. Hacker is Stanley Resor Professor of Political Science and director of the Institution for Social and Policy Studies at Yale University. An expert on economic inequality and contemporary governance, he is a frequent commentator on public policy and civic affairs, a regular adviser to leading policy makers in the United States and other advanced industrial societies, and the author or coauthor of five books, numerous journal articles, and a wide range of popular writings on American politics and public policy, with a focus on health and economic security. His most recent book is *Winner-Take-All Politics: How Washington Made the Rich Richer and Turned Its Back on the Middle Class* (New York: Simon & Schuster, 2011), written with Paul Pierson. With the support of the Rockefeller Foundation, he directs the Economic Security Index, a multiyear project examining economic insecurity in the United States, and he currently serves as a member of the High-Level Expert Group on the Measurement of Economic Performance and Social Progress, housed at the Organization for Economic Cooperation and Development. He recently won the Heinz Eulau Prize of the American Political Science Association for his 2013 article "The Insecure American," written with Philipp Rehm and Mark Schlesinger.

Michael Konczal is a fellow at the Roosevelt Institute, where he works on financial reform, unemployment, inequality, and a progressive vision of the economy. His blog, Rortybomb.com, was named one of the "25 Best Financial Blogs" by *Time Magazine*. His writing has appeared in *Boston Review, American Prospect, Washington Monthly, The Nation*, Slate.com, and *Dissent*, and he's appeared on *PBS NewsHour*, MSNBC's *Rachel Maddow Show*, CNN, Marketplace, and other media outlets.

Mark Lytle is Lyford Paterson Edwards and Helen Gray Edwards Professor of Historical Studies at Bard College, and the Mary Ball Washington Professor of American History, University College Dublin (2000, 2004). He is the author of *The Gentle Subversive: Rachel Carson, Silent Spring and the Rise of the Environmental Movement* (New York: Oxford University Press, 2007); *America's Uncivil Wars: The Sixties Era from Elvis to the Fall of Richard Nixon* (New York: Oxford University Press, 2006); and *The Origins of the Iranian-American Alliance, 1941–1953* (New York: Holmes and Meier, 1987).

Jeff Madrick is director of the Bernard L. Schwartz Rediscovering Government Initiative at the Century Foundation, a regular contributor to the *New York Review of Books* and a former economics columnist for the *New York Times*. He is editor of the magazine *Challenge* and visiting professor of humanities at Cooper Union in New York City. He is the author of *The Case For Big Government* (Princeton: Princeton University Press, 2008), which won a nonfiction award from Pen America, and *Age of Greed, The Triumph of Finance and the Decline of America, 1970 to the Present* (New York: Alfred A. Knopf, 2011). His latest book is *Seven Bad Ideas: How Mainstream Economists Damaged America and the World.* (New York: Alfred A. Knopf, 2014) He has also written for the *Washington Post, Los Angeles Times, Institutional Investor, The Nation, American Prospect*, the *Boston Globe, Newsday*, the *Boston Review of Books*, and the business, op-ed, and Sunday magazine sections of the *New York Times*.

Kevin Mattson is Connor Study Professor of Contemporary History at Ohio University and serves as a faculty associate of the Contemporary History Institute. His work explores the broad intersections between ideas and politics in 20th-century America. He is author of *When America was Great: The Fighting Faith of Post-War Liberalism in America* (New York: Routledge, 2004), and *"What the Heck Are You Up To, Mr. President?": Jimmy Carter, America's Malaise and the Speech that Should Have Changed the Country* (New York: Bloomsbury, 2009).

Charles Postel is an associate professor of history at San Francisco State University. He has also taught at California State University, Sacramento, the University of California, Berkeley, and Heidelberg University. A historian of American political thought, he is the author of *The Populist Vision* (New York: Oxford University Press, 2007), a history of the original Populist movement of the 1890s. *The Populist Vision* received the Bancroft Prize in History and the Frederick Jackson Turner Award from the Organization of American Historians. His present book project is a new interpretative work on the post–Civil War reform movements that culminated in the Progressive Era. He is also researching conservatism and the historical origins of the Tea Party movement. Charles Postel earned both his BA in history (1995) and his PhD in history (2002) from the University of California, Berkeley.

Mark Schmitt is the Director of Political Reform at the New America Foundation, a former Senior Fellow at the Roosevelt Institute and a leading progressive writer and organizational leader, with a deep understanding of the importance of ideas in the political process. Most recently he was executive editor of *American Prospect*, a position he held since 2008. He guided the *Prospect* during a period when it won several awards, including the Utne Reader award for best political magazine, for its coverage of the policy and political battles of the first two years of the Obama administration. He was policy director to former Senator Bill Bradley in the 1990s and a senior advisor on Bradley's 2000 presidential campaign. Before joining the *Prospect,* he was a senior fellow at the New America Foundation.

Joseph Stiglitz is Senior Fellow and Chief Economist at the Roosevelt Institute, Professor at Columbia University, and University Professor at Columbia University. In 2001, he won the Nobel Prize in economics and he was a lead author of the 1995 Report of the Intergovernmental Panel on Climate Change, which shared the 2007 Nobel Peace Prize. During the Clinton Administration, he served as a member of the Council of Economic Advisers from 1993–1995 and as its chairman from 1995–1997. He has also served as chief economist and senior vice president of the World Bank from 1997–2000. He is the author of numerous books, including *Globalization and Its Discontents* (New York: W. W. Norton, 2003), *The Three Trillion Dollar War: The True Cost of the Iraq Conflict* (with Linda Bilmes) (New York: W. W. Norton, 2008), *The Price of Inequality: How Today's Divided Society Endangers our*

Future (New York: W. W, Norton, 2012), and *Creating a Learning Society: A New Approach to Growth, Development, and Social Progress* (with Bruce C. Greenwald), (New York: Columbia University Press. 2014).

Elizabeth Thom is a Senior Project Coordinator and Research Assistant in Governance Studies at the Brookings Institution. She received her bachelors degree from the University of Pennsylvania where she majored in Political Science and Hispanic Studies.

Dr. John M. (Jack) Thompson is Lecturer at the Clinton Institute for American Studies, University College Dublin. His most recent publication is an edited volume, with Hans Krabbenam, titled *America's Transatlantic Turn: Theodore Roosevelt and the Discovery of Europe* (New York: Palgrave Macmillan, 2012). He is a frequent commentator in Ireland on American politics and foreign policy. He earned his MA from Johns Hopkins University and his PhD from the University of Cambridge.

Dorian T. Warren is Associate Professor at the School of International and Public Affairs and at the Institute for Research in African American Studies at Columbia University. He is also Co-Director of the Columbia University Program on Labor Law and Policy, a fellow at the Roosevelt Institute, and an MSNBC Contributor. His research interests include labor organizing and politics, race and ethnic politics, urban politics and policy, American political development, community organizing, public policy, and social science methodology. His publications include "The Unsurprising Failure of Labor Law Reform and the Turn to Administrative Action," in the Russell Sage Foundation Project entitled *Reaching for a New Deal: President Obama's Agenda and the Dynamics of U.S. Politics* (New York: Russell Sage, 2010), "The American Labor Movement in the Age of Obama: The Challenges and Opportunities of a Racialized Political Economy" in *Perspectives on Politics* (September, 2010), and *Race and American Political Development* (coeditor with Joe Lowndes and Julie Novkov), (New Brunswick: Routledge, 2008).

David B. Woolner is senior fellow and Resident Historian of the Franklin and Eleanor Roosevelt Institute, senior fellow of the Center for Civic Engagement at Bard College, and associate professor of history at Marist College. He is currently writing a history of FDR's last 100 days, forthcoming from Basic Books, and is coeditor with Warren Kimball and David Reynolds of *FDR's World: War, Peace, and Legacies* (New York: Palgrave Macmillan, 2008); with Henry Henderson of *FDR and the Environment* (New York:, Palgrave Macmillan, 2005); and with Richard Kurial of *FDR, the Vatican and the Roman Catholic Church in America, 1933–1945* (New York: Palgrave Macmillan, 2003); and is the editor of *The Second Quebec Conference Revisited: Waging War, Formulating Peace; Canada, Great Britain and the United States in 1944–1945* (St. Martins Press, 1998). He has been visiting associate professor of history at Bard College and remains a member of the faculty of the Bard Prison Initiative. He serves on the editorial board of the *International History Review* and has been an Archives Bi-Fellow at Churchill College, Cambridge, and held the Fulbright Distinguished Research Chair at the Roosevelt Study Center in Middelburg, the Netherlands, where he remains an honorary fellow.

INTRODUCTION

DAVID B. WOOLNER AND JOHN M. THOMPSON

One of the alleged truisms of our political culture is that America is a center-right nation. This explains many aspects of our country that differentiates us from Europe, goes the argument, whether it is our lower tax rates, weaker unions, or the fact that the United States has never produced a strong, social democratic political party. It is also the reason, we are told, that ambitious Democratic leaders, from Franklin Roosevelt to Barack Obama, have faced such vigorous opposition to their agendas. As John Meacham argued on the eve of Barack Obama's historic victory in 2008: "We are at heart a right-leaning country."[1]

Shrewd observers of American politics, however, have always been skeptical of this claim; and the last eight years, in particular, would seem to call it into question. Indeed, policies implemented since 2008 read like a wish list of progressive causes: significant health-care and financial reform, the winding down of wars in Iraq and Afghanistan, the expansion of gay rights, improved conditions for repayment of student loans and passage of equal pay legislation, and executive action on climate change and immigration reform. The future also looks promising for the American left, as demographic shifts and changing attitudes in the electorate about social issues and fiscal policy offer the prospect of an electorate that is more open to progressive ideas than at any point since the 1960s.[2]

At the same time, there are clouds on the horizon. Cuts to programs such as Medicare, Medicaid, and Social Security loom as policy makers grapple with rapidly increasing health-care costs, a large budget deficit, and an aging population. The opposition looks less open to compromise than at any point in living memory, a fact that has been highlighted by the emergence of the Tea Party and the increasingly strident calls of many Republicans to repeal central planks of the New Deal and Great Society programs. What is more, many question the depth of support for core Progressive values among the left's leading politicians, such as Barack Obama and Hillary and Bill Clinton. Their willingness to contemplate cuts to the social safety net; their failure, at times, to aggressively confront Republican intransigence; and hawkish stances on aspects of national security have prompted many Progressives to question their commitment to their cause and to and urge members from the populist wing of the party, such as Elizabeth Warren, to be more assertive.

Given this complicated state of affairs, with reason for hope and seemingly intractable problems present in equal measure, it seems like a propitious time to evaluate the state of Progressive politics in America; to ponder its historical legacy, to examine contemporary policy challenges, and to ask probing questions about its future. In recent years there has been a steady stream of books about various aspects of American politics, with much of the focus on the conservative side of the aisle.[3] Far less attention has been paid to the left side of the political spectrum. To be sure, scholars such as Eric Alterman, Kevin Mattson, and Michael Kazin have published excellent books on the evolution of the American Left; however, they overlook important aspects of the historical record, do not delve deeply into current policy debates, and offer little indication of what the future may hold.[4]

The goal of this book, then, is to provide (in one volume) the first comprehensive analysis of the Progressive tradition in American politics. To do so, the book examines the ways in which Progressive politics, broadly defined as the mainstream left in the American body politic, has been shaped by changes in the global economy over the past four decades; the ways in which the shift of the American political system rightward during the final three decades of the twentieth century affected Progressive thinking; and whether the United States is now entering a period that will favor Progressive policies.[5] To accomplish this goal, we have adopted an interdisciplinary approach, bringing together historians, economists, journalists, lawyers, and policy experts. The book is organized in a broadly but not rigidly chronological manner. The first section considers Progressive politics from a historical perspective, including the challenge posed by the evolution of the conservative movement; the second examines contemporary policy priorities and challenges; the third considers critiques of various aspects of the Progressive agenda; and the final section looks to the future.

Over the course of our analysis, three principal conclusions emerge. The first is that, contrary to conventional wisdom, the Progressive movement is as important a part of the American political legacy as are conservative strains of thinking. The contributions made by progressives during the eras of Theodore Roosevelt and Woodrow Wilson, Franklin D. Roosevelt, and Lyndon Johnson played at least as important a role in establishing the contours of American politics today as those made by conservative heroes such as Thomas Jefferson, Alexander Hamilton, James Madison, and Ronald Reagan.[6] This should allow us to dismiss any notions that conservative politics represent a strain of thinking that is more genuinely American than that offered by Progressives. The substantial and mostly positive historical record amassed by Progressive presidents and activists should also serve as a guide for today's challenges. How were previous obstacles overcome? To what extent should we demand "purity" from our leaders? At the same time, we must acknowledge that the Progressive legacy is mixed. A partial list of blemishes might include imperialism advocated and practiced by Theodore Roosevelt; the racism of Woodrow Wilson; internment of Japanese-Americans during FDR's tenure; and the ways in which the Vietnam War tainted the presidencies of JFK and LBJ.

Most historians agree that the decades following Johnson's presidency was a period of time in which conservatives were ascendant. Beginning with the presidency of Richard Nixon, Republicans occupied the White House for twenty-eight of the next forty years. More importantly, beginning with Ronald Reagan, conservatives began to chip away at the achievements of Teddy Roosevelt, Wilson, FDR, and LBJ. This included establishing lower tax rates, especially for wealthy Americans and corporations; sustained and largely successful efforts to disempower unions; the reduction of regulations and consumer protections; and, most recently, undermining access to abortion, affirmative action, and voting rights. However, the tide may be turning. Hence, the second theme of this book is that Progressives face, in many respects, the most promising environment in years. Demographic trends seem to indicate that Democratic candidates will face an easier path to the presidency than Republicans for the foreseeable future, as the Progressive base—minorities, young voters, urban whites, and women—expands while the conservative base shrinks. The domination of the Republican Party by older voters, rural whites, and corporate interests offers Progressives a chance to establish an electoral college majority as traditionally conservative states such as Virginia, Florida, and Colorado increasingly move into the toss-up or even Democratic columns. Meanwhile, changes in the national and global economy and society have lent a saliency to Progressive policies that they have not enjoyed in years. The growing numbers of Americans that lacked health insurance made passing the Affordable Care Act politically feasible, just as abuses on Wall Street in recent years made financial reform possible. Similarly, the unilateralism and incompetence that characterized the Bush administration's approach to national security provided an opportunity for Progressives to advocate and implement a more multilateral, sober, and cautious foreign policy.

Even as they look forward to a favorable political environment, however, Progressives should acknowledge the difficulties they will continue to face in the coming years. Therefore, the final theme of this volume is that for the next decade or two, American politics will, for the most part, remain gripped by partisanship and gridlock. The American political system, for instance, was designed to slow change and limit drastic reforms. This fact has been highlighted in recent years by the ability of conservatives in the Senate to cripple federal agencies and prevent presidential appointments to judgeships, while Republican appointees on the Supreme Court overturn decades of Progressive case law and some Republican governors and/or legislatures hinder implementation of the Affordable Care Act at the state level. This concerted effort to delay and even reverse Progressive policy achievements indicates the emergence of another significant roadblock: the emergence of a conservative political culture that is growing more hostile to Progressive ideas and that increasingly views compromise as tantamount to surrender. Such obstacles make it tempting for Democratic leaders to accept the dilution of Progressive policy goals in the interest of scoring political victories. And, if all of these challenges were not enough, despite the demographic trends working in favor of the American left, it is still nearly impossible to get the base of the movement to vote in off-year elections. This means that Progressives will probably have few opportunities for instituting significant reforms and that they will need to take advantage of them when they arise.

The book's main themes unfold over the course of four sections. The first section analyzes the evolution of Progressive politics during the twentieth century. In particular, this group of historians considers the legacy of Progressive political achievements, the relationship of the movement to conservatives, and the foundation that has been laid for the twenty-first century. Charles Postel kicks things off with a fresh take on the origins of Progressive politics. He argues that the progressive political agenda of figures such as Theodore Roosevelt and Woodrow Wilson was influenced, to a large degree, by the farmer-labor movements of the last few decades of the nineteenth century and that these ideas cohered in part in the face of the emergence of a distinctive set of conservative ideas. Next, Alan Brinkley and David Woolner explain how Franklin D. Roosevelt established a foundation for modern Progressive politics and in the process transformed the relationship between the American people and their government and the United States and the rest of the world in the years 1933 to 1945. In the third chapter, Kevin Mattson describes the emergence of what he calls the politics of frustration for progressives in the second half of the twentieth century. Finally, John M. Thompson contends that the Tea Party does not represent a new movement in American politics, as is often claimed, but is simply the latest episode in a decades-long effort by conservatives—one that has largely succeeded—to capture the Republican Party and to move it to the right.

Drawing upon these lessons from history, the second section of the book focuses on the Progressive movement today. The policy experts in this section take stock of the most pressing policy priorities and the prospects for progress and reform. First, Jeff Madrick takes a look at the evidence and concludes that the only way to achieve progressive policy goals such as reducing inequality and increasing growth is to accept the need for a better and more active federal government. Next, with the financial and political clout of Wall Street quickly recovering in the wake of the Great Recession, Mike Konczal breaks down the Dodd-Frank financial reform act and concludes that it has considerably more merit than many believe. In chapter 7, Mark Schmitt tackles one of the most intractable problems in America today: the dysfunctional state of our political system. Schmitt argues that, although there are no easy answers, reform is imperative if we are to address pressing problems such as inequality. Next, Jacob Hacker makes the case that only smart government policies can deal with the

mounting problem of economic insecurity for American workers and their families. In chapter 9, Dorian Warren examines the linkages between labor, race, gender, and poverty and finds that, although things appear in some ways worse than
they have in decades, there are also grounds for cautious optimism. Shifting to
an international context, Rosa Brooks analyzes America's place in the world and
concludes that the prospects for a progressive foreign policy remain relatively
bleak. In chapter 11, Mark Lytle examines the problem of climate change within
the context of the Progressive tradition and international politics and concludes
that the Obama administration has generally adopted the right balance between
acting on the scientific evidence and respecting state sovereignty. Finally, Ellen
Chesler anchors her essay in FDR's iconic Four Freedoms and sees the fight for
human rights and women's rights as an international cause in which considerable
progress has been made.

The third section takes a step back from the minutiae of policy debates to ask
more fundamental questions about the state of progressive political culture. First,
Jonathan Alter tackles a question that is bitterly debated on the left side of the political spectrum: why is Barack Obama—who clearly sympathizes with Progressives
on many issues—regarded by many as so frustratingly moderate? The answer, he
concludes, is multifaceted. The current political context—Americans still distrust
the idea of big government—is one part of the story; Obama's determination to
not give conservatives ammunition for portraying him as an angry black man also
plays a role, as does Obama's own inherent caution as a politician and leader. Next,
Christopher Caldwell asks, What do conservatives think of the left's agenda? Not
much, is the short answer, and he offers advice on alternative approaches.

The final section of the book offers some predictions and advice for the future.
Nobel Prize–winning economist Joseph Stiglitz argues that Progressives know what
needs to be done—the focus should be on jobs and wages, education, health and
home, opportunity and security—and even how to do it. The problem is that toxic
politics keep getting in the way. In the concluding essay, E. J. Dionne and Elizabeth
Thom acknowledge these substantial challenges but argue that, though the left has
yet to fully rise to the challenge, "the political tides in the United States still run in a
progressive direction." It is up to Progressives to be more aggressive about restoring
middle- and working-class wage growth, which they sees as the key battleground in
the near future.

It is no accident that the essays in this anthology offer a complicated, at times
contradictory, and not always optimistic analysis of the state of the Progressive
movement in the United States. Such complexity is necessary when describing politics in a big country with a large and diverse population and a system of governance
that was designed more than two centuries ago. At the same time, we are convinced
that Progressives have a vital role to play and that the country will be more prosperous if the ideas contained in this book play a role in shaping the future of American
politics.

Notes

1. Jon Meacham, "We're a Conservative Country," *Newsweek*, October 18, 2008, http://www.newsweek.com/meacham-were-conservative-country-92333, last modified July 30, 2014. See also John Micklethwait and Adrian Wooldridge, *The Right Nation: Conservative Power in America* (New York: Penguin Press, 2004); Marco Rubio, Speech at the Conservative Political Action Conference, February 9, 2012, http://www.rubio.senate.gov/public/index.cfm/press-releases?ID=ab463882-0fe4-4cad-b191-f8426824a860, last modified July 30, 2014.

2. Ruy Teixeira and John Halpin make this case in "The Obama Coalition in the 2012 Election and Beyond," Center for American Progress, December 2012.

3. Joel Aberbach and Gillian Peele, eds., *Crisis of Conservatism?: The Republican Party, the Conservative Movement and American Politics after Bush* (New York: Oxford University Press, 2011); Geoffrey Kabaservice, *Rule and Ruin: The Downfall of Moderation and the Destruction of the Republican Party, From Eisenhower to the Tea Party* (New York: Oxford University Press, 2012); Donald T. Crichtlow, *Phyllis Schlafly and Grassroots Conservatism: A Woman's Crusade* (Princeton, NJ: Princetone University Press, 2005); Lisa McGirr, *Suburban Warriors: the Origins of the New American Right* (Princeton, NJ: Princeton University Press, 2001); Rick Perlstein, *The Invisible Bridge: The Fall of Nixon and the Rise of Reagan* (New York: Simon $ Schuster, 2014); Rick Perlstein, *Nixonland: the Rise of a President and the Fracturing of America* (New York: Simon & Schuster, 2008); Donald Critchlow, *The Conservative Ascendancy: How the GOP Right Made Political History* (Cambridge, Mass:Harvard University Press 2007); Sean Wilentz, *The Age of Reagan: A History, 1974–2008* (New York: Harper Collins, 2008).

4. See, for example: Michael Kazin, *American Dreamers: How the Left Changed a Nation* (New York: Alfred A. Knopf, 2011) and Eric Alterman and Kevin Mattson, *The Cause: The Fight for American Liberalism from Franklin Roosevelt to Barack Obama* (New York: Viking, 2012). See also Sheila Collins and Gertrude Goldberg, eds., *When Government Helped: Learning from the Successes and Failures of the New Deal* (New York: Oxford University Press, 2014).

5. The word "progressive" is not easy to define. Some use it broadly, essentially as a synonym for liberal. Others employ it more narrowly, either to describe the left wing of the Democratic Party or as a label for the ideological descendants of the original Progressives, who place considerable emphasis on expertise and tend to favor technocratic solutions to political problems. In order to provide as full an account as possible of the left, we use the term in its broadest sense, though some contributors, such as Christopher Caldwell, have chosen a narrower definition.

6. To be sure, political memory is contested and each of these figures, with the obvious exception of Reagan, has been claimed at one time or another as a champion of the left. In addition, as Heather Cox Richardson points out in her new book, *To Make Men Free: A History of the Republican Party* (New York: Basic Books, 2014), for much of the party's history Republicans have debated the proper role of the federal government. What might be called a Hamiltonian wing has viewed the government in Washington as a legitimate and even necessary vehicle for addressing political and economic challenges, while a Jeffersonian strand of thinking tends to embrace a laissez-faire, states' rights view of Washington. In recent years, the Hamiltonians have been largely quiescent, aside from a few figures that wield marginal influence in the party, such as the columnist David Brooks of the *New York Times*.

Progressivism in America

PART ONE

ANTECEDENTS

1

TR, Wilson, and the Origins of the Progressive Tradition

CHARLES POSTEL

Theodore Roosevelt described the 1896 presidential campaign of William Jennings Bryan as "a gathering of social unrest," "anarchy," and "socialism." "Fundamentally," Roosevelt said, Bryan's Populist-Democratic insurgency "was an attack on civilization; an appeal to the torch." At the time he was serving as the head of the board of commissioners of the New York City Police Department. The newspapers reported that he suggested that the best solution to the Populist-Democratic revolt was to line its leaders "against a wall to be shot." He would later deny the report about firing squads. But his language was violent enough.[1] Roosevelt, of course, shared this apocalyptic assessment of Bryan's reform campaign with much of the rest of the political, academic, and business leaders of his region.

Sixteen years later, Roosevelt led his "Bull Moose" Progressive Party ticket in the 1912 campaign. The Socialist candidate, Eugene V. Debs, observed that Roosevelt "advocates doctrines which but a few years ago he denounced as anarchy and treason," noting that the "really progressive planks in the Progressive platform . . . [had been] taken bodily from the Socialist platform."[2] Debs, the former Populist, might have also said that these Progressive planks were drawn from the People's Party platforms of the 1890s. Meanwhile, Woodrow Wilson led the Democratic ticket. Wilson's political shift was perhaps no less dramatic. For years, he had aligned himself with the conservative wing of the Democratic Party. But in 1912 he ran on a reform platform that Bryan himself could and did support. When voters went to the polls, 75 percent of their ballots were cast for one of these three candidates—Wilson, Roosevelt, or Debs—candidates that embraced the sweeping reforms that we now know as Progressivism.

By the second decade of the twentieth century Progressivism appeared to be an unstoppable force in American politics. To understand its rise, we need to look at its origins. The short answer to the question of origins goes something like this: the roots of Progressivism can be found in the farmer-labor movements of the 1870s, 1880s, and 1890s. Antimonopolists, Grangers, Greenbackers, Knights of Labor, the Farmers' Alliance, Populists, and similar movements—movements that mainly took hold in the Midwest, West, and South—laid the ideological and political foundations of Progressive Era reform. Urban liberal coalitions of labor, women, and middle-class activists played a crucial role, often in conjunction with Populist and other farmer-labor movements. Historians have also pointed to a spectrum of constituencies from the new professional strata to the African American middle class, and they have traced other ideological currents on both sides of the Atlantic. But Elizabeth Sanders makes a powerful case when she argues that it was the "farmer-labor periphery" that produced the political wave that culminated in the great Progressive Era reforms.[3]

The 1912 election marked the Progressive high tide that swept in four constitutional amendments and two momentous acts of legislation. The Sixteenth Amendment opened the legal door for the progressive income tax. In the 1870s Grangers and Greenbackers had pushed a graduated income tax into national politics, and for some time it remained an essential demand of farmers and wage earners. They viewed such a tax as the best answer to the tariff, which was highly regressive, regionally inequitable, and one that mixed corporate money with congressional politics in menacing ways. They also saw the income tax as a means to address the growing crisis of economic inequality by redistributing ill-begotten wealth, and to finance needed infrastructure, from the National Weather Bureau, to road and harbor improvements, to public universities.

Pushed by representatives from the Populist states of the West and South, in 1894 Congress passed a small tax on incomes. Opponents argued before the Supreme Court that the tax was a form of confiscation and "communistic in its purposes and tendencies." Expressing what became the majority opinion, Justice Stephen Fields denounced the tax as "usurpation" and the stepping stone to a larger and more sweeping "assault upon capital."[4] The passage of the Sixteenth Amendment finally cleared the constitutional decks. Much like the 1894 tax, the graduated income tax of 1913 was small, since it only applied to the top 2 percent of incomes, and the very highest incomes were only taxed at a rate of 7 percent. But as the Populists had hoped, and as Justice Field had feared, this was only the beginning; by the mid-twentieth century the income tax served as an engine of wealth redistribution, income compression, and broader prosperity.

By replacing the selection of US senators by state legislatures with direct popular elections, the Seventeenth Amendment realized another reform originating in the farmer-labor agitation of the previous decades. The direct election of senators was a piece of the broader Populist vision of "direct democracy" to reform a political process where corporate lobbyists and party bosses worked their will on state legislatures in smoke-filled backrooms. Other pieces included the recall and the referendum. These latter forms of "direct democracy" would come to play an especially large role in the political agenda of Hiram Johnson, Bob La Follette, and other progressive Republicans, and through them Roosevelt's Bull Moose campaign.

Votes for women represented the most profound of the era's democratic reforms. Although its passage was delayed until after the war, the Progressive surge made it possible for the Nineteenth Amendment to be implemented. But here, too, it is important to remember that women's rights activism formed a powerful current of the farmer-labor movements of the 1880s and 1890s. This explains why Western states led the way on voting rights, starting in 1893 when Colorado became the first state to adopt women's suffrage by way of a referendum under a Populist administration.

And we must not overlook the disastrous Eighteenth Amendment, which was one of the most striking policy failures in American history. During the preceding decades, temperance campaigns and farm and labor reform often ran in tandem. Although the People's Party failed to endorse prohibition, many of the women attracted to Populism also saw alcohol restriction as a much-needed measure for public health and for the protection of women and children. This partly explains why support of prohibition mapped with the same geographic patterns of other Progressive Era reforms.

The Federal Reserve Act of 1913 established the country's first durable system of banking and credit regulation and a more accessible and elastic currency. Historians have justly emphasized the role of bank executives in shaping the Fed.[5] But too often overlooked is the extent to which the Fed also responded to the demands of farm and labor reform. Of course, Greenbackers and Populists preferred a proper central bank, housed in the Treasury Department, for example, and thereby subject to supervision by the electorate.[6] In this regard, it should be noted that Roosevelt's Bull Moose platform was closer to the original Populist ideas than the final product.

The Bull Moose platform also called for the "strong national regulation of inter-state corporations."[7] Despite his reputation as a "trustbuster," Roosevelt was less interested in breaking up corporate monopolies than in regulating corporations and in rationalizing industries to make them more efficient. The Federal Trade Commission Act of 1914 represented a major expansion of national regulation. Here, too, it is important to note that precisely the same ideas had been percolating since the closing days of the Civil War, with antimonopoly leagues campaigning against the speculative chaos—"everlasting smash" as they put it—that Wall Street unleashed on railroad systems and international trade.[8] The Grange, the Knights of Labor, and the Farmers' Alliances pursued similar ideals of rationalization, efficiency, and equity through regional and national systems of regulation.

As for the question of origins, then, Progressivism marked the culmination of decades of farmer and labor agitation. That is the short answer—an answer that helps explain the constituencies that allowed for the rapid success of Progressive reform in the first years of the twentieth century. The conservative triumph in the 1896 elections, with the ensuing collapse of the People's Party, masked a deeper current in American politics: the accelerated growth of the reform wings of both the Democratic and Republican parties, especially in the Midwest, West, and South. Part of this growth was the result of former Populists regrouping within the two main parties. The reform wings of both the Democratic and Republican parties were also strengthened by the recognition by party leaders of the potential of farm and labor reform votes for electoral success. This logic played out in the 1912 election. That was why Wilson reached out to Bryan and the western reform wing of his party. That was why Roosevelt turned for ideas and political support to reform Republicans of the Midwest and West and tapped Hiram Johnson, California's Progressive governor, as his Bull Moose running mate.

Locating the roots of reform in the farmer-labor periphery also sheds light on the class nature of Progressivism. Historians have done a fine job of delineating an elitist strand within Progressive reform, as upper- and middle-class reformers embraced notions of social improvement by way of providing expertise to the unenlightened and unwashed.[9] This strand wound through the Roosevelt and Wilson administrations and the wider reform coalitions. But that is only part of the story. Major Progressive Era reforms also had their roots in the political imagination and strivings of the men and women who worked America's farms, mines, factories, and railroads. Ordinary people with sunburned necks and calloused hands laid much of the foundation for key institutional structures of American political development. They did so with the ideal, partly realized, of making the United States a more equitable, secure, modern, and prosperous country.

The longer answer to the question of origins needs to address the immense complexity of the reform impulse. More precisely, it needs to address how such diverse phenomena gained the cohesion of what came to be known as the "Progressive movement," or "Progressivism." Because reform in the late nineteenth and early twentieth centuries took so many different shapes, and pursued such a kaleidoscope of often competing goals, historians have defined Progressivism in many different and often contradictory ways. Some historians have questioned whether it even makes sense to identify Progressivism as a specific phenomenon.[10]

To work through this complexity the historical context is important. These were decades of globalization, industrialization, urbanization, massive immigration, and a telecommunications revolution. Financial and industrial booms and busts were commonplace, and society was split apart by the concentration of wealth in too few hands and by the persistence of poverty and brutal insecurity for the working majority. These were decades when the corporation—railroad, banking, steel, oil companies—emerged as the master institution of American life. And this was a time when millions of men and women took part in tax clubs, consumer leagues, trade unions, professional societies, and farm and other voluntary associations that attempted to shape this fast-moving world.

Historians have struggled to locate common threads among these diverse efforts. Daniel Rodgers has astutely observed that reformers in that historical moment tended to employ three distinct clusters of ideas or "social languages." The first, and perhaps most pervasive, was antimonopoly and critiques of the inordinate power of corporations. The second was social cohesion and the desire to repair a split society. And the third was efficiency and the drive to bring rational order out of the helter-skelter of financial, industrial, and urban life. Within each of these clusters, however, rested competing and contradictory meanings. For muckrakers such as Ida Tarbell and farmer-labor politicians such as Robert La Follette, antimonopoly meant antitrust measures to break up concentrated capital. But for many reformers, from Farmers' Alliance leader Charles Macune to Teddy Roosevelt, concentration carried the potential for positive good. From this perspective, "antimonopoly" meant regulation and rationalization. Yet, the political and ideological contexts often gave these meanings more coherence than such differences might suggest; the multiple meanings of antimonopoly all questioned corporate prerogatives and power.

In that sense, the contours of Progressivism were partly defined by its conservative opposition. In the 1880s and 1890s conservative thought hardened and fastened on three interrelated ideas: so-called laissez-faire, the freedom of contract, and hard money. Here again, the farmer-labor movements of the day played a key role in the origins of this new conservative ideological system, as corporate, political, and academic elites sought to construct an ideological fortress to turn back the Populist challenge. This new doctrine has long been associated with the views of the Yale sociologist William Graham Sumner, as conservative academics, jurists, and business executives—whether directly influenced by Sumner or not—embraced the new ideological orthodoxy for which Sumner was the most outstanding publicist.[11]

Conservatives resisted farmer-labor demands for railroad regulation, income taxes, and other reforms with their notion of laissez-faire. Sumner's argument for laissez-faire rested on the classical liberal foundation of individual liberty. His ideal economic actor was "the forgotten man," his catchphrase for the striving middle-class entrepreneur, while his ideal government had neither the power nor the capacity to interfere in the natural workings of the private economy. But reality rarely intruded on these laissez-faire fantasies. Sumner may have written about "the forgotten man," but in its practical workings his new doctrine first and foremost defended the expanding prerogatives of giant banking and railroad corporations, not individual rights.[12] He considered the "aggregation of capital in few hands" as a natural and positive "social good," and the corporation proved the greatest of all aggregators.[13] As Brian Balogh has reminded us, the national government played a crucial role in "shaping both the market and the legal status of corporations that emerged as the key players in that market during the height of laissez-faire."[14] Conservatives had few objections to the government playing this role, and to its massive interventions on behalf of corporations: railroad subsidies, protective tariffs, bank charters, court action, strike breaking, and so forth. Sumner mainly accepted all of this with the telling exception of the tariff—telling because most of his laissez-faire colleagues did not share Sumner's qualms on this score. Most conservatives were untroubled by the fact that being both for and against government intervention—depending on whose interest was being served—was the practical essence of the laissez-faire system. The English observer James Bryce pointed out that "one half of the capitalists [in America] are occupied in preaching laissez faire as regards railroads, the other half resisting it" when it came to railroad subsidies and the tariff.[15]

Freedom of contract served as the indispensable conservative corollary to laissez- faire. "In our modern state, and in the United States more than anywhere else," Sumner reasoned, "the social structure is based on contract."[16] Contract served as the cornerstone of the social order, playing the vital role of structuring the relations between capital and labor. After the Civil War, plantation owners made use of fixed labor contracts as one of the means to bind newly freed slaves to extended terms of labor. Managers across corporate America employed so-called iron-clad contracts to compel workers to renounce the right to join a union (or to associate with those who might) as a term of employment. And conservative lawyers and judges marshaled freedom-of-contract arguments to combat legislation for shorter workdays, arbitration boards, and restrictions on child labor. Memorably, in *Lochner v. New York* (1905) the Supreme Court overturned a ten-hour-day law for employees of bakeries. The *Lochner* majority held that the law violated the freedom of workers to agree to toil for twelve- and fourteen-hour shifts six days a week as a condition of their employment—as if these workers had any choice in the matter if they wanted employment in their profession. In short, conservatives invented a freedom-of-contract dogma without any regard for either America's extensive history of regulatory legislation or for the real, practical despotism that many employers could and did wield over their employees.

In the face of farmer and labor demands for monetary and financial reform, conservatives responded with the rigid doctrine of hard money. During the Gilded Age, efforts to place the monetary system on the gold standard enriched Wall Street financiers and other creditors and impoverished the nation's farmers and debtors. These efforts also provoked a deflationary cycle that gripped the American economy, undermined the value of farmers' crops, created famines of cash and credit, stalled investment, and pushed industry into disastrous slumps. Farm and labor reformers argued that the channels of commerce required an elastic currency, based on paper, silver, or a combination of the two, and a national system of financial regulation. Such demands provoked a fevered response among business, political, and academic conservatives. They were known as "gold bugs" because they were gold fetishists; they convinced themselves that this particular metal represented a moral, naturally ordered, and superior civilization. To advocate paper or silver inflation was to threaten the foundations of the social structure. For the journalist William Allen White, Bryan's support of silver coinage represented "the apotheosis of riot, destruction, and carnage."[17]

Such highly charged ideological commitments deepened the social cleavages and fed the polarized politics of the Gilded Age. It was in this ideological context that police commissioner Roosevelt viewed the Populist-Democrats as an existential threat. And it was in this ideological context that the multitude strands of reform took the shape of a self-conscious Progressivism, defined in part by the confrontation with the conservative power of Supreme Court justices, political bosses, Wall Street financiers, and learned professors, all of whom stood pat on laissez faire, freedom of contract, and hard money. This poses the question of whether there would have been such enthusiasm for the pragmatism of William James and John Dewey without the persistent residue of dogmatic formalism within the academic establishment. Or, would there have been the experiential jurisprudence of Oliver Wendell Holmes Jr., or Louis Brandeis's critique of "industrial absolutism" without such decisions as *Lochner*? Or would there have been such dynamic progressive coalitions as the one that flourished in Hiram Johnson's California without the Supreme Court in *Santa Clara v. Southern Pacific* (1886) (which endowed railroad corporations with the rights of personhood), and without the subjugation of the state legislature to the railroad lobby?[18]

With McKinley's assassination in September 1901, the presidency fell into the hands of Roosevelt, who by this time was increasingly aligned with what was becoming the reform wing of the Republican Party. The conservative edifice cracked under the pressures of the new twentieth-century political realities and the financial panic of 1907. The election of 1912 showed just how badly damaged it was, holding on to barely a quarter of the popular vote. From time to time the old dogmas would reassert themselves in their old militant form: primary examples were the Liberty League and the corporate opposition to the New Deal and Taft, McCarthy, Goldwater, and Robert Welch during the early stages of the Cold War.[19]

Since the1970s the United States has witnessed the advent of a second Gilded Age, with a deepening crisis of economic inequality, aggressive expansion of corporate power, and a new hardening of conservative thinking. Especially within the milieu of Tea Party conservatism, the old trinity of laissez-faire, freedom of contract, and hard money has made a stunning comeback. The parallels between today's conservative commitments and those of the first Gilded Age are hardly accidental. Rather they reflect a distinct historical consciousness. As suggested by its name, the Tea Party movement is all about history lessons, and one of its central lessons is that America fell from grace with Progressive Era reforms. Scholars at the Heritage Foundation, the Cato Institute, and other conservative think tanks churn out books reviving Gilded Age dogmas. These ideas are publicized by conservative TV, radio, and Internet websites, which almost uniformly identify Roosevelt and Wilson with the "cancer" that has been gnawing at American freedom since the advent of the Progressive Era. Tea Party politicians, from Rick Perry to Ron Paul and Rand Paul, attest to this history and publish tracts about the evils of the Sixteenth and Seventeenth Amendments and the usurpations of the Federal Reserve.[20] In regard to the latter, gold is once again king of conservative economic thought. In 1990 Milton Friedman, the most influential conservative economist of the twentieth

century, dismissed gold advocates as "monetary monomaniacs."[21] Modern economies, according to Friedman and his fellow monetarists, had moved away from the
inflexible strictures of gold for a reason. But that was so yesterday. Today's conservatives have repudiated Friedman's monetarism in favor of the precious-metal religion
of the late nineteenth century.[22]

Perhaps today, as it was a hundred years ago, the rigid boundaries of conservative
thought define the contours of a new Progressive present. Perhaps that is the significance of a recent survey by the Pew Research Center that found the word "progressive" to be the most popular term in the American political lexicon.[23] Perhaps
that is the significance of President Obama's efforts to channel Theodore Roosevelt,
kicking off his 2012 campaign with a pilgrimage to Osawatomie, Kansas, where
Roosevelt had delivered his celebrated "New Nationalism" speech.[24] Perhaps that
is the significance of Proposition 30 in California, a 2012 referendum that, in the
spirit of the original "direct democracy" advocates, imposed higher income taxes
on the wealthy. Perhaps that is the significance of the changes in the New York City
mayor's office, where a man who invokes the old Progressives for solutions to what
he decries as the "second Gilded Age" replaced a Wall Street plutocrat.[25] Perhaps a
flexible, dynamic, multidimensional progressive majority is taking shape in the face
of an inflexible, unidimensional, and highly ideological bloc of conservative billionaires, politicians, judges, policy makers, and opinion shapers.

There are, however, striking differences with the past. First of all, the ideological
alignment of the two main political parties presents distinctive institutional hurdles.
In the late nineteenth and early twentieth centuries, Democrats and Republicans
represented fractured coalitions of interest, geography, and ideology. Both parties
had their corporate conservative and farmer-labor reform wings. Both parties had
their factional divisions over gold and silver, income taxes, tariffs, antimonopoly,
and corporate regulation. This allowed for cross-party coalitions and legislative log-
rolling that opened doors of opportunity when it came to passing reform legislation. Today, one party continues to function as an ideological coalition much as it
did in the past. Conservative Democrats can and do find common ideological and
political ground with conservative Republicans. However, such common ground
has virtually disappeared for Progressive Democrats. The reason for this is simple: the other party has forged a historically remarkable level of ideological cohesion. Republicans have their differences on foreign policy and to a lesser extent on
certain social issues. They also disagree about strategies to achieve common goals.
But the striking reality of the historical moment is the extent of agreement around
these common goals, especially when it comes to questions of political economy.
In the name of free markets and laissez-faire policies, Republicans have adopted a
nearly uniform hostility toward progressive income taxes and the social safety net.
The same goes for their opposition to the regulation of the health-care industry, the
financial sector, and carbon emissions. At the state level, Republican governors and
state legislators, employing freedom of contract arguments, have been marching in

lockstep to undermine labor protections and trade union rights. In 2011 and 2012 fifteen states passed legislation to dismantle public sector unions, and nineteen states introduced "right to work" laws.[26] And hard money is the uniform preference of national Republicans, with six of the party's nine presidential candidates in the last election promising to restore the gold standard.[27] At the end of the nineteenth century, conservatives showed ideological commitment and were blessed with resources. That remains the case. But what has changed is the historic level of domination realized by the conservative faction of one of the two main political parties. This conquest may prove short lived, but in the present historical moment it presents new hurdles for progressive reform.

Another difference was the prominent role that socialism played during the Progressive Era. The years immediately prior to the First World War represent the high-water mark of socialist politics in the United States. Part of a movement of diverse constituencies—from former Oklahoma Populists, to émigré radicals in lower Manhattan—American Socialists held some 1,200 public offices, led numerous trade unions, and exercised considerable influence on the intellectual and cultural scene. In both the positive and negative sense, the historian Alan Dawley observed that "it was true to say: no socialism, no progressivism." In the positive sense, the influence of such reformers as Florence Kelley and Upton Sinclair flourished within the "open boundary" between socialism and progressivism. And, in the negative sense, many Progressives sought to construct safe barriers to more dangerously radical alternatives; Roosevelt never tired of reminding his more conservative friends that without reform socialism would be knocking on the door.[28] Today, the Progressive brand of politics lacks the leavening of such a broad-based anticapitalist movement, although anticapitalist sentiment is more widespread than is usually allowed. The Pew Research Center reports that 31 percent of Americans have a positive view of the term "socialism," and 40 percent have a negative view of "capitalism."[29] But such sentiments lack the organizational force that allowed socialism to play such a significant role in early-twentieth-century reform.

Perhaps the most crucial difference is that Progressive Era reform accompanied the construction of American apartheid. During the post–Civil War decades the US government completed its efforts to confine the Indians to desolate reservations. The Chinese Exclusion Acts built up the walls of white nationalism. And by the 1890s new Jim Crow segregation laws formalized a regime of racial caste across the South and beyond. Soon thereafter, poll taxes, literacy tests, and the "white primary" effectively stripped African Americans of the franchise. Roosevelt had ties with Republicans who expressed sympathy for black rights, and as president he famously invited Booker T. Washington to the White House. But the more closely he identified himself with Progressivism the further he moved from notions of racial justice. At the 1912 Progressive Party convention in Chicago, white southern delegates demanded a "lily-white" policy. As John M. Parker, a Progressive leader from Louisiana put it: "Hereafter, we will have white primaries all the way through, and the white men of this country are going to rule." Northern delegates, such as Matthew Hale of Massachusetts, acceded the point: "We are saying to you people from the south, 'Your attitude on the negro problem is right, and ours is wrong.'" Roosevelt acceded the point, too.[30]

For his part, Woodrow Wilson directed his administration to complete the segregation of federal offices in Washington. Historians usually explain Wilson's racial viewpoints by taking note of his Virginia roots. But a deeper historical question would be to ask how was it that white southern Democrats formed such a major constituency of Progressive reform? Or, inversely, how could Progressivism have served as one of the pillars of the party of white supremacy and lynching law? And the answer lies in the mechanisms by which Progressive reform left intact the southern system of race and caste. Take the progressive income tax, for instance. White southerners, even relatively prosperous ones, understood that they would not be paying much of this tax; it would be paid mainly by New Yorkers. Accordingly, the states of the lower South were the first to ratify the Sixteenth Amendment, and they did so, reassured that this expansion of federal authority would not disturb southern race relations and white supremacy.[31] The same principle was behind southern Democratic support for currency reform, banking regulation, and other Progressive objectives. Political reforms such as the direct election of senators and the direct primary may have ruffled the feathers of the conservative old guard, but white southern Progressives recognized that as long as poll taxes and white primaries were firmly in place, such "direct democracy" measures would only reinforce the white power system of *herrenvolk* democracy.

This confluence of racism and Progressivism also had its farmer-labor roots. In the 1870s the farmers' Grange movement strongly opposed the Reconstruction experiment in multiracial democracy and demanded the restoration of the power and place of the white planter class. In the early 1890s the whites only Farmers' Alliance provided a rural voting bloc behind the new segregation laws. There were, of course, countervailing trends, as the Knights of Labor organized both black and white workers. And occasionally political circumstance led to political coordination between white reformers and African Americans, such as the "fusion" agreements made by black Republicans and white Populists in North Carolina. But even within the context of the Knights of Labor, and even considering the moments of "fusion" politics, white reformers rarely challenged the logic of segregation and white supremacy. With few exceptions, white farm and labor movements accepted the white nationalist notion of a white republic. And this legacy would undermine progressive reform through the New Deal and deep into the twentieth century.[32]

Today, the politics of white nationalism, xenophobia, and other forms of bigotry must be discussed in hushed tones and disguised in race-neutral language. In that sense, we have thankfully come a long way from the Progressive Era, when leading Democrats proudly wore the badge of white supremacy and when influential

Republicans spoke boastfully of the "master race." And perhaps also thankfully, the partisan alignments of racial politics have also changed. On the one hand, African Americans, Latinos, and other national minorities comprise major and growing Democratic constituencies, both at the national level and in the biggest states. On the other hand, the hardline conservative core of the Republican Party is steadily cornering the political market in white nationalism and xenophobia—even if this occurs mainly in whispers and carefully crafted code. It is an ominous sign that in the second decade of the twenty-first century one of the two main American political parties relies so heavily on racial resentment for political mobilization. But this new racial alignment may also carry great promise. One of its consequences is that it allows for at least the possibility of politically successful progressive coalitions that are not bound to a racist bloc within their own ranks. And if there is to be a new wave of progressive renewal perhaps it will bring to shore far more humane and universal notions of equality and social justice.

Notes

1. TR to Henry Cabot Lodge, April 8, 1897, TR to Cecil Arthur Spring-Rice, October 18, 1896, TR to Albert Shaw, November 4, 1896, *The Letters of Theodore Roosevelt*, Elting E. Morison, ed. (Cambridge, MA: Harvard University Press, 1951).

2. "Eugene V. Debs Says Moose Party Stole Socialist Planks," *Chicago World*, August 15, 1912, in Brett Flehinger, *The 1912 Election and the Power of Progressivism: A Brief History with Documents* (Boston: Bedford/St. Martin's, 2003), 177–178.

3. Elizabeth Sanders, *Roots of Reform: Farmers, Workers, and the American State, 1877–1917* (Chicago: University of Chicago, 1999).

4. William M. Wiecek, *The Lost World of Classical Legal Thought: Law and Ideology in America, 1886–1937* (New York: Oxford University Press, 1998), 136–139.

5. James Livingston, *Origins of the Federal Reserve System: Money, Class, and Corporate Capitalism, 1890–1913* (Ithaca, NY: Cornell University Press, 1986).

6. Charles W. Macune, et al., "Report of the Committee on the Monetary System," in Nelson A. Dunning, *Farmers' Alliance History and Agricultural Digest* (Washington, DC: Alliance, 1891), 124–130.

7. "Progressive Platform, Adopted at Chicago, August 7, 1912," *Machinists' Monthly Journal* 24 (October 1912), 934–935.

8. *Monthly Circular of the National Anti-Monopoly Cheap-Freight Railway League, Document IV* (New York: National Anti-Monopoly Cheap-Freight Railway League, August 1867).

9. Linda Gordon, "If the Progressives Were Advising Us Today, Should We Listen?" *Journal of the Gilded Age and Progressive Era* 1 (2002).

10. Daniel T. Rodgers, "In Search of Progressivism," *Reviews in American History* 10 (December 1982), 113–32; Peter G. Filene, "An Obituary for 'The Progressive Movement,'" *American Quarterly* 22 (1970): 20–34.

11. This ideology is often referred to as "Social Darwinism," a term its adherents did not use and that implies a perhaps exaggerated influence of Darwin on Sumner and other American conservatives. See Richard Hofstadter, "William Graham Sumner: Social Darwinist," in *Social Darwinism in American Thought* (Boston: Beacon Press, 1944). In juridical terms, this ideology has been labeled with such designations as "legal formalism," "orthodox ideology," and "legal classicalism." See Wiecek, *The Lost World of Classical Legal Thought*, 3. The designation used

in this paper is "conservatism," as this was the term often used by its adherents and had spe-
cific meaning in the historical context. See Robert Green McCloskey, "The World of William
Graham Sumner," in *American Conservatism in the Age of Enterprise, 1865–1910* (Cambridge,
MA: Harvard University, 1951).

12. R. Jeffrey Lustig, *Corporate Liberalism: The Origins of Modern American Political Theory,
1890–1920* (Berkeley: University of California, 1982).

13. McCloskey, *American Conservatism*, 50.

14. Brian Baloch, *A Government Out of Sight: The Mystery of National Authority in Nineteenth-Century
America* (Cambridge, UK: Cambridge University Press, 2009), 3. See also William J. Novak,
"The Myth of the 'Weak' American State," *American Historical Review* 113 (June 2008),
752–772.

15. James Bryce, *The American Commonwealth, Vol 2* (London: Macmillan, 1891), 292.

16. William Graham Summer, *What Social Classes Owe to Each Other* (New York: Harper &
Brothers, 1883), 21–22.

17. R. Hal Williams, *Realigning America: McKinley, Bryan, and the Remarkable Election of 1896*
(Lawrence: University Press of Kansas, 2010), 91, 128.

18. Louis Menand, *The Metaphysical Club: A Story of Ideas in America* (New York: Farrar, Straus
& Giroux, 2001), 337–375; Paul Kens, *Judicial Power and Reform Politics: The Anatomy of
Lochner v. New York* (Lawrence: University Press of Kansas, 1990); Wiecek, *Lost World of
Classical Legal Thought*, 152–156; Baloch, *A Government Out of Sight*, 331–333; Michael Paul
Rogin and John L. Shover, "Progressivism and the California Electorate," *Political Change in
California: Critical Elections and Social Movements, 1890–1966* (Westport, CT: Greenwood,
1970), 35–61.

19. Phillips-Fein, *Invisible Hands*, 3–25; Geoffrey Kabaservice, *Rule and Ruin: The Downfall
of Moderation and the Destruction of the Republican Party, from Eisenhower to the Tea Party*
(New York: Oxford University Press, 2012; Lisa McGirr, *Suburban Warriors: The Origins of the
New American Right* (Princeton, NJ: Princeton University Press, 2002);

20. David E. Bernstein, *Rehabilitating Lochner: Defending Individual Rights Against Progressive
Reform* (Chicago: University of Chicago, 2011); (Rick Perry, "The Progressive Era: Remaking
the Constitution with the Sixteenth and Seventeenth Amendments," in *Fed Up! Our Fight to
Save America from Washington* (New York: Little, Brown, and Company, 2010), 39; Ron Paul,
The Revolution: A Manifesto (New York: Grand Central, 2008); Rand Paul, *The Tea Party Goes
to Washington* (New York: Center Street, 2011).

21. Milton Friedman, "Bimetallism Revisited," *Journal of Economic Perspectives* (Vol. 4, No. 4, Fall
1990), 85–104.

22. Matt O'Brien, "Why Did Republicans Turn Against the Fed?" *New Republic*, September 27,
2011; Charles Postel, "Why Conservatives Spin Fairytales About the Gold Standard," *Reuters*,
September 17, 2013.

23. "Little Change in Public's Response to 'Capitalism', 'Socialism'," Pew Research Center for the
People and the Press, December 28, 2011.

24. "Full Text of President Obama's Economic Speech in Osawatomie, Kans.," the *Washington
Post*, December 6, 2011.

25. Benjamin Wallace-Wells, "The Dream of a Middle-Class New York," *New York*, January 6–13,
2014, 23–28; Amy Traub, "It's Not Just New York: The New Era of Progressive Urban Politics,"
The American Prospect, January 15, 21014.

26. Gordon Lafer, "The Legislative Attack on American Wages and Labor Standards, 2011–2012,"
Briefing Paper #364, Economic Policy Institute, October 31, 2013.

27. Ralph Benko, "The Gold Standard: A Litmus Test for GOP Candidates," *Forbes*, July
5, 2011.

28. Alan Dawley, *Struggles for Justice: Social Responsibility and the Liberal State* (Cambridge,
MA: Harvard University Press, 1991), 99–101.

29. "Little Change in Public's Response to 'Capitalism', 'Socialism'," Pew Research Center for the People and the Press, December 28, 2011.

30. Sidney M. Milkis, *Theodore Roosevelt, the Progressive Party, and the Transformation of American Democracy* (Lawrence: University Press of Kansas, 2009), 167–176.

31. A note of thanks to Robin Einhorn for sharing her insights into the southern origins of the federal income tax.

32. Charles Postel, *The Populist Vision* (New York: Oxford University Press, 2007), 173–203.

2

Franklin Roosevelt and the Progressive Tradition

ALAN BRINKLEY AND DAVID B. WOOLNER

For the first 125 years of US history, most American presidents were relatively weak—overshadowed by Congress, the courts, and the political parties. Most presidents enjoyed great prestige but seldom great power. Only in times of great crises did they have real authority. "If Lincoln had lived in times of peace," Theodore Roosevelt once said, "no one would remember his name."[1] But by the beginning of the twentieth century, the presidency began experiencing a remarkable transformation. No longer were presidents simply dignified symbols with little influence. They were increasingly bold and active men who transformed the character of the office and of the government.

The birth of the presidency of progressivism came from Theodore Roosevelt and Woodrow Wilson but most of all from Franklin Delano Roosevelt. He was undoubtedly the most important president of the twentieth century. FDR changed the character of government more profoundly than any president since the advent of the Constitution; he was also the only president to serve more than two terms (he was elected four times). His New Deal helped to produce a stunning expansion of the role of government in American life.

The New Deal was a remarkably diverse set of reform efforts that reflected not only the unusually eclectic ideologies of the people who worked in Roosevelt's administration but also Roosevelt's willingness to tolerate a broad range of ideas. There were New Deal programs of great daring and originality, and New Deal programs that were surprisingly clumsy and unimaginative. There were New Deal programs that were strikingly liberal, even radical, and New Deal programs that were decidedly conservative. Some New Deal programs worked while others failed. Some New Deal goals were achieved and some were not: including what was arguably the single most important such goal—ending the Great Depression, which Roosevelt could not accomplish until the Second World War necessitated the kind of massive federal spending in the economy that seemed inconceivable just a few short years before.[2]

The purpose of this essay is to explore the progressive legacy of the New Deal, to highlight those aspects of the New Deal that have left an enduring legacy in American life; to reflect upon how the diverse policies and programs that emerged under Roosevelt came to form what one might call the "liberal concept of the state"[3] and to underscore how FDR fundamentally transformed the relationship between the American people and their government as well as the relationship between the United States and the rest of the world in the years 1933 to 1945.

No evaluation of the New Deal's legacy would be complete without attention to the legacy of Franklin Roosevelt himself and the impact of his leadership on his successors and on other leaders worldwide. Ironically, however, Roosevelt himself was not always the powerful, committed figure he appeared to be.

Most Americans did not know that FDR had polio, and was completely paralyzed from the waist down. Nor were they aware that he was largely confined to a wheelchair, and unable to walk without the assistance of an elaborate system of braces, crutches, and canes. He and his aides worked hard to hide this aspect of FDR's life from the public, ensuring that no one would see him in his wheelchair outside the White House or his home. Moreover, during the last years of his life (and his presidency), he was desperately ill. But this too was concealed from all but a few of those who were closest to him.[4]

Roosevelt was also a leader without strong ideological beliefs or principles and is often criticized for his apparent lack of conviction. He "was content in large measure to follow public opinion," the historian Richard Hofstadter once wrote, and thus he charted no clear path.[5] He allowed the existing political landscape to dictate his course, the historian James MacGregor Burns lamented, instead of reshaping the Democratic Party to serve his own purposes.[6]

Such complaints were common among Roosevelt's contemporaries as well, most of all among those who had invested the greatest hopes in him. At times there even seemed to be something slippery about him, given his eagerness to please everyone with whom he talked, his ability to persuade people expressing two opposing views that he agreed with them both, and his tendency to allow seemingly contradictory initiatives to proceed simultaneously.

"When I talk to him, he says 'Fine! Fine! Fine!'" Senator Huey Long of Louisiana once complained. "But Joe Robinson [the Senate majority leader and one of Long's ideological nemeses] goes to see him the next day, and again he says 'Fine! Fine! Fine!' Maybe he says 'Fine' to everybody."[7] Henry Stimson, Roosevelt's secretary of war from 1940 on, was constantly frustrated by this enigmatic man, so much so that not long after Roosevelt died, Stimson privately expressed relief that in Harry Truman, he finally had a president willing to make a clear-cut and unequivocal decision. Roosevelt's fundamentally political nature—his rejection of all but a few fixed principles and his inclination to measure each decision against its likely popular reaction—may have been a significant weakness, as some of his critics have claimed (or his greatest strength, as others insist). But this prevaricative tendency was the essence of the man.

Roosevelt believed in capitalism, as all but a few Americans did. He also firmly believed that, at a time when liberal capitalist democracies were under siege in many parts of the world, government had a responsibility to save capitalism from its own difficulties: and among the things necessary to save it was assistance to the victims of its collapse. But he had few deep commitments beyond his faith in government and in democracy. As such, to the frustration of more principled people around him, he was endlessly flexible, always compromising, frequently dissembling, and never fully trustworthy or loyal to the people he worked with.

But despite (and perhaps even because) of these apparent weaknesses, Roosevelt was a great leader. His paralysis from polio was surely one of the most important aspects of his life from the early 1920s until his death. It gave him much of the steely determination that made him president and that allowed him to survive four national campaigns. It also gave him much of his public demeanor of sunny, garrulous optimism: for Roosevelt, like many disabled individuals, went to great lengths to distract people from his disability by being conspicuously cheerful and self-confident—an image he skillfully conveyed not just to those around him but also to the entire nation and even the world. Whatever the reasons, Roosevelt presented himself as a beacon of confidence and optimism, and in the panicked environment in which he entered office that alone was a significant achievement.

The firm, confident voice, the smiling optimism, the cock of the head, the up-tilted cigarette holder, the beaming smile: all of these traits helped many desperate people to believe that there was hope in their leadership and that the head of their nation was not just a bureaucrat but a symbol of their highest aspirations. And that image has survived for over sixty years as a potent model of presidential leadership to many Americans.[8]

Roosevelt's ideological flexibility, frustrating as it may have been to those around him, was in fact one of his greatest strengths as a leader. For it was responsible for one of the New Deal's most conspicuous and valuable features: its commitment to pragmatic experimentation. Roosevelt inherited a political world constricted in countless ways by fervently held principles on both the left and the right. Conservatives hewed on principle to the gold standard, to a balanced budget, to the sanctity of private contracts, to the obligation to protect capital whatever the cost, and above all to the belief that the invisible hand of the market must be permitted to govern the affairs of society without any interference from the visible hand of the state. Some people on the left were hostile to capitalism itself and insisted on punishing the wealthy. But into that ideologically constricted world, Roosevelt introduced a willingness to consider striking innovations, to cast aside deeply held inhibitions, to treat beliefs not as fixed and inviolable principles but as things to be tested and, if necessary, revised or repudiated. There were, of course, many things he would not do. There were certain principles he would not abandon or important new ideas he was slow to embrace or to which he was always resistant. But much of what was important about the New Deal was a result of the degree to which Roosevelt was open to what he liked to call the "spirit of persistent experimentation."[9]

Critics and admirers alike have argued that the New Deal reflected nothing but pragmatic responses to immediate problems. Hofstadter described it as little more than a "chaos of experimentation."[10] In a sour memoir published after his falling out with the president, Raymond Moley (Roosevelt's erstwhile advisor) wrote: "To look upon these programs as the result of a unified plan was to believe that the accumulation of stuffed snakes, baseball pictures, school flags, old tennis shoes, carpenter's tools, geometry books, and chemistry sets in a boy's bedroom could have been put there by an interior decorator."[11] But it also reflected Roosevelt's instinct for "action and action now" as he said in his first inaugural, and his belief in, if nothing else, the obligation of the leaders of government to work aggressively and affirmatively to deal with the nation's problems.

"Take a method and try it," Roosevelt liked to say. "If it fails, admit it frankly and try another. But above all, try something."[12] In a rapidly changing world of increasing uncertainty and complexity, there is much to be said for the legacy of ideological flexibility and spirited experimentation that the New Deal bequeathed to American public life.

Roosevelt formed a new and powerful national coalition of voters that made the Democratic Party—a weak minority party for nearly forty years before his election—into the dominant party in the United States for nearly forty years to come. Of course, the New Deal coalition no longer survives in anything like the form it assumed in the 1930s, 1940s, and 1960s, and the Democratic Party no longer dominates American politics in the way it did—but significant elements of that coalition remain important to American political life.

The New Deal made the Democrats the preferred party for people of liberal, progressive, or leftist inclinations in the United States, many of whom had previously considered the Republican Party—the party of Theodore Roosevelt—and many other reformers, more reliably progressive. But the growing conservatism of the Republican Party, along with the charisma and political acumen of FDR, helped move a broad coalition of progressives into the Democratic Party, where they still are today.

The New Deal also helped create a strong and enduring alliance between the Democratic Party and organized labor, which owed much of its economic strength to such landmark pieces of labor legislation as the National Labor Relations Act (NLRA) and the Fair Labor Standards Act. Roosevelt was at first reluctant to pass the NLRA (or "Wagner Act" as it is often called), but he realized that many Democrats supported strong unions, so he acted accordingly. The ability of unions to shape their members' political views has declined significantly since then, but the alliance with labor organizations survives as a distinctive and important part of the Democratic Party.

The New Deal made the Democratic Party the party of African Americans and most other minorities. African Americans were mostly Republican in the first seventy years after the Civil War, which was a tribute to Lincoln and to the predominant role his party played in the abolition of slavery. Roosevelt made them Democrats, but not because the New Deal committed itself to the African Americans civil rights struggle, which was already slowly taking root in the social landscape of the 1930s. On the contrary, the Roosevelt administration was mostly timid about civil rights issues (with the significant exception of Eleanor Roosevelt). But the New Deal did provide African Americans with desperately needed social services. The Roosevelt administration also appointed more blacks to positions of responsibility within government and exhibited a greater sympathy for their larger aspirations for equality than had any previous administration with the exception of Lincoln's. As Mary McLeod Bethune once noted, the Roosevelt years represented "the first time in the history" that African Americans felt that they could communicate their grievances to their government with the "expectancy of sympathetic understanding and interpretation." By 1936 over 90 percent of African American voters were voting for Roosevelt and the Democrats.[13]

Another way in which the New Deal has left an enduring legacy on modern America is in its transformation of parts of the nation's physical landscape: the New Deal era saw the most expansive and ambitious public works construction of any period in American history. The 1930s was, in fact, a period of great public works building in much of the industrial world, and particularly in nations where there were strong governments attempting to not only end the Depression but also to create a physical image of (and monuments to) themselves. In this respect, the America of the New Deal had something in common with Germany, Italy, and the Soviet Union.

Almost certainly the most conspicuous (and controversial) legacy of the New Deal is its contribution to the creation of the modern American welfare state or social safety net. These contributions took several forms, but the most enduring fall into two categories.

One category was the wide range of new programs and protections that have helped mostly middle-class people: mortgage protection for homes and small farms; insurance of personal bank deposits; income tax deductions for interest on home mortgages; and many other economic benefits and protections that have provided increased security and opportunity for middle-class Americans.

The other significant contribution is the equally wide range of programs that established the basic structure of the formal welfare state for the remainder of the twentieth century: unemployment insurance, pensions for the elderly, aid to the disabled, and perhaps most controversial, assistance to single mothers. These were all products of the Social Security Act of 1935, the single most important piece of social welfare legislation in American history.

Not every New Deal program enjoyed such a signifant impact on American life. The National Industrial Recovery Act of 1933, although perhaps the most ambitious program the New Deal ever created, was a disastrous failure. But other programs were of great importance. The New Deal's Agricultural Adjustment Act, and succeeding farm legislation, for example, gave American farmers a range of new protections against the instability of the agricultural market—protections many farmers had been fighting to obtain for a generation or more. New Deal labor legislation, both Section 7a of the 1933 National Industrial Recovery Act, as well as the more important National Labor Relations Act of 1935 noted above, established organized labor as a powerful and protected force within the industrial economy, able to bargain collectively with employers who had previously refused to negotiate with them and to play an enduring role in the distribution of resources and political power in the industrial world.

In the latter years of the New Deal, in the aftermath of a serious recession in 1937–1938, and in response to the obstinacy of the Depression that five years of New Deal efforts had mitigated but failed to end, Roosevelt began experimenting with other approaches to economic policy, most notably with what was coming to be known as "Keynesian" economics. An ill-advised effort to balance the budget by cutting government spending precipitated the disastrous 1937–1938 recession. A vigorous new program of spending and investment launched in early 1938 helped bring the economy back to at least limited life. Out of that partial success emerged the growing belief that government could influence the economy through its monetary and fiscal policies and through its control over the money supply and its ability to raise and lower spending and taxation.

To many younger New Dealers, the power of these fiscal and monetary instruments was a revelation. No longer would it be necessary to search for ways to reform capitalist institutions in order to revive the economy and produce economic growth. Even unreformed institutions could be helped to work better through the intelligent application of fiscal and monetary policies. It now seemed possible to manage capitalism without managing the institutions of capitalism: to help the economy revive without engaging in the politically and bureaucratically difficult effort to force capitalists to change their behavior or restructure their corporations. To the most exuberant Keynesians, this discovery meant that the greatest dilemma of the modern industrial world had been resolved, that the problem of monopoly—the problem that had preoccupied and frustrated more than two generations of reform efforts—need no longer preoccupy modern society; that it would be possible to lead the way to economic growth not by focusing on producers but by helping consumers—by pumping money into the hands of the millions of men and women who created the market demand for what capitalists produced.

The New Deal never fully embraced the Keynesian revolution, and indeed no subsequent American government ever fully embraced it. In recent years, fiscal policy as an instrument of economic management has been utilized infrequently, largely due to a fear of deficits and because of the increasingly global character of the economy. Monetary policy has emerged as the centerpiece of government intervention in the economy, although Keynesianism has had a significant, if perhaps brief, revival with the enormous stimulus package the Obama administration enacted early in 2009. Nevertheless, the New Deal helped create the belief that government not only had a responsibility to create or sustain prosperity but that it could do so without intruding too directly into the affairs of the capitalist world. In other words, the New Deal helped transform the relationship between the American people and their government. And in so doing, it fashioned a new liberal conception of the state that—although beleaguered and battered—in many respects remains with us.

* * *

And how might we assess the Roosevelt legacy in terms of foreign policy? Here, too, we must acknowledge that FDR has had an enormous impact not only in shaping America's role in the world but also in helping to shape a new conception of foreign policy among those who view themselves as progressives.

In a 1924 article published in *Foreign Affairs* entitled "American Foreign Policy: a Progressive View," Robert Morss Lovett takes note of the historical tendency in the United States for conservative governments (which he classified as those dedicated to "the maintenance of the status quo in domestic matters") to develop "an aggressive policy in foreign affairs," while those governments "whose chief outlook is toward the progressive improvement of existing conditions" tend to want to free themselves "from the complications of foreign policy."[14]

Given this tendency, Lovett also notes it is perhaps natural that progressives should be "comparatively indifferent to foreign policy," and that their leaders, as such, should be considered the most pronounced of isolationists.

If one looks at the experience of the early 1930s, when the United States found itself in the midst of the Great Depression, Lovett's historical characterization would seem to be correct. Given the depth of the economic crisis facing the United States, the American government dedicated itself, as FDR said in his first inaugural "to putting our own national house in order."

But we should not forget that the financial crisis that brought on the Great Depression was not confined to the United States. Indeed, America's suffering was but one part—albeit a large part—of a worldwide economic collapse that had enormous consequences on the course of the twentieth century.

In Europe and parts of Asia, the hardships caused by the global economic crisis led to the rise of fascist dictatorships in Germany, Italy, and Japan—anti-democratic regimes bent on the regimentation of their economies at home and the use of force to achieve their objectives abroad.

Meanwhile, torn asunder by the devastating effects of the Great Depression, and bitter about American involvement in the First World War, the US public turned its back on the rest of the world and disavowed its international responsibilities. In the absence of American support, the League of Nations foundered, and the enemies of democracy flourished. Piece by piece Hitler's Germany expanded at the expense of its neighbors, Italy invaded Abyssinia, Franco launched his fascist crusade in Spain, and the Japanese invaded China. Restrained by neutrality laws passed in the mid-1930s that did not distinguish between aggressor and victim, FDR could do little to assist the targets of aggression; by the end of the 1930s the United States found itself confronting a new world war.

There is no question that Roosevelt's response to the international dimension of the world crisis was dictated by in part by the tenets of isolationists and in part by his concern over the state of the US economy. Hence, he confined himself to periodically testing the limits of American isolationism by engaging in limited diplomacy in the mid- to late 1930s, and once war broke out, he gradually increased America's support to those who opposed fascism until December 7, 1941, when America found itself under attack and in the war.

But the key to understanding FDR's response to the international dimension of the crisis that America faced in the 1930s and 1940s rests with his conviction that the internal and external crises were linked. Hence, for Roosevelt—and many of his advisors—it was the economic deprivation caused by the global meltdown in the 1930s that stood as the root cause of fascism and hence the outbreak of the war itself.

FDR also believed that the absence of American political, military, and economic leadership during the 1930s was a major contributing factor in the world's decent into conflict. As the war intensified, therefore, he became more and more convinced that the United States must fashion a comprehensive response to the global crisis that included maintaining and strengthening key provisions of the New Deal at home, while simultaneously expanding American leadership abroad.

His goals here were essentially twofold: first, he wanted to prevent the reemergence of isolationism in the United States after the war—and this meant above all else maintaining "a healthy peacetime economy" and hence expanding the basic socioeconomic reforms of the New Deal. Second, he wanted to commit the United States to the creation of a new international order that was underpinned not merely by US economic power and military might, but primarily by American moral leadership—on the extension of the values he so eloquently expressed in his 1941 call for a world established on four fundamental human freedoms: freedom of speech and expression, freedom of worship, freedom from want, and freedom from fear.

FDR proposed this "greater conception" as the very antithesis of the "so-called new order of tyranny which the dictators seek to create with the crash of a bomb." His was a "moral order" that above all else was based on the fundamental concept as he said in his four freedoms address that "freedom means the supremacy of human rights everywhere" and in articulation of these values he committed his government and the people of the United States "to support those who struggle to gain those rights and keep them."

It was the attainment of the Four Freedoms that in essence became the war aims of the United States during the Second World War. But dedicating the United States and the American people to the realization of these ideals over the long term was another matter. Clearly such a monumental shift in US foreign policy would require a good deal of thought and effort, and the question we must address is how FDR proposed achieve this goal.

Fortunately, US policy during the war provides us with a guide as to how FDR hoped to secure this fundamental shift in America's relations with the rest of the world.

His first aim was to convince the American people that they had no choice but to live up to their international responsibilities. Indeed, the advent of air power made it clear that America's security was intimately connected to the security of other parts of the world. Perhaps the best articulation of this conviction can be found in FDR's fireside chat of February 1942 when, in an extraordinary example of presidential leadership, he asked the American people to "take out their maps"—purchased as requested by the White House in advance of the chat—so that they could physically see that the Second World War "is a new kind of war," not only in its "methods and weapons but also in its geography." It is, he went on, warfare on "every continent, every island, every sea"—and most significantly—"every air-lane in the world."[15]

This last point is critical. FDR insisted that the advent of air power meant that the American people had to adopt a new way of looking at the physical location of the United States. No longer could they afford to embrace the hemispheric view that encouraged the idea that the United States, positioned as it was between two oceans, was set apart from the other continents. They now had to adopt a global vision (based largely on polar map projections) that saw the United States as intimately linked with the rest of humanity. Moreover, this shift involved far more than merely a change in the way Americans interpret geography or view the placement of North America on a map; it also involved a psychological shift that encouraged not only "global thinking on the geographical plane," but also universal thinking on an "ideological plane."[16]

As such, and as he said in the same February 1942 radio address, "This great struggle has taught us increasingly that freedom of person and security of property anywhere in the world depend upon the security of the rights and obligations of liberty and justice everywhere in the world."

Viewed from this perspective the struggle to help America's Allies defeat the Axis on other continents became synonymous with the struggle to defend America and American values wherever that need may arise. The two, in short, were indistinguishable as it was impossible in "One World" to separate American security needs from those of other peoples.[17]

Based on these concepts, FDR was able to argue that "isolationism" (or what we might more correctly define as "unilateralism") was not only naive but also dangerous, for it was imperative in the wake of the twin crises that struck the world in the 1930s and 1940s for the United States to stay actively engaged with the rest of the world.

Engagement, of course, is not always easy. But in the wake of the most destructive war in human history, FDR arrived at another of his core convictions: that Great Power cooperation was essential to the preservation of world peace. This made it necessary to recognize that one of the key—if not *the* key—elements of postwar stability and security lay in cooperation with the Soviet Union.[18]

Contrary to later public perceptions, this approach was not based on ignorance or naiveté but rather on the firm recognition that Soviet power was here to stay.

Which brings us to the second facet of FDR's wartime foreign policies: the creation of the international institutions necessary to achieve the twin aims of Great Power cooperation and continued American engagement in world affairs. Here the goal was to secure the construction of a new political, strategic, and economic order that was based on the extension of American moral and military power through the United Nations and the extension of American economic power through the creation of the International Monetary Fund, World Bank, and a new multilateral economic system that would open up the world's markets and natural resources to freer trade.

We do not have space in this essay to go into the details of this effort. However, taken together, these measures, much like those of the New Deal, resulted in a permanent restructuring of the world's social, economic, and strategic makeup. They form the basis of the new world order that has given rise to the globalization of the world's economy and the American-led multilateral security system that exists via the UN, NATO, SEATO, and the myriad of other international economic and security organizations that the United States has played a leading role in since 1945. In short, FDR used the war to construct both the rhetorical and physical structure in which American leadership could operate, and in so doing he transformed the relationship between the United States and the rest of the world.

And what lessons might we draw from this? The first is that the growing militarization of US foreign policy has made us weaker not stronger; as FDR taught us, American credibility and moral leadership are far more important and powerful than our profound military might.[19] Second is the need to recognize that the moral imperative in US foreign policy—a moral imperative put at grave risk by the advent of the so-called enhanced interrogation techniques under President George W. Bush—means that we would be wise to shift our focus from the use of military force to the rule of law and the use of both the domestic and international criminal justice system in the prosecution of our so-called war on terror—to treat this struggle not as a "crusade for freedom" but much like the war on drugs: as an effort to root out criminal activity. This would lower the international status of the terrorists and increase the stature of the United States. And, finally, we should never forget the one lesson above all else that FDR embraced as the Second World War drew to its ultimate close: that our security and prosperity at home is intimately linked to security and prosperity abroad. As he said in his famous Economic Bill of Rights speech of January 1944:

> We have come to a clear realization of the fact that true individual freedom cannot exist without economic security and independence. Necessitous men are not free men. People who are hungry and out of a job are the stuff of which dictatorships are made.[20]

Viewed from this perspective, and from the perspective of the decades of relative prosperity and security that followed FDR's death in 1945, one can argue that the lessons of history teach us that FDR was correct when he insisted that America's security is directly tied to the security and well-being of all peoples—"everywhere in the world". And the only way to ensure our security and freedom in the long run is to recognize that military might and economic power are not enough, that if we really want to live in a world where America is secure, we need to understand, as he said, that freedom ultimately means "the supremacy of human rights everywhere."[21]

* * *

When one looks at the history of the Western industrial world since the end of the Second World War, it is hard not to be astonished at the remarkable changes that have occurred in the lives of ordinary people: there have been striking increases in standards of living throughout the Western world, dramatic improvements in housing and diet, a great increase in leisure, and a rise of new forms of entertainment and comfort. This achievement does not solve all the world's woes, to be sure. But the lifting of hundreds of millions of people out of poverty into affluence is one of the great, if still incomplete, feats of modern history. It is not, of course, an achievement that can be attributed solely or even largely to the New Deal or to US leadership in the postwar world. But it is, in part, a product of the liberal vision or liberal concept of the state that Franklin Roosevelt and his government helped to legitimize: a model of economic growth that—in spite of all of the clamor on the right about the perils of deficit spending—is still relevant to our own troubled times.

In the midst of the greatest economic crisis in the history of the industrial world, and at a time of darkness and fear and growing despair, New Deal liberals—and liberals worldwide—dared to dream of an economic future fueled by an engaged and committed government in which prosperity could be universal, in which unemployment could be eliminated, and in which the lives of ordinary people might be elevated and transformed. That may not be the only, or even the greatest, aspiration for a modern society. But it is an aspiration that not only helped the New Dealers transform the nature of the American state in both peace and war but also helped create the world we have come to know: a world that now stands in jeopardy in many ways, a world that could use something similar to a New Deal to help us recover from our own current crisis and to move us forward into a new era of progress.

Notes

1. Theodore Roosevelt, "The Conditions of Success," an address delivered to the Cambridge Union, Cambridge University, May 26, 1910.

2. David Kennedy, "What the New Deal Did," *Political Science Quarterly* (Summer 2009): 251–268.

3. See, for example, Alan Brinkley, "The New Deal and the Idea of the State," in Steve Fraser and Gary Gerstle. eds. *The Rise and Fall of the New Deal Order, 1930-1980* (Princeton, NJ: Princeton University Press, 1989), 85–86.

4. For more on FDR's struggle with polio see Hugh Gallagher, *FDR's Splendid Deception* (New York, Dodd, Mead & Co., 1985) and James Tobin *The Man He Became: How FDR Defied Polio to Win the Presidency* (New York: Simon & Schuster, 2013).

5. Richard Hofstadter, *The American Political Tradition and the Men Who Made It* (New York: Alfred A. Knopf, 1948), 316.

6. James MacGregor Burns, *Roosevelt: The Lion and the Fox* (New York: Harcourt Brace Jovanivich, 1956), 287–288.

7. Alan Brinkley, *Voices of Protest: Huey Long, Father Coughlin, and the Great Depression* (New York: Alfred A. Knopf, 1982), 58.

8. One of the most inspired recollections of the impact that FDR's leadership had on Depression-era America can be found in Bill Moyers's piece recalling his cotton-picking father's faith that he had "a friend" in the White House between 1933 and 1945 (Bill Moyers, "Moyers & FDR," *The Nation*, December 10, 2007, 9.

9. Franklin D. Roosevelt, Address to Oglethorpe University, Atlanta, Georgia, May 22, 1932, in *Franklin D. Roosevelt, The Public Papers and Addresses of Franklin D. Roosevelt, Vol. I* (New York: Macmillan, 1933).

10. Richard Hofstadter, *Age of Reform: From Bryan to FDR* (New York: Alfred A. Knopf, 1955), 307.

11. Raymond Moley, *After Seven Years: A Political Analysis of the New Deal* (New York: Harper & Row, 1939), 369–370.

12. Richard Hofstadter, *The Age of Reform*, 307.

13. David B. Woolner, "African Americans and the New Deal," *Next New Deal: The Blog of the Roosevelt Institute*, February 5, 2010. For more on the African American experience during the New Deal see Harvard Sitkoff, *A New Deal for Blacks: The Emergence of the Civil Rights as a National Issue: The Depression Decade* (New York: Oxford University Press, 1978).

14. Robert Morss Lovett, "American Foreign Policy: A Progressive View," Foreign Affairs, September 1924, 49.

15. Franklin D. Roosevelt, Fireside Chat, "On the Progress of the War," February 23, 1942, Franklin D. Roosevelt, Master Speech File, 1898–1945, FDR Presidential Library, Hyde Park, NY.

16. Alan K. Henrikson, "FDR and the 'World Wide Arena,'" in *FDR's World: War Peace and Legacies*, eds. David B. Woolner, Warren Kimball and David Reynolds (New York: Palgrave Macmillan, 2008), 46.

17. David B. Woolner, "Epilogue: Reflections on Legacy and Leadership: The View from 2008," in *FDR's World: War, Peace and Legacies*, ed. David B. Woolner, Warren F. Kimball, and David Reynolds, 229.

18. David B. Woolner, "Epilogue: Reflections on Legacy and Leadership," in *FDR's World*, 230.

19. For more on the militarization of US foreign policy see, Andrew Bacevich, *The New American Militarism: How Americans Are Seduced by War* (New York: Oxford University Press, 2013).

20. Franklin D. Roosevelt, "Annual Message to Congress on the State of the Union, January 11, 1944," Franklin D. Roosevelt, Master Speech File, 1898–1945, FDR Presidential Library, Hyde Park, NY.

21. Franklin D. Roosevelt, "Four Freedoms Address to Congress," January 6, 1941, Franklin D. Roosevelt, Master Speech File, 1898–1945, FDR Presidential Library, Hyde Park, NY.

3

From the Politics of Hope to
the Politics of Frustration

FDR's Legacy and the Quandaries of Postwar Liberalism

KEVIN MATTSON

> The existence of Franklin Roosevelt relieved American liberals . . . of the
> responsibility of thinking for themselves.
> —Arthur Schlesinger Jr.[1]

FDR's New Deal expounded big ideas, and while it is true—as his critics
charge—that FDR was no political philosopher and that much of the governmental activity that emanated from this remarkable period appears sporadic (and may
even be characterized as lacking a central ideology), a cursory reading of FDR's
major speeches conjure overarching themes and a unifying vision: that Americans
should model political initiative on the unity provided during "war" and think of
themselves as a "trained and loyal army" solving domestic problems; that "interdependence on each other" should push Americans beyond old-school economic
individualism and laissez-faire; that positive freedoms (freedom *to*) now trumped
negative freedoms (freedom *from* authority); that "every man has a right to life, . . . a
right to make a comfortable living" under "an economic constitutional order"; that
a faith in governmental action and the ideal of "enlightened administration" would
lead the country to better times.[2]

FDR also believed that the executive branch stood for national unity, due to its
singularity and embodiment in one person elected nationwide. The Executive was
therefore the rightful branch of government to rule and guide the country out of crisis into something that affirmed the nation's ideals of equality and democracy. This
was a pillar of the New Deal, both domestically and internationally, thanks to the
dawn of the Second World War. And this idea worked its way into the private lives
of ordinary Americans, who saw FDR as a larger than life, paternalistic figure who
spoke soothingly during fireside chats and who touched their lives directly, even

though he was miles away. His clenched, up-arching chin and broad grin seemed to symbolize government itself.[3]

The president's unified conception of his own leadership—as the commander in chief of a domestic "army"—fueled the flurry of programs that came from the White House or that the White House helped confirm coming from the halls of Congress (FDR was great at taking other peoples' ideas and affirming the hell out of them). From shoring up failed banks during the One Hundred Days to the decision to move left in 1935 by supporting labor unions, promoting extensive public works, creating Social Security, and slamming a hefty tax on the wealthiest Americans, FDR projected a sense of confidence that he acted for the people, for the nation's best interest, firmly and strongly. He might have "welcomed" opposition from his enemies, those with wealth and power, but that was because he was certain the people would watch his back. Rex Tugwell commented that FDR was "a man with fewer doubts than anyone I had ever known."[4] Of course, this attitude gave rise to the more troubling legacies of FDR's presidency—his desire to "pack" the Supreme Court and his secrecy in engaging the United States in Second World War. But whatever the case, FDR's foot soldiers—the citizens of the domestic army—confirmed his self-confidence over the course of four elections. Confidence mixed with bold action from a unified and energetic executive were immortalized in FDR's most famous words, "The only thing we have to fear is fear itself."

However, since his death FDR's legacy has proved difficult for most liberal presidents to match. A potent combination of renewed vigor on the right and changes in American political culture after Vietnam and Watergate has led to what might be called the "politics of frustration."

THE RIGHT RESURGENT
AND LIBERALISM FRUSTRATED

Consider the New Deal's legacy in the context of FDR's successor, Harry S. Truman. Here the act of stepping into power was stepping into a gigantic shadow. Chosen as vice president to placate southern Democrats who feared that Henry Wallace, a progressive man of the left (if not a man of political astuteness), might be chosen in his stead, Truman was largely unschooled in FDR's decision making. Indeed, Truman met only twice with the president in his capacity as vice-president. Suddenly out of necessity a certain humility and doubt entered the presidency, mixed with another side to Truman's persona—the cranky and impulsive one. Sounding in retrospect like a forerunner to George W. Bush's presidential style, Truman once snapped, "I'm here to make decisions, and whether they prove right or wrong I am going to make them."[5]

Truman faced a much feistier right flank than FDR. FDR and liberalism certainly had their opponents during the 1930s, but in the postwar period, the right became that much louder and their contentions resonated. This made Truman's challenge—to craft a liberal vision for a society not in the throes of a Depression but rather in the throes of a growing prosperity more apparent as the years wore on—much more difficult. Just how much the emergency of the Depression helped FDR became evident. It also empowered an organized, well-financed opposition to the new president. The National Association of Manufacturers (NAM) invested big dollars in fighting Truman's policies. The *Wall Street Journal* proved a constant critic of Truman, as did popular right-wing op-ed writers, Westbrook Pegler and Fulton Lewis, Jr. In addition, the influential Senator Robert A. Taft—"Mr. Republican"— opposed most of what Truman tried to implement.[6] More famously, the deep pockets found within the American Medical Association (AMA) mobilized against Truman's attempt to reform the health-care system.[7]

One year after assuming the office of the presidency, the backlash against FDR's legacy and Truman's own presidency became explicit. Nineteen forty-six would bring large numbers of Republicans into office, including two key political figures who had an enormous impact on the future of American politics: Congressman Richard Nixon and Senator Joseph McCarthy (and yes, the two of them were often allied). During the 1946 campaign, Nixon stole populist language and updated it for the times, speaking up for a "new forgotten man walking the streets" (listen to that FDR rhetoric!). He suggested ordinary citizens would oust the socialist New Deal bureaucrats who were suppressing free-market prosperity. Nixon spoke for the automobile dealers, insurance brokers, ranchers, and bankers who helped recruit him to run in 1946. They loved his sharp rhetoric about a forked road ahead—one path "advocated the New Deal" based on "government control in regulating our lives," the other envisioned "individual freedom and all that initiative can produce." He promised to rally those faceless white collar employees around anger and frustration. His campaign literature asked: "Are you satisfied with present conditions? Can you buy meat, a new car, a refrigerator, clothes you need? . . . Where are all those new houses you were promised?" This played along with the Republican slogan of 1946—"Had Enough?"—that was a brainchild of an advertising executive named Karl Frost. Translated into a policy agenda it meant: Sick of regulations, public housing, rent control, bureaucratic government in general? Want more *stuff*? Vote Republican and get it. Nixon was a white-collar populist who united people around their "fierce desire . . . to regain control of their own lives." As such, 1946 and the years to follow became just as much Nixon's as Truman's.[8]

The right's language was effective, and belies the notion that a "liberal consensus" reigned during America's postwar years. Still, it should not allow us to ignore Truman's liberal vision. Though historians usually focus on the "Fair Deal" proposed in 1949, Truman had outlined his liberal vision years earlier. On September 6, 1945, Truman presented Congress with the longest set of demands ever laid out by a president. He called it "one of the most important messages of my administration." It contained the twenty-one points of domestic legislation that, as he put it, "spelled out the details of the program of liberalism and progressivism which was to be the foundation of my administration."[9] Truman called on Congress to extend unemployment benefits, raise the minimum wage, and strengthen the FEPC (Fair Employment Practices Committee, the arm of government that could best aid civil rights). He warned against lifting wartime price controls—administered at the time by the Office of Price Administration (OPA)—an organization that ironically Richard Nixon had worked for alongside the liberal economist John Kenneth Galbraith—even though "some groups in business may be tempted to substitute for this long-range war-time thinking, a short-range policy designed to secure prices high enough to provide immediate profits . . ." Truman also championed the possibility of "a full production peace-time economy." He seemed to endorse the idea that public works could make up for free markets, boldly calling for "a national reassertion of the right to work for every American citizen able and willing to work—a declaration of the ultimate duty of Government to use its own resources if all other methods should fail to prevent prolonged unemployment—these will help to avert fear and establish full employment." Here he played up the Economic Bill of Rights FDR had set out during the last two years of the Second World War: rights were no longer just about freedom from government but also freedom from economic insecurity, which required governmental action. After endorsing slum clearance and support for veterans, Truman ended by saying, "I shall shortly communicate with the Congress recommending a national health program to provide adequate medical care for all Americans and to protect them from financial loss and hardships resulting from illness and accident."[10]

But Truman's vision failed to materialize. Republicans resisted these policies with considerable success. Conservatives such as Richard Nixon were confident that 1946 would be their year, especially since the Office of Price Administration (OPA) was scheduled to close. As citizens debated what should happen to the OPA, its chief administrator warned of an "inflationary joyride."[11] Citizens organized "Save the O.P. A." rallies, and labor unions threw their weight behind the agency, believing it could correct a future "wage-price spiral." In spite of this political and grassroots initiative, Congress, in the words of historian Meg Jacobs, produced a "severely weakened price control bill that made OPA into a paper tiger."[12] Truman fought this bill and lost. And when another bill came his way, similar to the previous one, he dropped his opposition and signed it, figuring there was no better option.[13] As a result, prices shot upward, and Truman appeared more a big talker than a deliverer. He threatened to open up his left flank, but that was increasingly being filled by the popular (and vocal) Henry Wallace, the man many liberals wished had gotten the presidency over Truman, who would run against him on a third-party ticket in 1948.[14]

The OPA struggle became a pattern: inspiring rhetoric that ended in political failure. Of course, Truman had his victories, especially on civil rights. But the bolder liberal vision of regulation and government activism—building on the New Deal legacy within an era of growing prosperity—was either defanged or defeated. The OPA went up in flames; the Employment Act of 1946 did nothing to ensure the "full employment" Truman hoped for; the Republicans passed antilabor union legislation (the Taft-Hartley Act) over Truman's veto; and national health care was dead out of the starting gate. All that was left for Truman was to use these defeats as cudgels against his enemies: he enjoyed berating a do-nothing Congress and squeaked into the presidency on his own terms in 1948. Here was the "give 'em hell" rhetoric mixed with an admission that the results would stop short of success. Here, in other words, was a politics of frustration.

Just as troubling were the limits Truman felt in terms of his ability to craft a liberal foreign policy. FDR believed that he could charm the Soviets into a postwar peace. Truman had no such illusions, as he watched the Soviet Union absorb much of Eastern Europe and provide inspiration—if not direct support—for pro-Communist forces in places like Greece and Turkey. Truman made "anti-Communism" a central tenet of postwar liberalism. In 1947 he famously told Congress, in language that, in retrospect, sounds overreaching, "I believe it must be the policy of the United States to support free peoples who are resisting attempted subjugation by armed minorities or by outside forces."[15] This was a huge promise. The "Truman Doctrine," as it would be called, came to define much of his foreign policy, giving aid to those who pronounced themselves enemies of Communism. And yet, this boldness held within its heart a simultaneous fear of the right. There was a growing sense that the conservative doctrine of "rollback" and toughness made liberals appear vacillating, even if they supported the ambitious doctrine of containment in which Truman believed. As conservatives dropped isolationism for "anti-Communism" and argued that the line between liberalism and Communism was blurred, Truman was dismayed, in 1949 especially, when the Soviets gained atomic parity with the United States and China turned "red." Truman was hemmed in by conservatives such as Joseph McCarthy who made the president—even with his bold doctrine—look weak on Communism. When he learned that North Korea had invaded South Korea, he immediately called for war without officially declaring it (that was still for Congress to do). Although he did stop short of the aggressive intentions of General MacArthur, who wanted to extend the war into China and perhaps beyond (Nixon and McCarthy supported this aggressive vision), Truman committed himself to containing Communism but provided few specifics as to how the Korean War might end. As Truman's biographer, Alonzo Hamby, points out, "The Korean War confronted Truman with the most serious international crisis of his presidency. It wholly rearranged the priorities of his administration, consigned the Fair Deal to limbo, left his presidency in tatters, and did grave damage to his morale."[16] Korea also foreshadowed the Vietnam War and the possibility that America might grow overcommitted in the world. If the goal was to support so-called free peoples across the globe, where would that end?

The politics of frustration became more pronounced when liberals learned the identity of Truman's choice for his successor: former Illinois governor, Adlai Stevenson. Thanks to his sharp intellectual qualities, academics loved Stevenson. But Stevenson's professorial airs and the fact that he came from an old aristocratic family with money provided an opportunity for conservative critics—especially someone like Richard Nixon, the bulldog vice-presidential candidate who served as a counterweight to Eisenhower's softness—to tag liberalism as elitist and fey. Stevenson, after all, did sound professorial when he explained why he refused to make a false promise that he could end the Korean War—now drawn out for two years—or provide easy solutions to any other problem. There was no "give 'em hell" tones to his words on the campaign trail: "Let's talk sense to the American people," Stevenson advised.[17] If this approach did not lead to victory, he said, "Better we lose the election than mislead the people; and better we lose than misgovern the people."[18] This was, quite simply, the price Stevenson believed was necessary to combat McCarthyism—which by 1952, like the Korean War, was also into its second year—and the superficialities of the media (1952 was the first time that television played a big role in politics, especially during Richard Nixon's famous "Checkers Speech"). Though most historians find it hard to believe *anyone* could have defeated the war hero Eisenhower in 1952, Stevenson's own rhetoric—his airy and deliberative manner had earned him the nickname "egg-head"[19] by the time the campaign was in full swing—hints at a liberal difficulty in making bold cases and stark declarations in its attempt to connect with average citizens.[20]

Stevenson's airy tones help explain why the toughness of John F. Kennedy—with his biography of military heroism during the Second World War—appealed to liberals, despite the man's youth, Catholicism, and vagueness. Kennedy projected a more tepid, cautious, and sometimes technocratic view of power, what Arthur Schlesinger Jr.—a passionate supporter—called a "sense of cool, measured, intelligent concern."[21] Some historians characterize JFK's style as that of a "stoic," due in part to masking the serious physical pain he suffered.[22] Kennedy held on to the belief that intelligence could shape the future of American politics, but he appeared more vigorous than Stevenson (who still wanted the nomination in 1960). Although he often stacked his own ranks with liberals—including Ted Sorensen, Arthur Schlesinger Jr., and John Kenneth Galbraith—he considered himself a "realist."[23] Indeed, he conceived of liberals such as Schlesinger as lightning rods who would allow him to move in a more centrist direction; Galbraith's liberal economic visions and suggestions for more robust activism on the part of the federal government were safely contained by making him an ambassador to India, not a major economic advisor. Kennedy tucked these people into back corners as best he could and turned to his own managerial style for governing. Without going into detail, it seems fair to characterize Kennedy's presidency as reactive—prodded by events, both at home and abroad (the best book on Kennedy and the civil rights movement, for instance, is aptly entitled *The Bystander*). This is not to say that JFK didn't love power or that he didn't sometimes use inspiring rhetoric about a "New Frontier." But he didn't see himself the way FDR did: as a commander of troops at home shaping the destiny of the nation. He believed in a sort of post-ideological politics and moved from putting out one political fire to the next.[24]

LBJ: A RETURN TO THE POLITICS OF HOPE

Kennedy's leadership style contrasted sharply with that of his successor. Lyndon Baines Johnson was the most important liberal leader in the postwar period. He did more than anyone to merge FDR's unified vision of the executive and the cause of liberalism. LBJ—more than even Harry Truman—married himself to FDR's legacy. He cut his political teeth administering a New Deal program, the National Youth Administration, in Texas; won election to Congress in 1937 on a defense of FDR's decision to pack the Supreme Court (!); and, in one of those many disturbing psychological stories associated with him, told a journalist that FDR had been "just like a daddy to me."[25]

Unlike Truman, Stevenson, and JFK, Johnson was liberal to his core and dreamed along FDR lines. Johnson famously told Walter Heller, a chief economic advisor: "I want you to tell your friends—Arthur Schlesinger, Galbraith and other liberals—that . . . I'm no budget slasher. If you looked at my record, you would know that I am a Roosevelt New Dealer. As a matter of fact, to tell the truth, John F. Kennedy was a little conservative to suit my taste."[26]

Johnson loved using power, having cut his teeth in the Senate where he possessed "the soul of a legislator" (a trait that allowed him to become something of a legislative-executive twin master).[27] Consider first the way LBJ used JFK's assassination. Addressing Congress, LBJ explained that the country must "do away with uncertainty and doubt" and "from the brutal loss of our leader we will derive not weakness, but strength; that we can and will act and act now."[28] Armed with a bloody shirt, LBJ projected a vision of executive power both simple and declarative. "When you have something to do, don't sit there," he once said. "Do it, and do it fast."[29]

Johnson's power wasn't just historic, it was also deeply personal and often weird. Much like his successor, Richard Nixon, Johnson rooted power in everyday psychology. He made his staff swim naked with him in the White House pool and invited them into the bathroom ("I had never before seen a president taking a shit," his speechwriter Richard Goodwin recalled).[30] In Lance Morrow's words, LBJ's "grossness was an exercise and tactic of power."[31] Indeed, he had a physical presence that FDR lacked. Johnson intimidated opponents by towering over them physically—often seating them in a chair with short legs and taking the highest chair in the office for himself—and by berating them, sometimes for hours, even twisting their arms or touching them inappropriately. It was called the "treatment," what Ben Bradlee of the *Washington Post* described as feeling like "a St. Bernard had pawed you all over."[32] The first time he met LBJ, Bill Moyers was struck by "the sheer presence of the man. And I thought, 'That's what power is.'"[33]

It was power that got things done for others. Johnson pushed the Civil Rights Act—crafted by his predecessor—that had lingered through the summer of the March on Washington up to the time of Kennedy's assassination. LBJ came at it with a moral sense of righteousness Kennedy lacked. He told stories in the White House about Zephyr Wright, a college graduate and African American who drove the then vice-president's car from Washington to Texas on numerous occasions. "When they had to go to the bathroom, they would pull off on a side road, and Zephyr Wright, the cook of the Vice President of the United States, would squat in the road to pee," Johnson once explained. "That's wrong. And there ought to be something to change that."[34] So LBJ worked with his vice president, Hubert Humphrey, to pass the landmark laws of the civil rights movement: the Civil Rights Act of 1964—which was passed without amendments and with solid backing—and the Voting Rights Act of 1965.

But where LBJ really carried FDR's torch of liberalism was through his committing the country—just two months after his assumption of the presidency—to an "unconditional war on poverty." This announcement made some members of his Council of Economic Advisers nervous. They worried about overreach, but LBJ, like FDR, insisted upon ambitious goals.[35] Of course, there had been some movement under Kennedy to confront poverty, especially in relation to juvenile delinquency. But LBJ, working with Congress, unleashed a flurry of programs that made the first nine months of 1965 replicate the feeling of FDR's original First Hundred Days—massive, sweeping legislation, "a long-distance run . . . completed at the pace of a sprint."[36] He formulated the Economic Opportunity Act that set up work-training programs for the unemployed (Job Corps), created Community Action Programs (CAP) that would engage citizens at local level to combat poverty ("maximum feasible participation" that created headaches for mayors), generated Volunteers in Service to America (VISTA) (another grassroots initiative), and provided loans to those businesses that helped put the unemployed back to work.[37] Much of this would falter. But a good share of his "war on poverty" endured, including Head Start, Legal Services Corporation, and the permanent establishment of food stamps. Most significant was the passage of Medicare for the aged, which was built upon and remains as popular as Social Security, and the "piggybacking" of Medicaid, a less popular program for the poor.[38]

And yet many liberals watched LBJ with unease. Some of this had to do with LBJ's manner and character: he appeared to many to be crude and vulgar. This was particularly true of many of Kennedy's liberal intellectuals (Schlesinger especially). As one friend of Johnson recounted: "The real liberals—never truly accepted Johnson. I don't know why, because he was more liberal than the most liberal of them . . . It's partly style, partly the fact that he's from Texas. They would tell you, 'He's good and he's wise and he's effective, but well, he just isn't our kind of a guy . . .'"[39]

Perhaps most importantly, the Vietnam War led many liberals to break with his administration, a fact that heightened Johnson's inbred paranoia. The war, like the Great Society and civil rights legislation, was rushed. The Tonkin Gulf Resolution gave Johnson carte blanche without declaring war. Johnson believed Congress should not "sanction" but rather "support the war."[40] As he initiated "Rolling Thunder" and agreed to escalate troop numbers from 1965, Johnson grew increasingly suspicious about dissent within his own ranks and society at large.[41] The "imperial presidency" was born.[42]

That Vietnam destroyed liberalism's prospects in America and tore the country apart are truisms. There's no need to repeat the story here. But we need to understand its legacy for our own world. If we jump from the disaster of the Vietnam War to Richard Nixon's Watergate scandal (and there were direct linkages between the two), we get closer to the world of contemporary liberals. For when liberals applauded the exposure of Nixon's abuse of power as they pressed for his impeachment, they helped deepen the distrust in government that had emerged as a result of America's involvement in Vietnam, a distrust that would do their own cause implacable harm going forward.[43] From the 1970s onward, liberals faced a conundrum: armed with a vision based upon the use of power and a martial, high-minded spirit of national mobilization, there was now plummeting trust in and growing cynicism about executive power and war. America had entered the age of the post-imperial presidency.[44]

A RETURN TO THE POLITICS OF FRUSTRATION: CARTER, CLINTON, AND OBAMA

Revisiting the tenures of the Democratic presidents after Vietnam and Watergate reinforces the challenges faced by contemporary liberals. Jimmy Carter described himself as a fiscal conservative (so too had FDR).[45] He was certainly a centrist; he hadn't opposed Vietnam until late in the war and strongly opposed George McGovern's presidential candidacy in 1972. Both Vietnam and Watergate left a huge scar on Carter's political thinking. One of his numerous speechwriters, James Fallows, remarked, "It often seemed to me that 'history', for Carter and those closest to him, consisted of Vietnam and Watergate."[46] The first film (and there were many) Carter watched in the White House was *All the President's Men*. In his journals, he explained how he "felt strange occupying the same living quarters and position of responsibility as Richard Nixon."[47] The shadow you step into—clear also in the case of Harry Truman—shades the rest of your presidency.

Carter ran as a populist and "outsider" in 1976 (who wouldn't have?). But it meant that he never really squared himself with the halls of power in Washington—that is, with Congress and a scrutinizing press corps inside the Beltway (both armed with

memories of Vietnam and Watergate and a sensibility of *never again*). Carter possessed none of the near-magical legislative skill of LBJ. As such, Carter's presidency
could be boiled down to the logic of entrapment: he was paralyzed by the specters
of Vietnam and Watergate and a fear of repeating the mistakes of his predecessors.

His highest ambition was to create a National Energy Policy (NEP) in order
to confront the oil crisis that had stymied America since 1973. Carter developed
his plan in secret,[48] assisted by Secretary of Energy James Schlesinger. It was rather
technocratic, but Carter tried to inject his Sunday-school teacher moralism into it,
with some potent rhetoric, tipping his hat to FDR and LBJ. He called for the "Moral
Equivalent of War." That the acronym MEOW was used more often than not underscores Carter's difficulty in garnering the martial spirit. Carter stumbled over the
legacy of Vietnam and Watergate, which fueled not only a mounting distrust of politicians but also the type of conspiratorial thinking that suggested the energy crisis
was really a hoax perpetrated by oil companies to drive up costs. He found a language of sacrifice—often nurtured by war tropes—to fail in the face of the cynicism
of the so-called me decade. Carter's NEP focused on "the centralization of federal
energy planning," balanced with decontrol.[49] But lobbyists whittled down the plan,
so when passed in 1978 it lacked the shared sacrifice and constraints on consumption that Carter wanted.[50] Such was the fate of the post-imperial presidency.

Carter took pride in his skilled conduct of diplomacy, his belief that foreign
policy should place particular importance on the protection of human rights, and
the fact that he never put boots on the ground or embroiled America in a war.
But these achievements were undermined by the Soviet invasion of Afghanistan
and the hostage crisis in Iran. Facing reelection in the midst of these two events
Carter announced his "rose garden" strategy, saying he would focus on the work
of being an executive rather than spend time campaigning for a second term. This
move was initially popular. But as time went on, there grew a generalized fear of
weakness on the part of the presidency. The argument that Carter had kept us out of
war—something that resonated with many liberals—now appeared as fecklessness.
The final part of the story is well known: Carter was beaten in 1980 by a man who
ironically claimed that FDR was one of his role models.

What about Bill Clinton? No liberal either, Bill Clinton was a self-professed "centrist," having gained his first experience in public office a governor of Arkansas and
developing his political thought with the Democratic Leadership Council (DLC),
an organization Arthur Schlesinger called (unfairly in my mind) "a quasi-Reaganite
formation" that worshipped "the free market."[51] Clinton aimed to win back Middle
America to the Democratic Party. And he announced the end of LBJ's Great Society
by proclaiming, "The era of big government is over."[52]

Nevertheless, Clinton held romantic visions of political power. His mind bub-
bled with ideas about welfare reform, job retraining programs, and public service
(the ambitions outlined in *Putting People First*). But his most important initiative
was health- care reform. Like Carter, Clinton pursued this policy in secret, having

his wife, Hillary Clinton, and others work behind closed doors to construct what became a 1,350-page proposal. It was complicated, and when it failed, Clinton's vision of leadership shifted. As Joe Klein remarks, "Clinton had spent most of his life dreaming of a heroic, Rooseveltian presidency of great acts and grand gestures. But that dream ended with health care."[53]

What replaced it was policy constructed around polling. Though he fought Congress on a government shutdown, he also codified a reactive politics. He rejected the principled rethinking of liberalism within the DLC for the polling of Dick Morris and Mark Penn.[54] Perhaps the best example of this was his simultaneous support for and critique of a Republican version of welfare reform. Clinton feared that the policy would be draconian, but after listening to his pollsters, he signed on to the legislation and then campaigned for reelection as an opportunity to fix the law. During his second term, things turned grim—if not absurd—when the House of Representatives voted to impeach the president (once again, the legacy of Watergate). Any return to a "Rooseveltian presidency" now appeared impossible, and Clinton found himself entertaining lame ideas about fighting ATM fees and what Mark Penn would later call "micropolitics."[55]

On foreign policy, he left behind a model of snap executive action about a humanitarian crisis—one that was bold but less risky all at once. In 1999 Clinton allied himself with NATO and received a non-binding authorization from the Senate to carry out airstrikes against the brutal Slobodan Milosevic. The aim was to defend innocent civilians and send a message: "If President Milosevic will not make peace, we will limit his ability to make war." The House's vote eventually tied on the Senate's original non-binding agreement (impeachment hung in the air). Congress never declared war and eventually gave the president shrugging support. Clinton seemed to find a way to justify limited military action or what might best be called a micro-war carried out by a weakened executive.[56]

Like President Clinton, Barack Obama faced limits to his ambitions from the outset. In part, these limits were the product of the era he was raised in and has governed. He came of age not only after the golden era of the civil rights movement (a member of the so-called Joshua Generation) but during the "malaise" decade and the Reagan era. After studying political theory, he did a stint in community organizing—a refuge from traditional representative governmental structures. He learned the art of listening to citizens to mobilize them at the grassroots level (some characterize community organizing as antipolitics, more direct than mediated or representational action). Obama assumed the presidency on the heels of George W. Bush, who had tried to reinvigorate the "imperial presidency" of Johnson and Nixon. The biographical details and the timing add up to a presidency hemmed in not just by a louder conservative movement but by its own sense of limits.

Hence, Obama was more JFK than LBJ. It wasn't just his youth but his cool persona that allowed some—including Kennedy's speechwriter, Ted Sorensen—to compare Obama to JFK.[57] He had a knack for powerful rhetoric on the campaign trail (one of his favorite speeches being Kennedy's "Ask Not What . . .") but often turned technocratic or aloof when it came to governing as president (in contrast to FDR's fireside chats).[58]

His signature policy—aside from the stimulus package—was health-care reform. Obama was certainly more effective than Clinton here, but consider how the Affordable Care Act's rollout left many Americans fuzzy at best and annoyed with a bungled website. That the policy's start-up aligned with a government shut-down certainly didn't help. But even in its origins, Obama's policy was stymied. Note the scandal surrounding its first proponent, Tom Daschle, for example; then it had to swim up the tide of public opinion already soured by TARP (not Obama's own policy but one that he carried forth) and the stimulus, which did far more good than it got recognition for.[59] Just barely winning on health care also made it more difficult for Obama to move forward on much of anything else, including a jobs bill (which went nowhere in his first term). There was no return to boldness like FDR's in 1935.[60] Ironically, throughout his presidency, liberals would prod the pres-ident to be more like Truman ("Give 'em hell, Barry")—an odd model, considering Truman's feistiness was as much about his own political defeat as it was about an aggressive criticism of his opposition.[61]

Obama's foreign policy offered a sensible reaction to the perils of the Iraq War and a vision grounded in a reading of Reinhold Niebuhr on the need for humil-ity and limits. During the Arab Spring, Obama seemed beholden to "leading from behind," meaning talk loud at times but don't use a big stick.[62] When Obama felt a line had been crossed in Syria—akin to Slobodan Milosevic's actions for Clinton—Americans witnessed one of the most bizarre episodes in diplomatic his-tory, with the president, for the first time in a long time, asking for Congress's support and vote for action and then having an offhand remark by Secretary of State John Kerry open up an alternative to military action. Since then, Obama has tried to steer a difficult foreign policy course, including carrying out pinpointed actions against Muslim fanatics in Iraq and Syria and short-term humanitarian initiatives—trying to avoid full-fledged engagement.

CONCLUSION

Given the difficulties they faced, some would argue that the Carter, Clinton, and Obama presidencies were failures. I think that a more accurate conclusion would be to view them as presidencies operating within the strictures inherited from history. They are certainly *rearguard*, that is, more JFK and more Truman than FDR and LBJ. They were presidencies that couldn't get out of the shadows of Vietnam and Watergate (and then later Iraq), during a time when liberalism lost influence. FDR's legacy of boldness and military valor offered little, other than a sense (to paraphrase Lou Reed) that those were different times.

So here we are with the contemporary quandary of liberalism: Liberals desire bold action on an array of issues but also fear the abuses (and the historical paranoia that abuses prompt) of executive power. The language of national sacrifice based on emergency wartime analogies consistently fall on deaf ears. This is rooted not just in historical experience (Vietnam, Watergate, the Clinton scandal, and Iraq) but in a long-term philosophical distrust in power, a suspicion that is indebted to what John Dewey called the "old" liberalism (or classical liberalism) in contrast with the "new."[63] When honest, liberals admit that power *can* corrupt (not that it always does). As much as liberals need to defend unified action to tackle problems, they must also protect *procedural* fairness. They must protect against the language of "decisionism" and the overreach of those who can grow isolated in political office.

Because of this, I think the future of liberalism will be tentative, humility fueled, focused on backcourt dribbling and defense of existing programs, worried about overstretch, hemmed in, and likely reactive rather than visionary or glowing with the language of war. More Truman, less FDR; more Obama, less LBJ. Like Obama's foreign policy, it might cite big principles—spreading democracy and promoting human rights—but be wary of rushing to action, because action can sometimes do more harm than good. Maybe we should call this version of post-war liberalism "Clinton-Obamaism" for lack of a better term. It's a liberalism that doesn't believe—as George W. Bush's henchmen did—we can or should overcome a "Vietnam legacy." This is a liberalism chastened by history and weakened by our predecessors' mistakes and misjudgments. This is a liberalism that moves where it can with caution. It is necessarily more reactive, aware of "backlash" and the ironies of history. And it's a liberalism that faces the overwhelming fact of American political life today: that confidence in the idea of government, at least in the abstract, continues to plummet.[64]

It's not a happy thing to say this; after all, our problems are immense. The American middle class—those citizens FDR wanted to defend against the vagaries of capitalism—is shrinking, poverty levels are growing, voting rights violations are returning, global warming threatens us in ways almost unimaginable. Authoritarian regimes in the Middle East and around the world deserve rebuke for abuse, authoritarianism, and genocide. And yet to think that these problems will be tackled by bold military valor and strong executive power at home is to hope for something difficult, if not impossible. The only thing we're left with is a chastened liberalism that will struggle to combat the paralysis that a politics of frustration always threatens.

Notes

1. Arthur Schlesinger Jr. "Two Years Later—the Roosevelt Family," *Life*, April 7, 1947, 113.
2. FDR, "Commonwealth Club Speech" and "First Inaugural Address," in *Great Issues in American History*, ed. Richard Hofstadter (New York: Vintage, 1969), 355, 350, 349.

3. Betty Winfield, *FDR and the News Media* (Urbana: University of Illinois Press, 1990), 104–105; see also Robert McElvaine, ed., *Down and Out in the Great Depression: Letters from the "Forgotten Man"* (Chapel Hill: University of North Carolina Press, 1983).

4. Tugwell quote, Jeff Shesol, *Supreme Power: Franklin Roosevelt vs. the Supreme Court* (New York: Norton, 2010), 507.

5. Alonzo Hamby, Man of the People: *A Life of Harry S. Truman* (New York: Oxford University Press, 1990), 313.

6. James Patterson, *Mr. Republican: A Biography of Robert A. Taft* (Boston: Houghton Mifflin, 1972).

7. For more on this, see Elizabeth Fones-Wolf, *Selling Free Enterprise: The Business Assault on Labor and Liberalism, 1945–60* (Urbana: University of Illinois Press, 1994) and Kim Phillips-Fein, *Invisible Hands: The Making of the Conservative Movement from the New Deal to Reagan* (New York: Norton, 2009).

8. Roger Morris, *Richard Milhous Nixon* (New York: Holt, 1990), 331; Stephen Ambrose, *Nixon* (New York: Simon and Schuster, 1987), 119; Conrad Black, *Richard M. Nixon* (New York: Public Affairs, 2008), 73, 12; Stephen Ambrose, *Nixon*, 120–121; Richard Nixon, *Memoirs*, 37; John Patrick Diggins, *The Proud Decades* (New York: W.W. Norton, 1989), 102; Richard Nixon, *The Memoirs* (New York: Simon and Schuster, 1990), 42.

9. Harry Truman, *Memoirs*, Volume 1 (Garden City: Doubleday, 1955–1956), 481–483.

10. *Public Papers of the Presidents of the United States: Harry S. Truman, 1945* (Washington, DC: Government Printing Office), 273, 279, 281, 290, 309.

11. Lizabeth Cohen, *A Consumers' Republic: The Politics of Mass Consumption in Postwar America* (New York: Knopf, 2003), 102.

12. Meg Jacobs, "'How About Some Meat'," *Journal of American History* 84 (1997): 937.

13. Alonzo Hamby, *Man of the People*, 381.

14. Norman Markowitz, *The Rise and Fall of the People's Century* (New York: Free Press, 1973), 147.

15. George McKee Elsey, *An Unplanned Life* (Columbia: University of Missouri Press, 2005), 149.

16. Alonzo Hamby, *Man of the People*, 534.

17. Jeff Broadwater, *Adlai Stevenson and American Politics: The Odyssey of a Cold War Liberal* (Woodbridge, CT: Twayne Publishers, 1994), 116.

18. Jeff Broadwater, *Adlai Stevenson*, 116.

19. See Richard Hofstadter, *Anti-Intellectualism in American Life* (New York: Knopf, 1963).

20. For more on this, see my *Just Plain Dick: Richard Nixon's Checkers Speech and the "Rocking, Socking" Election of 1952* (New York: Bloomsbury, 2012).

21. Quoted in Robert Dallek, *An Unfinished Life: John F. Kennedy, 1917–1963* (Boston: Little Brown, 2003), 279. On this characterization more broadly, see Bruce Miroff, *Pragmatic Illusions* (New York: McKay, 1976).

22. Robert Dallek, *An Unfinished Life*, 73.

23. Robert Dallek, *An Unfinished Life*, 178.

24. See Bruce Miroff, *Pragmatic Illusions*.

25. Michael Janeway, *The Fall of the House of Roosevelt: Brokers of Ideas and Power from FDR to LBJ* (New York: Columbia University Press, 2004), 149.

26. Quoted William Leuchtenberg, *In the Shadow of FDR* (Ithaca, NY: Cornell University Press, 2001), 137.

27. G. Calvin Mackenzie and Robert Weisbrot, *The Liberal Hour: Washington and the Politics of Change in the 1960s* (New York: Penguin, 2008), 69.

28. Quoted in Robert Dallek, *Flawed Giant: Lyndon Johnson and His Times* (New York: Oxford, 1998), 56.

29. Eric Goldman, *The Tragedy of Lyndon Johnson* (New York: Dell, 1969), 20.

30. Richard Goodwin, *Remembering America* (Boston: Little, Brown, 1988), 256.

31. Lance Morrow, *The Best Year of Their Lives* (New York: Basic, 2005), 207.

32. Robert Dallek, *Flawed Giant*, 5.

33. Robert Schlesinger, *White House Ghosts* (New York: Simon and Schuster, 2008), 163.
34. Robert Dallek, *Flawed Giant*, 113.
35. Irwin Unger, *The Best of Intentions: The Triumphs and Failures of the Great Society* (New York: Doubleday, 1996), 79; see also Robert Caro, *The Passage of Power* (New York: Knopf, 2012), 545.
36. Irwin Unger, *The Best of Intentions*, 104; Gavin MacKenzie and Robert Weisbrot, *The Liberal Hour*, 113.
37. Robert Dallek, *Flawed Giant*, 79.
38. David Farber, *Age of Great Dreams* (New York: Hill and Wang, 1994), 108.
39. Quoted Dallek, *Flawed Giant*, 124.
40. Arthur Schlesinger, Jr., *The Imperial Presidency* (New York: Popular Library, 1974), 181.
41. Robert Dallek, *Flawed Giant*, 376.
42. Robert Dallek, *Flawed Giant*, 252–3. One of the sadder legacies of this paranoia was how Hubert Humphrey moved from being a vice president who warned Johnson about the perils of Vietnam to being an apologist for the war—something that not only shattered his personality but also hurt his prospects in 1968. See my account of a 1967 meeting between Galbraith, Schlesinger, and James Wechsler and Hubert Humphrey where Humphrey defended the war while admitting it was a "morass": Kevin Mattson, *When America Was Great: The Fighting Faith of Postwar Liberalism* (New York: Routledge, 2006), 178–179.
43. H.W. Brands, *The Strange Death of American Liberalism*, (New Haven: Yale, 2001), 124–125.
44. The term is obviously Arthur Schlesinger Jr.'s. It's ironic to note that Schlesinger started his career writing romantic and glowing accounts of presidential power—in his works on the New Deal and certainly in his hagiographic memoir about JFK. But by the late 1960s, Schlesinger was questioning presidential prestige and power.
45. Jimmy Carter, *Keeping Faith: Memoirs of a President* (Fayetteville: University of Arkansas Press, 1985), 74.
46. James Fallows, "The Passionless Presidency," *Atlantic Monthly*, May 1979, 38.
47. Jimmy Carter, *Keeping Faith: Memoirs of a President*, 29.
48. Haynes Johnson, *In the Absence of Power* (New York: Viking, 1980), 188–189.
49. John C. Barrow, "An Age of Limits: Jimmy Carter and the Quest for a National Energy Policy," in Gary Fink and Hugh Davis Graham, eds., *The Carter Presidency: Policy Choices in the Post-New Deal Era* (Lawrence: University of Kansas, 2001), 163.
50. Haynes Johnson, *In the Absence of Power*, 292–293.
51. Quote in Kenneth Baer, *Reinventing Democrats* (Lawrence: University of Kansas, 2000), 81.
52. Sean Wilentz, *The Age of Reagan* (New York: Harper, 2008), 364. Wilentz points out that Clinton qualified this bold statement with talk about community and responsibility toward others, but that many saw the take-away in the bolder first words.
53. Joe Klein, *The Natural: The Misunderstood Presidency of Bill Clinton* (New York: Broadway, 2002), 138.
54. Joe Klein, *The Natural*, 135–136.
55. For more on Mark Penn's legacy in the world of Clintonism, see my "Microman," *The Guardian*, April 11, 2008: http://www.theguardian.com/commentisfree/2008/apr/11/microman
56. Clinton almost found the airstrikes ineffective and thus came close to sending in ground troops. The situation would have been quite different if that had happened: See John Harris, *The Survivor* (New York: Random House, 2005), 373–375.
57. Richard Wolffe, *Renegade* (New York: Crown, 2009), 84.
58. Jonathan Alter, *The Promise: President Obama, Year One* (New York: Simon and Schuster, 2010), 106.
59. Jonathan Alter, *The Promise*, 79–83.
60. Richard Wolffe, *Revival* (New York: Crown, 2010), 202.

61. See here Robert Kuttner, "Give 'Em Hell, Barry: What Barack Obama can Learn from Harry Truman's Inspired Use of Partisanship," *The American Prospect*, March 27, 2010; and Thomas Frank, "Health Care and the Democratic Soul: It's Time for Obama to Channel Harry Truman," *Wall Street Journal*, August 25, 2009.

62. Ryan Lizza, "The Consequentialist," *The New Yorker*, May 2, 2011, 55. It should be pointed out that these were not Obama's own words.

63. See John Dewey, *Liberalism and Social Action* (1935; Amherst: Prometheus, 2000). On the long history of distrust in government, see Garry Wills, *A Necessary Evil* (New York: Simon and Schuster, 1999).

64. http://www.huffingtonpost.com/2013/09/13/government-trust-poll_n_3922684.html

4

Progressive Politics and the Rise of the Modern Right

JOHN M. THOMPSON

In February 2009 CNBC editor Rick Santelli took to the floor of the Chicago Board of Trade to criticize President Barack Obama's plan to help homeowners who were struggling to pay their mortgages. Santelli slammed the administration for "promoting bad behavior" among "losers" and expressed the frustration of Americans who did not want to "pay for [their] neighbor's mortgages that has an extra bathroom and can't pay their bills." But Santelli's "rant," as it quickly came to be known, was more than an expression of frustration with possible solutions to the housing crisis; it embodied, more broadly, a fear among conservative Americans that their country, under the leadership of a progressive president, was evolving in a manner that they found terrifying. Santelli noted that Cuba had "moved from the individual to the collective" and in doing so had wrecked their economy. He warned that something similar was happening in America and announced that it was "time for another tea party."[1]

Santelli's outburst had a galvanizing effect on conservatives, with dozens of grassroots organizations forming across the country with names such as "Tea Party Patriots," "Tea Party Express," and "FreedomWorks." The Tea Party movement, as it quickly became known, presented itself as a grassroots movement with a libertarian bent that focused on "individual freedom, fiscal responsibility and limited government," as Matt Kibbe and Dick Armey, the leaders of FreedomWorks, wrote in *The Wall Street Journal*.[2] Observers on both sides of the aisle saw the Tea Party as a new and powerful force in American politics.[3]

However, viewing the Tea Party, and conservative politics in America more broadly from a historical perspective underscores the fact that, although the Tea Party has certainly been influential, it is anything but novel. Instead, it is merely the latest iteration in a long-term effort by conservatives to move the Republican Party rightward. Indeed, in their "Tea Party Manifesto," Kibbe and Armey wrote that the Tea Party was "not seeking a junior partnership with the Republican Party, but a hostile takeover of it."[4] This attempt by conservatives to take control of the Republican Party has been ongoing for decades, and as events in recent years demonstrate, it has largely succeeded.

THE RISE OF THE RIGHT

William F. Buckley, founder of the *National Review*, famously wrote in the magazine's mission statement, "A conservative is someone who stands athwart history, yelling Stop, at a time when no one is inclined to do so, or to have much patience with those who so urge it." He was referring to what conservatives saw as the urgent need to undo the dramatic changes that had occurred in American political life as a result of the New Deal. However, when it came to the nature of the Republican Party, Buckley sought something radically different than the status quo; he wanted to transform it into a vehicle for the conservative worldview, rather than an organization that treated such ideas as a constant threat to electability and respectability.[5]

The origins of the modern conservative movement can be traced to the mid-1950s, when activists such as Buckley began to challenge moderates and liberals for control of the Republican Party. This occurred simultaneously at different levels. Among the conservative elite, such as Buckley, there was a drive to assemble an intellectually compatible coalition of libertarians, traditionalists, and anti-Communists. Organization also occurred at the grassroots level around the country, as individuals such as Phyllis Schlafly and groups such as the John Birch Society mobilized in order to protect the country against Communism, big government, and other perceived threats that they believed the still-dominant liberals were ignoring or even promoting.[6]

Numerous sources provided the intellectual foundations for this movement, but the common point of departure was a profound distrust of the federal government. Partly this embodied a Jeffersonian view of the US Constitution, in which all power not explicitly granted to the federal government was to be preserved for the states as an essential means of preserving individual liberty.[7] This strand of thought was particularly influential in the South during the decades prior to the Civil War, where it served as a crucial justification for protecting the institution of slavery, and then for decades after 1865 as Southerners fought to deny civil rights to African Americans.[8] Crucial contemporary influences included the horrors of totalitarian regimes in Nazi Germany and the Soviet Union and the work of intellectuals and writers such as Friedrich Hayek and Ayn Rand.[9]

Imbued with this antigovernment ethos, conservatives were hostile not only to liberals and the Democratic Party but also to moderate Republicans such as Dwight Eisenhower. We often overlook the fact that, for much of the twentieth century, the Republican Party and conservatives had a tense relationship. A large bloc of conservatives could be found in the Democratic Party, especially in the South, as a legacy of the Civil War, and many Republicans were moderates or even liberals in the tradition of Theodore Roosevelt and Robert LaFollette. Hence, Republicans frequently clashed over ideas, with presidential nominating contests often serving as proxy fights for control of the party. Conservative elites and activists such as Buckley sought to marginalize the liberals and moderates and to move the party rightward. However, the conservative grassroots included extremist groups such as the John Birch Society, whose founder, Robert Welch, once accused Eisenhower of treason. The goal of Buckley and others was to marginalize figures such as Welch while harnessing the enormous energy of these groups. It was a complicated balancing act that has never been fully realized.[10] The susceptibility to conspiracy theories, antielitism, and anti-intellectualism that animated the John Birch Society and McCarthyism remained strong influences. As Richard Hofstadter observed at the time, these characteristics have long been part of American political culture and have by no means been limited to conservatives. However, they were much more prevalent on the right after the early 1950s.[11]

Nevertheless, the beginnings of a movement to capture the Republican Party were underway and began to bear fruit. Perhaps the first notable manifestation of the processes of conservative mobilization at the national level was the 1964 presidential nomination of Barry Goldwater. The US Senator from Arizona's libertarianism and strident anti-Communism, summarized in his 1960 book *The Conscience of a Conservative*, embodied the intellectual strands of the coalition that elites such as William F. Buckley had sought to assemble and that energized grassroots conservatives around the country.[12] The fact that Goldwater lost the election to Lyndon Johnson in one of the most lopsided results in history appears, in retrospect, far less important than the role that Goldwater played in serving as a vehicle for assembling a national conservative coalition that could vie for control of the Republican Party.

Goldwater was also in the vanguard of the so-called Southern Strategy. Using campaign rhetoric that appealed to the fears and prejudices of whites, particularly in the South, Goldwater and others such as George Wallace began the process of detaching states from the former Confederacy—and many whites in other parts of the nation—from the Democratic Party. The "solid South" had voted overwhelmingly for the Democratic Party since the Civil War era, and conservatives saw in the Civil Rights Act an opportunity to redraw the electoral map. This strategy coincided fortuitously with a significant demographic shift, as millions of Americans abandoned the Northeast and Midwest for the South and Southwest.[13] Richard Nixon's presidential campaigns in 1968 and 1972 used subtle language about states' rights, law and order, and busing—Nixon expanded his targets to white ethnic voters in the urban North in 1972—and Reagan used a similar strategy in 1976 and 1980.[14] When Lyndon Johnson signed the Civil Rights Act in 1964, he supposedly told an aide that the Democratic Party had lost the South for a generation. The process evolved more slowly than Johnson predicted, but over time his forecast came true.[15]

If Goldwater's campaign in 1964 demonstrated that there was a sizeable constituency for a conservative Republican message, it also highlighted the fact that such a
message was still seen as too extreme by a majority of Americans. Johnson used this
fact to his advantage during the campaign, perhaps most memorably in the television advertisement "Daisy," which implied none too subtly that Goldwater would
use nuclear weapons recklessly.[16] Indeed, even though Nixon was elected with the
(admittedly grudging, at times) support of conservatives in 1968 and 1972, he was
forced to govern as a moderate in many respects, as with his establishment of the
Environmental Protection Agency.[17]

This all seemed to change in 1980 with the election of Ronald Reagan. His platform of strong anti-Communism—he famously called the Soviet Union an "evil
empire"—hostility to federal spending, and conservative social values harnessed,
for the first time in a Republican president, the ideas that initially drew the support of conservative activists in the 1950s. Reagan's tenure coincided with the
emergence of many of the features that we identify with the modern Republican
Party. Grover Norquist's Americans for Tax Reform and the supply-side school
of economic theory came to prominence during these years, laying the foundations for an emphasis on low marginal tax rates, especially for high earners.[18]
Evangelical Christians also began to wield considerable political influence in
the party during the 1980s. This was seen in the influence of figures such as Pat
Robertson, who challenged George H. W. Bush for the Republican presidential
nomination in 1988 and formed the Christian Coalition.[19] Countering what was
seen as liberal domination of the federal judiciary was another hallmark of the
Reagan years. The president nominated staunch conservatives Antonin Scalia and
Robert Bork to the Supreme Court and elevated William Rehnquist to the position of Chief Justice.[20] The Federalist Society, an organization dedicated to promoting an originalist interpretation of the Constitution that is influential among
leading conservative members of the legal profession, was also founded during
Reagan's tenure.[21]

In retrospect, however, it is clear that Reagan's governing style was more moderate than his rhetoric. Although he oversaw significant tax cuts, he also accepted
a number of tax increases proposed by Congress. His harsh anti-Soviet rhetoric
also should be viewed in the context of his historic summit meetings with Mikhail
Gorbachev, which culminated in the Intermediate-Range Nuclear Forces Treaty.
Signed in 1987, this treaty eliminated nuclear and conventional ground-launched
ballistic and cruise missiles with intermediate ranges. Social conservatives were
routinely frustrated with Reagan's unwillingness to advocate more forcefully for
their priorities. These included school prayer and overturning the Supreme Court
decision *Roe v. Wade*, which legalized abortion. While they were pleased with the
nominations of Scalia and Rehnquist to the Supreme Court, they were suspicious
of another, Sandra Day O'Connor, who was somewhat more moderate on the question of reproductive rights.[22]

Reagan's relative moderation, which underscored his skill in reading the political zeitgeist and the continued appeal of the New Deal framework, was an indication that the country—including many Republicans—was not ready to embrace the full extent of the conservative platform. It also reflected the reality that Democrats still controlled Congress, and could block appointments—such as that of Bork—and policies that could be portrayed as extreme. However, as George H. W. Bush discovered, the Republican Party was increasingly hostile to moderates. Conservatives, long suspicious of his bona fides, reacted in dismay as he staked out centrist positions on issues such as the environment and the ban on assault weapons. Far more important, however, was the tax increase that Bush signed into law in 1990. Though it was not substantially different than those increases signed by Reagan, it earned him the enmity of many conservatives, a fact that was reflected in the vigorous challenge he faced from Pat Buchanan for the Republican Presidential nomination in 1992.[23]

Further proof of the growing power of conservatives in the party was furnished by the rise of Newt Gingrich to the Speakership of the House in 1994. As Thomas Mann and Norman Ornstein have argued, Gingrich's strategy for retaking the House—Republicans had been in the minority since the mid-1950s—involved extreme, confrontational tactics that had not been seen in that chamber in the modern era. They were designed to accomplish interrelated goals. Gingrich and his lieutenants strove to unite Republicans into a cohesive parliamentary minority that opposed Democrats on every issue, instead of finding areas of compromise, as had been the norm. They also sought to delegitimize the House as an institution in the eyes of the public, in order to undermine the popularity of the Democrats who were running it. Gingrich's tactics succeeded brilliantly, as demonstrated in the 1994 election, in which the Republicans retook the House with a substantial majority. The "Republican Revolution," as the media dubbed it, brought to Washington a number of populist conservatives who were even more confrontational than Gingrich, such as Rick Santorum, John Boehner, and Mark Sanford. These men and others like them would play a central role in shaping the nature of the party in the future.[24]

Several factors seemed to indicate that the Republicans had overreached during the 1990s and would return to a more moderate stance. These included Gingrich's ignominious departure from Congress amid accusations of impropriety and challenges to his leadership from other Republicans, the distaste among most Americans for the Republican-led impeachment of President Bill Clinton in 1998, Clinton's popularity when he left office, and the narrow and controversial victory of George W. Bush in the 2000 presidential election, along with his embrace of what he called "compassionate conservatism." However, the new president and his principal political advisor, Karl Rove, were determined to avoid the fate of Bush's father and to keep conservatives in the party satisfied. He therefore pursued a program of massive tax cuts that disproportionately benefited the wealthiest Americans, a vigorous prosecution of the so-called war on terror, and a controversial invasion of Iraq in 2003. Bush and his advisors were also notably indifferent to domestic policy.

As journalists and former administration officials have documented, Bush displayed a striking lack of intellectual curiosity, and Rove dictated the approach in a White House in which political operatives dominated policy discussions.[25]

Bush's tenure also coincided with the emergence of a powerful conservative media and internet presence. Fox News, owned by Rupert Murdoch and run by Roger Ailes, a former advisor to several Republican presidential candidates, emerged by the early 2000s as the preferred news outlets for conservatives and has dominated the ratings for cable news networks for most of the past fifteen years. With its high production values, celebrity program hosts, and unabashed partisan slant, Fox has revolutionized the way that Americans watch cable news and has been an important factor in the tendency of conservatives to circumvent traditional media outlets. This has been bolstered by the emergence of other prominent conservative voices. The *Wall Street Journal*, for instance, had long been a respected publication that focused on business and corporate news. However, ever since its purchase by Rupert Murdoch in 2007, the paper has evolved into a conservative general newspaper and a challenger to the left-of-center *New York Times*. Meanwhile, blogs such as the *Drudge Report* and *RedState* have given conservatives influential platforms in the social media sphere.[26]

However, the emergence of these new opinion leaders has been a mixed blessing from the perspective of many leaders in the Republican Party. Although they have contributed to the declining influence of traditional sources of media (which Republicans have long accused of a liberal bias) and enhanced the ability of conservatives to disseminate their worldview, these new voices have also facilitated greater scrutiny of officeholders, sapped the ability of party leaders to control the policy agenda, and increased the influence of grassroots activists. The result has been further radicalization of the party, along with swift and often harsh judgment of those politicians who are perceived to have failed in one respect or another.

George W. Bush, for example, in spite of his determination to avoid the mistakes of his father, is seen by many on the right as having been too moderate. His failure to cut the level of federal spending, his cooperation with Democrats in crafting legislation in the areas of education reform and Medicare, and his decision to support a massive bailout for the financial markets in 2008 led many conservatives to conclude that he was essentially a R.I.N.O. (Republican in Name Only).[27] What most saw as the incompetence of the administration in handling the occupation of Iraq and the chaos in New Orleans in the aftermath of Hurricane Katrina further alienated many in the party. The resounding loss in the 2008 presidential election of John McCain—a staunch conservative who had a history of ideological heterodoxy—further convinced many activists that the only way to ensure control of the White House, and sufficiently conservative governance, was to place priority upon ideological purity. This may have led to only moderate success in placing Tea Party–endorsed politicians in national office, but it has also had an enormous impact on the country's political system: Republicans have embraced ever more extreme positions and have been notably reluctant to compromise with Democrats.

THE REPUBLICAN PARTY TODAY

The gradual takeover by conservatives has resulted in a Republican Party that, in spite of its success in reshaping important facets of American politics over the past forty years, faces a number of structural problems. One is that, outside of cutting taxes, especially for the wealthiest Americans, and a rhetorical commitment to cutting the size of government, Republicans today betray a striking indifference to policy.[28] As the behavior of Republicans in Congress since 2008 has demonstrated, this was not just an anomaly that characterized the Bush administration. One manifestation of this has been the relative lack of legislative activity by the Republicans in the House of Representatives. As Jonathan Bernstein has observed, 100 days into the 113th Congress, Republicans had failed to introduce any substantial legislation, in marked contrast to earlier Congresses.[29]

Instead, Republicans in Congress have tended to focus on investigating the Obama administration or on proposing symbolic legislation that has no chance of passing, such as repealing the Affordable Care Act. What is more, in recent years, Republicans in Congress and around the country have routinely taken numerous (and often contradictory) stances on many policy issues. Perhaps the most striking example relates to social insurance. Paul Ryan, a member of the House of Representatives from Wisconsin who is regarded by many Republicans as the leading policy intellectual in the party, crafted several versions of a budget between 2008 and 2012 that would have begun to privatize Social Security and Medicare. Meanwhile, during the 2010 election campaign, a prominent tactic in the campaign strategy of congressional Republicans was the contention that *Democrats* planned to cut Medicare, as part of the Affordable Care Act.[30]

The fact that the Republican Party no longer takes much interest in policy is at least partly a product of the increasingly ideological nature of the party. Rather than crafting policies to deal with the most pressing problems—as Democrats have sought to do with health care and climate change—Republicans tend to favor the same prescription regardless of the facts of the particular problem: tax cuts and/or reducing the size of the federal government. As Matt Grossman and David Hopkins have argued, this makes it incredibly difficult for the party to participate responsibly in the process of running the country.[31] The American political system, which was designed by the framers of the Constitution to prevent any branch or any individual from gaining too much power, cannot function when one of the parties refuses to compromise. However, the threat of primary challenges from more conservative candidates has greatly increased the tendency of Republican members of Congress to prioritize doctrinal purity. The result has been a striking increase in problems of governance, including less legislation, more contentious confirmation battles, frequent threats to shut down the government, and brinksmanship regarding raising the federal debt ceiling. To be sure, Democrats are not blameless in this turn of events, but they find such dysfunction much more troubling than Republicans. As polling data indicates, whereas liberals generally see compromise as a necessary part of governance, Republicans overwhelmingly prefer their elective representatives to refuse to settle for anything less than complete victory.[32]

Republicans in Congress are responsive to this strand of thinking and, ironically, have successfully used it as a tactic for portraying the Democratic Party as the chief source of dysfunction and polarization. As Senate Minority Leader Mitch McConnell noted about initiatives during President Obama's first term, Republicans "worked very hard to keep our fingerprints off of these proposals. Because . . . the only way the American people would know that a great debate was going on was if the measures were not bipartisan. When you hang the 'bipartisan' tag on something, the perception is that differences have been worked out, and there's a broad agreement that that's the way forward."[33] In other words, Republicans have embraced, for most of the Obama era, opposition to progressive initiatives not because they oppose them in substance—often they do, but not always—but rather because that is what Republican voters demand and because it increases disapproval ratings for the president.

This determination to oppose Democratic ideas has been reinforced by a massive network of lobbyists and political action committees. Grover Norquist's Americans for Tax Reform foreshadowed the nature of things to come, as elected Republican officials today are subjected to a constant stream of pressure to adhere to conservative principles, usually through some combination of campaign contributions and report cards. The Club for Growth, a particularly influential group, advocates libertarian economic positions, with a particular focus on tax rates. The Heritage Foundation, once a respected conservative think tank, has evolved into an aggressive political pressure organization under the leadership of Jim DeMint, the former Senator from South Carolina. This atmosphere, as many observers have noted, makes it difficult for Republican legislators to engage in the compromises with Democrats that are essential for the political system to function.[34]

The relative indifference of the party to policy is also bolstered by the fact that conservatives increasingly receive their information mainly from conservative sources, resulting in a political culture where Republicans, and even their elected officials, are impervious to nonpartisan empirical evidence and scholarship. This phenomenon has become so common that many observers have taken to calling it "epistemic closure."[35] This may explain why Republicans appear to be much more susceptible to false information and conspiracy theories. This tendency has been particularly evident in many of the various pseudo-scandals during President Obama's tenure, which have included questioning the president's nationality and religion, the existence of so-called death panels in the legislation for the Affordable Care Act, or the unwillingness of many Republicans to believe polling data that predicted Obama's victory in the 2012 Presidential Election.[36] As Cass Sunstein and Adrian Vermeule predicted, attempts to counter such falsehoods, even when supported by an overwhelming amount of evidence or data—as in the case of climate change denial[37]—have been largely unsuccessful.[38]

Epistemic closure is only one source for the hostility to compromise among Republicans. More broadly, it is becoming increasingly clear that most conservatives believe that the country is in the process of changing for the worse, and they are desperate to halt this transformation before it becomes irreversible. As Stan Greenberg, James Carville, and Erica Seifert found in a series of focus groups in 2013, Republican voters are convinced that they are "losing politically and losing control of the country," and that President Obama "imposed his agenda, while Republicans in DC let him get away with it."[39]

To an extent, this sense of irreversible change originates in the changing demographics of the country. As Greenberg, Carville, and Seifert observe, Republicans have an "acute sense that they are white in a country that is becoming increasingly 'minority.'"[40] President Obama's election exacerbated this sense of change. He appears to serve as a powerful symbol of the ways in which the traditional balance of power between white Americans and their minority countrymen is changing. Indeed, Michael Tesler has found that Obama's election to the presidency has greatly increased the extent to which overt racist sentiment, rather than the coded appeals used for decades after the civil rights movement, has shaped partisan preferences among white voters.[41]

Perhaps the most dramatic manifestation of the sense of urgency felt by conservatives has been the emergence of the so-called Tea Party movement after 2009. As Rick Perlstein notes, the notion that the Tea Party represents a radical break from traditional conservative politics is mistaken. Instead, we should view the Tea Party as only the most recent manifestation of a long-running conservative tendency: over-reaction to control of the presidency by a progressive.[42] The short-lived American Liberty League, formed in 1934 by conservative Democrats and Republicans who sought to mobilize opposition to Franklin Roosevelt, was but the first iteration in a pattern that has been recurring for decades.[43]

Where the Tea Party differs from earlier conservative counter-reactions is in the degree of influence that it has been able to exercise over the Republican Party, pushing virtually all Republicans at the national level even further to the right.[44] The threat of primary challenges from more conservative Republicans and the increasing importance placed on ideological purity differ sharply from early phases of the party and from the current state of affairs among Democrats.

That is why the frequent mention of a civil war in the Republican Party is misleading.[45] The disagreements that observers frequently characterize as a fight between establishment Republicans and more conservative insurgents for control of the party is not usually a consequence of ideological differences. Because most Republicans do not care that much about policy, and agree broadly on the need to cut taxes and government spending on programs they perceive as benefiting primarily the poor and minorities, the real fight is mostly over tactics and rhetoric.[46] In other words, both wings of the party favor conservative policy stances. The main difference is that pragmatists tend to see occasional compromises—such as voting to fund the federal government—as a necessary step to retaining electability in national contests. The insurgents, meanwhile, place more emphasis upon ideological purity. The main measure of this is opposition to Democratic policies. It is this refusal to cooperate with Democrats under any circumstances that is the principal reason why we have not seen progress on issues such as climate change. The same may be said about the right's bewildering opposition to the recent promotion of a market-based solution to the health care crisis via the individual mandate. Republican activists care less about the specifics of policy than about the degree to which their elected officials are willing to oppose Democrats, especially President Obama.

That is why it is important to acknowledge is that many self-identified members of the Tea Party are not necessarily hostile to the federal government in every instance.[47] Rather, their main target appears to be federal programs that they perceive to be designed to primarily benefit undeserving Americans. Partially, this reflects an extreme libertarian belief that poverty is something that only happens to those who fail to work hard and are predisposed to look for handouts from the government. Also influential in this strand of thinking is a strong racial component, with Tea Partiers identifying nonwhite Americans as the most likely to take advantage of social insurance but also as being the least deserving of such help, given their alleged unwillingness to work. Tea Partiers and other conservatives also believe that the Democratic Party's commitment to expanding social insurance, in the form of programs such as the Affordable Care Act, is a deliberate tool to increase "dependency" among the poor and minorities and thereby increase the likelihood that these Americans will vote for their candidates.[48] This was the fundamental premise of Mitt Romney's infamous comments in 2012, in which he argued that 47 percent of Americans would vote for President Obama "no matter what" because they "are dependent upon government" and "believe that government has a responsibility to care for them."[49]

The ability of the Tea Party to push the Republican Party rightward should not be viewed as a new phenomenon, and is only the latest phase in a long-term process that began in the 1950s. However, while this shift of the Republican Party is the result of a decades-long campaign by conservatives, its consequences have only become fully apparent in recent years, perhaps most notably in regard to the drastic increase in partisanship.[50] While some of this is due to increased homogeneity in the two main political parties—the most conservative Democrat in Congress is now more liberal than the most moderate Republican—a number of scholars have concluded that most of the increase in partisanship is a result of the increasing radicalization of the Republican Party. In other words, the success of the Tea Party and their conservative predecessors in reshaping the culture of their party over the last six decades have been the principal cause of the increasingly divisive nature of American political life.[51]

Of course, many Republicans are aware of the extent of the challenges they face. This can be seen in the tentative suggestions of compromise on issues such as immigration by party leaders such as Jeb Bush, the former governor of Florida, and Senator Marco Rubio (though such efforts usually encounter fierce opposition, as was the case for Bush and Rubio).[52] There is even a movement afoot to reform the party. Ross Douthat, a thoughtful columnist for the *New York Times*, has been active in this regard for several years.[53] More recently, a group led by Yuval Levin, an intellectual who was an advisor to President George W. Bush, and Ramesh Ponnuru, an editor at the *National Review*, released a manifesto with the title *Room to Grow: Conservative Reforms for a Limited Government and a Thriving Middle Class*. This document implicitly recognizes that the Republican Party can no longer rely on the formula championed by Ronald Reagan—cutting taxes and government spending, except for national security—and needs to do more to address rising concern among many Americans about stagnating wages and income inequality.[54]

However, as E. J. Dionne, Jonathan Chait, and others have noted, these would-be reformers are severely limited by the political culture of the party, especially the requirement that Republicans demonstrate ideological purity. The result is a tendency to focus more on rhetoric and electoral positioning than upon coherent policy proposals.[55] This is partly a product of the party's lack of interest in policy. At least as important, however, is the fact that Republicans who are too vocal about reform tend to be punished severely: a number of prominent Republicans have been, in effect, excommunicated from the party for diverging too drastically from acceptable doctrine. Perhaps the most notable example of this is David Frum, the former speechwriter for George W. Bush who was fired from the conservative think tank American Enterprise Institute in 2010 for criticizing the Republican Party's decision to oppose, in toto, efforts to reform health-care reform instead of negotiating a compromise agreement.[56]

CONCLUSION

In spite of the many problems facing the Republican Party, it is unlikely that we are about to enter a period of Democratic dominance similar to the New Deal era. To be sure, demographic factors and the unpopularity of the Republican Party mean that Democrats will probably enjoy an advantage in presidential contests for the foreseeable future.[57] Perhaps more importantly, progressive priorities also appear set to serve as the starting point for many political debates in the coming years. This includes economic issues such as income inequality and social issues such as gay marriage and climate change.

At the same time, just as Democrats will probably enjoy a structural advantage in presidential elections, Republicans probably can look forward to natural majorities in the House of Representatives and the Senate, given the tendency of Democrats to cluster in large urban areas—accruing large majorities in a relatively small number of contests—and the fact that Republican strongholds are, in large part, found in small towns, rural areas, and less densely populated states.[58] Conservatives also control the Supreme Court, meaning that many progressive policies are vulnerable to judicial review. What is more, Republicans will probably capture the presidency in some years because voters tend to blame economic downturns on the party that holds the presidency. In other words, progressives will likely face a political landscape in which their priorities are popular but difficult to enact.

However, the most troubling aspect of today's Republican Party is the manner in which it will likely oppose progressive priorities. Differing approaches to policy problems will not, by definition, lead to political dysfunction. After all, Democrats have repeatedly demonstrated an ability to incorporate the ideas of their opponents into legislation. The individual mandate in the Affordable Care Act was, after all, introduced into political debates by the Heritage Foundation, so a conservative Republican Party is not inherently problematic.[59] Instead, progressives should be concerned by demands from conservative voters for total opposition to Democratic initiatives and the increasing tendency of their elected representatives to do just that. This means that deal making will be elusive and, in a political system in which compromise is a sine qua non to passing legislation, crucial problems such as immigration and climate change will be enormously difficult to address through the legislative process.

Notes

1. Lauren Sher, "CNBC's Santelli Rants About Housing Bailout," February 19, 2009, http://abcnews.go.com/blogs/headlines/2009/02/cnbcs-santelli/. Accessed August 14, 2014.
2. Dick Armey and Matt Kibbe, "A Tea Party Manifesto," *The Wall Street Journal*, August 17, 2010, http://online.wsj.com/news/articles/SB10001424052748704407804575425061553154540. Accessed August 14, 2014. Armey left FreedomWorks in 2012.
3. Mark Lilla, "The Tea Party Jacobins," *The New York Review of Books*, May 27, 2010, http://www.nybooks.com/articles/archives/2010/may/27/tea-party-jacobins/?page=1;   Peggy Noonan, "Why It's Time for the Tea Party," *Wall Street Journal*, September 17, 2010, http://online.wsj.com/news/articles/SB10001424052748703440604575496221482123504; Articles accessed August 14, 2014.
4. Armey and Kibbe, "A Tea Party Manifesto."
5. William F. Buckley, "Our Mission Statement," November 19, 1955, *National Review Online*, http://www.nationalreview.com/articles/223549/our-mission-statement/william-f-buckley-jr. Accessed June 18, 2014.
6. Kim Phillips-Fein, "Conservatism: a State of the Field," *Journal of American History* 98 (December 2011): 729; Donald T. Crichtlow, *Phyllis Schlafly and Grassroots Conservatism: A Woman's Crusade* (Princeton, NJ: Princeton University Press, 2005), 37–108; Lisa McGirr, *Suburban*

Warriors: The Origins of the New American Right (Princeton, NJ: Princeton University Press, 2001), 70.

7. Lance Banning, *The Jeffersonian Persuasion: Evolution of a Party Ideology* (Ithaca, NY: Cornell University Press, 1978), 116–117, 261, 264–265; Thomas Jefferson, First Inaugural Address, March 4, 1801, http://millercenter.org/president/jefferson/speeches/speech-3469. Accessed August 5, 2014.

8. David Brown and Clive Webb, *Race in the American South: from Slavery to Civil Rights* (Edinburgh: Edinburgh University Press, 2007), 67, 153, 277.

9. Alan Brinkley, *The End of Reform: New Deal Liberalism in Recession and War* (New York: Vintage Books, 1996), 157–160; Crichtlow, *Phyllis Schlafly*, 41; McGirr, *Suburban Warriors*, 152–154.

10. Rick Perlstein, *Before the Storm: Barry Goldwater and the Unmaking of the American Consensus* (New York: Hill and Wang, 2001), 153–158; Donald Critchlow, *The Conservative Ascendancy: How the GOP Right Made Political History* (Cambridge, MA: Harvard University Press, 2007), 57–59; Geoffrey Kabaservice, *Rule and Ruin: The Downfall of Moderation and the Destruction of the Republican Party, from Eisenhower to the Tea Party* (New York: Oxford University Press, 2012), xv–71.

11. Richard Hofstadter, *Anti-Intellectualism in American Life* (New York: Vintage Books, 1962), 3–5; Hofstadter, *The Paranoid Style in American Politics* (New York: Vintage Books, 2008), 3.

12. Perlstein, *Before the Storm*, 63–68, 171–200, 511–516; McGirr, *Suburban Warriors*, 111–146.

13. McGirr, *Suburban Warriors*, 21.

14. Perlstein, *Before the Storm*, 429–470; Rick Perlstein, *Nixonland: The Rise of a President and the Fracturing of America* (New York: Scribner, 2008), 202–568; Critchlow, *The Conservative Ascendancy*, 177; Thomas J. Sugrue and John D. Skrentny, "The White Ethnic Strategy," 171–192, in *Rightward Bound: Making America Conservative in the 1970s*, eds. Bruce Schulman and Julian Zelizer (Cambridge, MA: Harvard University Press, 2008).

15. Lewis L. Gould, *Grand Old Party: a History of the Republicans* (New York: Oxford University Press, 2014), 362–363; Dan Carter, *The Politics of Rage: George Wallace, the Origins of the New Conservatism, and the Transformation of American Politics* (Baton Rouge: Louisiana State University Press, 1995).

16. Perlstein, *Before the Storm*, 412–415.

17. Perlstein, *Nixonland*, 129–130, 281–289; Crichtlow, *Phyllis Schlafly*, 183–211.

18. Jude Wanniski's *The Way the World Works* (New York: Gateway Editions, 1978) was a crucial influence during the Reagan administration and helped popularize supply-side ideas in conservative circles. Wanniski was an adviser to Congressman Jack Kemp, one of the first supply-siders in government, who served as a mentor to Paul Ryan. Stephen Miller, "Jude Wanniski, 69, Provocative Crusader for Supply-Side Economics," *New York Sun*, August 31, 2005, http://www.nysun.com/obituaries/jude-wanniski-69-provocative-crusader-for-supply/19386/. Accessed August 22, 2014.

19. Sara Diamond, *Roads to Dominion: Right-Wing Movements and Political Power in the United States* (New York: Guilford Press, 1995), 228–256.

20. Critchlow, *The Conservative Ascendancy*, 172–219; Robert Dallek, *Ronald Reagan: the Politics of Symbolism*, viii, 123; Michael Schaller, *Reckoning with Reagan: America and its President in the 1980s* (New York: Oxford University Press, 1992), 41.

21. Steven M. Teles, *The Rise of the Conservative Legal Movement: The Battle for Control of the Law* (Princeton, NJ: Princeton University Press, 2008), 135–180.

22. James P. Pfiffner, "The Paradox of President Reagan's Leadership," *Presidential Studies Quarterly* 43 (March 2013): 81–100; Schaller, *Reckoning with Reagan*, 41.

23. Critchlow, *The Conservative Ascendancy*, 227–239.

24. Thomas Mann and Norman Ornstein, *It's Even Worse Than It Looks: How the American Constitutional System Collided with the New Politics of Extremism* (New York: Basic Books, 2012), 31–43.

25. Ron Suskind, "Why Are These Men Laughing?" *Esquire*, January 2003; Matt Latimer, "A Love of Power Helped End a Conservative Revolution," *Washington Post*, September 20, 2009.

26. Steve Coll, "The King of Foxes," *New York Review of Books*, April 3, 2014, http://www.nybooks.com/articles/archives/2014/apr/03/roger-ailes-king-of-foxes/; Nicholas Lemann, "Fear Factor," March 27, 2006, *New Yorker*, http://www.newyorker.com/archive/2006/03/27/060327fa_fact; Mark Bowden, "Mr. Murdoch Goes to War," *The Atlantic*, July 1, 2008, http://www.theatlantic.com/magazine/archive/2008/07/mr-murdoch-goes-to-war/306867/. Accessed August 5, 2014.

27. John D. McKinnon, "Rescue Tests Bush's Conservative Legacy," *Wall Street Journal*, September 29, 2008, http://online.wsj.com/news/articles/SB122264902427584171. Accessed August 5, 2014.

28. The commitment to tax cuts has shifted increasingly, in some influential corners of the party, toward reducing rates mainly for the wealthiest Americans. The *Wall Street Journal*, for instance, regularly bemoans the "lucky duckies" who are too poor to be liable for federal income tax. See, e.g. "The Non-Taxpaying Class," November 20, 2002, http://www.wsj.com/articles/SB1037748678534174748. Accessed December 15, 2014.

29. Jonathan Bernstein, "GOP Quits Public Policy," *Salon*, April 23, 2013, http://www.salon.com/2013/04/23/gop_quits_public_policy/. Accessed May 22, 2014.

30. Ryan Lizza, "Fussbudget: How Paul Ryan captured the G.O.P., *New Yorker* August 6, 2012. http://www.newyorker.com/reporting/2012/08/06/120806fa_fact_lizza?currentPage=all; Jennifer Steinhauer, "Ads Use Medicare Cuts as Rallying Point," *New York Times*, October 30, 2010, http://www.nytimes.com/2010/10/31/us/politics/31medicare.html. Accessed July 3, 2014.

31. Matt Grossman and David Hopkins, "The Ideological Right vs. the Group Benefits Left: Asymmetric Politics in America," paper prepared for presentation at the 2014 Midwest Political Science Association, p. 20, http://matthewg.org/papers/ideologicalright.pdf. Accessed December 15, 2014.

32. Pew Research Center for People and the Press, "Political Polarization in the American Public: How Increasing Ideological Uniformity and Partisan Antipathy Affect Politics, Compromise and Everyday Life," June 12, 2014, http://www.people-press.org/2014/06/12/section-4-political-compromise-and-divisive-policy-debates/. Accessed June 17, 2014.

33. Joshua Green, *The Atlantic*, January 4, 2011, http://www.theatlantic.com/magazine/archive/2011/01/strict-obstructionist/308344/. Accessed June 19, 2014.

34. Jennifer Steinhauer, "A Conservative Leader Was Less So in Congress," http://www.nytimes.com/2012/03/02/us/politics/chris-chocola-of-club-for-growth-was-less-fiscally-conservative-in-congress.html; Jennifer Steinhauer and Jonathan Weisman, "In the DeMint Era at Heritage, a Shift From Policy to Politics," *New York Times*, February 23, 2014, http://www.nytimes.com/2014/02/24/us/politics/in-the-demint-era-at-heritage-a-shift-from-policy-to-politics.html; Ralph Hallow, "As Main Street Deepens Schism in GOP, Conservative War Against Compromise Heads to Amelia," *Washington Times*, April 10, 2014, http://www.washingtontimes.com/news/2014/apr/10/as-main-street-deepens-schism-in-gop-conservative-/?page=all. Articles accessed July 4, 2014.

35. Julian Sanchez, "Frum, Cocktail Parties, and the Threat of Doubt," March 26, 2010, http://www.juliansanchez.com/2010/03/26/frum-cocktail-parties-and-the-threat-of-doubt/; Noah Millman, "Who Closed the Conservative Mind," April 8, 2010, http://theamericanscene.com/2010/04/08/who-closed-the-conservative-mind. Articles accessed June 17, 2014.

36. For birtherism, see "The Psychology of the Birther Movement," *New York Times*, April 21, 2011, http://www.nytimes.com/roomfordebate/2011/04/21/barack-obama-and-the-psychology-of-the-birther-myth; for death panels see Jim Rutenberg and Jackie Calmes, *New York Times*, August 13, 2009, "False 'Death Panel' Rumor Has Some Familiar Roots," http://www.nytimes.com/2009/08/14/health/policy/14panel.html?_r=0; for Republican skepticism about polling data in the autumn of 2012, see David Hill, "Outweighed

Republicans Skeptical of Polls' Left Tilt," *Washington Times*, September 25, 2012, http://www.washingtontimes.com/news/2012/sep/25/outweighed-republicans-skeptical-of-polls-left-til/?page=all. Articles accessed June 17, 2014.

37. Pew Research Center for People and the Press, "Fewer Americans See Solid Evidence of Global Warming," October 22, 2014, http://www.people-press.org/2009/10/22/fewer-americans-see-solid-evidence-of-global-warming/. Accessed June 17, 2014.

38. Cass R. Sunstein and Adrian Vermeule, "Conspiracy Theories," Harvard University Law School Public Law & Legal Theory Research Paper Series, University of Chicago Law School Public Law & Legal Theory Research Paper Series Paper No. 199, and University of Chicago Law School Law and Economics Research Paper Series Paper No. 387, January 15, 2008.

39. Stan Greenberg, James Carville, and Erica Seifert, "Inside the GOP: Report on Focus Groups with Evangelical, Tea Party, and Moderate Republicans," Democracy Corps, October 3, 2013, p. 1.

40. Greenberg, Carville, and Seifert, "Inside the GOP," p. 5. See also Maureen A. Craig and Jennifer A. Richeson, "On the Precipice of a "Majority—Minority" America: Perceived Status Threat From the Racial Demographic Shift Affects White Americans' Political Ideology," *Psychological Science*, April 3, 2014, http://pss.sagepub.com/content/early/2014/04/02/09 56797614527113. Accessed June 17, 2014.

41. Michael Tesler, "The Return of Old-Fashioned Racism to White Americans' Partisan Preferences in the Early Obama Era," *Journal of Politics* 75 (January 2013): 121.

42. Rick Perlstein, "The Grand Old Tea Party," *The Nation*, November 5, 2013, http://www.the-nation.com/article/177018/grand-old-tea-party#. Accessed June 18, 2014.

43. Frederick Rudolph, "The American Liberty League, 1934–1940," *American Historical Review* 56 (October 1950): 19–33; David Woolner, "The Tea Party Movement: Successor to the American Liberty League?" *Next New Deal*, July 1, 2010, http://www.nextnewdeal.net/tea-p arty-movement-successor-american-liberty-league. Accessed August 19, 2014.

44. Vanessa Williamson, Theda Skocpol, and John Coggin, "The Tea Party and the Remaking of Republican Conservatism," *Perspectives on Politics* 9 (March 2011): 35–36.

45. Jonathan Martin, Jim Rutenberg, and Jeremy W. Peters, "Fiscal Crisis Sounds the Charge in G.O.P.'s 'Civil War'," *New York Times*, October 19, 2013, http://www.nytimes.com/2013/10/20/us/fiscal-crisis-sounds-the-charge-in-gops-civil-war.html?pagewanted=all; Molly Ball, "Is This the End of the GOP Civil War?" *The Atlantic*, May 6, 2014, http://www.theatlantic.com/politics/archive/2014/05/thom-tillis-wins-north-carolina-primary-is-this-the-end-gop-ci vil-war/361834/. Articles accessed June 18, 2014.

46. Jonathan Bernstein, "There Is No Republican Civil War," *Bloomberg View*, April 7, 2014, http://www.bloombergview.com/articles/2014-04-07/there-is-no-republican-civil-war. Accessed June 18, 2014.

47. This fact is reflected in the most recent budget plan released by the leading Republican on domestic policy issues, Paul Ryan. It includes only mild cuts to Medicare and Social Security—which are popular among Tea Party voters—but would impose much larger cuts on the Affordable Care Act and Medicaid, which are seen by Republicans as primarily benefiting the poor and minorities. See Danny Vinik, "The Ryan Budget Doesn't Just Sin Against the Poor: It Sins Against Math, Too," *The New Republic*, April 10, 2014, http://www.newrepublic.com/article/117333/paul-ryans-budget-bad-poor-and-bad-math. Accessed June 18, 2014.

48. Williamson, Skocpol, and Coggin, "The Tea Party and the Remaking of Republican Conservatism," 32–35; Greenberg, Carville, and Seifert, "Inside the GOP," 10–13.

49. "Romney's Speech From *Mother Jones* Video," *New York Times*, September 19, 2012, http://www.nytimes.com/2012/09/19/us/politics/mitt-romneys-speech-from-mother-jo nes-video.html?pagewanted=all&_r=0. Accessed June 18, 2014.

50. Drew Desilver, "Partisan Polarization, in Congress and Among Public, is Greater than Ever," Pew Research Center, July 17, 2013, http://www.pewresearch.org/fact-tank/2013/07/17/

partisan-polarization-in-congress-and-among-public-is-greater-than-ever/. Accessed June 18, 2014.

51. Seth Masket, "Mitigating Extreme Partisanship in an Era of Networked Parties: An Examination of Various Reform Strategies," March 2014, Center for Effective Public Management at Brookings, p. 3; Kabaservice, *Rule and Ruin*, xvi; Nolan McCarty, "What We Know and Don't Know About our Polarized Politics," *Washington Post*, January 8, 2014, http://www.washingtonpost.com/blogs/monkey-cage/wp/2014/01/08/what-we-know-and-dont-know-about-our-polarized-politics/. Accessed June 18, 2014.

52. Beth Reinhard, "After Cantor Loss, GOP Fissures Appear on Immigration Position," *Wall Street Journal*, June 13, 2014, http://online.wsj.com/articles/after-cantor-loss-gop-fissures-appear-on-immigration-position-1402695863. Accessed on June 19, 2014.

53. See, for instance, Ross Douthat and Reihan Salam, *Grand New Party: How Republicans Can Win the Working Class and Save the American Dream* (New York: Anchor Books, 2008).

54. Yuval Levin and Ramesh Ponnuru, eds., *Room to Grow: Conservative Reforms for a Limited Government and a Thriving Middle Class*, YG Network, 2014, p. 3; Sam Tanenhaus, "Can the G.O.P. Be a Party of Ideas?" *New York Times*, July 2, 2014, http://www.nytimes.com/2014/07/06/magazine/can-the-gop-be-a-party-of-ideas.html?rref=homepage&module=Ribbon&version=origin&region=Header&action=click&contentCollection=Home%20Page&pgtype=article&_r=0. Accessed July 3, 2014.

55. E. J. Dionne, "The Reformicons," *Democracy Journal* 33 (Summer 2014): 34–51; Jonathan Chait, "Why Republicans Love Taxing the Poor," and "Best New Republican Climate Ideas Still Pretty Bad," *New York*, May 22 and June 17, 2014, http://nymag.com/daily/intelligencer/2014/05/why-republicans-love-taxing-the-poor.html and http://nymag.com/daily/intelligencer/2014/06/best-new-gop-climate-ideas-still-pretty-bad.html. Accessed June 19, 2014.

56. See, for instance, Howard Kurtz, "Conservative David Frum Loses Think-Tank Job After Criticizing GOP," *Washington Post*, March 26, 2010, http://www.washingtonpost.com/wp-dyn/content/article/2010/03/25/AR2010032502336.html; "Republicans and ObamaCare," *Wall Street Journal*, March 23, 2010, http://online.wsj.com/news/articles/SB10001424052748704117304575138071192342664?mg=reno64-wsj&url=http%3A%2F%2Fonline.wsj.com%2Farticle%2FSB10001424052748704117304575138071192342664.html; David Frum, "When Did the GOP Lose Touch With Reality?" *New York*, November 20, 2011.

57. Ben Highton, "A Big Electoral College Advantage for the Democrats is Looming," *Washington Post*, April 28, 2014, http://www.washingtonpost.com/blogs/monkey-cage/wp/2014/04/28/a-big-electoral-college-advantage-for-the-democrats-is-looming/. Accessed on June 19, 2014.

58. John Sides, "How the Senate is Biased Toward Republicans," *Washington Post*, January 31, 2014, http://www.washingtonpost.com/blogs/monkey-cage/wp/2014/01/31/how-the-senate-is-biased-toward-republicans/; Jonathan Chait, "The House Is Republican And It Ain't Going Back," *New Republic*, November 3, 2010, http://www.newrepublic.com/blog/jonathan-chait/78892/the-house-republican-and-it-aint-going-back. Articles accessed June 19, 2014.

59. James Taranto, "ObamaCare's Heritage," *Wall Street Journal*, October 19, 2011, http://online.wsj.com/news/articles/SB10001424052970204618704576641190920152366?mod=wsj_share_tweet&mg=reno64-wsj&url=http%3A%2F%2Fonline.wsj.com%2Farticle%2FSB10001424052970204618704576641190920152366.html%3Fmod%3Dwsj_share_tweet. Accessed July 3, 2014.

PART TWO

PROGRESSIVE POLITICS TODAY

Progressivism and Government

Building the Case for a Dignified and Decent Life for All

JEFF MADRICK

A leading left-of-center think tank wrote recently that it had opened its doors "with the ambitious goal of uniting a new generation of Americans behind a progressive vision for the future built upon equality, justice, and opportunity for all." This definition of progressivism is widely accepted, but it is also inadequate.

Being progressive now eludes America, and the American Left's expectations have been unwittingly but sharply reduced. Will future historians look back and say a nation with the highest child poverty rate in the developed world was progressive? A nation in which many people go hungry every night? A nation that tolerates extreme inequality of income—a distribution of income, by the way, which cannot possibly reflect the natural distribution of the talents of its citizens? A nation whose young today are finding fewer jobs than at any time since the Second World War? A nation in which the unemployment rate of black people has consistently been twice as high as that of whites for a generation? A nation with a modest Social Security system that would rather cut benefits further rather than raise taxes? A nation that undermines its workers' retirements by allowing companies to eliminate defined benefits plans and adopt 401(k)s? A nation with a highly unequal public education system and completely inadequate pre-K education? A nation that threatens to reduce health-care benefits for its elderly?

Take a look at where our country stands today. As the Congressional Budget Office reports, between 1979 and 2007, before the financial crash, the income after taxes of the top 1 percent increased 275 percent. The next 19 percent rose by 65 percent, the next 60 percent rose by 40 percent, and the bottom 20 percent rose by only 18 percent.[1]

Government policies should moderate—not increase—rising inequality. But between 1979 and 2007, the share of social transfer payments to low-income households declined, while taxes took a smaller piece of incomes as the average federal tax rate fell. A comparison using Luxembourg Income Study data shows that of the 14 major OECD countries, US tax and transfer policies reduce upper quintile incomes least and raise lower quintile incomes least.[2]

Through the weeds, some shoots sprouted. The expansion of the Earned Income Tax Credit, originally introduced under Ronald Reagan, has reduced poverty substantially. But it is limited too much to those who make enough money to take advantage of it. George W. Bush created the drug program for the elderly, but it had inadequate controls over prices. More children were successfully covered for health care under President Clinton, and Obama's Affordable Care Act is an admirable program despite its imperfections. But even after his reelection in 2012, we don't yet know whether it will succeed.

A progressive America is the only choice for the nation to remain humane, optimistic, flexible, and prosperous. The only avenue to get there is a fully committed and funded government. Meeting this objective requires more than a small adjustment in the nation's thinking about what its people owe each other, and in particular a more profound period of self-criticism on the part of the left. What has kept us from maintaining our progressive values and implementing necessary policies has been the rise of antigovernment attitudes since the 1970s.

The economy changed beginning in the 1970s, not least because of new attitudes toward government policies, attitudes that were often biased against workers, higher wages, and the poor. These policies included excessively tight money, union busting, ever lower minimum wages after inflation, tolerance of Wall Street pressures, tax cuts for the wealthy, and a less generous welfare system. As a result, wages for the lower half of the distribution, as political scientist Lane Kenworthy has shown, were no longer linked to a rising GDP whereas in the 1950s wages rose with GDP.[3] Today, those in the lower half of the distribution receive far more of their income from transfer payments than wages.

This chapter challenges three widely held assumptions of America's left wing. First, it argues that the slogan "equal opportunity for all," or its close cousin, "a level playing field," is not a satisfactory prescription for progressivism. It is progressivism light. Second, the market failures school of economics, which predominates among the left orthodoxy of economists, is also too ambiguous to be a progressive economic philosophy. Government as gap filler is not progressivism. Three, progressivism requires a clear view of government as a conductor, agent, and instigator of change. Americans do not have such a view of the purpose of government and frequently lock themselves into assuming that government should only do the kinds of things that it has already done.

I am not a philosopher, and I will not spend much space trying to define progressivism. But we require some sense of our ultimate objective. I have a simple but for me meaningful idea about it. At some point during the Enlightenment in Europe, an idea took hold that individuals could lead full lives. John Stuart Mill urged that man become "a progressive being," in *On Liberty*, by which his individuality could fully develop. This advance in individual development depended above all on progress in science, medicine, agriculture, and technology. It also depended on the rise of prosperity, which was based on growing productivity. Rising individual incomes created a sense of self-empowerment, a sense that one could control one's life, expand one's interests, become both expert and broadly cultured, and enjoy leisure time. Maintaining prosperity to advance and afford progressive policies may be nowhere more important than in America, which from the beginning always had an economic advantage in accessibility to land and better wages compared to the Old World, even in the difficult early industrial era. Prosperity can promote economic progressivism, and progressivism, if it creates adequate wages to support demand and a sense of optimism for most people, can promote economic prosperity.

Democracy is critical but not sufficient in itself to make full lives possible. In the end, a democracy of people committed to what? The right to choose and the freedom to speak are central progressive rights. But majority rule does not by definition protect minority needs.

The pursuit of freedom or liberty is also not an adequate objective. "Freedom" may be the most misleading word in the political realm. Does freedom alone lead to full lives? For many, freedom means the abolition or minimization of government rules or market intervention—individualism is all that is needed to fulfill lives. To others, as noted, it means government programs that level—*partly*—the economic starting place.

The American version of progressive aims was expanded from the start by the Declaration of Independence: life, liberty, and the pursuit of happiness were "unalienable" rights. The adoption of the word "happiness" to replace Locke's "estate," (or, as we'd say, "property") has been written about too often to add anything. But at what other time in history were men and women of an entire country promised they had a chance to be happy?

This to me is a central progressive idea. I can't define happiness with any precision, and it is usually not a useful word to use when surveying people about how satisfied they are. But I see it as the fulfillment of individual lives. As the British philosopher Alan Ryan describes it, "Negatively, [its] aim is to emancipate individuals from the fear of hunger, unemployment, ill health and a miserable old age, and positively to attempt to help members of modern industrial societies flourish in the way Mill . . . wanted them to."[4] I'd like to see the definition of progressivism include a promise of a *dignified* and *decent* life for all. A level playing field or equal opportunity is a not adequate; it is a subset of crude individualism.

* * *

I'd attribute much of the failure of progressivism in America to myths about the limits of government, which this chapter will address. The contemporary aversion to government has built up over thirty years, much of it led by economists. It culminated in the government shutdown in October 2013. I will argue that maintaining both prosperity and a progressive way of life will require a significant increase in taxes—not now, while the economy is weak—but over time, because government is central to a dignified and decent life for all Americans.

Yet it remains conventional wisdom in America today that higher levels of taxes and more government spending diminish America's prosperity. Shortly after the government shutdown in October, 60 percent of Americans thought government should *not* do more to solve America's problems. The claim that bigger government is now a social and moral wrong strikes a deeply intuitive chord, not only among those on the right but also among many on today's left. In both Europe and the United States, many persist in believing the high budget deficits of recent years were caused by social spending, but they were not. This myth, so easy to create and make credible, is used in a battle against true progressivism.

This contemporary ideological turn in America, best exemplified by the reversal of the faith in the New Deal and the Great Society, has a long bipartisan pedigree. It has become so obvious to so many over the last generation that big government and high taxes are the culprits, it hardly seems to require demonstration any longer. "Closed case: tax cuts mean growth," once wrote former Tennessee Republican Senator Fred Thompson, who can't seem to imagine there could be an alternative argument.[5]

What is discouraging is that many of today's Democrats only partially disagree. Many Democrats had a hand in persuading the public of the dangers of big government. The triumph of Republicans in the 1994 congressional elections reinforced the perception that American public opinion had turned against government, and Clinton abided by the sentiment. "The era of big government is over," said President Clinton with fanfare in his 1996 State of the Union address in January, the year of his presidential reelection bid. He had successfully raised taxes on better-off Americans with passage of a tax increase in 1993, but they would largely be used to reduce the federal deficit, not develop new social programs. The Democratic Leadership Council, which Clinton helped found in the mid-1980s, continued to urge Democrats to think twice where tax increases and the new social programs that require them were concerned. The "American Dream Initiative" in 2006, put forward by the DLC, proposed paying for modest new proposals only by closing tax loopholes, and demanded that no new programs should be enacted without a way of financing them. In 2008 the leading presidential candidates only agreed to raise taxes on high-income Americans. Without more tax money—"pay-go," as it was called—there could be few social initiatives. The Republicans had won strategically. America was stuck with minimal changes to the safety net and minimal new funds for transportation, education, and research.[6]

Federal deregulation went hand in hand with such attitudes about government. As the Financial Crisis Inquiry Commission concluded, the deregulation of the financial community was a primary cause of the financial crisis of 2008, whose aftermath we are still living with. The lax federal oversight under George W. Bush took an increasingly obvious toll, most clearly in the credit crisis of 2008, and hundreds of billions of dollars of losses accrued at major financial institutions. But this represents only part of the story; federal oversight of other sectors of the economy, including food production, the pharmaceutical industry, and the air and transportation industries all suffered, as did the people of New Orleans in the aftermath of Hurricane Katrina.

Deregulation had an early adherent with the Nixon administration in the early 1970s, but Jimmy Carter was a sincere believer, and aside from airline and trucking deregulation (which was arguably sensible) he gave priority to financial deregulation and in the process helped give enormous power to commercial and investment banks. Under Clinton, this trend continued with the result that much of the New Deal regulatory apparatus was rolled back. In 1999, for example, the Clinton administration supported the passage of the Graham-Leach Act, which did away with the separation of commercial and investment banking required under the 1933 Glass-Stegall Act, a move which at the time was taken in large part to allow for the merger of Citicorp and Travelers Group, creating one of the first of the destructive behemoths that would earn the moniker "too big to fail" at the onset of the Great Recession.[7]

When Clinton had hundreds of billions of dollars of budget surpluses to bestow in the late 1990s, he left federal spending on transportation, education, and poverty programs below the spending levels reached as a proportion of national income (the Gross Domestic Product) under his Republican predecessors, George H. W. Bush and even under President Reagan. To meet his social goals, Clinton generally resorted to tax credits, and the adoption of tax-advantaged programs to provide help for the working poor and to expand health insurance, retirement savings, and the affordability of college education—despite the reduced growth of military spending made possible by the end of the Cold War.

Such an approach was part and parcel of the greater reliance on free markets. A tax credit may encourage savings by exempting investment from income tax until retirement or raise incentives to work by creating a tax credit even as one's income rises. But the market does the rest of the work, it is assumed, not government. "Market incentives" became the new buzz phrase among middle-of-the road Democratic economists. Most important, such an approach also had the great virtue of not requiring a tax increase. But it was costly to government, as tax revenues were lost in the process. Meanwhile, with Clinton's encouragement, Wall Street hadn't had such a friendly hearing from Democrats in anyone's memory.

Some reforming of social programs was certainly necessary. Using subsidies rather than outright handouts often makes sense. Markets do have efficient distributive capacities that should be utilized when possible. But the new focus did not represent the return of clear-eyed pragmatism that it promised. Quite the opposite, it was an ideological turning point that moved the nation to the adoption of an antigovernment faith. "We know government doesn't have all the answers," Clinton said in his State of the Union Address. But even though some progressive programs were indeed overly ambitious and failed, no one ever promised that government had all the answers. By citing this straw man, Clinton had joined those who painted the government with an ideological broad brush of disapproval, and he brought the Democratic Party with him.

Enter President Obama, who—advised by the fiscally conservative former treasury secretary, Larry Summers, and the former head of the New York Federal Reserve, Timothy Geithner—would demand a summit on the budget deficit even before he took the oath of office. The new president's misguided focus on the deficit ultimately resulted in the creation of the fiscally conservative National Commission on Fiscal Responsibility and Reform, led by Erskine Bowles and Alan Simpson. In the end, President Obama had the good sense not to accept their findings, and endured criticism for it for some time. Still, for most of his first term, once his helpful and courageous stimulus package had been passed in early 2009, his attention continued to be consumed more by the budget deficit than the need to create jobs, with dire consequences for the long-term unemployed. Meantime, Bowles and Simpson continued to spread their gospel of balancing the budget.

Excepting the tax cuts, the American Recovery Act was an excellent piece of legislation, addressing issues of the poor and middle class alike. But Obama did not boast about it. He ducked behind the Clintonite veil of treating government warily. He rarely talked about poverty. By his second term, the new buzzword was middle-out reform, or something like that, always emphasizing the middle class but not proposing new taxes on the great middle or much help for the poor.

Today, the budget deficit should be a *distant* secondary concern. The lack of economic growth is America's main economic problem. But the nation can't get its mind off the deficits after years of being fed exaggerations about it by policymakers and think tanks. Perhaps the best example of this ill-timed obsession with the deficit can be found in President Obama's acceptance of sequestration, which killed jobs and took the heartbeat out of the American economy by reducing government spending at a time when we could least afford it.

* * *

Is there any truth to the idea that more government will slow growth? No. Government has grown faster than the economy for the past one hundred years and the rate of economic growth has barely changed. Two mainstream economists, the University of Chicago's Nancy L. Stokey, and Sergio Rebelo of Northwestern, carefully measured growth and effective tax rates since the adoption of the income tax. The authors, hardly left-wing economists, concluded that, "This large rise in income tax rates produced no noticeable effect on the average growth rate of the economy."[8]

Lane Kenworthy has compared the rise of government revenues in America as a proportion of GDP to economic growth. In the early 1900s, government revenue as a percent of GDP was about 10 percent, including state and local governments, and by the 1990s or so it leveled out at about 37 percent. Yet economic growth contin-ued at roughly the same rate over the entire period. It wiggled around some—after all we had a Great Depression and some slow growth after the early 1970s, not to mention the recent Great Recession. But the rate over time largely remained the same, growing at about 1.2 percent a year (per capita).[9]

Here's what is maybe more telling. Sweden and Norway also experienced a rapid growth in their economies over these years but with government revenue reaching approximately 60 percent of GDP. Yes, you may remember that Sweden had a hic-cup in the early 1990s, when the country's tax revenues reached 65 percent of GDP. Some critics charged that this was an indication that Keynesianism was failing, but as Kenworthy notes, once Sweden got government revenues back down to 60 per-cent of GDP the country did just fine. So maybe that's a reasonable cut-off point. We are a long way from that point.

These examples are pretty persuasive. So too is the work of another mainstream economist, Peter Lindert, who looked very closely at the relationship of GDP and the size of government and found no dampening effect.[10] The reason is that govern-ment performs many growth-enhancing tasks. These include policies that encour-age women to work and maintain their careers, such as ample paid leave with a guaranteed return to the same jobs level as in the past. In many European nations, university is free, as is pre-k education. Health care is either cheaper or free to all, and the quality is good. Government enhances growth.[11]

Jon Bakiya and Joel Slemrod have examined how different tax rates might affect economic growth through incentives to work and invest. Here, after an exhaustive study in which they massaged their data in every conceivable way, these two con-ventional economists found no relationship between higher tax rates and lower growth. In fact, they find no measurable relationship at all between tax rates and growth—despite the loud proclamations about the perils of high taxes from such nationally known economists as Martin Feldstein and Robert Barro.[12] Political sci-entist John Mahon has recently tried to see whether high tax rates reduced freedom, the main concern of conservatives. But that's not all he did. He stacked the case against high tax advocates by comparing tax rates to measures of freedom done by conservative organizations such as the Heritage Foundation. He found that highly taxed states are freer.[13]

With all this research to support more use of government, why has the modern progressive case been so tepid? The influence of the right in orthodox economics has clearly pulled the left well to the center. Take, for example, books from such Obama advisers as Cass Sunstein, the co-author of *Nudge,* which suggests that proper market incentives will adequately change behavior or enhance social jus-tice. The left has embraced ideas such as "entrepreneurial" government, which was especially popular during the Clinton presidency. It advocates only modest infra-structure investment. Some in the self-defined left still believe finance, if unfettered, will spread capital magnanimously around the world to generate prosperity. Their major poverty program is the aforementioned Earned Income Tax Credit, borrowed from Friedman, not a tax-and-spend policy like Social Security. The EITC is a good program, but it is not adequate. "Tax-and-spend" and "industrial policy" remain tainted terms.

Adopting market incentives is often a good idea, and there has been a healthy ascendance of such ideas. But they are not sufficient and should be viewed as a complement to—and not a replacement for—true progressivism. The Great Recession has shown us this. We have the EITC, but we still have high levels of poverty that have not recovered in the expansion (and we still have one of the highest childhood poverty rates in the developed world).[14] We have about seven million sixteen- to twenty-four-year-olds today that neither have a job nor are studying. The employment-to-population ratio of twenty-one year olds to twenty-four year olds is the lowest for any age group in America. The proportion of teens working at summer jobs has fallen sharply since 1980. We have a complete break between rising productivity—the supposed source of a growing standard of living—and actual wages. The US Census Bureau reports that household incomes have not grown, stagnating at about 1997 levels.

Above all, we rarely think of government as a necessary and sometimes sufficient agent of *change*. The greatest threat to a decent American society—and I'd also argue, to prosperity—is when a narrow view of government confronts fundamental change.

Why are we so bad at the relatively new idea of pre-K, for example? In many European nations, 90 to 100 percent of four-year-olds are going to high-quality schools, and they usually start at three years of age. In the United States less than 70 percent of four-year-olds attend school, and these are of a highly mixed, largely unregulated quality. We have not dealt with this fundamental change in our knowledge of how important early development is to full and decent lives, and to Americans who can eventually contribute to the economy.

The current battle over the budget deficit is another example of our new misunderstanding of government's place in our lives. Almost every major budget balancing plan presented in the United States called for more social spending cuts (and sometimes defense cuts) than tax increases. One or two—aside from the plan of the congressional progressive caucus—were almost equal in tax hikes and social spending cuts. It is as if there is a law of economics that you cannot raise taxes more than you cut social spending. As previously noted, this stems from a contemporary political bias with no basis in economic evidence. Some economists have even claimed that social spending cuts stimulate more growth than do higher taxes when these cuts are used to reduce the budget deficit, but this argument does not hold up against the evidence and has been soundly discredited.[15] Indeed, in spite of the fact that the United States is the least-taxed rich country in the world, a great many economists have joined the anti-deficit campaign in America, including notable Democratic ones and members in good standing of the market failures schools.[16]

Milton Friedman wrote in the *Preface* to a 2002 edition of *Capitalism and Freedom* that people's experience with growing government since 1962 had convinced them his antigovernment philosophy was right. In fact, the conservative movement's great friend was not correct in his simplistic observations. Friedman and others attributed the damaging hyper-inflation of the mid 1970s to government spending and the ensuing budget deficits, as well as to the easy money policies of the Federal Reserve. By the late 1970s, most of America was convinced that government was the issue. It was effective simple politics and bad analysis. In Reagan's debate with Jimmy Carter before the November presidential election, he told Americans they had to live with inflation, not because they lived too well, but because government did. The well-said message stuck in the mind of the public. After the debate, Reagan's approval ratings rose markedly in public opinion surveys, and he won easily a week later.[17]

Friedman offered a good deal of libertarian ideology but little evidence that big government was the root of the problem. The causes of inflation in the 1970s were more complex than rising government spending or the growing money supply—which were the factors that Friedman emphasized. Rising government budget deficits can contribute to inflation, but other equally and even more prominent causes in this complex decade included the eightfold hike in oil prices by the Organization of Petroleum Exporting Countries (OPEC), worldwide crop failure, a sudden downshift in productivity growth not anticipated by any economist (including Friedman) and the fall in the value of the dollar. As for the size of government, federal expenditures were approximately only one percentage point higher in the first half of the 1970s as a proportion of GDP than they were in the first half of the 1960s, yet the Bureau of Labor Statistics reported that annual inflation started to rise to double digits in the early 1970s, and annual consumer price inflation was only slightly more than 1 percent in the early 1960s. Moreover, it is important to note that even in the worst years of the 1970s, the budget deficits as a proportion of the economy were no larger than they were during the worst years of George W. Bush's administration in the early 2000s, when inflation was under control.

But Friedman's argument about the dangers of government was politically effective for a variety of reasons, including weariness over the Vietnam War, the Watergate scandal, the so-called counterculture, national desegregation policies, and a rising right-wing public relations effort. It also found reinforcing echoes in American nostalgia for an artificial laissez-faire past.[18]

In his early campaigning for the Republican presidential campaign in 2008, Mike Huckabee, governor of Arkansas and admirer of Reagan, put the old American myth simply. "The greatness of this country has never been in its government," he said in a speech before the New Hampshire primary. "Any time the government gives something to us, they first have to take something from us."[19] Milton Friedman told historian Frank Bourgin that the closest we came to a laissez-faire economy was in the 1800s. But America never had a laissez-faire government. Government was active in America even when it was small. And it has been essential both to growth and the provision of an ever-more decent life for more and more Americans.

* * *

Indeed, if we look back at our past, we will find many examples of government intervention in our economy and of the progressive use of government to expand opportunity and improve the quality of life for all Americans. Take, for example, Thomas Jefferson's call for the government regulation of land sales, so as to ensure that it remained relatively inexpensive and accessible to small farmers. Or the demand from John Calhoun, the powerful and persuasive congressman from North Carolina, who joined House Speaker Henry Clay in insisting that the federal government invest in what they called "internal improvements"—the construction of major roads and canals, which became known as "the American system."[20]

Another great progressive achievement of these years was public education. The Founding Fathers were generally committed to providing education for the people. Jefferson was one of the early leaders. But it was local government, particularly in New England (long after Jefferson), which encouraged and directed serious investment in primary schools through local taxation, mostly of property, beginning in the 1820s or so. By 1850 the public school system before the Civil War was the first major example of an income redistribution policy in America because all property owners paid taxes and provided free education even for the poor. Originally, in fact, families were required to pay tuition for their children to cover part of the costs, but these charges were eventually eliminated.

By international standards, schooling in America was a giant success. More than half of the school-age population was enrolled in primary school by 1850.[21] The resulting literacy and rudimentary math skills contributed significantly to America's economic growth.[22]

After the Civil War, the nation entered a new age of rapidly advancing industrialization and mass production. Coal, steel, and machinery grew into enormous industries with corporations of enormous size.[23] In this period, the federal government, through donations of land, aggressively subsidized the development of the transportation network critical to the expansion of industry—the railroads. A reasonable figure is that it provided approximately half the financing for the revolutionary and highly productive national transportation system through such land donations.[24]

Similarly, government donated land to enable agricultural and technical colleges to finance themselves. These "land grant" colleges—made possible by the 1857 Morrill Act and extended in 1862, with the strong support of President Lincoln—were dedicated to the study of agriculture and the "mechanical arts." Cornell University, the University of California at Berkeley, Ohio State, Pennsylvania State, Rutgers in New Jersey, Texas A&M, and the Massachusetts Institute of Technology, among many others, were founded under this program, which laid the foundation for one of America's exemplary achievements: the state university system.

In addition to these developments, federal guarantees of equality, best exemplified by the passage of the fourteenth and fifteenth amendments, also came about in the wake of the Civil War, inspired in part by Lincoln's belief in the power of the federal government. According to Eric Foner, however, the laws and amendments passed in the Reconstruction period represented not a continuation of the rights and freedoms articulated in the US Constitution but rather an abrupt change. It may be "tempting," Foner argues, "to view the expansion of citizens' rights during Reconstruction as the logical fulfillment of a vision articulated by the founding fathers but for pragmatic reasons not actually implemented when the Constitution was drafted." Yet, he asserts that

> [the] boundaries of exclusion had long been intrinsic to the meaning of American freedom. Reconstruction represented less a fulfillment of the Revolution's principles than a radical repudiation of the nation's actual practice for the previous seven decades. Indeed, it was precisely for this reason that the era's laws and constitutional amendments aroused such bitter opposition. The underlying principles—that the federal government possessed the power to define and protect citizens' rights, and that blacks were equal members of the body politic—were striking departures in American law.[25]

Unfortunately, for decades the fourteenth and fifteenth amendments were rarely enforced. By the 1880s the Supreme Court limited their application, effectively affirming the right of states to enforce Jim Crow laws that mandated segregation in public places.[26]

Indeed, in the latter decades of the 19th century, a conservative turn dominated the nation, much as it has since the 1970s. As industrialization exploded, and jobs and the pursuit of fortune became more available, the nation seemed to tire of its battles for social justice. With the growth of the industrial economy, life changed radically. Twenty-six percent of Americans lived in cities in 1880 compared to 46 percent by 1910. The growing cities became centers for diphtheria, yellow fever, and tuberculosis. Working and living conditions could be abysmal, and life expectancy fell sharply in urban centers compared to rural America. Involuntary unemployment became a constant reality, though one often denied since the unemployed were frequently viewed as simply indolent.

In spite of these problems, the federal government resisted efforts to develop new social programs. Government intrusion was thought—as it is today—to be counterproductive.[27] The preservation of freedom was the principle cited to justify the rise of poverty, disease and squalor, and now limited government.[28]

But with the rise of the Progressive Era, the political pendulum, as Arthur Schlesinger Jr. put it, began to swing the other way. In the minds of a growing number of Americans—even prosperous Americans—suffering and unequal

opportunity could not be dismissed so easily as the inevitable and justifiable consequence of further economic growth. Social Darwinism was being displaced by
the social gospel that preached communal responsibility—and with it a shift in the
meaning of freedom.

Still, federal government spending, if much larger than before the Civil War,
remained a relatively small proportion of the nation's total income. Part of this
stems from the Progressive Era emphasis on new regulations, the breakup of trusts
and monopolies and the extension of democracy—through such moves as the passage of the seventeenth and nineteenth amendments—rather than on new social
programs.[29]

At the state and local level, however, spending on health programs, city services,
and education rose rapidly. Here, the development of elaborate and expensive sewer
and water systems made it possible for cities to grow without the constant threat
of disease, rendering cities themselves major sources of wealth and innovation.[30]
Government also financed new research and dispensed the invaluable vaccines.[31]
And the progressive era also brought about creation of the Federal Reserve—a central bank at last.

As evidenced by the experience of the 1920s, however, resistance to the uses
of government—despite the early advances of progressivism—remained. It would
require the stock market crash of 1929, countless people losing their savings in failed
banks, and the frightening levels of unemployment in the early 1930s, to convince
the nation to adopt new policies for a complex, industrialized economy. Still, government spending, even in the midst of the Great Depression, and despite a surge
in growth after 1931, did not reach levels as a proportion of the GDP that would
lift the nation out of the Depression. It would take the surge of military spending in
1941 and 1942 of nearly 10 percent of the GDP—what one commentator has called
the "New Deal on steroids"—that led to full employment by stimulating demand for
goods and services and providing military and civilian employment to millions.[32]

After the Second World War, almost all economists feared a reprise of the
Depression. It was hard to imagine what could replace all the lost military demand.
But the opposite occurred. After a stagnant year in 1947, the economy grew as rapidly on average as it ever did, and the incomes of most working Americans grew
faster than ever, despite the allegedly heavy burden of the New Deal. The highest tax
bracket reached approximately 90 percent, where it remained until 1964. Roosevelt
had proposed a G. I. Bill of Rights in 1943, among other things, to provide aid for
veterans to go to college and buy a home. Congress raised objections, but in 1944,
the G. I. Bill was passed. By the late 1950s, half of the returning 16 million soldiers
financed college or other training programs as a result. Millions of mortgages were
guaranteed.[33] The nation was thus directed toward education and home buying.

Dwight Eisenhower, once president, drew the ire of the Republican right wing
by proposing to expand Social Security coverage to another 10 million workers—to
include farm workers and professionals such as teachers, accountants, and dentists.

Eisenhower said that it was simply clear that not everyone could save enough for retirement.[34] Eisenhower also advocated the development and federal financing of a national highways system, calling it necessary for national security.

Between 1948 and 1970, the share of spending in GDP by federal, state, and local governments rose from 16.5 percent to 27.5 percent, which is nearly nine percentage points. Much of this increase was in social expenditures. Yet productivity, wages, and overall GDP grew very rapidly. What is the complaint then in light of all this success? It is hard to escape the conclusion, as noted earlier, that government did not hurt but significantly helped economies to grow.

* * *

Judging by the careful assessment of economic achievements by nations with high taxes and large governments, and judging by American history itself, active and sizable government has been critical to growth and prosperity among the world's richest nations, including the United States. Any impact on incentives and any displacement of private spending due to high taxes have been more than compensated for by spending programs and regulatory functions that enhance growth. If tax revenues are used to invest productively in the nation's human capital, as well as its infrastructure, legal system, and the fair distribution of economic rewards, they will expand the economy. If programs are established that make broad use of the nation's human capital—its educated and healthy public—as well as its transportation infrastructure, its legal system, and the fair distribution of economic rewards, they will contribute to growth. These programs create the tools and assets that enable the private markets not only to function but also to provide a broad-based prosperity that benefits us all.

In light of all this, it may seem surprising that the financial crisis of 2008 and the Great Recession did not result in a return to progressive policies for very long. One important reason is that the success of New Deal and later progressive programs reduced the suffering. We now have unemployment insurance, Social Security, Medicare, Medicaid, TANF, food stamps, the EITC, the Child Tax Credit, and a minimum wage, however inadequate. None of these were yet available to reduce the misery and insecurity that we faced at the start of the Great Depression. Obama's stimulus, based on Keynesian theory, did forestall a more serious recession and begin a recovery. The United States recovered its pre-crisis GDP by 2010, whereas much of Europe remains below its pre-crisis level. Yet, in such an environment, the ideological shift to the right was not as readily challenged. The fear of big government held strong.

* * *

The lessons of economic history show that we should not back away from true progressivism because it is politically unacceptable. Strong and growing government is part and parcel of a progressive society. When we winced in the past at the prospect of strong government—after the Civil War and in the 1920s—we suffered. We are wincing again. If we want to enter the twenty-first century as a strong, prosperous, and progressive nation, we should replace our obsession with the federal budget deficit with a demand for higher taxes. With more money, many worthwhile programs could be initiated to provide a decent, dignified life to all Americans while enhancing prosperity at the same time.

We could easily raise taxes five full percentage points of GDP, which would add up to some $800 billion a year. This would leave our revenue rate still near the bottom of the pack among the richest nations. Which taxes should be implemented? There are many to be considered: a VAT, a carbon tax, a financial transactions tax, higher income tax rates, even a wealth tax.

Progressives should talk actively and openly about the programs the nation needs. These should include aggressive investment in infrastructure, expansion of research and development, a national pre-K system, a higher minimum wage, and an extended unemployment insurance system.

But progressives should also talk more boldly about a significant increase in Social Security benefits, a more effective Medicaid system, a living wage, cash distributions to families in poverty for each child (perhaps with conditions that the parents attend classes on children's needs, go to regular pediatric appointments, and meet nutritional minimums or perhaps with no conditions at all), a government-as-last-resort jobs program, up to one-year paid job leave for new parents, a program to make college free, and the near elimination of poverty.

Perhaps these ideas seem impractical and wide eyed to those who make Washington their stomping grounds. But unemployment insurance seemed like utopian thinking to Americans in the 1850s, as did Social Security to Americans in the 1910s. Nevertheless, those who believed in these ideas kept fighting against the odds. This might be another way of defining progressivism: a determination to battle against the status quo even though the battles are often lost—until they are won. It is in this spirit that today's progressives should carry on the struggle to create a dignified and decent life for all, knowing full well that future victory is not guaranteed. But the effort to transform our government into an active instrument of social and economic justice must continue.

Notes

1. "Trends in the Distribution of Household Income Between 1979 and 2007," *Congressional Budget Office*, Report, October 25, 2011, https://www.cbo.gov/publication/42729.
2. Janet C. Gornick and Markus Jänitti, *Income Inequality: Economic Disparities and the Middle Class in Affluent Countries* (Stanford: Stanford University Press, 2013).
3. Lane Kenworthy, "America's Social Democratic Future," *Foreign Affairs*, January–February, 2014, http://www.foreignaffairs.com/articles/140345/lane-kenworthy/americas-social-democratic-future.

4. Alan Ryan, *The Making of Modern Liberalism* (Princeton, NJ: Princeton University Press, 2012), 25.

5. Fred Thompson, "Closed Case: Tax Cuts Mean Economic Growth," *Wall Street Journal*, April 4, 2007.

6. Stephen Rose, "What's Not the Matter with the Middle Class," *The American Prospect*, Sept. 4, 2006, http://www.prospect.org/cs/articles?articleId=11943.

7. Mitchell Martin, "Citicorp and Travellers Plan to Merge in Record $70 Billion Deal: A New No. 1: Financial Giants Unite," *New York Times*, April 7, 1998, http://www.nytimes.com/1998/04/07/news/07iht-citi.t.html.

8. Jeff Madrick, "They Can Strengthen the Economy," in *10 Excellent Reasons Not to Hate Taxes*, ed. Stephanie Greenwood (New York: New Press, 2007), 36.

9. Lane Kenworthy, "America's Social Democratic Future," *Foreign Affairs*, January/February, 2014, http://www.foreignaffairs.com/articles/140345/lane-kenworthy/americas-social-democratic-future.

10. Peter Lindert, *Growing Public, Social Spending and Economic Growth since the Eighteenth Century* (Cambridge, UK: Cambridge University Press, 2004).

11. Ibid.

12. Joel Slemrod, and Jon Bakija, *Taxing Ourselves: A Citizens Guide to the Debate over Taxes*, (Cambridge, MA: MIT Press, 2008).

13. *Challenge Magazine.*

14. "Comparative Child Well-being across the OECD," in the OECD 2009 report, *Doing Better for Children*, http://www.oecd.org/els/family/43570328.pdf.

15. Howard Schneider, "An Amazing Mea Culpa from the IMF's Chief Economist on Austerity," *Washington Post*, January 3, 2013, http://www.washingtonpost.com/blogs/wonkblog/wp/2013/01/03/an-amazing-mea-culpa-from-the-imfs-chief-economist-on-austerity/.

16. See, for example, Jeff Madrick, *Seven Bad Ideas: How Mainstream Economists Have Damaged America and the World* (New York: Knopf, 2014).

17. William Greider, *Secrets of the Temple: How the Federal Reserve Runs the Country* (New York: Simon and Schuster, 1989), 218.

18. Jeff Madrick, *Age of Greed* (New York: Knopf, 2011), 26–51.

19. Elizabeth Holmes and Amy Chozick, "Bruised in Iowa, Clinton, Romney Change Styles," *Wall Street Journal*, January 7, 2008.

20. Frank Bourgin, *The Myth of Laissez-Faire in the Early Republic* (New York: HarperCollins, 1990), 169.

21. Charles Sellers, *The Market Revolution* (Oxford: Oxford University Press, 1991), 367–369.

22. Peter H. Lindert, *Growing Public: Social Spending and Economic Growth Since the Eighteenth Century* (New York: Cambridge University Press, 2004), 88–99.

23. Eric Foner, *The Story of American Freedom* (New York: W.W. Norton, 1998), 59. Foner cautions that wage labor was an ambiguous term, since full-fledged industrial armies of manufacturing workers hardly existed in Lincoln's time. It was the historically small business that still dominated in the new economy.

24. Alfred Chandler, *Scale and Scope, the Dynamics of Industrial Capitalism* (Cambridge, MA: Belknap Press, 1990), 112.

25. Foner, op. cit., 107.

26. See discussion of *Plessy v. Ferguson* (1896), in Foner, op. cit., 132.

27. Price Fishback, et al., *Government and the American Economy: A New History* (Chicago: University of Chicago Press, 2007), 261–262.

28. Foner, op. cit., 113.

29. The Seventeenth Amendment to the US Constitution established the direct election of US Senators to Congress; the Nineteenth Amendment granted women the right to vote.

30. Environmental protection agency website. http://www.epa.gov/msw/timeline_alt.htm

31. Laurie Garrett, *Betrayal of Trust:The Collapse of Global Public Health* (New York: Hyperion, 2000), 10–11.

32. David B. Woolner, "FDR Put Humanity First. The Sequester Puts it Last," *Next New Deal*, March 1, 2013, http://www.nextnewdeal.net/fdr-put-humanity-first-sequester-p uts-it-last.

33. The United States Department of Veteran Affairs, History of the G. I. Bill, http://www.gibill. va.gov/GI_Bill_Info/history.htm.

34. Dwight D. Eisenhower Statement to Congress on Social Security, August 1, 1953, *Social Security Administration*, Presidential Statements, http://www.ssa.gov/history/ikestmts. html#special.

Financial Reform after the 2008 Crisis

MICHAEL KONCZAL

INTRODUCTION

The need to suddenly regulate the entire financial system wasn't a burning topic in advance of the 2008 election. At the time, there were significant ideas and plans on a number of policy frontiers under consideration by the candidates. Foremost among these were the discussions about how to bring about universal health care and the relative importance of the technical, though crucial, policy consequences of mandates to purchase health care, as well as the importance of public options designed to ensure competition in health-care exchanges. Though the specifics weren't hammered out, activists, interest groups, and politicians also put immigration reform, global warming, and the election of public-sector unions onto the public stage. As the year progressed, a public effort to stimulate the economy through deficit spending and public investment also became a key issue.

But financial reform was rarely debated during the election. When it did come up, it usually involved some element of housing relief and bankruptcy reform designed to target the massive wave of foreclosures hitting the mortgage market that year. It is important to note that when it came to the issue of financial reform, there were no built-up coalitions of advocates demanding solutions, as was the case for, say, immigration reform; nor were there any deeply researched competing policy solutions built up over decades as there were for health care. Think tanks had little expertise in financial reform, and virtually all were caught off guard by the collapse of the financial sector. This meant that in the face of the worst financial crisis since the onset of the Great Depression, policy makers lacked a core set of policy goals or instruments, or the institutions ready to make them happen. These had to be created in real time.

Not only were systemic reforms to the financial sector not under debate, the general principles necessary to address such an effort were also missing. However, by mid-2009, in the wake of the election, a series of reforms goals were outlined by Congress and the administration, and a year later were passed into the Dodd-Frank

Financial Reform Act. Much of this reform drew on a long tradition of Progressive thought about regulations and the economy. Much of it did not. Progressive and liberal financial reform has a long and conflicting tradition in this country that raises questions about the role of the state and the market when it comes to regulating this crucial and complicated sector of our economy.

WHERE WE ARE COMING FROM

In examining the Great Recession and the congressional reaction to it, it is worth contrasting what happened with what came before. In the past three decades there has been a conscious turning away from the New Deal and Progressive Era approach to regulation. Since the Carter presidency, the general tenor of liberal regulatory policy has been deregulatory. This accelerated and became a mantra during the 1990s and the Clinton presidency. The concept of "market logic" was predominant in policy circles. Competition was seen as the ultimate good, and government was limited to some regulations of the margins. In keeping with this view, "financial reform" received a good deal of attention. President Carter started the repeal of regulations for commercial banking, and President Ronald Reagan allowed Wall Street to write the laws necessary for mortgages to be turned into private-label securitization.[1] Under President Clinton, the Glass-Steagall Act, which separated commercial and investment banking, was repealed, and the explosive, unregulated growth of derivatives was consciously left outside the regulatory umbrella.[2] Moreover, by 2008, all of the major policy proposals of that year's election campaign—from health-care exchanges to carbon pricing—reflected this logic.

The changes in the regulatory structure of the financial sector in the Carter-Reagan-Clinton years led to an explosion in the size, concentration, and the profitability of the financial system. The top five banks went from holding 17 percent of industry assets to holding 52 percent. Corporate profits went from a baseline of around 5 percent in 1950 to 40 percent in the 2000s, and the pace of the growth of finance in GDP doubled.

What guided macro-economic and regulatory policy in this period? As Bob Litan and Jonathan Rauch wrote in the 1998 book *American Finance for the 21st Century*, which was originally prepared as a report to Congress by the Treasury Department making the case for the removal of Glass-Steagall, there were three simple principles that guided their approach to financial regulation: "an enhanced role for competition; a shift in emphasis from preventing failures of financial institutions at all cost toward containing the damage of any failures that inevitably occur in a competitive market; and a greater reliance on more targeted interventions to achieve policy goals."[3]

This vision is relevant because it's precisely the vision of financial reform that collapsed in the financial crisis of 2008. Indeed, every element of it failed. The financial markets became more concentrated and more profitable instead of more competitive after deregulation was completed in the late 1990s. Bad actors, from subprime lending to those who gamed mortgage-backed securities, weren't investigated during the housing bubble, and criminal prosecutions and other forms of penalty have been absent in the aftermath of the crisis. Furthermore, in the middle of a crisis, regulators blinked and backstopped the entirety of the financial sector through a broad-yet-obscure series of Federal Reserve programs, programs the Fed refused to properly disclose to the public. Gains were privatized; while potential losses were socialized both through the risks taxpayers were exposed to in the form of bailouts, and through the unwillingness of the federal government to provide struggling homeowners with any kind of direct support.

Thus the old logic of financial reform was out the window, with a major question mark in its place. A new system had to be created, one that looked further to the Progressive past of the regulation of markets.

GOALS

To understand what kinds of regulations are needed in the wake of the 2008 crisis, it's best to start with an outline. So what are the goals of financial reform? The goals mentioned below are not exhaustive, but they provide a good first pass for what financial reform is meant to accomplish if it is to be successful. These are the goals that have animated financial reforms for a century, and they are central to the debate that broke out in 2009 about how to avoid a repeat of the most recent financial crisis.

1. Preventing Panics and Avoiding Bailouts

As we saw in the financial crisis of 2008, one of the core goals of a system of financial regulation must be to maintain the stability of the financial market while also avoiding bailouts and the lack of accountability that follows from them. This is easier said than done, because financial panics have had a long history in the twentieth and twenty-first centuries. Banking is a crucial component of the financial sector because it also involves the payment system that allows for the functioning and growth of markets. But given its speculative and leveraged nature it is also prone to rapid collapse. Moreover, because it turns short-term funding into long-term assets—what economists call "maturity transformation"—it is also prone to runs and panics.

The legal scholar Anna Gelpern has compared crisis responses throughout the world in the twentieth century. She found a remarkable consistency across all of them. She describes bailouts as a type of containment, where the same questions come up over and over again. The government needs to figure out whether it will suspend regulations, rewrite or otherwise not enforce contracts, and redistribute losses, including those to the taxpayer. Gelpern argues that simple, transparent and evenly distributed measures are the right way to balance needs and prevent collapse while still maintaining fairness.[4]

Bailouts are a special form of government subsidy. Subsidies are government actions designed to bring about a specific outcome (e.g., people buying homes or employers hiring people and giving them health care). However, bailouts are viscerally different than, say, the mortgage interest tax credit. Unlike subsidies that incentivize individuals to take certain actions, bailouts are subsidies designed to prevent something—the failure of a firm, for example.

Bailouts are *ex post* phenomena, meaning that they occur when the firm is already about to fail. We already have rules and laws that are designed in advance to allocate losses when firms go under, ranging from the numerous chapters of bankruptcy to the limited liability corporation itself. However bailouts are not put into place in advance. They are executed only when a firm is about to go under.

Bailouts are unfair then, because they prevent the normal winners and failures of the market from taking place. Our economy is very good at forcing businesses to absorb the cost of their failures. Those who stand to gain the most in good times also stand to lose the most in bad times. Bailouts prevent this from happening, so those who gained in good times also don't lose in the bad times. Who absorbs those losses instead? The government or rather the taxpaying public it represents. Or, as one phrasing goes, bailouts "privatize the gains, and socialize the losses." As a result of popular outcry about the decision of the federal government to bail out the banks in 2008–2009, the bailout plan was changed from a direct infusion of cash to the purchase of equity shares so the public might get something back in return.[5] This diluted the shares of other equity holders while providing the public with the opportunity to make gains on any potential market upswing in the overall financial health of a given firm. Doing so certainly appears to improve the fairness of the plan, but it still doesn't address our fundamental discomfort with bailouts. When bailouts break the link between market actions and consequences, firms may take on more risk, thinking that they will be insured. This is referred to as moral hazard, and it can further generate the problems we are looking to solve.

Bailouts are also ad hoc. In 2007 and 2008, not all firms were treated equally. This gives bailouts the appearance of being arbitrary. Bear Stearns received a bailout from the government, but at the last minute Lehman Brothers didn't. This type of arbitrary behavior can quickly turn into abuse, especially when the procedures can be bent or broken for powerful or connected firms. These ad hoc processes often amplify our concerns about inequality, and about the ability of powerful firms to use the government for their benefit.

2. Transparency

A second goal of financial reform is ensuring transparency. This too has a long history within the financial reform movement. As the Progressive legal scholar and activist Justice Brandeis argued in the early twentieth century, the term "publicity" was synonymous with what we refer to as either disclosures or transparency:

> Publicity is justly commended as a remedy for social and industrial diseases. Sunlight is said to be the best of disinfectants; electric light the most efficient policeman. And publicity has already played an important part in the struggle against the Money Trust. The Pujo Committee has, in the disclosure of the facts concerning financial concentration, made a most important contribution toward attainment of the New Freedom. The battlefield has been surveyed and charted. The hostile forces have been located, counted and appraised. That was a necessary first step—and a long one—towards relief. The provisions in the Committee's bill concerning the incorporation of stock exchanges and the statement to be made in connection with the listing of securities would doubtless have a beneficent effect. But there should be a further call upon publicity for service. That potent force must, in the impending struggle, be utilized in many ways as a continuous remedial measure.[6]

Transparency here means that financial information is broadly accessible to all market participants. The idea here is to prevent the concentration of market power within key financial institutions. Transparency is meant to dislodge market power but also to allow financial intermediaries to discipline and regulate each other. More transparency can lead to markets growing even faster. Some estimates of the Dodd-Frank Act have shown that transparent derivatives markets allow for even more transactions at lower costs.

This has specific consequences. One of the biggest areas of growth in the financial sector has been in financial assets like mutual funds and hedge funds. The regulations of mutual funds make it so consumers and market participants have reliable information when it comes to both the fees that are charged and the techniques that are used to take risks and make money. This, in turn, allows for actual competition on both getting better results and reducing the costs of the fees. During the past decades, fees on mutual funds have come down significantly as a result. Hedge funds, however, are not required to disclose their costs in the same way, and so their fees have exploded.

3. Consumer and Investor Protection

Preventing consumers from being ripped off is another core goal of financial regulations. Again, we can turn to Justice Brandeis to summarize the argument:

> The archaic doctrine of caveat emptor is vanishing. The law has begun to require publicity in aid of fair dealing. The Federal Pure Food Law does

not guarantee quality or prices; but it helps the buyer to judge of quality by requiring disclosure of ingredients. Among the most important facts to be learned for determining the real value of a security is the amount of water it contains. And any excessive amount paid to the banker for marketing a security is water. Require a full disclosure to the investor of the amount of commissions and profits paid; and not only will investors be put on their guard, but bankers' compensation will tend to adjust itself automatically to what is fair and reasonable. Excessive commissions—this form of unjustly acquired wealth—will in large part cease.

But the disclosure must be real. And it must be a disclosure to the investor. It will not suffice to require merely the filing of a statement of facts with the Commissioner of Corporations or with a score of other officials, federal and state. That would be almost as ineffective as if the Pure Food Law required a manufacturer merely to deposit with the Department a statement of ingredients, instead of requiring the label to tell the story.[7]

Here the goals can range from making sure that consumers understand the products available to them to ensuring that they have a cop on the beat to check and challenge wrongdoing. The government has a role to play in nudging or otherwise ensuring that certain products and conditions of quality are met. Above all, consumer and investor protection involves information and accountability. Consumers should have good information about what they are buying and recourse if something goes wrong.

But by the time the 2008 crisis hit, these protections were no longer in place. As a result, homeowners were issued loans without knowing the terms, or the terms were changed or forged after the fact. Worse still, when foreclosures were initiated, they were often processed by middlemen who had a financial incentive in seeing the mortgage fail. Moreover, these practices didn't just affect individual families; they also affected institutional investors, who need legal recourse if fraud has occurred. These are the issues that were at the heart of the mortgage-backed securities that were sold to institutional investors throughout the housing bubble and that played such a significant role in the recent financial crisis.

4. Efficient Allocation of Capital

The last and final goal of financial reform is to ensure that capital is allocated where it is best available for investment in the real economy, or the parts of the economy focused on producing goods and services. We've seen many instances in the lead-up to the financial crisis where capital had been allocated not to benefit investors but instead toward products designed to fail. The efficient allocation of capital is of course closely linked to the others just mentioned as the fair distribution of financial resources involves getting capital to individuals who need it on terms that are likely to be repaid, and to businesses that need it for investment and growth. In recent years, however, we've seen that finance has become just as much about removing capital from firms—independent of their ability to grow, invest or innovate—as it has been about traditional investing. Indeed, the "shareholder revolution" of the past thirty years has fundamentally changed the goal of the financial sector, with the extraction of capital as paramount.[8] As the economist J. W. Mason has found, during the height of the housing bubble, the corporate sector was paying more in stock buybacks and dividends than they were making in cash. This is not a system that is consistent with a growing, innovative economy.

With these four goals in mind, we can focus on how the financial reforms associated with Dodd-Frank try to tackle these problems. What are the instruments and regulations that policy makers used to try and reform the financial sector? And how do the current efforts at reform compare to the earlier Progressive and liberal vision of regulating the economy, as opposed to the more deregulatory approach of the past three decades?

In examining these questions, it is important to emphasize that the period from the late 1970s to 2007 is best described as an era of "re-regulation" instead of "deregulation." It is not so much that there was less regulation or state structuring of the capital and financial markets but rather that the purpose of the regulations was vastly different than those imposed during the New Deal. Indeed, the purpose of regulation in the post-Carter era was to give Wall Street and the finance sector maximum flexibility, with a legal framework designed to punish individual bad actors and process failure. It was this framework that failed in the Great Recession. But what tools should we design to replace it?

PRICES AND COMPETITION

Under Dodd-Frank, prices and the more general idea of competition are understood to require regulatory structures and rules to function properly. Before this, however, Wall Street itself would structure competition. The assumption was that financial firms would hold the necessary amount of capital to remain solvent and that derivative funds would do whatever was best for managing risk. This did not happen.

As a result, there's been a push under Dodd-Frank to rely on more structural limitations within firms and a renewed role for price information structured through government regulations. Take derivatives, for example. Most derivatives, after Dodd-Frank, are now required to trade through specialty institutions called clearinghouses and exchanges, designed to help manage risk and make the price information from this market public. Those derivatives that don't trade through exchanges will be required to hold more capital as insurance against risk than they would otherwise. There's already evidence that this system has both increased trading volume but decreased the price, consistent with the process of making price information public and using competition to drive down costs.

Another interesting development in the wake of the 2008 crisis has been bringing the concept of a "public utility" to the regulation of credit card fees charged to merchants, a fee referred to as "interchange." Under the public utility approach, direct rate regulations are set by the Federal Reserve. This regulation became the most lobbied reform to be repealed in the aftermath of Dodd-Frank, with an effort almost succeeding in 2011. This expansion of the concept of "public utilities" is essential to the Progressive vision and will become more important in the future after Dodd-Frank.

LIMITATIONS AND REQUIREMENTS

Placing limitations on the structure of financial institutions is far more in keeping with the Progressive and/or New Deal approach to regulation. As noted, the deregulatory era encouraged consolidation, not only among different firms but also across business lines. A prime example of this phenomenon can be seen in the rise of hedge funds. Over the past thirty years, it became more and more common for the major financial institutions to create divisions or groups located within a given financial firm whose sole purpose was to place bets and gamble with the firm's own ability to make money. These divisions—or hedge funds—in essence were designed to turn bad luck or bad practices—some would say "fraud"—into profits. The "Volcker Rule" initiative, named after the former Federal Reserve chairman and finalized at the end of 2013, was designed to bring an end to these practices. Under the new Volker rules, financial firms will no longer engage in these activities, which in turn means that they will no longer be exposed to the major risks associated with running a hedge fund. In taking these steps to isolate hedge funds from the largest financial firms, the Volker rule represents a remarkable break from the previous status quo.

Limitations on the size of financial firms is another issue that was debated intensely as the reforms that became Dodd-Frank were developed. Here, popular calls to "break up the banks" led to the drafting of an amendment to Dodd-Frank in support of this measure. The effort to break up the big banks failed to pass the Senate as Dodd-Frank was being drafted, with the amendment calling for the breakup receiving only thirty-three votes. But the debate over size continues, with many experts arguing that breaking up the banks is necessary for a working financial system. Those advocating size limitations have several arguments going for them. The first is that if the firms were smaller, they'd be both easier for their management to run and easier to fail gracefully, without taking down the whole system. Some regulators argue that if the government insists that the large banks must face bankruptcy if they fail in the future, the chances that such a bankruptcy could proceed in a calm and orderly fashion—without bringing about a major disruption or serious disaster in the overall financial sector—are slim at best. As such, it would be far better to limit the size of the major banks rather than rely solely on the threat of bankruptcy and hope to limit their risk-taking activities.

THE SAFETY NET

As mentioned earlier, another important tool for the stabilization of the financial sector is the ability of the Federal Reserve to act as a lender of last resort. And during the financial crisis, the Federal Reserve extended these tools to firms acting like banks that weren't traditionally conceived of as banks.[9] These "shadow banks" were like banks in the sense that they were subject to runs when creditors panicked about their loans.

Dodd-Frank attempts to standardize the process by which the Federal Reserve can provide liquidity for the shadow banking sector. Dodd-Frank strips out previous language from the Federal Reserve Act that was used to execute the emergency lending facilities (Sec. 1101). The Federal Reserve can no longer use its 13(3) powers to provide support in "unusual" circumstances for an "individual, partnership, or corporation." That language has been removed and replaced with "program or facility with broad-based eligibility." Dodd-Frank explicitly writes into the Federal Reserve Act that "any emergency lending program or facility is for the purpose of providing liquidity to the financial system, and not to aid a failing financial company." Going further it writes "[T]he Board shall establish procedures to prohibit borrowing from programs and facilities by borrowers that are insolvent."

PRUDENTIAL REGULATIONS

Another requirement of Dodd-Frank involves forcing banks to hold more types of capital. During the deregulatory period the emphasis was on trusting both banks and the ratings agencies to carry out these actions. As Alan Greenspan wrote in his 1998 speech, "The Role of Capital in Optimal Banking Supervision and Regulation," this "use of internal credit risk models" could serve as a "possible substitute for, or complement to, the current structure of ratio-based capital regulations." As Greenspan had argued elsewhere, at that point, "[s]upervision has become increasingly less invasive and increasingly more systems—and policy—oriented. These changes have been induced by evolving technology, increased complexity . . . not to mention constructive criticism from the banking community."[10]

Since then, there's been significant pushback against this model, with a focus on blunter, and significantly higher, capital requirements. Higher capital requirements serve a wide variety of purposes, including solvency, risk management, ending "too big to fail" through resolution, preventing liquidity crises in the shadow banking sector, right-sizing the scale and scope of our largest financial institutions, and designing financial regulations with an eye toward preventing bubbles.

* * *

One way to gain a greater understanding of the specifics of new financial regulation is to compare it to the banking and financial reforms passed during the New Deal and to examine the extent to which the new reforms mirror the New Deal. This is a particularly useful exercise because the pieces match up quite well.

RESOLUTION AUTHORITY: FDIC

The elements of Dodd-Frank designed to try and manage a failure of a large financial institution, generally called "resolution authority," are similar to the FDIC's legal authority to carry out the collapse of a commercial bank. Indeed the processes are mirrored on each other, with the FDIC explicitly tasked with this responsibility under Dodd-Frank. The general idea is the same—ensure that the process is continuous, while making certain those who gained the most in good times, like the equity holders, take the losses.

The process is designed explicitly to try and prevent bailouts and other unfair practices. The FDIC needs written recommendation that requires "an evaluation of the likelihood of a private sector alternative to prevent the default of the financial company" as well as "an evaluation of why a case under the Bankruptcy Code is not appropriate for the financial company" before they can start the procedure. The default setting in the law is that the private sector alternative is always better to government action and that the Bankruptcy Code is always better than resolution. This is consistent with the logic of those who want the government to commit to as little action as possible.

If the FDIC starts to resolve a failing financial company using its liquidation powers, what strict, legal limitations does it have to follow? There's a section titled "Mandatory Terms and Conditions for all Orderly Liquidation Actions" (Sec. 206) that can give us a start. If there's a liquidation, the FDIC has to wipe out shareholders if necessary and "ensure that the shareholders of a covered financial company do not receive payment until after all other claims and the Fund are fully paid" and hit creditors to "ensure that unsecured creditors bear losses in accordance with the priority of claim provisions." The government isn't allowed to redo TARP or AIG and buy equity in the firm to keep it alive: the FDIC rules state that they will "not take an equity interest in or become a shareholder of any covered financial company or any covered subsidiary." The FDIC can't act for "the purpose of preserving the covered financial company."

The new law also requires the FDIC to fire management to "ensure that management responsible for the failed condition of the covered financial company is removed" and fire board members to "ensure that the members of the board of directors . . . are removed." There's explicit legal language that allows FDIC to claw back compensation so that claimants "may recover from any current or former senior executive or director substantially responsible for the failed condition of the covered financial company any compensation received during the 2-year period preceding" (Sec. 210). It's difficult to imagine a firm really excited about going through such a procedure.

CONSUMER FIANCIAL PROTECTION BUREAU (CFPB): SECURITIES ACT

The original Securities Act was designed to use disclosures, information, and enforcement to bring a sense of security to the marketplace. The Consumer Financial Protection Bureau (CFPB) functions exactly the same way. Indeed, the amount and variety of financial instruments that consumers face every day is astounding compared to a century ago. But these instruments are essential for every part of functioning in society, from buying groceries to saving for important life goals like education, housing, and retirement.

The idea of the CFPB is not to make instruments "safe" for consumers. It's to provide clear information, basic requirements, and crucial enforcement. During the Greenspan era, fraud in the subprime market was routinely ignored by regulatory authorities. Consumer enforcement responsibilities were divided across a dozen agencies, where it was a minor priority and ultimately an orphan mission that nobody was really responsible for carrying out.

DERIVATIVES REFORM: SECURITIES AND EXCHANGE ACT

Here again, this is designed to take the cutting edge financial products of their respective days, stocks, and derivatives, and bring transparency to their markets. The Securities Exchange Act was designed to force price transparency for stocks so that everyone could see (and benefit from) the price information transmitted through the entire market. The same is being done with derivatives. As of this writing, the Commodity Futures Trading Commission (CFTC), tasked with derivatives enforcement, is collecting derivative information that moves through the new exchanges that have been set up, and will make this information accessible to market participants.

SHADOW BANKING
REGULATION: GLASS-STEAGALL

Dodd-Frank consciously does not try and reinstate Glass-Steagall. As President Obama's treasury secretary, Jack Lew, said during his confirmation, he believes it is an "anachronism," out-of-date and no longer relevant. Time will tell whether that is the correct call. But the general idea of balancing the regulatory environment between investment banks and commercial banks is still applicable. There is increased regulation of the largest financial firms, with special focus on preventing immediate failures while also making sure that failures are manageable and don't spread to the wider financial markets. This helps prevent certain types of regulatory abuse, where investment banks act as commercial banks without any type of proper regulatory framework.

CONCLUSION

Dodd-Frank represents a major shift in the approach to financial regulations. In addition to trying to counter serious problems that were exposed by the financial crisis, Dodd-Frank also draws on a long tradition of Progressive and New Deal liberal approaches to regulations. These approaches worked to build a level of mass prosperity that built a middle-class nation. If we hope to have an economy that works again in the future, we'll need to continue to build on this strong tradition.

Notes

1. Private-label securitization is the process that created bonds out of individual mortgages, instruments that are seen as a major driver of subprime mortgages, the housing bubble, and large housing losses.
2. The 1933 Banking Act, normally referred to as Glass-Steagall, had several parts, but the best-known section involved preventing commercial banks from acting as investment banks. This was repealed to allow for the mergers related to Citigroup.
3. See Robert Litan and Jonathan Rauch, *American Finance for the 21st Century*, (Washington, DC: Brookings Institution Press, 1998).
4. Gelpern, Anna, "Financial Crisis Containment" (May 7, 2009). *Connecticut Law Review*, Vol. 41, No. 4, May 2009. Rutgers School of Law-Newark Research Papers No. 047.
5. The bill that became TARP went through several revisions, but the final approach of purchasing warrants that gave taxpayers an upside of the stabilization was seen as a massive improvement over earlier versions.
6. Louis D. Brandeis, *Other People's Money and How the Bankers Use It* (New York: Cosimo Classics, 2009), 92.
7. Louis Brandeis, *Other People's Money*, 103–104.
8. The Shareholder Revolution consists of the intellectual and institutional changes, starting in the 1970s, that refocused the corporate sector toward generating returns for those holding

stocks. This has changed everything from executive pay to having a narrower focus on stock prices as a metric of firm health.

9. Regulators gave access to the discount window to Goldman Sachs, GMAC, and GE Capital in the middle of the crisis, all firms that would normally not have access to that lending.

10. Remarks by Chairman Alan Greenspan, *Bank Regulation*. Before the Independent Community Bankers of America National Convention, San Antonio, Texas, March 2005.

|| 7 ||

Reopening the American Political System

MARK SCHMITT

I. THE POLITICS THE NEW DEAL MADE

In 1935, in midstream of the New Deal, a political scientist coined the aphorism, "new policies create new politics."[1] It was a good description of how programs such as Social Security and public regulation were already shaping the political norms, processes, and expectations of the decades that followed. The New Deal demonstrated to Americans what government could achieve: it could save capitalism; rescue individuals, families, and communities from disaster; and it could build a foundation of security that in turn created the middle-class nation of the second half of the twentieth century. More importantly, it showed the power of popular democracy to make affirmative change. It revealed that a complex, dispersed process, designed to protect powerful minorities—one that for the previous century had often been paralyzed and always vulnerable to the influences of wealth and corruption—could take action, expand popular participation, achieve compromise, observe and correct errors, and build broad consensus around a vision of government that few Americans could have imagined.

While not without obstacles and bitter compromises—ranging from the octogenarians of the Supreme Court to the stubborn segregationists whose consent FDR needed to carefully negotiate legislation—the politics forged in the New Deal era were robust and adaptable and for decades set the terms for how America would be governed. Moreover, it is important to remember that the political give and take of the New Deal did not represent the natural order but rather a specific, hard-won achievement. As such, the post–New Deal political structure differed greatly from the politics dominated by the wealthy that prevailed in the late nineteenth century and again throughout the 1920s. It was also unlike the Progressive Era politics of the period in between, with its reliance on elite expertise and limited public participation. (Women couldn't vote until after the Wilson administration.) After the New Deal, the political system—at both the legislative and administrative level—was able to identify problems, find common ground on solutions, and combine the growing capacity of the administrative state with a gradually more pluralistic and inclusive democratic process: African Americans won the all-important right to vote in 1965; the principle of one-person/one-vote, wiping out wildly undemocratic districting schemes in almost every state, was affirmed by the Supreme Court in a series of decisions around the same time; and finally, in the 1970s, newly elected members of Congress finally had the clout to break down the entrenched power of older, Southern committee chairs—a power that presidents Roosevelt, Truman, Kennedy, and Johnson worked carefully around in order to open Congress to innovation and real debate.

Needless to say, the post–New Deal political order didn't accomplish all that it set out to accomplish right away. It took another thirty years to overcome the entrenched power that blocked basic civil rights and another seventy to grind out the passage of the last great piece of New Deal reform: universal access to health insurance. The post–New Deal order also made its share of mistakes: the overreliance on expert advice and dismissal of ideological conflict characterized by John F. Kennedy's 1962 Yale commencement address (economic questions were "subtle challenges for which technical answers, not political answers, must be provided"), for example, or the careless rush to create antipoverty programs in the Great Society and the backlash it created. But even the conservative reaction of the Reagan and first Bush administrations fits smoothly into the norms of post–New Deal politics, trimming programs that had grown unwieldy and paring back high tax rates but always with both broad public consent and evidence-based policy choices. Reagan, for example, raised taxes after it became clear he had cut them too far, worked with Democrats to save Social Security rather than privatize it, and retained and even expanded the US Department of Education after vowing to eliminate it.

II. THE BREAKDOWN OF THE OLD ORDER

The New Deal political order is a story from history, however. Today, from elections to legislation to the basic functions of the executive branch, and in the states as well as in Washington—government has failed to play its role in finding pragmatic solutions to widely recognized problems. Average worker pay has stagnated for decades, and government has been unable to act. Each year the warnings from scientists about climate change get starker, and Congress does nothing. Immigration and infrastructure investment remain unaddressed. The Republican Party retains enormous power despite divorcing itself from both evidence-based policy judgments and the views of the median voter. Given the economic, social, and environmental challenges of the near future, nothing is more urgent than repairing the dysfunction of government, restoring trust, and rebuilding the promise of American democracy—regardless of ideology or what one sees as the appropriate policy response.

It is useful to compare today's political dysfunction with the post–New Deal order for two reasons. First, such an exercise does not involve juxtaposing today's politics against an alternative vision of a deliberative-democracy utopia in which everyone participates and listens thoughtfully to the views of others. The political order from the 1930s through the late 1990s was messy, full of ugliness and moments when the entire structure seemed at risk (during the McCarthy era, for example). But it had a way of coming back into alignment over time. Second, contrasting the post–New Deal order with today's dysfunction reminds us that the more productive political actions of the recent past were not necessarily a natural development. It came about as a consequence of the creative activities of a set of leaders, ranging from FDR to the Justices of the Warren Court to the members of Congress elected in 1974 who opened up the closed committee system.

To address the current fundamental crises of the American economy and society, nothing is more urgent than to get the political process moving again. But we lack even a rough consensus on where to start. To gain a better understanding of the challenge we face, it may be helpful to recognize that much of the current analyses of today's political dysfunction falls into five basic categories given below:

Partisanship: America's two major political parties are now divided along ideological lines, with none of the idiosyncratic overlap that for much of the twentieth century created a space for bargaining and consensus. Centrist lawmakers, as well as elected officials who represented districts that were more liberal or more conservative than their parties, created a kind of transactional fluidity to American politics, allowing coalitions to form along many different lines. There were pro-labor Republicans, antichoice Democrats, Republicans who favored tax increases and stronger programs for the poor, and Democrats who opposed them. There were Republicans who kept their hold on Democratic-leaning districts, in part by supporting public programs for their districts, and the opposite.

Now the split between the parties is complete, and there are only a handful of members of Congress who represent districts won by the other party's presidential nominee. In the Senate, the conservative Democrats have been replaced by extremely conservative Republicans and moderate Republicans by generally liberal Democrats. Instead of complex coalitions, politics is just a matter of counting chips, like an endless two-person game of *Risk*, and the result is usually stalemate. But stalemate is not neutral; it serves the interests of the already advantaged.

Polarization: Elected legislators seem to respond to their party's ideological extremes, rather than seeking consensus or seeking to reach the median voter. As Jacob Hacker and Paul Pierson (as well as Norman Ornstein and Thomas Mann) have noted, polarization is asymmetric—it is primarily a phenomenon of the Republican Party, beginning before the emergence of the "Tea Party" in 2009.[2] As measured by roll call votes the average House Republican became 175 percent more conservative over the period between 1975 and 2010, in a steady shift to the hard right.[3] As Ornstein and Mann put it, "The GOP has become an insurgent outlier in American politics. It is ideologically extreme; scornful of compromise; unmoved by conventional understanding of facts, evidence and science; and dismissive of the legitimacy of its political opposition."[4]

Both the partisanship and the polarization of Congress are echoed and reinforced in partisan media and in the general public. The "median voter," who was once believed to anchor American politics and pull it back from the extremes, seems to have disappeared.

Institutional failure: Congress in particular is poorly designed to function under conditions of ideologically aligned and polarized parties. If the United States had a parliamentary government, as in most other Western democracies, the party that won a victory comparable to the Democrats' in 2008 would be free to implement the policy program on which it campaigned and would be held accountable for its success or failure. In the United States, with veto points throughout the system—as perhaps best exemplified by the minority party's ability to block action in the Senate, and the endlessly complicated interaction between the budget process and other legislation—this is almost impossible. In 2009 and 2010, the minority party, as well as individual legislators, were able to delay, disrupt, and (in the case of climate change legislation) completely block the agenda on which Barack Obama, sixty senators, and the widest majority in the House of any party since 1993 were elected. Unable to respond adequately to the recession, and burdened with a health-care plan that appeared partisan and was made far more complex than necessary, the Democrats were held accountable not for the failure of their policies but rather for their failure to overcome Republican obstruction. We now have parliamentary parties without the institutions that in a parliamentary system allow the majority party to enact its agenda and to be held accountable for its success or failure.

Congress is not the only institutional structure that leads to dysfunction. Electoral structures, particularly winner-take-all elections, exacerbate polarization, as do closed primaries.[5] Pervasive mistrust of government makes coherent public action even more difficult, but that mistrust is stoked by certain actors in the political process who benefit from it, and government failure reinforces and legitimates mistrust in what has become a vicious cycle.

Active efforts to limit participation: The story of American democracy since Theodore Roosevelt and Woodrow Wilson had been one of steady expansion of voting and civic participation, to include women, and forty-five years later, African Americans, and then young adults in the process; to make votes count through the principle of one-person, one-vote; and eventually to bring down the smaller hurdles that made participation difficult, such as limited voting hours and distant polling places, long registration delays, or residency requirements. In the 1990s further expansions, through such provisions as automatic registration at motor vehicle and human services offices, or same-day registration, garnered increasing opposition. Still, the expansion of the franchise still crawled forward. Today, however, there is an all-out attack on the right to vote, with almost every state that has full Republican control of government immediately passing new voter-identification requirements, often designed in a way that, presumably by intention, disproportionately affect younger, minority, or poor voters. Texas's law, for example, which the Supreme Court permitted to take effect in 2014 even though it had been overturned by a Federal District Court in a sweeping decision, would allow those who showed a concealed-carry weapons permit to vote, while not accepting a student ID as valid identification. Not since the last days of Jim Crow has the right to vote itself been so deeply contested.

Influence of economic inequality: The role of money in the political process, which is not limited to campaign contributions, distorts decision making, takes many promising policy options off the table, deepens public distrust, and in turn reinforces economic inequality.

Often this is described simply as "campaign finance," or as a consequence of the Supreme Court's 2009 decision in the *Citizens United* case, which pared back one element of campaign finance law that restricted independent spending by corporations. But we should think of the problem of money in politics more broadly, as the intersection between the profound economic inequality that has defined the United States since the 1980s and the political process. Here, economic inequality, deep socioeconomic separation, political polarization, and the disparity of political power cycle upon one another in a self-reinforcing pattern.

As the deep economic divide of recent decades has entered public consciousness, most recently through Thomas Piketty's surprise best-seller *Capital in the 21st Century*, there is broad consensus that while some kinds of economic inequality, such as gains acquired through innovation and risk taking, are legitimate and even desirable, inequality created or reinforced through the political process (sometimes referred to as "rent seeking") is more troubling.[6] A system in which concentrated political and economic power work in lockstep to reinforce the advantages of those who have already won the economic race will surely stifle economic and social dynamism. The gridlock of our political system, which has been unable to act on well-understood priorities such as climate change and immigration, is one indication that this is occurring; economic stagnation since the onset of the Great Recession (except for the wealthiest) is another. Moreover, inequality of political influence is widening, along with the wealth gap: Adam Bonica of Stanford University has shown that the top 0.01 percent of political donors (just 25,000 people) now make up more than 40 percent of all political giving, up from just 10 percent in 1982. In the same period, the richest 0.01 percent's share of all national income went from less than 2 percent to almost 6 percent.[7]

Political scientist Robert Dahl drew a distinction between *dispersed inequality*—in which the economic, political, and social elites were not necessarily the same group—and *cumulative inequality*, in which the winners in one sphere reinforce their advantages in the others, closing out new entrants. Not too long ago, it was plausible to argue that inequality in American politics was to some extent dispersed. Labor unions and mass-membership organizations, for example, could mobilize the many to counteract the economic power of the wealthy few. The ideological overlap between the political parties and across regions created an environment in which constantly shifting coalitions could achieve changes such as the bipartisan State Children's Health Insurance Program in 1997. But the ideological consolidation of the parties, and the unprecedented efforts, (especially at the state level) to break the countervailing power of institutions like labor unions and community organizations, has created a very different market for power: one in which economic inequality systematically reinforces itself through the political process often through mere inaction. Hence, the paralysis of the political process is not entirely an accident. It helps to consolidate and reinforce the power of the already powerful. The "policy drift," to use Hacker and Pierson's phrase, that follows from inaction leads in the direction of a shrinking social safety net, greater risk passed on to individuals rather than shared at more resilient levels of society, and far greater gains by those who are already winners.

This cumulative inequality is the primary challenge to American democracy and effective governance in the twenty-first century. Athough corruption, particularly quid pro quo corruption, is transactional and ever changing, inequality of influence and access is systemic, self-reinforcing, and surely more pervasive than the handshake deal between a donor and a senator. Recent books by political scientists Martin Gilens and Andrew Gelman have shown in persuasive detail that the policy preferences of the well-off consistently prevail over those of the middle-class and poor.[8]

III. TOWARD SOLUTIONS

Many of the causes of governmental dysfunction are simply baked into the cake of American politics and will never change. Partisan alignment—the fact that we now have one clearly conservative party and one clearly moderate-liberal party (one with a base in the South and Midwest, the other with a base on the coasts)—is a perfectly natural condition. The world in which there was significant ideological overlap between the parties is a historical anomaly that dates back to the era immediately after the Civil War. It took more than a century and some realignments along the way for our parties to become divided along ideological lines, but it happened.

One family of solutions is rooted in pure nostalgia for the customs and forms of the politics of the 1970s and 1980s. In a recent book, Jason Grumet of the Bipartisan Policy Center—an organization formed by retired members of Congress and lobbyists—rejects most structural solutions (e.g., campaign finance reform) and instead waxes nostalgic for a time when senators hung out together at the US Senate barber shop. But as Ornstein has pointed out, members of Congress don't hang out together because they don't want to work together, not the other way around.[9]

Other structural solutions are more promising: the elimination of filibusters for executive-branch appointments other than the Supreme Court has removed one veto point that had rendered several courts and federal agencies dysfunctional. The next step would be to eliminate the filibuster for legislation, although many senators, especially veterans, are wary of letting the institution become, like the House, purely majoritarian, while losing the qualities of open debate and amendment that give individual senators the power to put ideas on the agenda.

There's no doubt that the drawing of district lines, for both state legislatures and Congress, has something to do with the dysfunction of government and with asymmetric polarization. The majority of Republican members of Congress hold such safe seats that they worry more about primaries from more conservative challengers than about Democratic opponents in the general election, and thus, they are distanced even further from the median voter. And while ten or twenty congressional districts might be more competitive if some neutral or objective redistricting process had been used, the reality of most single-member districts is that they will lean toward one party or the other. It is also the case that Republican members of Congress who represent districts that merely lean Republican do not generally seem to vote in a more moderate way than members who represent heavily Republican districts.

And just as the New Deal government's proven capability to solve problems and build a modern economy (including, for example, rural electrification and a stable financial system) *reinforced* confidence in self-government and strengthened democracy, today our doubts about government's capacity—some real, and others stoked by those with an interest in a feeble government—has *weakened* our confidence in democratic self-government, leaving it even more vulnerable.

Because radical economic inequality and the explosion of money in politics are the defining phenomena of the last decade, the remainder of this chapter will focus on their intertwined relationship. Here, too, confusion reigns. Indeed, even on the most basic question of *why* we want to restrain the influence of money in politics, we are uncertain and lack both a reliable legal principle and a clear story to tell the public about the problem and the possibilities for a better world.

For forty years, laws governing money in politics have been guided by the logic of preventing corruption—or its more ambiguous cousin, "the appearance of corruption." Limits on contributions to candidates have been permitted by courts only because large contributions from a single donor, like any financial conflict of interest, might distort an elected official's decisions. But limits designed to achieve any other purpose—such as promoting political equality—have been held to violate the Constitution. This logic precedes the *Citizens United* decision of 2009 by decades.

But the concept of corruption is too narrow to capture all the ways in which money and economic inequality distort democracy. Nevertheless, this narrow view has shrunk even further thanks to the recent Supreme Court decisions on campaign finance regulation, with the most recent decision, *McCutcheon vs. FEC*, stating explicitly what the *Citizens United* majority ruling merely hinted at: that the Court views only the prevention of quid pro quo corruption—meaning a specific promise of action by an elected official in exchange for a contribution—as a valid basis for regulation of any kind of political spending. Because quid pro quo corruption is difficult to spot and harder to prove, this is a weak foundation on which to build any kind of structure to offset the real distortions of democracy by money and the way it governs who can run, which ideas are on the agenda, and who elected officials spend their time listening to.

One approach to defining the foundational principle upon which to build a case against the detrimental effects of economic inequality on democracy has been to widen the scope of the concept of corruption to encompass more of the real ways in which money—and those who have it—dominate the political process. Zephyr Teachout's historical reconstruction of the concept of corruption, for example, has shown that corruption was a deep concern of the Founding Fathers. Teachout also shows that the Founders' definition of corrupt activity went far beyond the transactional corruption of the quid pro quo. In *Corruption in America*, Teachout defines corruption as much more than simply the idea that donors have access to or leverage over elected officials.[10] Corruption, she says, "refers to excessive private interests in the public sphere; an act is corrupt when private interests trump public ones in the exercise of public power."[11] Her solutions center on structural changes that would keep legislators focused on the public interest.

On a similar track, Harvard law professor Lawrence Lessig, whose best-known work is based on a study of Congress and lobbying, has developed the concept of "dependence corruption": when elected officials are wholly dependent on a fairly small number of donors, they will naturally hesitate before taking actions that might offend those donors.[12] This concept is far more useful and accurate than the phrase "appearance of corruption" in describing the real dynamic between candidates and elected officials and the few large donors or boosters on whom they are wholly reliant. For one thing, it clears away the issue of intent or character as responsible, honest legislators with a strong commitment to the public interest are every bit as dependent as the unprincipled mercenaries of the television series *House of Cards*. "Good people caught in a bad system" is not only a more accurate description of the real workings of money in politics; it also avoids the paralyzing cynicism that flows from the message that most politicians are corrupt.

While reasonable limits on campaign contributions and disclosure of contributions and spending serve an essential purpose, that purpose is limited. Even the most expansive conceptions of corruption fail to capture much of the distorting effect of money in politics. Our mental picture of the elected official who should do one thing but does another because he's been subtly or not-so-subtly nudged by his donors, hardly applies to the many legislators who vote the way they do because their view of the public interest happens to be the same as that of their donors and their strongest supporters. Still, we should not lose sight of the fact that money can distort democracy in two ways: it can alter legislators' actions after they're elected, or it can alter who gets elected.

In the New Deal to 1990s era—an era of rough political consensus and a broad political center that shaped many of our assumptions about political money—there were many centrist politicians with loose ideological commitments who could be nudged and lobbied by donors and potential donors. But in an environment of more polarized parties and strongly held ideological commitments, money is more likely to elect true believers, for whom the traditional model of postelection corruption doesn't quite apply. A more comprehensive framework for thinking about money in politics needs to recognize the distortion of political outcomes by money at all stages in the process and not just when a donor visits a senator and reminds him of his indebtedness.

A long-standing dream of reformers, embodied in the Fair Election Campaign Act as passed in 1974, has been to move beyond corruption, and establish *political equality* as a fundamental principle governing money and democracy. If policy were based on the idea that all voters and all candidates should start on as close to an equal footing as possible, and that all voters should have roughly equal capacity to influence elections, it would open the door to policies that might include ceilings on total spending in a campaign (as in the original FECA); contribution limits so low that many more people could afford to make them ($100 per person, for example); triggers that might level the playing field by providing public funding or other advantages for candidates who are outspent; or even non-voluntary public financing. The Constitutional amendment to reverse *Citizens United,* in the version that won fifty-four votes in the Senate in September 2014, but failed to proceed, would have inscribed "the fundamental principle of political equality for all" in our founding document for the first time.

Unfortunately, without such an amendment or a major change in jurisprudence, courts are likely to look skeptically at the idea that political equality is a core value that justifies restrictions on spending or expression. Even the more liberal mid-1970s Supreme Court in *Buckley vs. Valeo* described the idea of political equality as "wholly foreign to the First Amendment," and Chief Justice John Roberts found that a single mention of the idea of "levelling the playing field" (on a website that had not been cited by either party to the case) justified overturning one provision of Arizona's public financing law. Even the most basic and minimal measure of political equality—that of one person, one vote—was not clearly embraced by the Supreme Court until 1964 in a series of decisions that could easily have gone the other way.

The Supreme Court is not wrong to see political equality as an awkward concept without clear boundaries. Money is hardly the only source of inequality in politics—incumbents have an advantage over challengers; celebrities often have an edge; media figures and columnists have unequal influence in shaping the public's political views. Further, much political inequality reflects differences in organizational strength. Although, as a definitive recent study by three political scientists showed, the well-off are better organized and better mobilized. A pluralistic, Madisonian democracy needs to respect the intensely held views of well-organized and passionate minorities. Often what appears to be inequality of money—such as the resources of the National Rifle Association—really reflects the intensely held positions of a well-organized community. Because pluralistic politics ultimately allocates unequal political power, it cannot maintain equality at every stage.

Advocates of political reform now speak in shifting and indirect language. We denounce corruption, knowing that the word resonates with the public and that is the only reliable legal premise for reform. But much of what we call corruption is really inequality of influence. We criticize "dark money" and call for disclosure, even though neither corruption nor inequality would be significantly affected by disclosure alone. We focus solely on elections, because they are a legal zone subject to regulation, even though electoral campaigns are just one aspect of deep political inequality. And while some see the current drive for an amendment to the Constitution as "the salvation of American politics," to use the words of Senator Harry Reid, the reality is that this represents little more than a gesture of anger at the power of the wealthy. It is hard to find in all of this a clear and persuasive framework for defining the problem of political equality and its solution.

IV. POLITICAL OPPORTUNITY: A NEW FOUNDATION FOR NEW POLITICAL REALITIES

What should a useable framework for political reform achieve? First, it should rest on an accurate description of what's wrong with the current political process. Second, it should lead to policy responses that are achievable, not today but in the next five or ten years, and that would also be effective. It should serve the dual purpose of creating a plausible legal and constitutional justification for policy, and conveying a clear and accessible story about solutions for the public and policy makers. Finally, it should not create further conflicts with rights to free expression but rather expand and enhance every person's freedom to speak about issues and candidates.

The key to such a framework is *expanding political opportunity*. Just as there are two ways to address purely economic inequality—by limiting gains at the top, or by expanding real economic opportunity for those who have not benefited from growth—there are two similar approaches to the influence of radical inequality in the political process. The traditional strategy has been to put a ceiling on the electoral and political voice of the very wealthy, which, as shown above, has both practical and constitutional limits. The alternative is to create structures that ensure opportunity for people, organizations, ideas, and visions that are currently shut out of the political process. The concept of *political opportunity* can provide not only a legal framework for a new generation of policy reforms but also a set of approaches that are more likely to be effective at balancing the voice of the well-off and breaking the cycle of cumulative inequality. "Opportunity" is an overused word in American political life, on both left and right, but political opportunity is a real and substantive concept with specific implications for effective policy. Political opportunity means

- that any candidate with a broad base of support, or who represents a viewpoint with broad support that wouldn't be represented otherwise, should have a chance to be heard, in elections and other contexts, even without support from big-dollar donors.
- that every citizen should have a reasonable opportunity to participate meaningfully in the political process, not just as a voter, but as a donor, a volunteer, an organizer, or by expressing his or her own views.
- that individuals should be free to express their political views, protected from coercion or direction by an employer or other institution.
- that the political system is structured to encourage organizing people, not just money, especially around issues affecting low- and moderate-income voters.

Political opportunity-based reforms will not only make the system fairer, giving voice to the voiceless and helping to offset the political influence of wealth, but they also hold the promise of restoring fluidity and creativity to the political process, as candidates compete on new ideas and new axes of conflict and compromise emerge, breaking the stifling duality of the current system.

A familiar metaphor in thinking about political money is that big money "drowns out" the voices of those who don't have it. That might have been the right way to think about money in a world of three broadcast networks, but in the modern world, communication is so rich, varied, and complex that it's difficult to drown out anyone. The real question is whether people and ideas can reach a threshold where they can be heard amid the noise. Somewhere after that threshold is reached, there are likely diminishing returns to additional political spending. In other words, efforts to limit spending at the top end are likely to have less of an impact on opportunity than reforms that help others be heard.

The first focus, then, should be on the barriers to entry into politics, the things that make it difficult for candidates and new ideas to reach the threshold where they are fully heard in the debate. While it is true, as shown above, that elections are only one way political influence can be allocated, they remain nonetheless the main gateway for people and ideas.

The most obvious reform that flows from the framework of political opportunity would be an expansion of programs like New York City's small-donor public financing system, which dramatically lowers the barriers to entry and make running for office a possibility for candidates who start with broad public support but may not have a base of money. And it gives ordinary citizens the opportunity to participate as donors. Results can be measured by the number of races that are competitive or have more than two viable candidates, as well as by the number of contributors.

Full-public financing systems such as those in Arizona or Connecticut have a similar effect, enabling candidates to run who don't have much money. Arizona's qualifying process—a process where a participating candidate must raise a base of $10 contributions—also enables ordinary citizens to participate in the money primary. Tax credits or vouchers for contributions, such as proposed by Yale law professor Bruce Ackerman and currently implemented in Minnesota, would similarly empower all individuals, even those who don't have $175 to donate to a campaign (the threshold for a small contribution in New York City). However, a candidate who was already well known, such as an incumbent, might have an advantage in attracting those vouchers or credits before competitors had a chance. A combination of matching funds and credits or vouchers, as proposed by Rep. John Sarbanes in his "Government by the People" legislation, might be the best approach, giving candidates a way to get started. This way, everyone, even those who can't spare $50, get a chance to contribute.

In his groundbreaking 2011 article, "The Participation Interest," Spencer Overton put forward a number of other proposals that would encourage citizen participation as donors and volunteers as well as voters, all of whom would also expand opportunity.[13] Small donor PACs, for example, which could accept contributions of no more than $250 but have more flexibility than other PACs, would encourage organizing and help causes that don't have wealthy supporters to be heard. There is some evidence that the disclosure requirement on contributions of more than $200 deters donors from making those modest contributions; raising that threshold to, say, $500 might make first-time donors more comfortable without opening a massive loophole.

Not all efforts to lower the barriers to entry into politics involve changing the rules, however. Technology has already dramatically changed the relationship between candidates and small donors. On the Democratic side, for example, ActBlue has made it possible for potential donors to identify candidates all across the country who they might support (often based on recommendations from friends or bloggers), and along with older projects such as EMILY's List, these tools have given candidates a way to raise their first money even if they don't have a wealthy base of supporters.

More recently, products such as NationBuilder appeared on the scene, offering candidates from any party (or no party at all)—as well as small organizations of all kinds—a basic suite of tools necessary to start a campaign, including the capacity to build and manage lists, launch a website, send mass e-mails, coordinate volunteers, accept credit card donations and—of real value—access a reliable voter file. NationBuilder's costs range from $19 to $999 a month, but previously most campaigns had to buy these services separately and put them together from scratch at much higher cost. It is, in effect, a turnkey startup campaign. Similarly, Run for America, a new organization intended to encourage young people to run for Congress, is structured as a B Corporation: that is, a company that's not a nonprofit but is intended to serve a public purpose. It would provide its candidates with basic campaign services at the lowest possible cost.

The declining effectiveness of broadcast television advertising, and the shift to targeted online communication, might also reduce the barriers to entry. Most candidates beyond the local level spend a large percentage of whatever money they have on television: this is because that's how it's always been done, and because political consultants have a vested interest in advertising commissions. But political scientist David Karpf predicts "a slow shift away from television among campaigns that is going to continue."[14] The combination of smart public-financing systems, technology that lowers the barriers to entry, and new ways to communicate with voters at lower cost could dramatically transform the landscape of money in politics. This could also reduce the incentives for candidates to create Super PACs or enlist outside spending.

Nor would all of the steps that fall under the framework of political opportunity involve raising money or lowering costs. Changes to voting structures, such as instant-run-off voting or ranked-choice voting, can give financially challenged candidates an opportunity to influence politics anyway, as other candidates compete for the second-choice votes of their supporters. These systems can reward organizing over money and discourage campaigns based on pure negative attacks. Innovations such as ranked-choice voting can both reduce the influence of money and the pressure to raise it and can be coupled to systems like small-donor matching funds to boost the effectiveness of each.

Finally, the dominance of money in shaping the debate outside of elections, such as through think-tank funding, paid research, lobbying, and grassroots lobbying, can be offset by restoring some of the infrastructure of independent, trusted resources. Yale law professor Heather Gerken has proposed treating lobbying in much the same way that the political-opportunity approach would treat campaign finance: public funding of experts to ensure that lawmakers have access to sound and balanced information from independent sources, without trying to block anyone else's right to lobby.[15] The elimination of independent sources of information such as the congressional Office of Technology Assessment in the mid-1990s is widely thought to have increased the influence of industry lobbyists. Restoring these public institutions, in a newer and more adaptable form, would help bring new ideas and information to the legislative process.

We should always be wary of promising more than any procedural reform, or combination of public and private reforms, can achieve. Nothing will be "the salvation" of American politics. Progressives who hope that fixing money in politics, ending the filibuster, or implementing ranked-choice voting will lead to a new era of liberal consensus will be disappointed (and so will conservatives, or centrists). The country is deeply divided, and our political structures awkwardly designed for such deep divisions. But it's all made worse by profound economic inequality that deepens and reinforces political inequality. To disrupt this closed and stagnant system, an approach based on a vision of political opportunity can map the way to reforms that will be legally and constitutionally sound—and one that will bring new voices, new perspectives, and new ideas to America's political discourse.

Notes

1. E.E. Schattschneider, *Politics, Pressures and the Tariff* (New York: Prentice-Hall, 1935), 288.
2. See Jacob Hacker and Paul Pierson, *Off Center: The Republican Revolution and the Erosion of American Politics* (New Haven, CT: Yale University Press, 2006).
3. Author calculation from voteview.org.
4. Thomas E. Mann and Norman Ornstein, "Let's Just Say It: The Republicans are the Problem," *Washington Post*, April 27, 2012, http://www.washingtonpost.com/opinions/lets-just-say-it-the-republicans-are-the-problem/2012/04/27/gIQAxCVUlT_story.html.
5. See FairVote's semi-annual "Monopoly Politics" report at www.fairvote.org.
6. Thomas Piketty, *Capitalism in the Twenty-First Century*, (Cambridge, MA: Belknap Press, 2014).
7. Adam Bonica and Nolan McCarty, Keith T. Poole, and Howard Rosenthal, "Why Hasn't Democracy Slowed Rising Inequality?" *Journal of Economic Perspectives* 27. 3 (Summer 2013), 111–112.
8. See, for example, Martin Gilens, *Affluence and Influence: Economic Inequality and Political Power in America* (Princeton, NJ: Princeton University Press, 2014) or Andrew Gelman, *Red State, Blue State, Rich State, Poor State: Why Americans Vote the Way they Do* (Princeton, NJ: Princeton University Press, 2009).
9. Norman J. Ornstein, "Trust is Not Enough to Break Through Washington Gridlock," *National Journal*, October 1, 2014, http://www.nationaljournal.com/washington-inside-out/trust-is-not-enough-to-break-through-washington-gridlock-20140930.
10. Zephyr Teachout, *Corruption in America: From Benjamin Franklin's Snuff Box to Citizens United*, 2014.
11. Ibid., p. 9.
12. Lawrence Lessig, *Republic, Lost: How Money Corrupts Congress* (New York: Twelve, 2012), 231.
13. Overton, Spencer, "The Participation Interest," *Georgetown Law Journal* 100.4.
14. Arielle Confino, "T.V.'s Role in Political Campaigns Diminishes," *GoLocal Prov News*, September 16, 2014, http://www.golocalprov.com/news/tvs-role-in-political-campaigns-diminishes.
15. Heather Gerken, "Keynote Address: Lobbying as the New Campaign Finance," *Georgia State University Law Review* 27.4, 1153–1160.

8

Insecurity, Austerity, and the American Social Contract

JACOB S. HACKER

On August 14, 1935, Franklin Roosevelt signed into law the Social Security Act, the cornerstone of America's distinctive framework of social protection. Seated at a table in the White House's Cabinet Room, he was flanked by Labor Secretary Frances Perkins, the first woman appointed to a presidential cabinet, and Representative David Lewis, a former coal miner and self-taught lawyer who championed the legislation. Standing nearby was Representative John Dingell of Michigan—the child of Polish immigrants (his original last name was Dzieglewicz) who introduced the first bill for national health insurance in Congress in 1933. Their presence was fitting, for as Roosevelt declared that day, the law was designed to provide ordinary workers and their families—women as well as men, children as well as adults, coal miners and sons of immigrants alike—with "some measure of protection" against the "hazards and vicissitudes of life."[1]

But Roosevelt did not just celebrate the law's safeguarding of "human needs"; in addition, he emphasized that the Act was part of an evolving "structure intended to lessen the force of possible future depressions" and to limit the need for the government to go "deeply into debt to furnish relief to the needy." Henceforth, Roosevelt proclaimed, the law would "provide for the United States an economic structure of vastly greater soundness."

Roosevelt's insistence that public insurance was good not just for those experiencing dislocations but also for the economy as a whole sounds jarring today. The dominant view is that Social Security, Medicare, and other similar programs are inefficient and unaffordable. Defenses of these programs stress their protection of "human needs" rather than their role in supporting a strong economy. Meanwhile, the many and vocal attacks on these programs emphasize their mounting costs, their supposed uncontrollability, and their alleged perverse incentives.

The leading economic spokesperson of the Republican Party, Representative Paul Ryan, suggests that we are transforming "the safety net into a hammock that lulls able-bodied people to lives of dependence and complacency, that drains them of their will and their incentive to make the most of their lives." Spending on this hammock threatens a "debt crisis," Ryan warns, in which "our finances will collapse, our economy will stall." The United States, he insists, must "change course"—and that change should take the form of dramatically cutting back the mandatory programs that DC insiders pejoratively refer to as "entitlements."[2]

To get a sense of the change in discourse, glance at figure 8.1, which shows the number of references to "entitlements" and "social insurance" in the tens of millions of English-language books scanned by Google. "Social insurance" was once a common term, used to describe programs and policies that provide broad risk protection that is more generous for lower-income and higher-risk groups. In the wake of the Social Security Act, the phrase rose dramatically in prominence. Starting in the 1970s and accelerating in subsequent decades, however, "entitlements" has risen to surpass "social insurance" in English-language books. The notion that many public programs are a form of insurance that is potentially beneficial to the economy has been eclipsed by the idea that these are runaway obligations that threaten our economic future.

This view has it almost exactly backward. Economic insecurity remains a pressing problem that only effective government policies can address. What's more, our

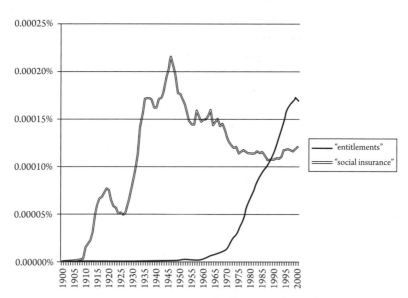

Figure 8.1 "Entitlements" vs. "Social Insurance" in English-Language Books. Source: Google Ngram Viewer, http://books.google.com/ngrams. Results represent a three-year moving average of occurrence of "entitlements" and "social insurance" in English-language books digitized by Google as a percentage of all one-word and two-word phrases, respectively.

society can afford to upgrade these policies. Indeed, we cannot afford to *not* upgrade these policies. Like the Great Depression, the financial crisis that began in 2007 has taught us important lessons about the limits of private responses to widespread economic risks. It is these private responses, such as workplace health insurance, that are inefficient and unsustainable. As they decline, more and more risk is shifting to workers and their families—in ways that likely hurt the economy overall. Far from a comfortable hammock, America's framework of social protection is becoming more threadbare and less complete.

This transformation is an opportunity as well as a threat. Because the United States relies more on inefficient and eroding private responses than any other rich nation, there is ample room for us to expand social protection while actually saving our society money and improving our economy. The greatest opportunity lies in health care, where we spend vastly more than other affluent nations for less coverage and poorer outcomes. But there is also an enormous amount of "money on the table" in the complex web of subsidies that encourage private employment-based benefits and retirement savings—subsidies that cannot and will not prevent the continuing shift of risk and whose benefits accrue mostly to the least vulnerable workers.

In short, critics are correct that the American social contract needs to be harmonized with a twenty-first-century economy and society. But contrary to their arguments, this means upgrading public social protections to cover the most significant risks and the most vulnerable Americans. We can increase security for workers and their families even as we make American social protection more efficient and its costs more controllable. The challenges we face are at least as much political as economic, which is why those seeking reform should be thinking at least as much about political realities as about policy alternatives.

THE INSECURITY CONSTELLATION

The financial crisis that began in 2007 has provided a harsh reminder that economic insecurity is still very much a part of American life. In the eighteen months between March 2008 and September 2009—according to a survey I designed with two fellow researchers—roughly half of Americans experienced at least one major employment dislocation within their family (involuntary unemployment or loss of more than a month of work due to sickness or injury) and more than half experienced at least one major health dislocation (major out-of-pocket expenses, much higher insurance costs, or loss of insurance altogether).[3] At the same time, Americans were, and continue to be, strikingly ill-prepared for major economic risks. Asked how long they could go without their current income before hardship set in, more than 70 percent said less than six months, and nearly half said less than two months (see figure 8.2).

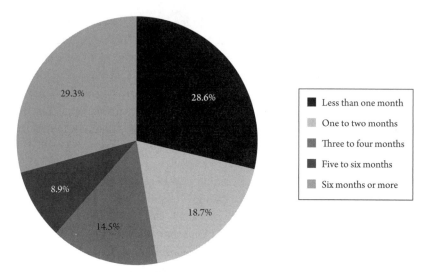

Figure 8.2 How Long Can Households Go Without Income Before Hardship Sets In? Source: Survey of Economic Risk Perceptions and Insecurity (SERPI). The SERPI was incorporated as a part of the 2008–2009 Panel Survey of the American National Election Studies (ANES), an online survey of a nationally representative sample of Americans who agreed to be interviewed monthly between January 2008 and October 2009. With financial support from the Rockefeller Foundation, the SERPI was fielded as the sole questions for the ANES panel in March (Wave 15) and September (Wave 21) of 2009; 2,084 respondents completed both waves of the survey. Results are weighted to replicate a nationally representative distribution of respondents. The question asked how long a respondents' household could go without income before "hardship" set in.

These pessimistic expectations are borne out by the evidence. Households that experienced major economic risks between March 2008 and September 2009 reported much higher levels of unmet basic needs: going without food because of the cost, losing one's house or rental, or going without health care because of the expense. Even among families in the third quartile of household income (annual income between $60,000 and $100,000), more than half of families who experienced employment or medical disruptions reported being unable to meet at least one basic economic need.[4]

Although the recent downturn cast insecurity in stark relief, these dislocations represent the culmination of a long-term trend rather than a sudden departure from stable conditions. Over the last generation, there has been a gradual but steady increase in the share of Americans experiencing substantial economic losses, such as big drops in income or major spikes in out-of-pocket medical costs.[5] The cumulative risk of such losses over a working life is very high. According to a recent examination using data from 1968 to the present, more than two-thirds of Americans will experience involuntary job loss by the age of sixty, and more than half will spend at least one year in poverty. And these risks have risen: between 1968 and 1988, roughly 12 percent of forty-five to fifty-year-olds experienced at a least a year in poverty. Between 1988 and 2008 (two decades that overwhelmingly predate the recent downturn), the chance was almost 18 percent.[6]

We often neglect rising insecurity, for at least two reasons. First, the gap between the most affluent Americans and the rest of society has grown dramatically.[7] These fortunate families have not experienced the same rise in economic insecurity as the less affluent, and their divergent experience looms large in media portrayals of the economy. Second, and more important, the changes of the last generation have yet to work fully through the age pyramid of American society. Changes in social benefits, especially those that affect retirement, often take decades to reach full effect. Shifts in labor markets usually have their greatest impact on less established workers. Thus, in many areas of social policy, older Americans reflect the economic order of forty or more years ago. Like a distant constellation whose light takes years to reach us, their much higher levels of economic security provide an image of the past: a world of widespread economic security in which a substantial amount of risk was pooled across workers and generations. Their children, and especially their grandchildren, are coming of age in a fundamentally different world—one that promises much greater insecurity and much more unequal prospects during their working lives and in retirement.

I have called this transformation the "Great Risk Shift," the long-term transfer of economic risk from broad structures of insurance, whether sponsored by the corporate sector or by government, onto the balance sheets of American families.[8] Unique among rich democracies, the United States fostered a social contract based on widespread provision of private workplace benefits. As figure 8.3 shows, our *government* framework of social protection is indeed smaller than those found in other rich countries. Yet when we take into account private health and retirement benefits—mostly voluntary, but highly subsidized through the tax code—we have an overall system similar in size to that of other rich countries. The difference is that our system is distinctively private.

This framework, however, is coming undone. The unions that once negotiated and defended private benefits have lost tremendous ground. Partly for this reason, employers no longer wish to shoulder the burdens they took on during more stable economic times. Employers also no longer highly value the long-term commitments to workers that these arrangements reflected and fostered. The resulting shifts are larger than any retrenchment program pursued by conservative critics of public social programs. Health insurance has become much less common in the workplace, even for college-educated workers. In the early 1980s, 80 percent of recent college graduates had health insurance through their job; by the late 2000s, the share had fallen to around 60 percent.[9] And, of course, the drop has been far greater for less-educated workers.

Meanwhile, employers have restructured retirement benefits to eliminate guaranteed payouts (so-called defined-benefit plans) and replace them with individual

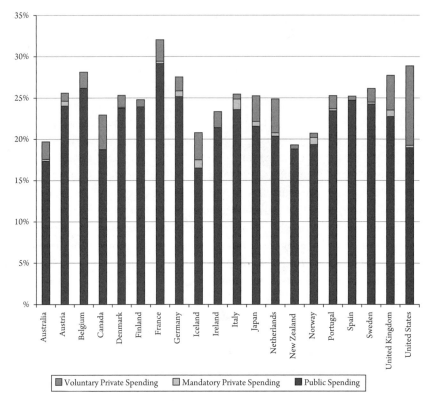

Figure 8.3 Public and Private Social Spending in Affluent Democracies, 2009. Source: OECD, "Social Spending During the Crisis: Social Expenditure (SOCX) Data Update 2012," http://www.oecd.org/els/soc/OECD(2012)_Social%20spending%20after%20the%20 crisis_Data.zip. All figures reflect net spending after taxes. In order to avoid double counting, the value of tax breaks that subsidize private social benefits has been ignored for the calculation of net public social expenditure.

savings accounts sponsored by employers (so-called defined-contribution plans).[10] These 401(k)s and other defined-contribution plans do not pool the risk of inadequate income in retirement, nor do they ensure participation or adequate contributions in the way that traditional plans did. As a result, retirement security is declining, with most younger workers holding retirement savings that are far too limited to provide them with a secure retirement even with Social Security. We are moving back toward a world in which only the well off can expect to retire comfortably in old age.

Debate over the American social contract is badly dated. A period of greater insecurity is already upon us, embedded in the limited savings and less secure benefits of younger workers. Still, the choices we as a society make today will help shape how the costs and benefits of our current framework are distributed. More importantly, they could usher in a new era of broad security—if we move to redirect resources that are currently used to underwrite a costly, unequal, and eroding private system.

THE HEALTH-CARE RENT IS TOO DAMN HIGH!

In one of the 2012 Republican presidential debates, there was an unexpected contestant named Jimmy McMillan, running under the banner of the Rent Is Too Damn High Party. (Perhaps recognizing how few Republican voters are renters, the candidate known for his odd facial hair changed the slogan for the campaign to "The Deficit is Too Damn High!") Given that McMillan hails from New York City, it is understandable why he chose to focus on housing costs. But if there is one form of rent that really is too damn high, it is the exorbitant amount that Americans pay for health care. In the lingo of economics, a "rent" is excess payment made to market actors because of their political or economic power. The rents in health care consist of enormously wasteful levels of spending that result from policies tilted toward the health-care industry within a market marked by vast imbalances of information and influence between patients and providers.

The good news is that getting control of these costs would vastly increase economic security both directly and indirectly—directly because health costs are a major threat to economic security in themselves, and indirectly because they are the biggest threat to America's long-term budget. Without "rent control" in health care, any larger reform goals will be crushed under the ever-growing burden of medical costs.

Tempers flare whenever international comparisons of health care are made. Yet certain basic facts cannot be ignored. The United States spends vastly more than other rich nations—almost twice as much per person as the next most profligate nation, Switzerland, and about $700 billion more overall in 2006 than you would predict based on our per capita income.[11] Furthermore, the main reason for this higher spending is not greater utilization of care: Americans visit doctors less often and spend less time in the hospital after treatment, they are younger on average, and there are fewer doctors and hospital beds per capita than is the norm among rich nations.[12]

Instead, the main reason we spend so much more is that our health care *prices* are so much higher than those found in other rich nations (see figure 8.4). High prices equal high incomes for providers, drug companies, medical device manufacturers, and other industry players. They do not, alas, equal better health outcomes. Despite all the excess spending, Americans live shorter lives and are in poorer overall health than citizens of most other rich nations, and rates of preventable deaths are higher.[13] The quality of American health care is not the sole (nor even the primary) reason for this poor performance. But at the very least, we are not getting very good value for our money.

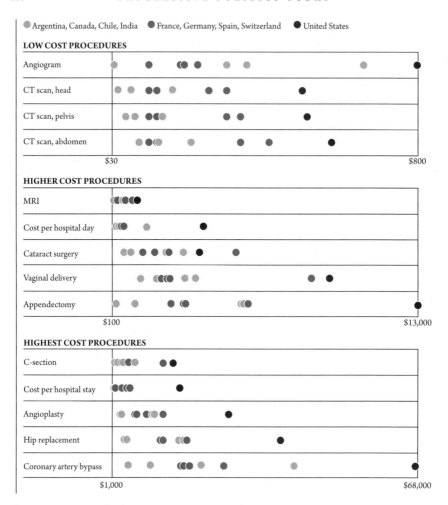

Figure 8.4 U.S. Medical Prices in Cross-National Perspective. Source: "The High Cost of Medical Procedures in the U.S.," *Washington Post*, March 2, 2012, accessed July 8, 2014, http://www.washingtonpost.com/wp-srv/special/business/high-cost-of-medical-procedures-in-the-us/. Data from International Federation of Health Plans.

These cost differences add up. If American expenditures had risen at the rate of Swiss expenditures between 1980 and 2010, we would have spent $15 trillion less on health care overall. Even in the jaded world of health costs, that is a lot of money (enough, for example, to send more than 175,000 kids to a four-year college).[14] Looking forward, America's long-term deficit problem is a health-care spending problem. Take out Medicare and Medicaid, and the federal budget is more or less balanced as far as the eye (or at least the Congressional Budget Office) can see.[15] Over the long term, demographic shifts, while real, pale in their effects to the pressures created by rising medical costs. Ever-escalating health spending means not just less disposable income for workers and their families but also less budgetary scope to upgrade benefits or invest in education, infrastructure, technology, and other critical sources of future growth. No health-care cost containment, no improved social contract.

Fortunately, this is an area where effective public and private efforts could make an enormous difference. Other countries control costs better than us for a simple reason: they create countervailing power to push back against all the industry players seeking higher incomes. These strategies do not require a "single payer," where the government acts as a public insurer for basic services. In Switzerland, insurance is private, though highly regulated; yet the government effectively sets prices. In other nations, the state oversees negotiations between providers and insurance funds. But no rich nation other than the United States leaves cost control to decentralized negotiations between private insurers and providers—negotiations in which increasingly consolidated and politically mobilized providers almost invariably hold the upper hand.

We do not need international experience to demonstrate this point. Medicare, the federal insurance program for the elderly and disabled, has controlled costs better than private insurers, pioneering new payment methods, such as prospective payment for hospitals, precisely because it has some measure of countervailing power.[16] Yet Medicare's power is limited. Not only does it cover the elderly and disabled alone but the medical-industrial complex has managed to limit Medicare's countervailing power in myriad ways. In 2006, for example, drug companies successfully insisted that a prescription drug benefit not allow direct insurance through Medicare (instead, private supplemental plans offer the benefit), nor involve any price negotiation by the federal government. As a result, companies have been able to charge exorbitant prices. Lipitor, a cholesterol drug used by many beneficiaries, costs on average $124 a month in the United States—and $6 in New Zealand. The nasal medication Nasonex runs $108 a month on average—and $29 in Canada.[17] On most dimensions, Canada and New Zealand are as market oriented as the United States. They just don't allow manufacturers with limited-duration monopolies thanks to patent protections charge whatever a distorted market will bear.

Faced with the reality of runaway prices, many critics of economic protections have argued that the problem is that patients don't have enough "skin in the game."[18] The solution, they insist, is to shift more risk and costs onto patients—especially Medicare beneficiaries—to increase their incentive to shop around and bargain for better prices. But health care is not a normal market. The asymmetry of information between providers and patients is huge. Shopping around, especially at the time of treatment, is often prohibitively difficult ("Wait, don't pull out my rupturing appendix; I want to see what the place down the street charges!"). And insurance creates its own Catch-22. High-tech care is simply too costly to finance without insurance. Yet insurance rightly protects the most costly patients whose expenses account for the vast bulk of our overall spending. (The costliest 10 percent of Medicare beneficiaries account for more than 60 percent of spending).[19] They cannot have "skin in the game" unless we allow them to lose all their skin.

Transforming Medicare's guaranteed benefits into a voucher that covers only a fixed amount of the cost of care, with the growing remainder falling onto older and disabled Americans, makes sense only if we pretend that health costs borne by individuals are fundamentally different from health-care costs borne by the federal government. Because such a shift will not control costs for all the reasons just mentioned—and may even cause costs to rise by reducing the pressure on federal policy makers to improve Medicare's efficiency—then reducing the federal government's commitment simply means shifting more costs and risks onto patients and their families. That is a poor bargain for today's older Americans. It is an even worse bargain for younger generations who are facing greater insecurity in the workforce today and will now be required to face greater insecurity in retirement as well.

Health-care cost control would be good for economic security in itself, and it would be very good for economic security when we consider the larger opportunity costs of ever-rising spending. In principle, such cost control is within our grasp. Extending Medicare to younger Americans, for instance, would give the program much greater leverage to hold down costs. It would also eliminate the current tension between Medicare and the Affordable Care Act (ACA) that has been created by the ACA's heavy reliance on slowing Medicare spending to finance new coverage for the nonelderly. Systemic cost-containment could be achieved through a variety of strategies, from an expanded Medicare program to a "public option" insurance plan for younger Americans without secure workplace coverage to so-called all-payer rate setting at the state or federal level to create standard prices across all insurers.[20] All of these would involve breaking open the demographic silos of our present inefficient system and fostering countervailing power on the purchasing side of health care. The problem, of course, is the politics—which is a topic this chapter will revisit. But the politics of increased cost control is arguably no less fraught than the politics of shifting ever more expenses onto Medicare beneficiaries—a constituency not exactly known for its quiescence. Instead of moving Medicare toward the private model of multiple plans and limited coverage, we should be doing the opposite: increasing the public bargaining power embodied in Medicare and extending its reach to younger Americans. This would not only allow the public sector to better control costs but would also create pressures on private insurers to adopt public innovations in cost control and care management as well.

A NEW SOCIAL CONTRACT

The road to reform runs through health-care cost containment. But where does it lead? Entire books are devoted to this question. But in the more limited space available here, let me introduce and explain some of the main goals.

The overarching goal, of course, is an affordable framework of security that provides adequate protection against the most pressing risks of our era. Yet achieving that goal requires a measure of pragmatism often lacking among advocates who compare the shining beauty of policy ideals to the messy reality of actual arrangements. To use a social-science term, our public-private system of social protection is "path-dependent."[21] The road already traveled makes some future routes very unlikely (the Swedish cradle-to-grave model of social services, for instance). Central aspects of our system, such as our heavy reliance on workplace benefits are likely to remain with us for some time to come. Reformers will need to work with what they have.

Yet they should also recognize that times have changed. When FDR signed the Social Security Act, economic insecurity was largely seen as a problem of drops or interruptions in male earnings, whether due to unemployment, retirement, or other costly events. Even as working women became the norm, America's social programs mostly failed to address the special economic strains that two-earner and single-parent families face. Whole categories of social protection that are nearly universal in other rich nations—from paid sick days to subsidized child care, to early childhood education that enriches children's capacities even when their parents are working—are largely absent in the United States.

Nor do existing programs adequately address the distinctive unemployment patterns that became increasingly prevalent as industrial employment gave way to service work, such as the rising problem of long-term unemployment. And the shift of workers from one economic sector to another that is characteristic of our current era often leads to substantial pay cuts and the need for specialized retraining, not just short-term income losses.

In short, US social policy has become less capable of cushioning the biggest risks that workers and their families face. Our framework of social protection is overwhelmingly focused on the aged, even though young adults and families with children face the greatest economic strains. It emphasizes short-term exits from the workforce, even though long-term job losses and the displacement and obsolescence of skills have become more severe. In many places, it embodies the antiquated notion that family strains can be dealt with by a second earner—usually a woman—who can easily enter or leave the workforce as necessary. Above all, it is based on the idea that job-based private insurance can easily fill the gaps left by public programs, even though it is ever clearer that job-based private insurance is not enough.

These shortcomings suggest that an improved social contract should emphasize portable insurance to help families deal with major interruptions to income and big blows to wealth. They also mean that these promises should be mostly separate from work for a particular employer and that social benefits should move from job to job. If this sometimes means corporations are off the hook, so be it. In time, they will pay their workers more to compensate for fewer benefits, and there are plenty of ways to encourage their contributions without having them decide who gets benefits and who does not.

By the same token, however, we should not force massive social risks on institutions incapable of effectively carrying them. Bankruptcy—which afflicts roughly 1.5 million mostly middle-class families each year—should not be a backdoor social insurance system.[22] Private charity care should not be our main medical safety net. And credit cards should not be supplemental income for families when times are tight. To be sure, when nothing better is possible, we may need to preserve even incomplete and inadequate safety nets. But the ultimate goal should be a framework of social insurance that revitalizes the best elements of the present system, while replacing those parts that work less effectively with stronger alternatives geared toward today's economy and society.

Which brings us to the final principle: measures to enhance security should be designed to enhance opportunity. Most of us think of these measures a way of helping those who have had bad fortune or have fallen on hard times. Yet, as FDR recognized, providing economic security generates far wider benefits for our economy and our society. Corporate law has long recognized the need to limit the downside of economic risk taking as a way of encouraging entrepreneurs and investors to make the risky investments necessary to advance in a capitalist economy. The law of bankruptcy and the principle of limited liability allow entrepreneurs to innovate with the security of knowing that they will not be financially destroyed if their risky bets fail.

The experience of major economic shocks is among the most unsettling events that families go through, leaving psychological, economic, and social traces—from reduced happiness to decreased labor-force attachment to family dissolution—for years and even decades to come. Workers who come of age during a recession experience poorer earnings and employment outcomes for at least twenty years.[23] Workers who lose a job face a significantly heightened risk of death compared with their continuously employed counterparts—even two decades after unemployment.[24] Although some degree of economic insecurity is part and parcel of a dynamic capitalist economy, families torn apart by economic risks are not in a position to adequately plan for or invest in the future.

Just as entrepreneurs need basic protections to foster risk taking, families also need a basic foundation of financial security if they are to feel confident in making the investments required to advance in a dynamic economy. All of the major wellsprings of opportunity in the United States—assets, workplace skills, education, investments in children—are costly and risky for families to cultivate. Providing security can encourage families to make these investments, aiding not just their own advancement but improving the economy as a whole.

REBUILDING THE THREE-LEGGED STOOL
OF RETIREMENT SECURITY

To see what such a framework might look like, let us return to one of the most glaring examples of the so-called great risk shift: the movement away from secure pension benefits in the private sector. America's framework for providing retirement security was historically referred to as a "three-legged stool," with Social Security, private pensions, and personal savings each carrying an important part of the weight of securing workers' retirements. As private defined-benefit pensions have disappeared, we have moved from the traditional three-legged stool of retirement security to a two-legged stool—Social Security and private savings (inside and outside of 401(k)s). Needless to say, this stool is much less stable than the last.

Today, Social Security is basically the only guaranteed pension left. Yet the role of Social Security has declined in the last twenty years as well, mainly due to cutbacks that occurred in the late 1970s and early 1980s. Looking forward, Social Security is expected to replace a smaller share of preretirement income than it did in the past. That is true even if Social Security pays promised benefits—an assumption that is safer than Social Security's doomsayers believe but still hinges on favorable economic and demographic trends and some adjustments in the program.

But if Social Security has grown modestly less generous, private pensions have essentially ceased to provide any risk protection to a large chunk of less-affluent workers. This is not a coincidence. The incentives for higher-income Americans to save have ballooned with the expansion of tax-favored investment vehicles like 401(k)s. Yet, because the tax breaks for these benefits are skewed toward higher-income Americans, most Americans receive modest benefits from these costly tax breaks. (In 2011, tax breaks for retirement pensions and accounts cost the federal government over $140 billion in forgone tax revenue). Roughly 80 percent of these tax subsidies for retirement savings accrue to the top 20 percent of the population. Only 7 percent accrue to the bottom 60 percent of the population.[25]

The reasons for this stark disparity are threefold—and they largely hold true with other tax-subsidized workplace benefits. First, lower-income Americans face lower marginal tax rates, making tax breaks for private benefits worth much less to them. Second, lower-income Americans are least likely to have access to tax-favored benefits. And third, lower-income Americans have the least discretionary income to contribute to tax-favored accounts (or pay for their rising portion of employment-based health premiums). Living paycheck to paycheck, they need the greatest incentive and assistance to save. Instead, the tax benefits for retirement are structured so that they provide the greatest rewards to higher-income workers. Not surprisingly, account balances in 401(k)s are highly tilted toward the rich. The typical account holder has less than $20,000 saved, and this counts only those who *have* 401(k)s. Overall, around 70 percent of defined-contribution pension and IRA assets are held by the richest fifth of Americans.[26]

All this strongly argues for preserving and even expanding the one guaranteed source of retirement security for most workers that we have left: Social Security. Though Social Security has a long-term deficit, dealing with it does not require abandoning the core elements of the program: guaranteed lifetime benefits paid on retirement, provided as a right, and linked to lifetime earnings. The shortfall can be relatively easily closed by making benefits and the payroll taxes that fund them more progressive and by tying benefits to future longevity so that fortunate generations that live longer than the last receive slightly less from the program than now promised. Because most of the gains in life expectancy over the last generation have been enjoyed only by higher-wage workers, increased progressivity should take precedence over longevity-based adjustments.[27]

In particular, the so-called wage cap on Social Security payroll taxes should be eliminated or at least substantially raised, and it should be applied to capital income as well as wages. As income has grown more unequal over the last generation, more and more of the highest wages are exempt from the Social Security payroll tax—which is capped at around $115,000 in annual earnings. Because high-income workers receive the lowest rate of return from Social Security, raising the cap results in far more revenue flowing into the program than new spending on benefits. In fact, eliminating the payroll-tax cap would by itself close the long-term funding shortfall.

Even with a secure Social Security system, today's workers will need other sources of income in retirement. As they are presently constituted, 401(k)s are not the solution. Too few workers are offered them, enroll in them, or put adequate sums in them, and they place too much of the risk of retirement planning on individuals, with too little information and insurance to help them build a secure retirement. Though many supporters of the present system argue that 401(k)s can be fixed with minor tweaks, such as requiring companies to automatically enroll their workers, these sorts of adjustments will not address the major problems: skewed tax subsidies, low contribution rates, leakage from the system when workers change jobs, and most fundamental of all, the fact that many employers do not offer a 401(k).

On the other side, some pension experts have proposed mandatory, government-managed accounts with a guaranteed rate of return that would supplement Social Security, forming a "second tier" of compulsory retirement savings that would largely replace 401(k)s.[28] For all their merits, these proposals face serious political and logistical obstacles. Instead, I propose a middle way: a more robust version of plans for "universal 401(k)s" that have received notice in recent years. Universal 401(k)s should be available to all workers. Employers would be encouraged to match employer contributions to these plans, and indeed, the federal government could provide special tax breaks to employers that offered better matches to lower-wage workers Automatic enrollment would be required, and the default contribution rate would be set at a level that would finance an adequate retirement along with Social Security. Moreover, the default investment option under 401(k)s should be a low-cost index fund with a mix of stocks and bonds that automatically shifts over time as workers age to limit market risk as workers approach retirement. Existing tax breaks for 401(k)s would be replaced with a retirement savings credit that would be placed in the accounts of all workers. Such a credit would be the same for all workers and, hence, a much larger share of the income of low-wage workers.

After my criticism of 401(k)s, it may come as a surprise that I think universal 401(k)s are the best route forward. Yet the difference between universal 401(k)s with strong incentives for contributions and the present system is profound. What's more, I recommend one additional change: requiring that 401(k) accounts be converted into a lifetime guaranteed income at retirement unless workers could show they had sufficient assets to weather market risk. These new annuities could be provided by private firms under strict federal rules or directly by the federal government. To help workers' plan ahead, 401(k) balances should be reported to account holders not as a cash sum but as their expected monthly benefit amount—just as Social Security benefits are reported. In essence, universal 401(k)s along these lines would bring back something close to a guaranteed private pension, with government, rather than employers, pooling the risk.

GETTING FROM HERE TO THERE

With apologies to the 1992 Clinton campaign, whose campaign handbook *Putting People First* summed up their appeal to the middle class, those seeking to upgrade the American social contract should be "putting politics first." By this, I mean that reformers must think not just about what policies would be better than our current crumbling framework but also about how our polarized and gridlocked political system could realistically take us from here to there. In this final section, I present five strategic maxims and suggest how they link to necessary changes.

Demography isn't destiny, but it's powerful. American society is changing fundamentally. Hispanics are becoming the largest minority group, and whites will represent a minority of the US population within a generation. Single and single-parent women—who strongly lean toward Progressive policies such as those outlined in this chapter—are a growing part of the electorate. And the shifts in the workforce discussed in this chapter have meant that an increasing number of workers, white as well as nonwhite, face the kinds of insecurity and financial strains once limited to the working poor.

In the short term, these changes have very mixed effects. In presidential election years, when turnout is high, they have resulted in a more progressive electorate; however, they have also activated political forces concerned about the transformations underway—forces willing to limit access to the ballot box, gerrymander districts, and sink enormous sums of money into elections to hold back the tide. Yet the arc of history bends toward a greater voice for less privileged Americans who will see value in greater security. Whether politicians will hear them depends on whether advocates create the ongoing pressure to develop viable options and keep them on the agenda.

Turning the tables. To create that pressure requires that Progressives take a page out of the conservative playbook. In the early 1980s two advocates of Social Security privatization presented what they called a "Leninist strategy" (yes, that was actually the title of their piece).[29] At its center was the idea that conservatives had to work diligently behind the scenes to shift policy toward their preferred outcome of private retirement accounts, which they hoped would eventually become the basis of privatization. Although the idea did not pan out—in part because those accounts were so much less attractive than previously thought—the strategy was sound. In American politics, big reforms are difficult to push through and as a result are rare. Many of the adjustments that are needed will come not through major legislative changes but rather through persistent improvement of present arrangements.

Nowhere is this more true than with regard to health care. The passage of the ACA was the biggest change in our framework of social protection since the creation of Medicare and Medicaid in 1965. But the law is a "starter home," as one backer called it—complex, sometimes contradictory, and on the whole insufficient to either provide universal insurance or seriously rein in costs.[30] This is not to argue that much more could have been achieved; given how close the law came to passage and how contested it remains today, the notion that a single-payer system could have passed if only President Obama had fought for it is fanciful. But advocates of the law will have to push it forward on multiple fronts—state and federal—if the ACA is to have anything close to its promised effects (much less go beyond them) to provide universal affordable coverage.

I have already suggested that these changes should seek to bring the successful international approach to cost control to bear on America's out-of-line prices. Another goal should be to allow a gradual movement away from employment-based coverage by creating the option for all employers to finance coverage through the new insurance exchanges set up to provide private options (these exchanges should also add a public option). In practice, this means shifting toward payroll-based contributions for coverage through the exchange—the Social Security model and the common way of financing coverage in other systems based on multiple private plans. If these payroll contributions were lower than the cost of private insurance, as they should be, the burden on employers would actually be lower than in the current system. At the same time, workers would be guaranteed portable coverage that moved from job to job.

A politics of "rent control." Perhaps the most lamentable feature of America's eroding framework of economic security is the degree to which it wastes resources that could be better applied to improve security or achieve other ends. Massive subsidies to encourage high-income taxpayers to save are mostly wasted resources, since these are the Americans most likely to save on their own. Paying two to three times as much for the very same health services delivered in other countries is wasteful—a transfer from taxpayers and cash-strapped patients to highly profitable and highly paid sectors of the economy. Yes, there is plenty of inefficiency and waste in government. But much of it involves excessive deference to and support for private-sector players that benefit from distorted markets that allow them to provide weak guarantees of security at exorbitant costs.

A politics of "rent control" would have two benefits. First, it would free up resources. If medical costs were restrained as effectively as they have been in other nations, many of our long-term budget problems would simply disappear. Second, a concerted campaign to roll back high rents that burden citizens and consumers would dispel some of the widespread doubts about the capacity of the public sector to address social problems—perhaps the greatest political barrier to a more secure future.

Reviving faith in government. As the journalist George Packer notes, we have lost our faith in "collective self-betterment."[31] Americans value and laud Social Security and Medicare but mostly see them as one-off successes rather than as a demonstration that social insurance is actually the best way to deal with insecurity. Trust in public officials has plummeted since the 1960s, reaching basement levels in recent years. A foundation of economic security cannot be built on the soft sands of public cynicism.

Our increasing spending on private social benefits—itself partly a reflection of this lack of faith—only makes the situation worse. The political scientist Suzanne Mettler has found that Americans do not see tax breaks, public loans, and other indirect forms of public aid as governmental, even if they cost the government billions.[32] Those who rely the most on these hidden benefits are also most skeptical of the state. Mistrust breeds mistrust, encouraging our leaders to rely on hidden forms of aid that fail to move the needle of public disillusionment. Mistrust also breeds mistrust because leaders are encouraged to avoid at all costs the rhetoric of public problem solving. Silence about what government can do thus further reinforces the vicious cycle.

Yet vicious cycles can become virtuous cycles when the dynamic is reversed. Reforms that demonstrate the value of public action, such as those outlined in this chapter, feed the reservoir of goodwill on which additional initiatives may draw. This was perhaps FDR's greatest insight. When he declared "the only thing we have to fear is fear itself," he did not mean our nation was safe from threat. Far from it: his point was that even well-grounded fears should not prevent us from finding solutions. The same holds true today. The growing sense of insecurity is paralyzing. It corrodes our faith in collective institutions and pushes our focus inward. To reverse this dangerous drift, we need to remember (and fight for) the basic ideal that FDR's Social Security Act embodied: that some economic risks cannot be addressed through individual or private action but require the faith in collective self-betterment that made our nation great.

Notes

1. "Signing of the Social Security Act" and "FDR's Statements on Social Security," Social Security Administration, accessed July 8, 2014, http://www.ssa.gov/history/fdrsign.html and http://www.ssa.gov/history/fdrsign.html.

2. Arthur Delaney and Michael McAuliff, "Paul Ryan Wants 'Welfare Reform Round 2,'" *Huffington Post*, March 20, 2012, accessed July 8, 2014, http://www.huffingtonpost.com/2012/03/20/paul-ryan-welfare-reform_n_1368277.html; "Paul Ryan Addresses NRI Summit," *National Review*, accessed July 8, 2014, http://www.nationalreview.com/corner/338905/paul-ryan-addresses-nri-summit-nro-staff.

3. Jacob S. Hacker, Philipp Rehm, and Mark Schlesinger, "The Insecure American: Economic Experiences, Financial Worries, and Policy Attitudes," *Perspectives on Politics* 11 (2013): 23–50.

4. Jacob S. Hacker, Philipp Rehm, and Mark Schlesinger, *Standing on Shaky Ground: Americans' Experiences with Economic Insecurity* (New Haven, CT: Economic Security Index Project, December 2010), http://www.economicsecurityindex.org/upload/media/ESI%20report%20final_12%2013.pdf.

5. Jacob S. Hacker, Gregory A. Huber, Austin Nichols, Philipp Rehm, Mark Schlesinger, Rob Valletta, and Stuart Craig, "The Economic Security Index: A New Measure for Research and Policy Analysis," *Review of Income and Wealth* 60 (2014): S5–S32.

6. Mark Robert Rank, Thomas A. Hirschl, and Kirk A. Foster, *Chasing the American Dream: Understanding What Shapes Our Fortunes* (New York: Oxford University Press, 2014), 36.

7. Facundo Alvaredo, Anthony B. Atkinson, Thomas Piketty, and Emmanuel Saez, "The Top 1 Percent in International and Historical Perspective," *Journal of Economic Perspectives* 27 (2013): 3–20.

8. Jacob S. Hacker, *The Great Risk Shift: The New Economic Insecurity and the Decline of the American Dream* (New York: Oxford University Press, 2008).

9. Based on analyses of the March Current Population Survey by Liana Fox and Elise Gould, "Employer-Provided Health Coverage Declining for College Grads in Entry-Level Jobs," Economic Policy Institute, July 18, 2007, accessed July 8, 2014, http://www.epi.org/publication/webfeatures_snapshots_20070718/.

10. Twenty-five years ago, 83 percent of medium and large firms offered traditional "defined-benefit" pensions that provided a fixed benefit for life; today, the share is below one-third. Instead, companies that provide pensions mostly offer "defined-contribution" plans like the 401(k), in which returns are neither predictable nor assured. Moreover, despite the expansion of 401(k) plans, the share of workers with access to a pension at their current job—either a defined benefit plan or a 401(k) plan—has fallen from just over half in 1979 to under 43 percent in 2009. See Hacker, *The Great Risk Shift*, chapter 5.

11. Carlos Angrisano, Diana Farrell, Bob Kocher, Martha Laboissiere, and Sara Parker, "Accounting for the Cost of Health Care in the United States," McKinsey Global Institute, January 2007, accessed July 8, 2014, http://www.mckinsey.com/insights/health_systems_and_services/accounting_for_the_cost_of_health_care_in_the_united_states.

12. Anderson, Gerard F., Uwe E. Reinhardt, Peter S. Hussey, and Varduhi Petrosyan, "It's the Prices, Stupid: Why the United States Is So Different from Other Countries," *Health Affairs* 22 (2003): 89–105.

13. National Research Council and Institute of Medicine, *U.S. Health in International Perspective: Shorter Lives, Poorer Health* (Washington, DC: The National Academies Press, 2013).

14. David Squires, "The Road Not Taken: The Cost of 30 Years of Unsustainable Health Spending Growth in the United States," *The Commonwealth Fund Blog*, March 21, 2013, accessed July 8, 2014, http://www.commonwealthfund.org/publications/blog/2013/mar/the-road-not-taken.

15. Henry J. Aaron, "Budget Crisis, Entitlement Crisis, Health Care Financing Problem—Which Is It?" *Health Affairs* 26 (2007): 1622–1633.

16. Chapin White, "Why Did Medicare Spending Growth Slow Down?" *Health Affairs* 27 (2008): 793–802.

17. International Federation of Health Plans, "2012 Comparative Price Report," March 2013, accessed July 8, 2014, http://www.slideshare.net/brianahier/international-federation-of-health-plans-price-report.

18. See, e.g., Paul Ryan, "The GOP Path to Prosperity," *Wall Street Journal*, April 5, 2011, accessed July 8, 2014, http://online.wsj.com/news/articles/SB10001424052748703806304576242612172357504; Joshua Gordon, "Health Care Reform Consensus and Increasing "Skin in the Game," Concord Coalition, May 14, 2013, accessed July 8, 2014, http://www.concordcoalition.org/tabulation/health-care-reform-consensus-and-increasing-skin-game-post-two-three; Bipartisan Policy Center, "Domenici-Rivlin Protect Medicare Act," November 2011, accessed July 8, 2014, http://bipartisanpolicy.org/sites/default/files/Domenici-Rivlin%20Protect%20Medicare%20Act%20.pdf.

19. Congressional Budget Office (CBO), *High-Cost Medicare Beneficiaries* (Washington, D.C.: CBO, 2005), 4.

20. For more on the public option and its promise, see Jacob S. Hacker, "Health-Care Reform, 2015," *Democracy* 18 (Fall 2010), accessed July 8, 2014, http://www.democracyjournal.org/18/6772.php.

21. This is the argument elaborated in Jacob S. Hacker, *The Divided Welfare State: The Battle over Public and Private Social Benefits in the United States* (New York: Cambridge University Press, 2002).

22. Katherine M. Porter, ed., *Broke: How Debt Bankrupts the Middle Class* (Stanford, CA: Stanford University Press, 2012).

23. Lisa B. Kahn, "The Long-Term Labor Market Consequences of Graduating from College in a Bad Economy," *Labour Economics* 17 (2010): 303–316.

24. Daniel Sullivan and Till Von Wachter. "Job Displacement and Mortality: An Analysis Using Administrative Data," *Quarterly Journal of Economics* 124 (2009): 1265–1306. See also Michael Luo, "At Closing Plan, Ordeal Included Heart Attacks," *New York Times*, February 24, 2010, accessed July 8, 2014, http://www.nytimes.com/2010/02/25/us/25stress.html.

25. Jacob S. Hacker, "Introduction: The Coming Age of Retirement Insecurity," *Meeting California's Retirement Security Challenge*, ed. Nari Rhee (Berkeley: UC Berkeley Center for Labor Research and Education, 2011), 7.

26. Ibid., 8.

27. Hilary Waldron, "Trends in Mortality Differentials and Life Expectancy for Male Social Security-Covered Workers, by Socioeconomic Status," Social Security Bulletin 67 (2007): 1–28.

28. See Hacker, "The Coming Age of Retirement Insecurity," for further elaboration of these proposals.

29. Stuart Butler and Peter Germanis, "Achieving a 'Leninist' Strategy," *Cato Journal* 3 (Fall 1983): 547–561.

30. That backer was Senator Tom Harkin, quoted in Hacker, "Health Care 2015."

31. George Packer, *Blood of the Liberals* (New York: Macmillan, 2001), 396.

32. Suzanne Mettler, *The Submerged State: How Invisible Government Policies Undermine American Democracy* (Chicago: University Press of Chicago, 2011).

9

Labor, Race, Gender, and Poverty in America

DORIAN T. WARREN

INTRODUCTION: POVERTY IN AMERICA

When he submitted the Economic Opportunity Act to Congress in 1964, President Lyndon B. Johnson declared a "war on poverty" in America. As he informed the nation during his first State of the Union address, "Our aim is not only to relieve the symptom of poverty, but to cure it and, above all, to prevent it."[1] Fifty years later, it is clear that the United States has not only failed to achieve this goal but may even be losing ground in the fight against poverty.

To be sure, there was a significant decrease in poverty in the 1960s, primarily due to the effects of Social Security on elderly poverty. The elderly poverty rate fell from 35 percent in 1960, to under 10 percent by the mid-1990s.[2] However, in recent years poverty has been on the rise, even before the Great Recession. Today, about 15 percent of Americans—more than 45 million—live under the official and very conservative federal government estimate of poverty.[3] Other estimates of those living "near poverty" put the number around 100 million, or 1 out of 3 Americans living in, or near, poverty.[4] Of course, it varies by race and gender. Women are much more likely to be living in poverty, as are African Americans and Latinos.[5] Roughly one in four African Americans and Latinos live in poverty.[6] Among wealthy nations, the United States leads in the category of child poverty, as about one in four children lives in poverty, according to the official US Census poverty definition.[7] Less conservative poverty measures indicate that nearly one in three children live in poverty, with America ranking thirty-sixth out of forty rich democracies.[8]

The statistics are even more alarming when examining what social scientists call "concentrated poverty," defined as living in a place where the poverty rate is 30 percent or more. This definition of poverty includes the dimension of residential segregation by race and class. Compared to 12 percent of white children, about one in three Latino children live in concentrated poverty and almost half of all black children (45 percent) live in concentrated poverty, while one in five Asian Americans and about four in ten Native American children live in concentrated poverty in America.[9]

EMPLOYMENT TRENDS

Poverty in America can only be understood in the context of jobs and employment. Americans who are unemployed, underemployed, working at low-wage jobs, or seeking full-time work (but only able to secure part-time employment) are much more likely to be living in poverty or near poverty. While the unemployment rate reached 10 percent at the height of the Great Recession, by late 2014 it had dropped to less than 6 percent (5.8 percent).[10] Yet there have always been racial and ethnic differences in unemployment in the United States, and the economic recovery has continued to be racially uneven. Since the 1960s, the African American unemployment rate has been at least twice that of white unemployment. In fact, the highest level of white unemployment has never reached the lowest level of black unemployment over this time.[11] And in many American cities African American unemployment reaches Depression-era levels at 20 percent or higher.[12]

However, unemployment is only one challenge facing American workers and especially workers of color; another is low-wage employment and flat wages. This is a long-term problem: wages have been stagnant for the last two or more decades. Most Americans were making the same amount in 2011 that they were in 1989.[13] Beginning in the 1970s and accelerating through the 1980s, 1990s, and 2000s, the US economy shifted from a primarily industrial, manufacturing-based economy to a post-industrial one defined by consumption and services. This shift resulted in the "bipolar" or "hourglass-shaped" economy we see today: there are lots of high-wage jobs at the top, lots of low-wage jobs at the bottom, but a dramatic loss of median-wage jobs in the middle.[14] The growing service sector of the economy has created millions of unstable, low-wage jobs with unpredictable schedules, little-to-no health care or pension benefits, and little-to-no ability for workers to have a voice at work.[15]

Low-wage work has continued to proliferate in recent years as a result of the structural changes in our economy, even in the so-called economic recovery. While mid-wage occupations were 60 percent of overall job losses in the recession, they only constituted 22 percent of jobs gained in the recovery.[16] Low-wage occupations, in contrast, made up roughly 60 percent of jobs gained in the recovery.[17] Roughly one in four Americans works in a low-wage job of some kind, defined as roughly $12 an hour or less. Again, this problem disproportionately affects workers of color. Whereas one in four whites worked in low-wage jobs in 2013—already a high number in itself—more than four in ten Latino workers worked in low-wage jobs, as did more than one in three African Americans.[18]

Unfortunately, as it stands now, there is little prospect for increasing the number of high-paying jobs. Sixteen of the twenty occupations with the largest numeric growth projected through 2020 are low-wage jobs that do not require a college degree.[19] To be fair, we are also creating a decent number of jobs at the other end of the spectrum (i.e., jobs requiring doctorates, master's or bachelor's degrees). But the vast majority of jobs being created are low skilled, low-wage jobs requiring a high school diploma or less.[20]

A related problem is the significant increase in Americans who want to work full time but are not able to. This "involuntary part-time work" is now a significant part of the employment landscape and is projected to continue to grow.[21] It is ironic that the labor movement fought for so long to reduce working hours: the forty-hour work week, weekends, the eight-hour day, and now it is in a position of fighting for *more* hours. In addition, the United States creates fewer high-quality jobs relative to our rich democratic peers. We are the only rich democracy that does not require employers to provide paid holidays or paid vacation. To be sure, many employers offer paid holidays and paid sick days, but these are not mandated by federal law.

In addition to unemployment, underemployment, low wage work, part-time work, and jobs with little to no benefits, what is referred to as "wage theft" has become a national epidemic and new employment norm. Wage theft is when workers' employers do not compensate them for all of the hours they work. In 2012 alone, government agencies recovered almost $1 billion from employers for workers victimized by wage theft.[22] This amount recovered is a conservative estimate and probably understates the problem. And according to one study, undocumented immigrant workers are particularly vulnerable to wage theft, experiencing stolen wages at rates higher than native-born workers.[23]

Another problem affecting American workers is segregation by race and gender in the workplace. One of the intentions behind the 1964 Civil Rights Act—one of the most significant legislative achievements of the civil rights movement—was to end employment discrimination and segregation based on race, ethnicity, nationality, and sex. What we know from social science research is that for about fifteen years we made progress in terms of desegregation in the workplace by race and gender. However, after 1980, this desegregation progress plateaued, and in many firms and occupations resegregation has occurred.[24] Racial and gender occupational segregation at the workplace is particularly problematic because they are a causal factor in systemic and persistent racial and gender wage disparities.[25]

In addition to race and gender occupational segregation affecting women workers, workers of color, and especially women of color, many workers face significant barriers even gaining access to the labor market. One of the most significant problems of the twenty-first-century labor market is the incredibly high incarceration rate in the United States. We incarcerate more people than the top thirty-five European countries combined.[26] Over two million Americans have had some contact with criminal justice institutions. And even though violent crime in particular has gone down significantly in the last decade, there is still a very high rate of incarceration.[27] This matters for labor market access because possession of a criminal record, as the sociologist Devah Pager points out, makes it very difficult to find a job.[28] Employers are extremely reluctant to hire formerly incarcerated men and women, which is a problem particularly affecting African American men. This problem is also compounded by disenfranchisement and exclusion from the political system. Felons in most states lose the right to vote, and some are permanently banned from voting. In some states it requires a governor's exoneration to restore your political rights.[29]

With these major transformations in the nature of the economy and work—low-wage work, part-time work, persistent occupational segregation, unequal labor market access—came public policies that redistributed income and wealth from the working- and middle-classes to the most advantaged Americans. The share of income going to the top 1 percent (and especially the top one-tenth of 1 percent) increased dramatically from the 1970s to the present, resulting in wage stagnation, increasing debt, and declining mobility for the majority of Americans.[30] But this wasn't the result of "natural" market forces; politics and public policies played causal roles in this outcome of increased inequality. As political scientists Jacob Hacker and Paul Pierson argue, the increased political power of business interests and the most affluent from the 1970s to the present also meant a greater likelihood of success on policies that benefit them, to the detriment of poor, working-class and middle-class Americans.[31] Whether through new policies that redistributed income and wealth upwards as the Bush tax cuts did, or through what Hacker calls "policy drift" (the ability to prevent updating public policies like the minimum wage to keep pace with changing conditions), business and economic elites have captured the American political system to achieve policy outcomes that benefit them over the vast majority of residents.[32]

THE DECLINE OF AMERICAN UNIONS

The changing nature of work and the economy, as well as public policies that benefit elites over the majority of Americans, coincided with the decline of the American labor movement, and particularly the bargaining power of workers vis-à-vis their employers.[33] As the number of union members declined dramatically over the last forty years, especially in the private sector, the bargaining power workers enjoyed in the immediate post–Second World War period to enable shared economic prosperity also declined, resulting in what Timothy Noah calls "The Great Divergence" between economic elites and everyone else.[34] This decline in workers' bargaining power through their unions has meant an increase in both economic inequality as well as *political inequality*. That is, the historic ability of organized labor to be a "countervailing power" to big business and elites has also eroded.[35]

Unions were once a vital part of the American labor market. In the mid-1950s, about one in three workers in the private sector were members of a union.[36] This degree of unionization had a powerful effect because of what is known as the "union threat" effect.[37] In other words, because unionization was so prevalent, even non-union workers benefited because firms and industries would raise wages to try and compete with unionized firms. Given the decline of unions in recent years, however, the union threat effect no longer plays a role in the labor market. In 1964 unionization rates were well over 20 percent, especially in the Midwest, and on both the East and West coasts. By 2005 most of the country had turned red in terms of low levels of unionization. And a significant gap has emerged between public and private levels of unionization.[38] The labor movement has mostly disappeared in the private sector even as it has remained fairly robust in the public sector. About one in three public employees are members of a union, compared to under 7 percent of private sector workers.[39] However, in the last several years we have witnessed high-profile attempts by conservative governors in states such as Wisconsin and Ohio to undermine the power of public sector unions in their states. Such attacks on union power by conservative officials appear likely to continue.[40]

In post-industrial and rich democracies, including the United States, unions play a key role in shaping labor market outcomes. Insofar as unions rectify the inequality in bargaining power between workers and employers, one of the original aims of the 1935 National Labor Relations Act, higher union density decreases wage inequality in the American labor market while increasing the purchasing power of consumers.[41] For instance, union membership raises median weekly earnings and reduces race and gender-based income gaps, and union workers are much more likely to receive health care and pension benefits than workers who are not members of a labor union.[42] This is particularly important within the context of the continuing rise in the numbers of American workers living in poverty. Joining a union increases earnings and fringe benefits, what is often referred to as the "union premium." The union premium is the difference between union and non-union wages and benefits after controlling for several employer and worker characteristics including occupation, education, race, and gender. In 2010, for instance, the overall union premium was 15.5 percent, 20.9 percent for African American workers, and 23.2 percent for Latinos.[43] There is also a union premium for women and women of color, particularly in the low-wage service sector of the economy where they tend to be overrepresented due to race, class, and gender occupational segregation.[44]

Related to the problem of falling unionization rates is the stagnation of the minimum wage. "Policy drift" is a central problem in this context. Even though our economy has changed and the economic context has changed, our minimum wage standard has not kept pace. For instance, even a worker who works full time and makes minimum wage still remains under the official government poverty level.[45] That is, a full-time worker at the minimum wage earned $15,080 in 2013, while the federal poverty line for a family of two that year was $16,078.[46]

CONCLUSION

What does all this add up to? Greater incarceration rates, declining minimum wage, wage stagnation, wage theft, declining unionization, the proliferation of low-wage jobs, and continuing patterns of occupation segregation by race and gender are at the heart of contemporary inequality and rates of poverty in the United States. As a result, we have become a much less mobile society than previously and are one of the least mobile societies, especially among rich democracies. The common myth of the American Dream, of people rising and falling accordingly to ability and hard work, bears little resemblance to this reality. Geography matters a lot in this context, and some places allow for less mobility than others. A 2013 article in the *New York Times* shows the pattern of decreasing mobility by region (see figure 9.1). Not surprisingly, due to its historic role as the foundation of the country's low-wage economy, it is more difficult to move up the socioeconomic latter in the Deep South than it is in most other parts of the country.[47]

This differs greatly by race. For African American children born in the lowest quartile, two out of three stay there, compared to one out of three white children. This amounts to very little mobility in twenty-first-century America.[48] Although the title of this essay is "Labor, Race, Gender and Poverty in America," it could just as easily be "Caste, Class, and Race," echoing the title of sociologist Oliver Cox's classic 1948 book. Cox challenged a school of thought in American sociology that conflated caste and race. Following Cox's argument, we should think about caste in America today more in line with poverty. Insofar as the American caste system closely matches our significant rates of poverty in the sense of *limiting mobility*, contemporary caste limits mobility based on a person's heredity or biological background, not his or her race.[49] This newer caste system is soft, but it is quickly hardening. We also have a class system and a system of racial stratification. They all overlap. We should not conflate those three systems, but we should instead recognize that even though they are conceptually, fundamentally different, they also overlap in important respects.

What can we do about this interrelated set of problems? There are some reasons for hope. In recent years there has been much more risk-taking and mobilization by low-wage workers, particularly among Walmart employees and fast-food workers, who since 2012 have engaged in one-day strikes in over 190 cities and towns across the country.[50] At 1.4 million workers, Walmart is the country's largest private employer. It is also the most anti-union company in the United States.[51] The symbol of Walmart and fast food companies like McDonalds or Burger King—as employers

In Climbing Income Ladder, Location Matters

A study finds the odds of rising to another income level are notably low in certain cities, like Atlanta and Charlotte, and much higher in New York and Boston.

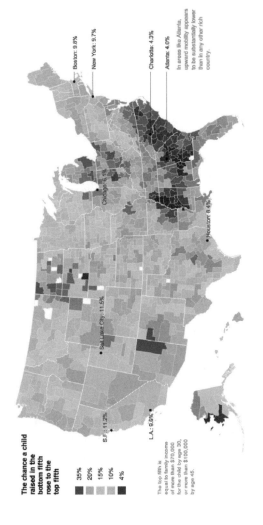

The chance a child raised in the bottom fifth rose to the top fifth

- 35%
- 20%
- 15%
- 10%
- 4%

The top fifth is equal to family income of more than $70,000 for the child by age 30, or more than $100,000 by age 45.

Boston: 9.8%
New York: 9.7%
Charlotte: 4.3%
Atlanta: 4.0%

In areas like Atlanta, upward mobility appears to be substantially lower than in any other rich country.

Chicago: 6.1%
Salt Lake City: 11.5%
S.F.: 9.6%
L.A.: 9.6%
Houston: 8.4%

E-MAIL   By DAVID LEONHARDT   PUBLISHED: JULY 22, 2013

Figure 9.1 Map of Upward Mobility for Children in the United States as published in the *New York Times*, July 22, 2013.

and multinational corporations—allow us to focus on the role of work and the workplace in contemporary inequality. It gets at the distinction between what Jacob Hacker calls *predistribution* versus *redistribution*.[52] Predistribution describes the distribution of wages, income, and other goods (health insurance, retirement security) in the labor market before government tax-and-transfer policies begin to operate. Redistribution refers to the broad range of government policies aimed at reducing poverty and inequality through a social safety net. Poverty researchers and advocates primarily focus on these policies: EITC, food stamps, Social Security, Medicaid and Medicare, etc. While we know these are important poverty- and inequality-reducing policies and programs, they often become the most common pathways to addressing inequality. This is to the detriment of the quintessential role predistributive processes play in creating and reproducing inequality via the workplace.

Over the last several years, coalitions of unions, community groups, and churches have begun organizing low-wage workers to take collective action directly against big employers in the service sector. As mentioned earlier, low-wage workers, overwhelmingly workers of color and female workers, have engaged in one-day strikes against the largest low-wage employers in America: Walmart and fast food companies such as McDonald's, Burger King, Wendy's, KFC, Taco Bell, Pizza Hut, Domino's Pizza, among others. Organizing under the demands of the "Fight for 15" and the right to organize collectively without retaliation, thousands of seemingly powerless low-wage workers are taking aim at the biggest and most powerful corporate actors at the center of the twenty-first-century American economy. Already, companies like Walmart have responded in both predictable and unpredictable ways. Predictably, Walmart and several of the fast food chains have responded the way employers usually do when workers demand a voice at work, higher wages, and better working conditions: with threats, bribes, and retaliation in the form of firing workers. All of these are illegal under our New Deal labor law regime—codified initially in the 1935 National Labor Relations Act. Yet we know from several decades of research that the law is terribly broken and offers very little protection or recourse for workers attempting to exercise their rights.[53] When workers attempt to unionize through National Labor Relations Board elections, 57 percent of employers threaten to close the worksite, 47 percent threaten to cut wages and benefits, and most egregiously, employers illegally fire pro-union workers in 34 percent of union election campaigns.[54] All of these tactics are illegal under the law, yet employers have become increasingly emboldened over the last thirty years to engage in such explicit behavior. And even when workers are able to overcome intense employer hostility and vote successfully for union representation, a year after the election, more than half (52 percent) are still without a collective bargaining agreement due to employer resistance to bargaining in good faith, which is also a violation of labor law.[55]

Yet unpredictably, these large and powerful employers epitomizing our contemporary—and future—low-wage economy have also responded in some cases by increasing wages and improving working conditions, albeit very quietly.[56] Just as important has been the communicative effect of these campaigns by low-wage workers engaging in visible collective action in an era when labor strikes are unheard of in contemporary America.[57] The predistributive politics of these low-wage workers and their allies, whether directly targeting employers or through local politics, has forced sustained attention in the public discourse around contemporary poverty, and economic and political inequality. Emerging in 2011 when a small group of protestors decided to form "Occupy Wall Street," a protest effort that spread to over a hundred American cities, income inequality and a broken national political system have continued to occupy local and national media attention.

Scholars have also responded to these visible claims of inequality defining the modern American political economy. From French economist Thomas Piketty's best-selling book, *Capital in the 21st Century*, to studies by political scientists showing the empirical relationship of economic inequality and political inequality and outcomes, social scientists have increasingly shed light on the symbiotic and self-reinforcing relationship between the inequalities generated by modern American capitalism and our national political system.[58] What is becoming increasingly clear is that growing poverty, income inequality, and the increasing concentration of wealth in America has led to the capture of American politics by organized business interests and the most affluent.[59] As it turns out, democracy might be very compatible with oligarchy.[60] Yet, much like their predecessors almost a hundred years ago, who emerged as a new and enduring base for the twentieth-century New Deal coalition, a new generation of low-wage workers—predominantly immigrants, blacks and Latinos—are organizing via community organizations, unions, and new kinds of worker organizations and their churches to advance social justice in America.[61]

Notes

1. Lyndon Johnson, "Special Message to the Congress Proposing a Nationwide War on the Sources of Poverty," March 16, 1964, http://www.presidency.ucsb.edu/ws/?pid=26109; Lyndon Johnson, "Annual Message to the Congress," http://www.presidency.ucsb.edu/ws/index.php?pid=26787. Last accessed October 1, 2014.
2. Gary V. Engelhardt and Jonathan Gruber, "Social Security and the Evolution of Elderly Poverty," in *Public Policy and the Income Distribution*, eds. Alan Auerback, David Card and John Quigley (New York: Russell Sage Foundation, 2006).
3. Carmen DeNavas-Walt and Bernadette D. Proctor, "Income and Poverty in the United States: 2013," *Current Population Reports*, US. Census Bureau, September 2014, http://www.census.gov/content/dam/Census/library/publications/2014/demo/p60-249.pdf.
4. Ashley N. Edwards, "Dynamics of Economic Well-Being: Poverty, 2009–2011," *Household Economic Studies*, U.S. Census Bureau, January 2014. http://www.census.gov/prod/2014pubs/p70-137.pdf.
5. Ibid, supra note 3.

6. Ibid.

7. Ibid.

8. Christopher Ingraham, "Child Poverty in the U.S. is Among the Worst in the Developed World," *Washington Post*, October 29, 2014, http://www.washingtonpost.com/blogs/wonkblog/wp/2014/10/29/child-poverty-in-the-u-s-is-among-the-worst-in-the-developed-world/. Last accessed October 31, 2014. UNICEF Office of Research, "Children of the Recession: The Impact of the Economic Crisis on Child Well-Being in Rich Countries," September 2014. http://www.unicef-irc.org/publications/pdf/rc12-eng-web.pdf.

9. Annie E. Casey Foundation, "Data Snapshot on High-Poverty Communities: Children Living in America's High-Poverty Communities," February 2012, http://www.aecf.org/m/resourcedoc/AECF-ChildrenLivingInHighPovertyCommunities-2012-Full.pdf.   Last accessed November 7, 2014.

10. Patricia Cohen, "Jobs Data Show Steady Gains, but Stagnant Wages Temper Optimism," *New York Times*, November 7, 2014, http://www.nytimes.com/2014/11/08/business/jobs-numbers-for-october-2014-reported-by-labor-department.html?_r=1,   accessed November 8, 2014. The November rate was also 5.8%: http://data.bls.gov/timeseries/LNS14000000, last accessed December 6, 2014.

11. Heidi Shierholz, "Likely That Nearly One in Five Black Workers Was Unemployed at Some Point in 2013," *Economic Policy Institute*, http://www.epi.org/publication/black-workers-unemployed-point-2013/, accessed October 31, 2014.

12. Algernon Austin, "High Black Unemployment Widespread Across Nation's Metropolitan Areas," *Economic Policy Institute Issue Brief #315*, October 3, 2011, http://www.epi.org/publication/high-black-unemployment-widespread-metropolitan-areas/.

13. Elise Gould, "Why America's Workers Need Faster Wage Growth—And What We Can Do About It," *Economic Policy Institute Briefing Paper #382*, August 27, 2014, http://www.epi.org/publication/why-americas-workers-need-faster-wage-growth/; Steven Greenhouse, *The Big Squeeze: Tough Times for the American Worker* (New York: Knopf, 2009).

14. Saskia Sassen, Saskia. *Globalization and Its Discontents: Essays on the New Mobility of People and Money.* (New York: The New Press, 1998); Erik Olin Wright and Rachel E. Dwyer, "The Patterns of Job Expansions in the USA: A Comparison of the 1960s and 1990s." *Socio-Economic Review*. 1: 289–325, 2003.

15. Desmond King and David Rueda, "Cheap Labor: The New Politics of 'Bread and Roses' in Industrial Democracies." *Perspectives on Politics*. 6.2 (2008): 279–297.

16. National Employment Law Project, "The Low-Wage Recovery and Growing Inequality," *NELP*, August 2012, http://www.nelp.org/page/-/Job_Creation/LowWageRecovery2012.pdf?nocdn=1.

17. Ibid.

18. Valerie Wilson, "Broad-based Wage Growth Is Essential for Fighting Poverty and Narrowing Racial Wage Gaps," *Economic Policy Institute*, June 19, 2014, http://www.epi.org/publication/broad-based-wage-growth-essential-fighting/, last accessed December 6, 2014.

19. Bureau of Labor Statistics, "Most New Jobs: 20 Occupations With the Highest Projected Numerical Change in Employment, "http://www.bls.gov/ooh/most-new-jobs.htm, last accessed December 6, 2014.

20. Ibid.

21. Maria E. Canon, Marianna Kudlyak and Marisa Reed, "Is Involuntary Part-time Employment Different after the Great Recession?," *Regional Economist*, Federal Reserve Bank of St. Louis, July 2014, https://www.stlouisfed.org/publications/re/articles/?id=2536.

22. Brady Meixell and Ross Eisenbrey, "An Epidemic of Wage Theft Is Costing Workers Hundreds of Millions of Dollars a Year," *Economic Policy Institute Issue Brief #385*, September 11, 2014, http://www.epi.org/publication/epidemic-wage-theft-costing-workers-hundreds/.

23. Center for Urban Economic Development, National Employment Law Project, and UCLA Institute for Research on Labor and Employment, *Broken Laws, Unprotected Workers: Violations*

of Employment and Labor Laws in America's Cities, 2009, http://www.unprotectedworkers. org/index.php/broken_laws/index.

24. Kevin Stainback and Donald Tomaskovic-Devey, *Documenting Desegregation: Racial and Gender Segregation in Private-Sector Employment Since the Civil Rights Act* (New York: Russell Sage Foundation, 2012).

25. Ariane Hegewisch and Heidi Hartmann, "Occupational Segregation and the Gender Wage Gap: A Job Half Done," *Institute for Women's Policy Research*, January 2014, http://www.iwpr.org/publications/pubs/occupational-segregation-and-the-gender-w age-gap-a-job-half-done/at_download/file.

26. The Pew Charitable Trusts, *Collateral Damage: Incarceration's Effect on Economic Mobility*, (Washington, DC, 2010).

27. Ibid.

28. Devah Pager, *Marked: Race, Crime, and Finding Work in an Era of Mass Incarceration*, (Chicago: University of Chicago Press, 2007).

29. The Sentencing Project, "Felony Disenfranchisement: A Primer," April 2014, http://www. sentencingproject.org/doc/publications/fd_Felony%20Disenfranchisement%20Primer.pdf.

30. Timothy Noah, *The Great Divergence: America's Growing Inequality Crisis and What We Can Do About It*, (New York: Bloomsbury, 2012); Thomas Piketty and Emmanuel Saez, "Income Inequality in the United States, 1913–1998," *Quarterly Journal of Economics*,118 (1), 1–39, 2013; Thomas Piketty, *Capital in the Twenty-First Century*, (Cambridge, MA: Belknap, 2014).

31. Jacob S. Hacker and Paul Pierson, *Winner-Take-All Politics: How Washington Made the Rich Richer—and Turned Its Back on the Middle Class*, (New York: Simon & Schuster, 2010).

32. Hacker and Pierson, supra note 31; Larry M. Bartels, *Unequal Democracy: The Political Economy of the New Gilded Age*, (Princeton, NJ: Princeton University Press, 2008); Martin Gilens, *Affluence and Influence: Economic Inequality and Political Power in America*, (Princeton, NJ: Princeton University Press, 2012); Nicholas Carnes, *White-Collar Government: The Hidden Role of Class in Economic Policy Making*, (Chicago: University of Chicago Press, 2013).

33. Hacker & Pierson, supra note 31; Noah, supra note 30; Chris Rhomberg, *The Broken Table: The Detroit Newspaper Strike and the State of American* Labor, (New York: Russell Sage, 2012); Jake Rosenfeld, *What Unions No Longer Do*, (Cambridge, MA: Harvard University Press, 2014).

34. Timothy Noah, supra note 30.

35. John Kenneth Galbraith, *American Capitalism: The Concept of Countervailing Power*, (Transaction, 1952); Kay Lehman Schlozman, Sidney Verba & Henry Brady, *The Unheavenly Chorus: Unequal Political Voice and the Broken Promise of American Democracy*, (Princeton, NJ: Princeton University Press, 2012); Rosenfeld, supra note 33.

36. Rosenfeld, supra note 33.

37. Lawrence Mishels and Matthew Walters, "How Unions Help All Workers," *Economic Policy Institute Briefing Paper #143*, August 26, 2003, www.epi.org/publication/ briefingpapers_bp143/.

38. Rosenfeld, supra note 33.

39. Bureau of Labor Statistics, "Union Members—2013," www.bls.gov/news.release/pdf/ union2.pdf, last accessed December 6, 2014.

40. Steve Fraser and Joshua B. Freeman, "In the Rearview Mirror: A Brief History of Opposition to Public Sector Unionism," *New Labor Forum* 20.3 (2011): 93–96.

41. Richard B. Freeman, *America Works: The Exceptional U.S. Labor Market*, (New York: Russell Sage Foundation, 2007); Rosenfeld, supra note 33.

42. Bureau of Labor Statistics, supra note 30; Paul Frymer, "Labor and American Politics," *Perspectives on Politics* 8.2 (2010): 609–616; Rosenfeld, supra note 33.

43. Janelle Jones and John Schmitt, "Union Advantage for Black Workers," *Center for Economic and Policy Research*, 2014, www.cepr.net/index.php/publications/reports/union-advantage-for-b lack-workers. Last accessed December 6, 2014. The authors show the "union premium" for black workers continues to hold as it is 15.6% for wages, 17.9% for employer-provided health insurance, and 19.1% for employer-provided retirement plans. The union premium is higher

for black workers with a high school diploma or less, although it still holds for those with college and advanced degrees.

44. John Schmitt and Nicole Woo, "Women Workers and Unions," *Center for Economic and Policy Research*, 2013, www.cepr.net/index.php/publications/reports/women-workers-and-unions, last accessed December 6, 2014.

45. David Cooper, "The Minimum Wage Used To Be Enough To Keep Workers Out of Poverty—It's Not Anymore," *Economic Policy Institute*, December 4, 2013, http://www.epi.org/publication/minimum-wage-workers-poverty-anymore-raising/.

46. Ibid.

47. David Leonhardt, "In Climbing Income Ladder, Location Matters," *The New York Times*, July 22, 2013, http://www.nytimes.com/2013/07/22/business/in-climbing-income-ladder-location-matters.html?pagewanted=all&_r=0. Last accessed October 1, 2014.

48. Tom Hertz, "Understanding Mobility in America," *Center for American Progress, http://cdn. americanprogress.org/wp-content/uploads/kf/hertz_mobility_analysis.pdf.*

49. Oliver C. Cox, *Caste, Class, and Race: a Study in Social Dynamics* (New York: Monthly Review Press, 1948).

50. Steven Greenhouse, "Strong Voice in 'Fight for 15' Fast-Food Wage Campaign," *New York Times*, December 4, 2014. http://www.nytimes.com/2014/12/05/business/in-fast-food-workers-fight-for-15-an-hour-a-strong-voice-in-terrance-wise.html.   Last   accessed December 6, 2014.

51. Nelson Lichtenstein, *The Retail Revolution: How Wal-Mart Created a Brave New World of Business*, (New York: Picador, 2010).

52. Jacob S. Hacker, "The Institutional Foundations of Middle-Class Democracy," *Policy Network, http://www.policy-network.net/pno_detail.aspx?ID=3998&title=The+institutional+foundations +of+middle-class+democracy.*

53. Paul C. Weiler, *Governing the Workplace: The Future of Labor and Employment Law*, (Cambridge, MA: Harvard University Press, 1990); Kate Bronfrenbrenner, "No Holds Barred—The Intensification of Employer Opposition to Organizing," *EPI Briefing Paper #235*, May 20, 2009, www.epi.org/publication/bp235.

54. Bronfenbrenner, supra note 53.

55. Ibid.

56. Susan Berfield, "Wal-Mart's Black Friday Strikes: Are the Workers Already Winning?," *BloombergBusinessweek*, November 28, 2014, http://www.businessweek.com/articles/2014-11-28/walmart-black-friday-strikes-are-the-workers-already-winning.   Last accessed December 6, 2014.

57. Rhomberg, supra note 33.

58. Bartels, Gilens, supra note 32; Piketty, supra note 30.

59. Ibid.

60. Jeffrey A. Winters, *Oligarchy*, (Cambridge, 2011).

61. Harold Myerson, "Labor's New Reality: It's Easier to Raise Wages for 100,000 than to Unionize 4,000," *Los Angeles Times*, December 7, 2014, www.latimes.com/opinion/op-ed/la-oe-meyerson-labor-organizing-20141208-story.html. Last accessed December 7, 2014.

10

Crafting a Progressive Foreign Policy in Today's World

ROSA BROOKS

What would it mean for the United States to have a truly progressive foreign policy? And how likely is it that we'll see such a thing in our lifetime?

In the foreign policy context, the very term "progressive" poses immediate difficulties. There's little enough agreement on what the term "progressive" means in the context of domestic politics, and the notion of "progressive foreign policy" is even murkier. Would a "progressive foreign policy" be one that hearkens back to the Progressive Era, for instance? It's one thing to look back with nostalgia on the domestic reforms of the Progressive Era, but American foreign policy in the Progressive Era was a decidedly mixed bag and not something most of those who today call themselves progessives would be inclined to praise.

It was during the Progressive Era that the United States became a distinctly interventionist and imperial power: Teddy Roosevelt's "splendid little war" gave the United States control over several Spanish colonial possessions, while Roosevelt's Corollary to the Monroe Doctrine established the United States as hemispheric cop, if not yet global cop.[1] Taft's "Dollar Diplomacy" had a distinctly ugly side, though it was later repudiated by Woodrow Wilson, who was the champion of international institutions and national self-determination. But Wilson also soon found himself advocating the use of force to promote free trade and "make the world safe for democracy." Indicative of the general confusion, some scholars view today's neo-conservative hawks as the rightful heirs to the Wilsonian tradition, while others insist that Wilsonian foreign policy traditions are the exclusive property of liberal democrats.[2]

For present purposes, we need not evaluate the progessivism of Progressive Era foreign policy, but we do need to give the term "progessive" some content. The Center for American Progress (CAP), a self-styled champion of modern progessivism, defines progessivism as "grounded in the idea of progress—moving beyond the status quo to more equal and just social conditions consistent with original

141

American democratic principles such as freedom, equality, and the common good."[3] That seems a reasonable starting point. Beyond that, we might add that modern progessives generally share the belief that affirmative government action is often required to prevent the wealthy and powerful from trampling upon the poor and powerless. Progressives tend to believe that extreme inequality and highly concentrated power can distort democratic politics—and though they may differ from one another on precisely where, when, and how governments should intervene, they generally share the view that government should play an active role in assisting the very worst off and diluting excessive concentrations of power and privilege. This implies some underlying progressive commitment to universalist conceptions of human dignity, human rights, and the rule of law.

In theory, then, a progressive US foreign policy should be characterized by a commitment to similar principles (a commitment to reducing at least the most savage and unjust forms of inequality; a commitment to the common global good rather than only national self-interest; a wariness of concentrated power; a commitment to inclusive, right-respecting politics; and a commitment to using governance structures to promote the common good). But articulating these principles in the abstract still tells us little about what a twenty-first-century progessive US foreign policy would look like. To delineate the contours of a progessive foreign policy, we first need to understand the global context in which the United States currently operates.

THE GLOBAL CONTEXT

The US today inhabits a world that is far more complex and interconnected than the world inhabited by Progressive Era leaders. This interconnected and rapidly changing world offers both unparalleled opportunities and unprecedented dangers, and it has both enabled and confounded progressive reforms. Above all, the United States now inhabits an uncertain world: one that is perhaps less predictable and intelligible than ever before.

COMPLEXITY AND INTERCONNECTEDNESS

On some level, everyone knows this. In fact, we've heard so much about globalization, complexity, interconnectedness, and uncertainty that we're often tempted to block out such claims, or dismiss them as platitudinous: *Been there, theorized that.* But we shouldn't be too quick to assume that we "get it." Mostly, we don't. We say things like, "Yes, of course, the global environment is complex, interconnected and uncertain," but we don't feel it in our bones.

We should feel it in our bones. We *need* to, because if we don't, we may make a variety of faulty assumptions about our ability to predict future events. To explain what I mean by this, let me start by trying to breathe some life into the clichés about complexity and uncertainty.

Consider both the nature of the changes that have occurred in the last century and the rate at which those changes have occurred. A hundred years ago, the world population was about 1.8 billion, and there were roughly sixty sovereign states in the world.[4] In 1914 the automobile was still a rarity; there were no commercial passenger flights and no transcontinental telephone service. Fifty years ago, global population had climbed to over 3 billion and there were 115 member states of the United Nations, but air travel was still for the wealthy, and the advent of the personal computer was nearly two decades away.[5]

Today, the globe contains 7 billion people living in 192 UN member states and a handful of other territories. These 7 billion people take 93,000 commercial flights a day from 9,000 airports,[6] drive 1 billion cars[7] and carry 7 billion mobile phones around with them[8]—phones they can use to monitor their heart rate, purchase stocks, post restaurant reviews, share family photos, tweet real-time information about unfolding events, or create and distribute how-to videos for aspiring bio-terrorists.

A hundred years ago, human activity inside the borders of one state could have but little direct or immediate effect on people living in other states. Today, that's no longer true: as we all know, a collapse in one state's stock market can trigger rapid meltdowns in other markets, destructive computer viruses can spread in hours or days, and carbon emissions in the United States and China can change sea levels in the Netherlands, or cause increasingly severe and unpredictable weather around the globe.

In many ways, the world's increasing complexity and interconnectedness has driven and enabled a variety of progressive developments. A hundred years ago, war was still seen as "politics by other means,"[9] and a fundamental prerogative of states—but the cataclysmic world wars of the first half of the twentieth century led states to accept (in principle, if not always in practice) the strict limitations on the use of force contained in the 1945 Charter of the United Nations.

The UN Charter itself—with its emphasis on peace, human dignity, equal rights, justice and "social progress"—reads like a progressive manifesto,[10] and since 1945, its progressive vision has been at least partially realized.[11] Interstate conflict has declined sharply since the end of the Second World War, and notwithstanding some obvious counter-examples, militarily powerful states are today far less free than in the pre-Charter world to use overt force to accomplish their aims.[12] Meanwhile, the UN structure offered at least a preliminary shift toward a more democratic form of international governance; despite the power imbalance built into the Security Council's voting rules and permanent membership, each state gets one vote in the General Assembly.

The United Nations also quickly became a venue for what the Charter termed "the progressive development of international law."[13] Today, the world has numerous international and regional courts and other dispute resolution bodies that provide a viable alternative to using force to resolve disputes,[14] and the decades after 1945 witnessed what some have termed "the human rights revolution,"[15] as nations codified their commitment to advancing human dignity and rights. In keeping with the Charter's requirement that colonial powers take steps "to develop self-government [and] assist" colonized populations "in the progressive development of their free political institutions," the era of European colonialism came to a largely peaceful end by the mid 1970s, and as they transitioned to independence, most former colonies became at least nominal democracies.

Meanwhile, medical and agricultural advances in the decades following the Second World War brought unprecedented health and prosperity to almost every part of the globe[16]—facilitated by the growing number of international organizations dedicated to health and development, from the World Health Organization and the World Food Program to UNICEF and the UN Development Program. More recently, the communications revolution has enabled exciting new forms of nongovernmental cross-border alliances to emerge, which empowers, for instance, global human rights organizations and environmental movements.

But looking around the world, few progessives would be inclined to declare victory. Even as increased global interconnectedness has enabled a range of progressive developments, the world has grown in certain respects both more unequal and more dangerous since the UN Charter was drafted in July 1945.

A very small number of states—the US being the primary culprit—have come to consume a disproportionate share of the world's resources, control a disproportionate share of global wealth, and produce a disproportionate share of the world's waste. By the year 2000, write Betsy Taylor and Dave Tilford, 5 percent of the world's population produced 50 percent of the world's solid waste; the United States, with "less than 5 percent of world population," was using "one-third of the world's paper, a quarter of the world's oil, 23 percent of the coal, 27 percent of the aluminum, and 19 percent of the copper."[17]

Wealth inequalities are even more glaring: in 2010, 39 percent of the world's wealth belonged to Americans.[18] A 2014 Oxfam report concludes that the richest 85 individuals on earth are currently worth more than the globe's 3.5 billion poorest people; overall, "the lower half of the global population possesses barely 1 percent of global wealth, while the richest 10 percent of adults own 86 percent of all wealth, and the top 1 percent account for 46 percent of the total."[19] In an interconnected world—in which the means of lethal violence have been democratized and dispersed,[20] and birth rates in poorer parts of the earth have substantially outpaced birth rates in the wealthiest regions[21]—these glaring inequalities create a rising risk of future resource-based conflict.

From a species-survival perspective, the world has grown vastly more dangerous since the Progressive Era. Even as life expectancy has increased and interstate conflicts have declined, humans have gained the unprecedented ability to destroy large chunks of the human race, and possibly the earth itself. In 1945 the development and use of the atom bomb opened the door to global cataclysm. In the twenty-first century, there are still an estimated 17,000 nuclear warheads in the possession of some nine nation-states[22]—and though the near-term threat of interstate nuclear conflict has greatly diminished since the end of the Cold War, nuclear material is now less controlled and less controllable.

Nuclear threats aren't the only thing that might plausibly keep us up at night: if you want to give yourself a good scare, do some bedtime reading on bio-engineered threats,[23] or even the various possible lethal epidemics that might start without help from malign human actors and then spread around the world in weeks, thanks to modern travel technologies. Or take a few moments to contemplate the potential impact of climate change, which could submerge coastal cities,[24] cause drought and famine, and fuel further regional and global resource conflict.[25]

UNCERTAINTY

Just as salient for progessives, our world has also grown more uncertain and unpredictable over the last century. We have more information than ever before, and vastly greater processing power; however, the pace of global change has far exceeded our collective ability to understand it, much less manage it.

For most of human history, major technological and social transformations occurred over hundreds or even thousands of years. For the average European peasant, life in the year 300 AD wasn't all that different from life in 800 or 1300 or 1700: daily life revolved around hunting, fishing, or agriculture; the manufacture of goods was on a small, pre-industrial scale; travel was by foot, horse, or ship. Much the same could be said for ordinary people living in Africa, Asia, and every other inhabited part of the globe. Even in the New World, where change was the norm for many European settlers, many Americans living in 1900 would have had more daily experiences in common with Americans living in 1800—or 1700, for that matter—than with Americans living today. We thus literally have no points of comparison for understanding the scale and scope of the risks faced by humanity today. Compared to the long, slow sweep of human history, the events of the last century have taken place in the blink of an eye.

From a global perspective, this should temper any pride we feel in recent progressive achievements and give us pause when we're tempted to conclude that today's trends are likely to continue. Perhaps life expectancy will continue to rise worldwide—but perhaps emerging diseases, climate change, and resource-related conflicts will turn a century of rising life expectancies into a mere blip on the charts. Perhaps the recent steep decline in interstate conflicts will continue—but perhaps seventy years of human history is too little to go on when it comes to spotting enduring shifts in the rate and lethality of conflict and violence.[26] Perhaps the lack of nuclear catastrophe since 1945 tells us that we have succeeded in managing nuclear risk—but perhaps we have merely had a run of mostly unmerited good luck.

Analysts often view such potential catastrophes as nuclear disaster as "high consequence, low probability" risks,[27] but even this assumes we have a solid basis for assessing the probability of various scenarios. But how do we compute the probability of a catastrophic event of a type that has never yet been seen? Does seventy years without global nuclear annihilation tell us that there's a low probability of nuclear catastrophe—or just tell us that we haven't had a nuclear catastrophe yet?[28]

Humans are generally poor forecasters and poor evaluators of probability and risk.[29] Faced with uncertainty, we fall back on a range of mental heuristics: we tend to assume, for instance, that the way things are is the way things are likely to remain. Sometimes, this is reasonable: the mountain that's been there for thousands of years will probably be there for another hundred. But we forget that the same logic doesn't hold for everything.[30] Lack of sudden, wholesale change sometimes signifies a system in stable equilibrium, but sometimes—as with earthquakes—pressure can build up over time, undetected.

Often, the problem is that we just don't know enough about how incredibly complex systems work: scientists studying tornados and tsunamis have gotten much better at understanding the conditions that lead to such weather events but still have little ability to predict their precise time and locations far enough in advance to do any good.[31] Throw in the confounding effect of climate change, and we're flummoxed—even though, in theory at least, the data we need for weather forecasting is far easier to measure and quantify than the data that would be required to predict future trends in governance, conflict, economic development, and public health. As a result, most foreign policy and international security "experts" have about as much ability to predict the geopolitical future as you or I would have to predict next winter's weather by looking out the window.

The events of recent decades should also undermine any confidence in our collective ability to predict geopolitical change. Most analysts assumed the Soviet Union was stable—until it collapsed.[32] Most scholars predicted that Egypt's Hosni Mubarak would retain his firm grip on power—until he was ousted.[33] Intelligence analysts didn't foresee Russia's Crimean land grab, or the rapid advances into Iraq made by extremist terror groups spilling over from Syria's civil war. How much of what we currently file under "stable" should more properly be categorized under "Hasn't Collapsed—Yet"?

Progressives in particular should take all this to heart, for if we take complexity and uncertainty seriously, we need to challenge some of progessivism's often submerged assumptions. For one thing, we should abandon any assumption that "progress" is somehow part of the natural order of things. Biological evolution isn't teleological, and neither is cultural, political, or technological evolution. Our world will surely change, but no one should assume it will change for the better, or that recent changes for the better are destined (or even likely) to endure.

Similarly, we should remain skeptical about our collective ability to predict, plan, or control outcomes. Progressives believe that government should play an active role in breaking up concentrated power and helping the least well off. I share that belief—but I also think we routinely overestimate our ability to correctly predict which interventions will be effective, in part because we routinely underestimate the complexity of the problems we try to tackle and the very substantial role played by chance.

All this has implications for delineating the contours of a truly "progressive" modern US foreign policy. Before I turn to that, however, let me spend a moment on the current position of the United States within this complex, perilous, and uncertain global environment.

THE US ROLE IN THE WORLD

Over the course of the last century or so, the United States went from being a bit player on the global stage to the dominant figure. The United States consumes a disproportionate share of global resources, produces a disproportionate share of the world's waste, and holds a disproportionate share of the world's wealth. We spend more on our military than China, Russia, the UK, France, Japan, India, Saudi Arabia, Germany, Brazil, Italy, South Korea, Australia, and Canada—combined. US power is polarizing, and the United States itself is as much reviled as admired, but few would dispute that the United States is currently the globe's most dominant economic and military power.

Nevertheless, US power has been declining.[34] In part, America's global power and influence are diminishing simply because numerous once-weak states have been growing stronger: Europe, despite its current woes, has become an economic and diplomatic force to be reckoned with. China, India, and Brazil have emerged as regional powerhouses with increasingly global reach. This is a trend that began decades ago: in his 1987 National Security Strategy, President Reagan noted, "The United States no longer ha[s] an overwhelming economic position vis-a-vis Western Europe and the East Asia rimland."[35] In 1990 President George H. W. Bush echoed this theme in his National Security Strategy: "It was inevitable that our overwhelming economic predominance after the war would be reduced."[36]

Inevitable or not, America's relative decline in global power isn't necessarily a bad thing, either for the world or for the United States itself. Remember *Gulliver's Travels*? True, it wasn't much fun for Gulliver to be the little guy in the land of Brobdingnagian giants—but it was just as unpleasant to be a giant among the Lilliputians.

The United States also has far less ability to act autonomously today than it had fifty or a hundred years ago. This is not a development unique to the United States, of course: every state's autonomy has declined as a result of globalization. Globalization has created collective challenges that no state, no matter how powerful, can address on its own, and collective goods that no state can reach on its own.

This isn't necessarily a bad thing, either: just as the twentieth century's two world wars spurred unprecedented changes in global governance, more recent collective challenges might spur further innovative global cooperation—to address collective environmental and public health problems, for instance. But it's unwise to be too sanguine: it's equally possible that the growth of collective problems will just create global paralysis, or a race to the bottom, as states try to grab scarce resources before others can, or protect themselves through aggression or isolationism.

US power and global influence have also declined in absolute terms. If global wealth inequality has increased in recent decades,[37] wealth inequality within the United States has increased even more rapidly.[38] The United States now has greater income inequality than any other state in the developed world—and most states in the developing world.

By many measures, we've hollowed out the American dream: American life expectancy ranks well below that of other industrialized democracies, and the same is true for infant mortality rates and elementary school enrollment rates. Meanwhile, we have the highest documented per capita incarceration rate in the world: 25 percent of the world's incarcerated people are in US prisons and jails.[39] On international health and quality of life metrices, the US has been losing ground for several decades.[40] The social safety net created by decades of progressive reforms has become badly frayed. Worse, the political system we rely upon for reform and repair seems itself to be broken; the US government shutdown of late 2013 offered a striking illustration of US political dysfunction.[41]

Add to this the divisive national security policies of the Bush administration— many continued, and some expanded, by the Obama administration—and it's no surprise that the United States has become less admired and less emulated around the globe.[42] Power comes not only from military and economic might but also from reputation, legitimacy, and credibility. As the United States grows palpably more internally dysfunctional, its ability to "get its way" globally has also declined.[43]

Nevertheless, American political leaders seem to share a bipartisan dedication to denying that American global power has declined. Indeed, America seems to suffer from a serious case of the Lake Wobegon effect:[44] "declinism" and "declinists" have entered the American political vocabulary, but only as purely pejorative terms.[45]

Perhaps this is itself another sign of decline: American "exceptionalism" wasn't always premised on a conviction of permanent US power and superiority. After all, when John Winthrop famously told the Massachusetts Bay Colony settlers that "wee shall be as a citty upon a hill" in 1630,[46] he was issuing a warning, not making a promise. Winthrop reminded the American settlers that the purpose of their new settlement was *not* worldly gain or power, but rather "service to the Lord":

If we shall fall to embrace this present world and prosecute our carnal intentions, seeking great things for ourselves and our posterity, the Lord will surely break out in wrath against us . . . . Now the only way to avoid this shipwreck [is] to do justly, to love mercy, to walk humbly with our God . . . . We must be willing to abridge ourselves of our superfluities, for the supply of others' necessities. . . . We must delight in each other; make others' conditions our own; rejoice together, mourn together, labor and suffer together . . . ."

Another progessive manifesto! If the settlers could live up to these requirements, declared Winthrop, "The Lord will be our God, and delight to dwell among us, as His own people, and will command a blessing upon us in all our ways . . . . He shall make us a praise and glory that men shall say of succeeding plantations, 'may the Lord make it like that of New England.'"

Winthrop's next and most famous words were uttered not in a triumphalist spirit, but as a reminder that the price of failure was high:

For we must consider that we shall be as a city upon a hill. The eyes of all people are upon us. So that if we shall deal falsely with our God in this work we have undertaken, and so cause Him to withdraw His present help from us, we shall be made a story and a by-word through the world.

Interestingly, the American people seem far more willing than their political leaders to acknowledge the decline of US power and influence. In poll results released in December 2013, the Pew Research Center found that "for the first time in surveys dating back nearly 40 years, a majority (53 percent) says the United States plays a less important and powerful role as a world leader than it did a decade ago. The share saying the U.S. is less powerful . . . has more than doubled—from just 20 percent—since 2004. An even larger majority says the U.S. is losing respect internationally."[47] What's more, Americans seem less committed than their political leaders to American exceptionalism: another Pew survey released in July 2014 found that "about three-in-ten [Americans] (28 percent) think that the U.S. 'stands above all other countries in the world', while most (58 percent) say it is 'one of the greatest countries in the world, along with some others'. . . . Three years ago, 38 percent said the U.S. stood above all others, while 53 percent said it was one of the greatest nations."[48]

Will US global power to continue to decline in the decades to come? Having issued such stern warnings about the dangers of predicting the future, I hesitate to advance a strong opinion. There is certainly nothing inevitable about continued US decline. But at a minimum, any sensible US foreign policy needs to rest upon the recognition that US power has waned substantially in the last two decades—and the distinct possibility that it will continue to do so in the decades to come.

A PROGRESSIVE FOREIGN POLICY
FOR THE TWENTY-FIRST CENTURY

Return to the original question: what would it mean to have a truly progressive US foreign policy in today's world? What might it mean to develop a forward-looking US foreign policy in a world characterized by so much complexity and uncertainty—a foreign policy that acknowledges the recent decline in US power, and at the same time remains true to the animating principles of progessivism? In this context, I think core progessive principles and hard-headed US self-interest both push in the same direction.

Start with progressive principles. If we take progressive values seriously, we should mourn the growing inequality and political dysfunction of domestic US politics, but we should not necessarily mourn the relative decline of US global power. The US record of advancing progressive values has been mixed, at best: our foreign policies in the decades since the 1920s have been as contradictory as those of the Progressive Era. We have promoted human rights but supported repressive dictators for reasons of ideology or convenience; we have helped craft some of the most progressive multilateral treaties but have declined to ratify the very treaties we helped create.[49] We have at times been a regional and global peacemaker but have at other times undermined the prospects for democracy and stability by financing ideologically motivated insurgencies. We have offered generous financial assistance to those in need, even as our own policies perpetuate global inequalities.

Might the world not be better off with a somewhat less dominant United States? If progressives believe that extreme inequality and high concentrations of power and privilege distort political decision making and undermine prospects for justice, we should presumably consider the emergence of a somewhat more level global playing field a positive development.

Yet it's not quite that simple. The United States has a mixed record of advancing progressive values, but few other states have consistently done better. A "more level global playing field" sounds like a good thing, but without rules and referees, level playing fields can easily become playgrounds for bullies. The departure of one 800-pound gorilla from the field sometimes just opens up space for other outsized and non-benign powers to emerge.

A progressive US foreign policy would presumably eschew unilateralism except in the most dire of emergencies but should not require national self-abnegation. On the contrary: though US global power has declined, the United States still has outsized power and influence and should not hesitate to use both when doing so can help foster the emergence of a more robust system of international governance—one with empowered institutions that are truly capable of constraining powerful states and nonstate actors through the equal enforcement of international law.

This was, in fact, the original vision of the United Nations system, before self-interest and then Cold War politics watered everything down: its early proponents took for granted that an effective United Nations—one truly capable of achieving the ends described in the Charter's preamble—would require a strong judicial system and a standing army, and assumed that the Security Council, which locked into place the post–Second World War power structure, would eventually evolve to become more broadly representative.[50]

The human rights revolution has made modern progressives more inclined to locate political legitimacy on the consent of individuals, rather than the consent of states. A truly progressive US foreign policy would promote a system of international governance with robust rights protections for individuals and nonstate groups; it would be a system built on the recognition that states currently remain the primary mode of political and social organization in the international sphere but also upon the recognition that new forms of social organization continue to evolve and may ultimately displace some (or perhaps even all) states. Such a progressive international system would seek to bring such new actors and organizations within the ambit of international law, both as responsible creators of law and as responsible subjects of law. It would seek new means of resolving thorny collective problems, from climate change to public health challenges to the threat posed by weapons of mass destruction.

A progressive US foreign policy would involve a US commitment to respect rule-of-law norms both domestically and in our multilateral and bilateral engagements. That means, among other things, avoiding hypocrisy: we need to play by the same rules we demand that others respect. (It's difficult to credibly condemn Russian interventionism in the Ukraine, for instance, while simultaneously defending the 2003 invasion of Iraq.) If we genuinely believe that the rules are wrong or outmoded—and sometimes they are—we should work collaboratively with other international actors to develop a fair process for changing the rules.

A progressive US foreign policy would also seek to foster more equitable sharing of global wealth, through more generous provision of financial support to international institutions by wealthy states, a greater willingness to forgive the international debt of poorer states, more foreign aid designed to help the world's neediest, and the elimination of protectionist policies such as US agricultural subsidies, among other things. It would champion fair and equitable access to what some have termed "the global commons": the earth's natural resources, the sea, the air, and even space. Perhaps most important, it would seek to do all these things through a reformed international governance system.

All this is implicit in a commitment to progessive values, but I believe it is also consistent with US self-interest—even, in fact, required by an honest assessment of US interests and prospects. Historically, every significant empire has eventually declined, and the United States is not likely to prove an exception. Making appropriate allowances for our limited ability to predict the future, current trends suggest that, at least in the near-term, the decline in America's relative global power is likely to continue.

We do not know, however, what form this decline will take. We don't know if it will be fast, or slow; we don't know if the American Empire is in for a hard landing, or a soft one. Will we crash, like the former Soviet Union? Or will a slow decline in power nonetheless leave us an intact and relatively influential nation, like the United Kingdom?

We don't know what our national future will look like. In fact, as I noted earlier, we can make fewer and fewer geopolitical predictions with confidence: the world has changed too much and too fast for us to accurately assess the probabilities of many types of events. (Perhaps this is why it's so tempting to stay in Lake Wobegon, with our eyes closed and our fingers crossed.) But paradoxically, perhaps this very uncertainty can be our lodestone, pointing realists and idealists alike toward a sensible, forward-looking global strategy.

Most of us understand the sound reasons to save for the future and purchase various forms of insurance. Similarly, Americans across the political spectrum still express substantial support for the maintenance of at least some minimal social safety net, in the form of unemployment benefits, Social Security, Medicare, and Medicaid.[51] This is so for a simple reason: all of us know we might someday *need* those benefits ourselves. Any one of us might someday face job loss or illness; all of us will eventually face old age.

In the international arena, the same is true. Every nation, including the still-powerful United States, faces the possibility of misfortune. Our economy could collapse, or our military power could decline. Empires, like individuals, can sink into poverty, illness, or simple old age. And empires, like individuals, would do well to hedge against the possibility of future misfortune.

On a global level, taking seriously the possibility of future misfortune requires us to invest in much the same kind of safety net we invest in domestically. Even those skeptical about the likelihood of future US decline should share a commitment to hedging against future misfortune; in fact, uncertainty can be a powerful tool for planning.

That may seem oxymoronic—but consider one of the twentieth century's most famous philosophical thought experiments, outlined in John Rawls's book, *A Theory of Justice,* in which Rawls applies a version of decision theory to derive optimal principles of justice. Imagine, said Rawls, rational, free, and equal humans seeking to devise a set of principles to undergird the structure of human society. Imagine further that they must reason from behind what Rawls dubbed the "veil of ignorance," which hides from them their own future status or attributes. Behind the veil of ignorance, wrote Rawls, people still possess general knowledge of economics, science and so forth, and can draw on this knowledge to assist them in designing a future society. Their ignorance is limited to their own future role in the society they are designing: "No one knows his place in society, his class position or social status, nor does anyone know his fortune in the distribution of natural assets and abilities, his intelligence, strength, and the like. I shall even assume that the parties do not know their conceptions of the good or their special psychological propensities."[52]

If we were collectively designing social structures and rules, but could not know our own future position in that social structure, what structures and rules would we come up with? Rawls concluded that in the face of such radical uncertainty about their own future positions, rational, free, and equal beings behind the veil of ignorance would be drawn toward a "maximin" (or "minimax") rule of decision, in which they would seek to the minimize their losses in a worst case scenario.[53] To put it in slightly different terms, since they don't know whether they'll be haves or a have-nots in the society they are designing, they should seek to build the kind of society in which they each will be *least* badly off even if they start with the fewest advantages.

To Rawls, this should lead those behind the veil of ignorance to support two core principles: the first relates to liberty ("each person [should] have an equal right to the most extensive basic liberty compatible with a similar liberty for others"), and the second relates to social and economic goods (social goods should be distributed equally, unless an unequal distribution would serve the common good and be "to the greatest benefit of the least advantaged," while "offices and positions [should remain] open to all under conditions of fair equality of opportunity."[54]

These are principles of justice progressives can readily embrace, and it is easy enough to see their operation domestically. A rational actor behind the veil or ignorance would presumably wish to live in a society committed to equal rights and equal opportunity, and with a robust social and economic safety net, for instance.

Two decades after the initial publication of *A Theory of Justice*, Rawls sought to apply a form of this thought experiment to the global order. In *The Law of Peoples*,[55] he argued that decent "peoples" (states, more or less)—whether liberal or nonliberal—would, from behind the veil of ignorance, reach agreement on a number of core principles that should govern international relations. The principles he came up with are, to a significant extent, those that already form the underpinning of today's international order. Among them are the following: "Peoples . . . are free and independent, and their freedom and independence are to be respected by other peoples; Peoples are to observe treaties and undertakings . . . . Peoples have the right of self-defense but no right to instigate war for reasons other than self-defense; Peoples are to honor human rights . . . . Peoples have a duty to assist other peoples living under unfavorable conditions," and so on.[56]

Rawls's arguments are complex, and I can't do justice to them here (or to the arguments of Rawls's many interpreters and critics). Fortunately, although Rawls sought to deduce what a truly "just" global order might look like, my agenda is much less lofty: it is limited to arguing that a crude, limited version of Rawls's thought experiment can help us delineate the contours of a sensible US global strategy—a "maximin" strategy that is reasonably best suited to protecting the interests of the

United States and its people, both in today's messy world and in a wide range of future messes.

Imagine, then, a crude version of Rawls's veil of ignorance, with only the United States behind it. This veil of ignorance doesn't require us to disavow what we know of history (our own or the world's), nor does it require us to disavow what we know of recent trends, present global realities, US values, or our current conception of the good. Our own veil of ignorance only hides the future from us: we don't know whether the US will be rich or poor, weak or strong, respected or hated, in twenty or fifty years from now.

Behind such a veil of ignorance, a maximin decision rule would lead us to prefer international rules and institutions that will maximize America's odds of thriving even in a worst-case future scenario. The further implication of such a Rawlsian thought experiment is this: if we consider it possible that the US will continue to decline in global power, we should use the considerable power we still have to foster the kind of international order most likely to benefit us if we someday lose that power.

American international lawyers—most on the liberal side of the political spectrum—are fond of highlighting the deep respect most of the framers of the US Constitution and most early Supreme Court justices had for international law, usually as part of an effort to convince current judges and public officials to show a similar respect.[57] Critics—usually, though not always, on the right—tend to counter that international law is a weapon of the weak:[58] the early American republic—young and powerless—*needed* international law, they argue, but the world's sole superpower does not.

I think this view is mistaken: to my mind, law is an essential tool for powerful states as well as weak states. But for the sake of the argument, assume that international law *is* primarily a weapon of the weak. This is no reason for the United States to ignore it. On the contrary: as a state that has grown manifestly weaker in recent years, and may soon be weaker still, we'd better learn to love international law. Odds are, we're going to need it. The same goes for a more robust and equitable international governance system. We can argue over whether the United States needs this right now, but reasoning from behind the veil of ignorance, we should surely hope for this in the future.

In the face of uncertainty about the future, rational self-interest thus dictates the same kind of foreign policy suggested by a moral or political commitment to core progressive values. It's impossible (and probably not desirable) to outline precisely what that would look like on an issue-by-issue basis, but let me highlight a few more principles that should animate a progressive US foreign policy.

In 2011 my former Pentagon colleagues Wayne Porter and Mark Mykleby published an important white paper calling for a new US "strategic narrative."[59] "America's national strategy in the second half of the last century was anchored in the belief that our global environment is a closed system to be controlled," they argue, "but we failed to recognize that dominance, like fossil fuel, is not a sustainable source of energy." To prosper in the face of complexity and uncertainty, assert Porter and Mykleby, the US needs "to move beyond a strategy of containment to a strategy of sustainment (sustainability); from an emphasis on power and control to an emphasis on strength and influence; from a defensive posture of exclusion, to a proactive posture of engagement."

Their paper is well worth reading and offers a blueprint for the kind of progressive foreign policy we need. It emphasizes humility when dealing with what we can and cannot control and the importance of understanding that our domestic policies are inherently related to our foreign policy. If we hope to shift from an unsustainable strategy emphasizing control and exclusion to a sustainable strategy emphasizing credible influence and engagement, we need, among other things, to mend our tattered domestic social safety net. We need the kind of progressive reforms of our health care and educational systems that others have already outlined in this book; we need to address the glaring (and growing) economic inequities that have reduced social mobility and left millions of Americans one setback away from poverty. Globally, credible US influence depends significantly on the degree to which others around the world perceive the United States as internally strong, equitable and just.

Meanwhile, engagement requires us to not simply build strong and just international institutions and demonstrate our own respect for the rule of law; engagement also requires us to deepen and broaden our interactions with those who live beyond our borders. This happens through generous and thoughtful development and humanitarian assistance and through a renewed emphasis on cultural, economic, scientific and educational collaborations and exchanges.

Since 9/11, US foreign policy has grown substantially more militarized, with resources and authorities flowing toward the security sector (the Defense Department, the intelligence community, and so on) and away from civilian diplomacy and development agencies. There is no quick or easy way to reverse this—at least in the near term, it is unlikely that Congress will be inclined to substantially increase funding for civilian foreign policy agencies. But there is another (and far cheaper) way to re-civilianize our foreign policy: the US government can encourage, fund, and enable more good old-fashioned public diplomacy—exchange programs, cultural programs, educational programs and the like. People-to-people ties do matter: they help the US foster international good will and develop the strong networks of friends and information sources that will stand us in good stead when harder times come—as they will.

The US is, and always has been, a nation of immigrants. Today modern transportation and communications technologies enable immigrants to maintain strong ties to their communities of origin in ways that were simply impossible a hundred years ago. Yet from a foreign policy perspective, our government does little to leverage the incredible diversity of the American public. This too should change.

CAN WE GET THERE FROM HERE?

I have focused so far on the principles that should animate a progressive twenty-first-century US foreign policy. I now want to turn to a different question: how likely is it that the US government will adopt such a foreign policy?

Not very likely, I'm afraid. While I believe many senior members of the Obama administration share the progressive vision I have laid out here, the administration has found it remarkably difficult to make this vision actually animate policy choices in anything close to a consistent way, and this is not likely to change in the next few years.

This is so for several reasons. For one thing, the president's current inner circle is made up largely of advisors with expertise and experience in domestic policy, rather than foreign policy. As a result, foreign policy has been something of an afterthought—to be addressed in times of crisis, but otherwise of secondary concern.

This relative foreign policy inexperience also translates into a reduced White House ability to understand, leverage, and control the nation's vast and complex national security bureaucracy. (The US Department of Defense, for instance, is the world's largest organization, employing more than three million people, including more than two million active duty military personnel.) Add in the intelligence community and the national security sub-components of agencies from the Justice Department to the Homeland Security Department and you have a sprawling, unwieldy machine that is remarkably difficult to reset.

When he took office in 2009, President Obama inherited a national security apparatus that had been set to "perpetual war." His administration has lacked both the determination and the bureaucratic savvy to know how to rein in this bureaucracy, however, and there's no significant domestic constituency pushing the White House to try harder. We can see this playing out on issue after issue. Take the White House's earlier determination to close Guantanamo: nearly six years later, little progress has been made, and the administration that promised to restore the rule of law has ended up supporting the indefinite administrative detention of scores of detainees—some of whom have been repeatedly determined to pose no security risk.

Overall, I don't think the Obama administration has been able to offer (much less implement) a coherent foreign policy. The administration's attitude toward armed conflict and the use of lethal force is only one case in point, but it certainly highlights the often-contradictory policies of the last six years. "Americans are deeply ambivalent about war," President Obama noted in a 2013 speech,[60] but he could equally have been speaking of himself. Obama campaigned on a promise to end the war in Iraq and "finish the job" in Afghanistan. But even as he continues to insist that the United States "cannot use force everywhere" and that "perpetual war . . . will prove self-defeating, and alter our country in troubling ways," he has nonetheless become embroiled in a series of military adventures, some of his own making.

Although the last US combat troops finally withdrew from Iraq in December 2011,[61] there are still as many American troops in Afghanistan today as when President Obama was first elected.[62] Obama also presided over a seven-month air campaign in Libya and dramatically accelerated a covert drone war that has so far killed an estimated 4,000 people in Pakistan, Somalia, and Yemen.[63] Indeed, taking into consideration both geographic scope and deaths caused by US drone strikes in these three states, one might well consider US drone strikes a third war.[64]

Nonetheless, the administration continues to insist in court filings that it can neither confirm nor deny the existence of US drone strikes. As a result, neither the American public nor the international community can accurately assess the costs of this conflict. We don't know if US drone strikes are in fact making the United States safer, or if they are further destabilizing already unstable regions and increasing extremist sentiment. What's more, US drone strikes are deeply troubling from a rule of law perspective. The US justifications of such targeted killings have been given mainly in short speeches and the occasional leaked internal document, leaving it unclear how the US decides what constitutes an armed conflict, and which organizations and individuals it considers to be targetable. The US refusal to even acknowledge most strikes means there is no way to determine whether internal policies or the law has been followed, and no way to remedy possible mistakes or abuses. The impact of this on already shaky global conflict prevention and sovereignty norms is troubling—and the impact on US moral credibility has already been devastating.

The ongoing civil war in Syria offers another example of the administration's contradictory attitude toward the use of force. Early in the Syrian conflict, the President resisted calls for US military intervention, noting the limits of US ability to alter the situation and the possible unintended consequences of using force to intervene in a complex internal conflict. But by declaring that the use of chemical weapons would cross "a red line," he tripped himself up in his own rhetoric: when evidence suggested that the Assad regime had used such weapons, Obama declared his intention to take military action in Syria—even in the absence of Security Council authorization.

To many Americans and much of the globe, this seemed more than a little disturbing: with more than a hundred thousand Syrians already killed with conventional weapons—a figure that has now climbed to two hundred thousand—why fixate on the deaths of a thousand more due to chemical weapons? Further, if the United States was willing to intervene militarily inside a sovereign state without Security Council authorization—for the third time, after Kosovo and the 2003 invasion of Iraq—what was left of the UN Charter's rule on sovereignty and the use of force?

President Obama's stated determination to intervene militarily in the Syrian conflict over Assad's use of chemical weapons caused an immediate and bipartisan uproar within the United States. Congressional and military leaders voiced skepticism: what would a limited series of air strikes actually accomplish, politically or militarily? What about the risks of escalation? Was the United States willing to drop bombs in order to make a point about chemical weapons, while remaining passive in the face of continuing civilian deaths from conventional weapons?

Ultimately, and rather ironically, a Russian-brokered compromise allowed the president to back away from his plans to use force in Syria in autumn 2013. Still more ironically, President Obama found himself, a year later, authorizing the use of US airpower to strike not at the Assad regime but at some of the Assad regime's bitterest enemies: the rebel fighters of the self-proclaimed "Islamic State."

The crisis over Syria remains an example of the ongoing tensions within the current administration, tensions between a principled foreign policy vision, on the one hand, and crisis-driven policy-making inflected by political expediency. The overall result has been a US foreign policy that is neither consistently progressive nor even particularly coherent.

This is fairly gloomy assessment. I wish I could say that the future prospects for a truly progressive US foreign policy are bright, but unfortunately I do not think they are. We currently have as progressive a president as we are likely to get; but even so, we have seen little progressive change. Given how broken our domestic political system has become, I don't have much hope for the next few administrations, either.

I said earlier that US global power has been declining, and I'd place good odds on a near-term continuation of that decline. The real question is not whether US power will continue to decline, but whether the American empire will have a soft landing, or a hard one. My guess is that if we end up with a soft landing, we will owe it not to our own wise policies but to the kindness of other states—or simple good luck.

Acknowledgments

Portions of this essay first appeared in shortened and modified form in several columns I published in *Foreign Policy* (www.foreignpolicy.com). I am grateful to Betsy Kuhn at Georgetown University Law Center for her invaluable assistance with proofreading and citations; any remaining errors are all my own.

Notes

1. "Chronic wrongdoing," declared Roosevelt, "or an impotence which results in a general loosening of ties of civilized society, may in America, as elsewhere, ultimately require intervention by some civilized nation, and in the western hemisphere, the adherence of the U.S. to the Monroe Doctrine may force the United States, however reluctantly, in flagrant cases of wrongdoing or impotence, to the exercise of international police power." Theodore Roosevelt's Annual Message to Congress for 1904; House Records HR 58A-K2; Records of the U.S.

House of Representatives; Record Group 233; Center for Legislative Archives; National Archives. http://www.ourdocuments.gov/ doc.php?flash=true&doc=56.

2. Walter Russell Mead, review of *The Crisis of American Foreign Policy: Wilsonianism in the Twenty-First Century*, by G. John Ikenberry, Thomas J. Knock, Anne-Marie Slaughter, and Tony Smith. *Foreign Affairs*, March/April, 2009, http://www.foreignaffairs.com/articles/64728/walter-russell-mead/the-crisis-of-american-foreign-policy-wilsonianism-in-the-twenty.

3. John Halpin and Conor P. Williams, "Progressive Traditions: The Progressive Intellectual Tradition in America," Center for American Progress, April 14, 2010, http://www.americanprogress.org/issues/progressive-moveme/report/2010/04/14/7677/the-progressive-intellectual-tradition-in-america/.

4. "List of Sovereign States in 1914," *Wikipedia, The Free Encyclopedia*, http://en.wikipedia.org/wiki/ List_of_sovereign_states_in_1914.

5. Steve Lohr, "The Beige Box Fades to Black," *New York Times*, April 18, 2002; Loyd Case, "30 Years, 30 Great Tech Events," *PC World* 31.3 (2013): 81–84.

6. "All Scheduled Flights Worldwide," http://www.flixxy.com/scheduled-airline-flights-worldwide.htm.

7. Daniel Tencer, "The Number of Cars Worldwide Surpasses 1 Billion; Can The World Handle This Many Wheels?," *The Huffington Post Canada*, February 19, 2013, http://www.huffington-post.ca/2011/08/23/car-population_n_934291.html.

8. Joshua Pramis, "Number of mobile phones to exceed world population by 2014," Digital Trends, February 18, 2013, http://www.digitaltrends.com/mobile/mobile-phone-wo rld-population-2014/.

9. "Carl von Clausewitz," *Wikiquote*, http://en.wikiquote.org/wiki/Carl_von_Clausewitz.

10. U.N. Charter, Preamble, 1945, http://www.un.org/en/documents/charter/preamble.shtml.

11. This is especially true of with respect to the progressive goals for social and economc reform articulated in Articles 3 and 4 of Chapter I of the Charter, calling for international co-operation in solving problems of "an economic, social, cultural of humanitarian character". See: *Charter of the United Nations, Chapter I: Purposes and Principles*, http://www.un.org/en/documents/charter/chapter1.shtml.

12. Human Security Report Project, "*The Decline in Global Violence: Reality or Myth?*," March 3, 2014, http://www.hsrgroup.org/docs/Publications/HSR2013/HSR_2013_Press_Release.pdf.

13. U.N. Charter, art. 13, para. 1(a), http://www.un.org/en/documents/charter/chapter4.shtml.

14. For example, the International Court of Justice, the International Tribunal for the Law of the Sea, and the World Trade Organization Appellate Body are among the international adjudicating bodies established to resolve interstate disputes. See, e.g., Cesare Romano, Karen J. Alter and Yuval Shany, *The Oxford Handbook of International Adjudication* (Oxford: Oxford University Press, 2014).

15. Akira Iriye, Petra Goedde, and William I. Hitchcock, eds., *The Human Rights Revolution: an International History* (New York: Oxford University Press, 2012).

16. Food and Agriculture Organization of the United Nations, FAOSTAT, Statistics: Production, http://faostat3.fao.org/faostat-gateway/go/to/browse/Q/*/E; "Modern Agriculture and Food Security: A History," Global Food Security, http://www.foodsecurity.ac.uk/issue/history.html; World Bank, Health, Nutrition and Population (HNP) Statistics Data Dashboards, http://datatopics.worldbank.org/hnp/HNPDash.aspx.

17. Betsy Taylor and Dave Tilford, "Why Consumption Matters," *The Consumer Society Reader*, eds. Juliet B. Schor and Douglas B. Holt (New York: New Press, 2000), 472.

18. Jack Ewing, "America's Dominance of Global Wealth Is Slipping," Economix (blog), *New York Times*, September 14, 2010, http://economix.blogs.nytimes.com/2010/09/14/americas-dominance-of-global-wealth-is-slipping/.

19. Oxfam, "Working for the Few: Political Capture and Economic Inequality," January 20, 2014, http://www.oxfam.org/sites/www.oxfam.org/files/bp-working-for-few-political-capture-economic-inequality-200114-summ-en.pdf.

20. Geneva Declaration Organization on Armed Violence and Development, "Executive Summary," *Global Burden of Armed Violence 2011* (2011), http://www.genevadeclaration.org/fileadmin/docs/GBAV2/GBAV2011-Ex-summary-ENG.pdf.

21. United Nations, Population Division, "World Fertility Patterns 2013," http://www.un.org/en/development/desa/population/publications/pdf/fertility/world-fertility-patterns-2013_slides.pdf.

22. World Nuclear Stockpile Report, Ploughshares Fund, http://www.ploughshares.org/world-nuclear-stockpile-report.

23. Stephen Hummel, Vito Quaranta, and John Wikswo, "The Biohacker: A Threat to National Security," *CTC Sentinel* 7 (Jan. 2014): 8–11, http://www.ctc.usma.edu/posts/the-biohacker-a-threat-to-national-security.

24. Anders Levermann, Peter U. Clark, et al., "The Multimillennial Sea-Level Commitment of Global Warming," *Proc. of the National Academy of Sciences USA* 110 (August 20, 2013): 13745–13750, http://www.pnas.org/content/110/34/13745.full.

25. Solomon M. Hsiang, Marshall Burke, and Edward Miguel, "Quantifying the Influence of Climate on Human Conflict," *Science* 341 (September 2013): 1235367, http://dx.doi.org/10.1126/science.1235367.

26. See, e.g., Nils Petter Gleditsch, ed., "The Forum: The Decline of War," *International Studies Review* (2013) 15, 396–419, http://stevenpinker.com/files/pinker/files/intl_studies_review.pdf.

27. Ian M. Threadgold, "Reducing the Risk of Low-Probability High-Consequence Events," *Society of Petroleum Engineers* (2011), http://dx.doi.org/10.2118/141763-MS; Bernice Lee and Felix Preston with Gemma Green, "Preparing for High-Impact, Low-Probability Events: Lessons from Eyjafjallajökull," Chatham House (January 2012), http://www.chathamhouse.org/sites/files/chathamhouse/public/Research/Energy,%20Environment%20and%20Development/r0112_highimpact.pdf.

28. See, generally, Rosa Brooks, "Apocalypse Soon!" *Foreign Policy* (February 20, 2013), http://www.foreignpolicy.com/ articles/2013/02/21/apocalypse_soon; Rosa Brooks, "Warning: Winter Metaphor Alert!," *Foreign Policy* (February 2014), http://www.foreignpolicy.com/articles/2014/02/13/warning_winter_metaphor_alert_snow_washington.

29. Eliezer Yudkowsky, "Cognitive Biases Potentially Affecting Global Risks," Machine Intelligence Research Institute (2008), http://intelligence.org/files/CognitiveBiases.pdf.

30. See, e.g., Jared Diamond, "That Daily Shower Can be a Killer," *New York Times*, January 23, 2013, http://www.nytimes.com/2013/01/29/science/jared-diamonds-guide-to-reducing-lifes-risks.html.

31. Nathaniel Rich, "The New Science of Disaster Prediction," *New Yorker*, November 19, 2013, http://www.newyorker.com/online/blogs/newsdesk/2013/11/the-new-science-of-disaster-prediction.html.

32. Leon Aron, "Everything You Think you Know about the Collapse of the Soviet Union is Wrong," *Foreign Policy*, June 20, 2011, http://www.foreignpolicy.com/articles/2011/06/20/everything_you_think_you_know_about_the_collapse_of_the_soviet_union_is_wrong.

33. Richard Cincotta, et al., "Seismic Shift: Understanding Change in the Middle East," The Stimson Center (May 2011), http://www.stimson.org/images/uploads/research-pdfs/Full_Pub_-_Seismic_Shift.pdf.

34. See, e.g., Charles Kenny, "Americans! Stop Worrying and Learn to Love Decline," *Politico*, January 7, 2014, http://www.politico.com/magazine/story/2014/01/decline-is-good-for-america-101749.html#.U9Z1mWyA3cs; Alec Tyson, "Most Americans Say U.S. is Great, but Fewer Say it's the Greatest," Pew Research Center, Fact Tank (blog), July 2, 2014, http://www.pewresearch.org/fact-tank/2014/07/02/most-americans-think-the-u-s-is-great-but-fewer-say-its-the-greatest/; Fareed Zakaria, "Are America's Best Days Behind Us?," *Time*, March 3, 2011, http://content.time.com/time/magazine/article/0,9171,2056723,00.html.

35. White House, "National Security Strategy of the United States," 1987, p. 3, http://nssarchive.us/NSSR/1987.pdf.

36. White House, "National Security Strategy of the United States," 1990, preface, http://nssarchive.us/NSSR/1990.pdf.

37. See, e.g., Derek Thompson, "The World's 85 Richest People are as Wealthy as the Poorest 3 Billion," *The Atlantic*, January 21, 2014. See also John Cassidy, "Forces of Divergence," *The New Yorker*, March 31, 2014. http://www.newyorker.com/magazine/2014/03/31/forces-of-divergence, and John Cassidy, Piketty's "Inequality Theory in Six Charts," *The New Yorker*, March 26, 2014. http://www.newyorker.com/news/john-cassidy/pikettys-inequality-story-in-six-charts.

38. Neil Shah, "U.S. Poverty Rate Stabilizes—for Some," *Wall Street Journal*, October 11, 2013, http://online.wsj.com/news/articles/SB10001424052702304500404579127603306039292.

39. Jon Fasman., "Why Does America Have Such a Big Prison Population?" *The Economist*, August 14, 2013, http://www.economist.com/blogs/economist-explains/2013/08/economist-explains-8.

40. Stephen Bezruchka, "The Hurrider I Go the Behinder I Get: The Deteriorating International Ranking of US Health Status," *Annual Review of Public Health* 33 (2012): 157–173, http://www.annualreviews.org/eprint/iESYF775U2MwVfrxfAR2/full/10.1146/annurev-publhealth-031811-124649; US Burden of Disease Collaborators, "The State of US Health, 1990–2010: Burden of Diseases, Injuries, and Risk Factors," *JAMA* 310(6) (2013): 591–606, http://jama.jamanetwork.com/article.aspx?articleID=1710486&utm_source=Silverchair%20Information%20Systems&utm_medium=email&utm_campaign=JAMA%3AOnlineFirst07%2F10%2F2013; Grace Wyler, "US Women Are Dying Younger than their Mothers, and No One Knows Why, *The Atlantic*, Oct. 27, 2013, http://www.theatlantic.com/health/archive/2013/10/us-women-are-dying-younger-than-their-mothers-and-no-one-knows-why/280259/.

41. See, e.g., Thomas E. Mann, "Admit it, Political Scientists: Politics Really Is More Broken Than Ever," *The Atlantic*, May 26, 2014, http://www.theatlantic.com/politics/archive/2014/05/dysfunction/371544/.

42. Andrew Kohut, "Reviving America's Global Image," Pew Research Global Attitudes Project, March 5, 2010, http://www.pewglobal.org/2010/03/05/reviving-americas-global-image/.

43. Andrew Kohut, et al., "Global Opinion of Obama Slips, International Policies Faulted," Pew Research Global Attitudes Project, June 13, 2012, Overview, http://www.pewglobal.org/2012/06/13/global-opinion-of-obama-slips-international-policies-faulted/; Chapter 3, http://www.pewglobal.org/2012/06/13/chapter-3-global-opinion-of-barack-obama/; Andrew Kohut, et al., "America's Global Image Remains More Positive Than China's," Pew Research Global Attitude Project, July 18, 2013, http://www.pewglobal.org/2013/07/18/americas-global-image-remains-more-positive-than-chinas/.

44. Recall Garrison Keillor's fictional Lake Wobegon, "where. . .all the children are above average." See, e.g., Lake Wobegon Effect," Oxford Reference, http://www.oxfordreference.com/view/10.1093/acref/9780199534067.001.0001/ acref-9780199534067-e-9348.

45. See, e.g., Eliot A. Cohen, "Obama Fails on National Security," *The Washington Post*, Sept. 14, 2012, https://www.google.com/url?sa=t&rct=j&q=&esrc=s&source=web&cd=7&cad=rja&uact=8&ved=0CEcQFjAG&url=http%3A%2F%2Fwww.washingtonpost.com%2Fopinions%2Fobama-fails-on-national-security%2F2012%2F09%2F14%2F6d361ab2-fd22-11e1-8adc-499661afe377_story.html&ei=SrbFU5T9IaXo8QHL6oDQBQ&usg=AFQjCNGi8eTBKfn0olvQFHG6ut2cMSSIww&sig2=AJ_7Rge237_nXojeGvbHhw&bvm=bv.71126742,d.b2U; Victor Davis Hanson, "Beware the Boom in American 'Declinism,'" CBS News-National Review, November 14, 2011, http://www.cbsnews.com/news/beware-the-boom-in-american-declinism/.

46. John Winthrop, *A Modell of Christian Charity* (1630), Hanover Historical Texts Project, https://history.hanover.edu/texts/winthmod.html.

47. Pew Research Center, "America's Place in the World, 2013," December 2013, http://www.people-press.org/2013/12/03/public-sees-u-s-power-declining-as-support-for-global-engagement-slips/.

48. Tyson, Pew Research, http://www.pewresearch.org/fact-tank/2014/07/02/most-americans-think-the-u-s-is-great-but-fewer-say-its-the-greatest/.

49. See, e.g., Matthew Bunn, "US Failure to Ratify Key Nuclear Conventions," Nuclear Security Matters-Belfer Center, March 12, 2014, http://nuclearsecuritymatters.belfercenter.org/blog/us-failure-ratify-key-conventions; David Welna, "Senate Fails to Ratify UN Treaty on Disabilities, NPR, December 5, 2012, http://www.npr.org/2012/12/05/166546008/senate-fails-to-ratify-u-n-treaty-on-disabilities; http://www.economist.com/blogs/economist-explains/2013/10/economist-explains-2; Keith Johnson, GOP Opposition Scuttles Law-of-Sea Treaty, *Wall Street Journal*, July 16, 2012, http://blogs.wsj.com/washwire/2012/07/16/gop-opposition-scuttles-law-of-sea-treaty/.

50. See, generally, Jared Genser and Bruno Stagno Ugarte, "The Evolution of the Security Council's Engagement on Human Rights," in *The UN Security Council in the Age of Human Rights* (Cambridge, UK: Cambridge University Press, 2014).

51. Bruce Stokes, "Public Attitudes Toward the Next Social Contract," New America Fdn./Pew Research Center, January 2013, http://www.pewglobal.org/files/pdf/Stokes_Bruce_NAF_Public_Attitudes_1_2013.pdf.

52. John Rawls, *A Theory of Justice* (Cambridge, MA: The Belknap Press of Harvard University Press, 1971), 11–12; *A Theory of Justice* was revised and republished in 1999. See John Rawls, *A Theory of Justice*. Rev. ed. (Cambridge, MA: Belknap Press of Harvard University Press, 1999).

53. See, generally, Rawls, *Theory*, chapters 26 and 27.

54. See Rawls, *Theory*, 83.

55. John Rawls, *The Law of Peoples, Critical Inquiry* 20.1 (Autumn 1993). *The Law of Peoples* was later revised and expanded, then published along with another essay in book form. See John Rawls, *The Law of Peoples* (Cambridge, MA: Harvard University Press, 2001).

56. Rawls, *The Law of Peoples, Critical Inquiry*, p. 46.

57. See, e.g., Harold Hongju Koh and Michael Doyle, "The Case for International Law: A Response to 'The War of Law,'" *Foreign Affairs* 92 (2013): 162–165, http://www.foreignaffairs.com/articles/140169/harold-hongju-koh-and-michael-doyle/the-case-for-international-law.

58. See, e.g., Robert Kagan, "Power and Weakness," *Policy Review* 113 (2002): 3–28, http://den-beste.nu/external/Kagan01.html; https://www.law.virginia.edu/pdf/workshops/0708/lee.pdf; Jack L. Goldsmith and Eric A. Posner, *The Limits of International Law* (New York: Oxford University Press, 2005).

59. Wayne Porter and Mark Mykleby, "A National Strategic Narrative," Woodrow Wilson International Center for Scholars (2011), http://www.wilsoncenter.org/sites/default/files/A%20National%20Strategic%20Narrative.pdf.

60. The White House, "Remarks by the President at National Defense University," May 23, 2013, http://www.whitehouse.gov/the-press-office/2013/05/23/remarks-president-national-defense-university.

61. As I write, however, renewed crisis in Iraq has led to the deployment of several thousand military advisors in Iraq, along with US airstrikes in both Iraq and Syria.

62. Ian S. Livington and Michael O. Hanlon, "Afghanistan Index," Brookings Institution, May 2014, http://www.brookings.edu/~/media/Programs/foreign%20policy/afghanistan%20index/index20140514.pdf.

63. Jack Serle, "September 2013 Update: US Covert Actions in Pakistan, Yemen and Somalia," October 1, 2013, http://www.thebureauinvestigates.com/2013/10/01/september-2013-update-us-covert-actions-in-pakistan-yemen-and-somalia/.

64. I have written more extensively about drone strikes and targeted killings elsewhere—see, for instance, Testimony from May 16 Senate Armed Services Committee Hearing on the AUMF, http://www.lawfareblog.com/wp-content/uploads/2013/05/Brooks_05-16-13.pdf; "10 Ways to Fix the Drone War," *Foreign Policy*, April 11, 2013, http://www.foreign-policy.com/articles/2013/04/11/10_ways_to_fix_the_drone_war; and "Drones and the International Rule of Law," *Journal of Ethics and International Law* (forthcoming), http://scholarship.law.georgetown.edu/cgi/viewcontent.cgi?article=2296&context=facpub.

11

The Progressive Tradition and the Problem of Global Warming

MARK LYTLE

Those who flooded into the nation's capital on January 20, 2009, to celebrate the inauguration of Barack Obama seemed confident that this president would launch the nation on a new course. Yet for all the promises he made that day, Obama did not fully address a fundamental issue facing the United States: in the face of global warming, how could the United States revive its consumer economy in a way that created more income equity but did not increase emissions of greenhouse gases? And how would the United States balance its consumption with that of Europe and the BRIC nations—Brazil, Russia, India, and China—whose rapid economic growth accelerated both warming and competition for natural resources? Success on the economic front threatened disaster for the environment and vice versa.

The dilemma Barack Obama faced in 2009 was a consequence of the economy Americans created over the twentieth century. As environmental historian John McNeill observed, "The modern United States was built on the premise of cheap [and plentiful] energy." Since that premise remained valid for most of the century, Americans embraced it almost without wavering. Abundant fresh water was another commodity Americans presumed as a birthright and built into their economic infrastructure over the twentieth century. They created a Western irrigation empire and made profligate industrial and residential use of freshwater resources. Here, too, evidence mounted that the initial assumption of an infinite water supply was increasingly untenable. Agricultural interests sparred with urban regions over the distribution of shrinking water resources. As McNeill pointed out, the insecurity of energy and water regimes means that "the social order of many societies . . . is probably at risk. Acute social strains, typical of modern times, will remain our fate as long as ecological disruptions, also typical of modern times, remains our practice."[1]

Those with a historical bent probably recognize that these warnings have a familiar ring. Reform-minded Americans in the early twentieth century believed the

United States faced a comparable resource crisis. Not only had the frontier closed, as Fredrick Jackson Turner announced, but also a once bountiful landscape showed tell-tale signs of despoiled nature in the pollution engulfing cities, the clear-cut forests from Maine to Minnesota, and the many species—migratory wild fowl, seals, bison, and the mighty whales—gone or near extinction. The titles of books and muckraking articles denounced, "The Slaughter of the Trees," *Our Wasteful Nation*, "A nation's profligate waste," and "America's Profligacy With Its Heritage." One muckraker warned, "In fifty years we will have the whole states as bare as China . . . ." Deforestation would produce floods that "ripped apart" the Mississippi Valley and its fertile delta. "We shall shiver in the cold and burn in heat never before felt. Like Chinamen our children will rake the soil for fuel or forage."[2]

Despite this note of impending doom, the early-twentieth-century reformers were an optimistic lot fired by a "can do" spirit. Conquering the West, launching a mighty navy with an empire to go with it, and producing a material abundance on an unprecedented scale were among the nation's signature achievements. Behind this success lay the advances in science and technology that gave birth to the progressive tradition. Though a common understanding of the term "progressive" has eluded generations of historians, we can make some claims about the movement's legacy. Central to the Progressive ideal were such notions as man's destiny to rule over and improve on nature, the capacity of science to unlock the secrets of man and nature, and the inevitable progress of mankind to higher states of material, moral, and spiritual being. No area of public policy more fully embodied the Progressive agenda than conservation, a program that first sought to preserve natural resources and guarantee their wise use, but eventually applied to almost all facets of contemporary society.[3]

Among those who placed conservation at the center of Progressive reform were Theodore Roosevelt and Gifford Pinchot. Along with his "high octane" personality, huge ego, and capacity for self-dramatization, Roosevelt brought to the presidency and Progressivism a passion for wild nature and the wild West, a belief in the "strenuous life" and "muscular Christianity," and a commitment to conservation. For Pinchot, conservation for use, as exemplified in the scientific forestry he learned in Europe, had the promise of promoting national well-being long into the future. Both Roosevelt and Pinchot championed the Progressive model of "disinterested" experts, engineers, and scientists who put the search for truth, the promotion of the public interest, and the utilitarian ideal of the "greater good of the greatest number" ahead of the special interests and the quest for personal gain that ruled what Mark Twain derided as "the Gilded Age." Their efforts led to the creation of the National Forest Service and a vast increase in the public lands and national parks, the Bureau of Reclamation and its expansive irrigation agenda for the arid West, the preservation of vital water power sites and coal reserves, and the drive to police the behavior of those whose greed and careless waste of resources threatened the nation's future.

Issues of sovereignty were one matter reformers faced. Often these federal initiatives intruded on what generally had been the provenance of the states. National Progressives in the Roosevelt camp saw new promise in a vigorous and interventionist federal government. They recognized that many issues such as railroad regulation, pure foods, and the protection of endangered species such as whales, seals, and migratory wildfowl, demanded interstate and transnational solutions. Consider, as an example, the American effort to ban pelagic (on the open seas) seal hunting. The vast majority of fur- bearing seals bred their pups on the Pribilof Islands in the Bering Sea. The acquisition of Alaska in 1867 made the islands and (so Americans thought) also the seals US property. Sealskins, like Buffalo robes, had become a highly valued commodity and attracted hunters in large numbers from Canada, Russia, Japan, and the United States. The United States gave a monopoly over the trade in sealskins first to the Alaskan Commercial Company (1870–1890) and then to Northern Commercial Company from 1890–1910. By then decades of indiscriminate slaughter, similar to the assault on the buffalo and whales, had reduced the population of fur seals from millions to around 150,000.

The problem of controlling hunters arose because unlike the Americans, Russians, and Japanese who hunted on land, Canadian seal hunters waited in boats for the mother seals that took to the open sea to forage for their pups. There they became easy prey. The Americans considered this piracy and sought to ban pelagic hunting. At a meeting in Paris in 1893, they demanded that the British official, representing the Canadian sealers, acknowledge that pelagic hunting was theft. The British countered by claiming that the commodities of the sea were free to anyone. Arbiters shaped a compromise that satisfied neither American nor Canadian sealers and opened the door to exploitation by the Russians and Japanese. In the meantime a group of American scientists determined that pelagic hunting had caused a dramatic decline in seal populations. That information led arbiters to conclude that, while hunting on the open seas might be legal, it was not sustainable. By 1898 the scientific evidence convinced Congress to ban American pelagic sealing, and the Russians and Japanese soon agreed to a moratorium. In 1911 Canada, Japan, Russia, and the United States agreed to a convention that banned pelagic hunting. So successful was this step that by 1940 fur seal populations had grown to over 2 million.

American conservationists who worried about a similar decline in migratory songbirds and wildfowl also had to contend with sovereignty issues, in this case between state and federal authority. Hunting was generally understood to fall under the regulatory authority of the states. In 1913 they persuaded Congress to pass the Federal Migratory Bird Bill based on the dubious premise that protecting birds fell under the Interstate Commerce Clause. Fearful the law would not withstand Supreme Court scrutiny, its proponents convinced the State Department to negotiate with Canada and Mexico the Migratory Bird Treaty of 1916. It solved the national sovereignty problem by freeing each nation to set its own rules. Where the Supreme Court might deny the federal government authority over the states to regulate bird hunting, it would be more inclined to uphold its authority to enforce an international treaty.[4]

Beyond sovereignty, the seal and migratory protection bills exemplify two additional principles that guided Progressives in their efforts to turn back the assault on nature. The first of these was a faith in the ability of science to define impartial standards. Without such guidance, officials often operated in the dark when weighing rules and regulations. How many trees could lumber men cut before a forest lost its capacity for renewal? How many seals, whales, and birds could hunters take before their populations became unsustainable and the species faced extinction? Progressives believed that scientists should and could answer those questions. Scientists, after all, first warned about the threat to seals and provided the guidelines that returned the herds to sustainable levels.

In their search for efficient regulations, scientists chose sustainability as a yardstick. Clearly the current practice of hunting species to the point of extinction or cutting timber without a plan for reforestation made no sense. To make resource consumption rational, and progressives valued rationality, regulators needed to determine in the cases of birds, seals, or whales the proper age, gender, and number that could be killed without undermining the species' sustainability and thus its commercial viability. For non-renewable resources such as fossil fuels and minerals, sustainability took the form of efficient use. Reducing waste extended the time to find new or alternative sources.

Progressive conservationists' gift to the modern environmental movement was their faith in sovereignty, science, and sustainability as a foundation for effective public policy. Obstacles arose, as they did in the case of whales and seals, when disputes over sovereignty and science blocked consensus over the proper path to sustainability. Perhaps the most significant contemporary issue on which the Progressive model has failed to achieve effective regulatory regimes is climate change. Evidence has mounted since the 1970s that human emission of greenhouse gases has raised global temperature at such a rate that ice caps and glaciers are melting and sea levels are rising. Some geologists now refer to the present as "the anthropocene," a geologic era in which humans, according to an *Economist* editorial, "have become a force of nature reshaping the planet on a geological scale—but at far faster than geological speed." Severe weather events such as tsunamis, hurricanes, droughts, floods, or tornados occur with greater frequency. As New York Governor Andrew Cuomo said in the wake of devestating Hurricane Sandy in 2012, "One hundred year storms now occur every two years," thus producing a new weather reality the world must adjust to.[5]

International concern over the threat of global warming first became widely evident in the wake of Earth Day I 1970. In 1971 MIT physicist Carroll Wilson invited experts to Stockholm to discuss mankind's impact on the climate. It was the first such meeting dedicated to global warming and ended by calling the world's attention to the dangers of greenhouse gases and particle pollutants. The widely circulated report closed with a Sanskrit prayer: "Oh, Mother Earth . . . pardon me for trampling on you."[6]

The following year the United Nations sponsored The United Nations Conference on the Human Environment. Delegates from 113 nations, scientists, and a host of NGOs gathered in Stockholm to discuss a range of environmental concerns. Sovereignty issues divided the delegates then and continued to be a source of conflict thirty-seven years later in Copenhagen. The so-called Group of 77, composed of the least-developed nations, mostly in the southern hemisphere, insisted that they should be free to pursue economic growth and receive development aid from the wealthier nations. They argued that since they created the least pollution and consumed the fewest resources they were entitled to pursue growth. Many of these poorer countries, such as Bangladesh, faced the gravest threat from global warming, but the G-8 generated most of the greenhouse gases, so only they could take effective action. India, represented by Indira Gandhi, associated itself with the Group of 77 as would China at later conferences, even though by 2006 China had overtaken the United States as a producer of CO_2 emissions.[7]

By the 1990s the post-Reagan Republican Party had repudiated, once and for all, the party's progressive tradition that once supported regulation, progressive taxation, and programs that promoted income redistribution or the reduction of poverty. The Republicans' hostility to science and to activist government as well as a precious regard for American sovereignty has framed their opposition to climate regulation. Tea Party activists and neoconservatives also have been highly nationalistic and even jingoistic in their approach to international affairs. They constantly attack the United Nations and seek to reduce American support as a threat to sovereignty. Foreign aid, other than military assistance, has been anathema. On the issue of climate change they followed the lead of the Global Climate Coalition (GCC) financed by leading corporations and individuals in the oil and gas, trucking, petrochemical, and automobile corporations. The GCC funneled money and research grants to scientists and think tanks that denied the existence of global warming.

George H. W. Bush occupied the White House when the Intergovernmental Panel on Climate Change (IPCC) issued its first report. In opposition to the GCC and other deniers, the Climate Change Panel endorsed a general scientific consensus that human activities were most likely, though not definitely, responsible for a measureable increase in global temperatures. Skeptics like the GCC either disputed the IPCC data or argued that natural climate patterns explained the rise. The media in its obsession with fairness gave disproportionate coverage to the handful of deniers even if they had little scientific expertise or clear-cut conflicts of interest.

The Bush administration sided with the skeptics, even as other G-8 members and independent government agencies acknowledged that the time had come to address the problem. Heavily influenced by GCC and other energy lobbies, the administration determined that the best way to discourage climate action was "to raise the many uncertainties." Thus, Bush faced a difficult decision when 172 nations, including 108 heads of state, gathered in 1992 for the Earth Summit in Rio de Janeiro. Would Bush attend? If so, what role would the United States play? The large majority of G-20 governments, including leading US allies, all supported the adoption of mandatory limits on greenhouse gas emissions. Ultimately, Bush did choose to attend; but instead of supporting the emerging consensus, he decided to frustrate the reformers. One hundred fifty delegates finally signed the "United Nations Framework Convention on Climate Change" of which one critic remarked that its "evasions and ambiguities left so many loopholes that policy makers could avoid any meaningful action," and most, the United States chief among them, did manage to avoid "meaningful action."[8]

By the time Bill Clinton became president in 1993, the Democratic Party maintained sole custody of the progressive tradition. Clinton signaled his willingness to make the environment a priority by selecting activist Al Gore as his vice president. Seizing control of Congress in 1994, conservatives led by Newt Gingrich and ex-exterminator Tom Delay, launched a counter-offensive against environmental regulation and climate action. They attacked evidence that the planet was warming and denied that human action threatened the environment. Profoundly suspicious of any multinational regulatory body that might undermine American sovereignty, they pushed to defund the United Nations. All the same, in its 1995 report, the IPCC issued its most unequivocal summation of current scientific thinking: "The balance of evidence suggests that there is a discernable human influence on climate change." Chastened by the 1994 Republican congressional triumph, Clinton, with one exception, chose not to spend his political capital fighting the climate fight, no matter how worthy the cause.[9]

That exception was Kyoto, a 1997 gathering of delegates from over 190 nations for the United Nations Conference on Climate Change. The United States proposed a modest return to emissions levels of 1990. The European Union called for more aggressive action. Once again the Group of 77 (G-77) countries, as well as India and China, insisted they should be exempt from any restrictions on development. As the delegates reached an impasse, Al Gore flew into Kyoto to forge a compromise. The resulting Kyoto Protocol acknowledged "that developed countries are principally responsible for the current high levels of GHG emissions in the atmosphere as a result of more than 150 years of industrial activity, and places a heavier burden on developed nations under the principle of 'common but differentiated responsibilities.'" Thus, the final protocol, adopted by some 191 nations, did bind industrial countries to significant emissions reductions beginning in 2008, while exempting the developing nations.[10]

The United States signed the Kyoto Protocol, but never ratified it. Sovereignty once again was at issue. Even before the Kyoto meeting began, the Senate had announced with a 95–0 vote that it would not ratify any treaty that exempted the less-developed countries, especially India and China. Fearful of the momentum Kyoto might produce, the Global Climate Coalition swung into action with a multimillion-dollar lobbying and advertising effort. Conservatives raised the phantom of world government as they warned Kyoto would place the global economy in the hands of less-developed nations. Worse yet, they claimed, a carbon tax would wreak havoc on the US economy.[11]

During the 2000 election campaign George W. Bush pledged to govern as a compassionate conservative. Bush also gave assurances that he would address the issues of alternative energy and climate change. As president, however, he followed the advice of his political guru Karl Rove and his vice president Dick Cheney who urged him to govern from the right. That became evident in his approach to global warming. On March 13, 2001, Bush sent a letter to the Senate in which he announced his withdrawal of American support for the Kyoto Protocol. "As you know, I oppose the Kyoto Protocol" Bush explained, "because it exempts 80 percent of the world, including major population centers such as China and India, from compliance, and would cause serious harm to the U.S. economy." He did back "a multi-pollutant strategy to require power plants to reduce emissions of sulfur dioxide, nitrogen oxides, and mercury," but rejected the idea "that the government should impose on power plants mandatory emissions reductions for carbon dioxide that Bush asserted was not a 'pollutant' under the Clean Air Act."[12]

Critics attacked this position on Kyoto because Bush acted unilaterally and in that way favored narrow American economic interests over those of the world community. As the world's single largest producer of greenhouse gases until 2006, the United States obviously impacted climate change. On the other hand, conservatives led by the Global Climate Coalition applauded the decision, especially since Bush adopted the GCC rationale for rejecting the protocol. He emphasized the economic disadvantages Americans would face if they complied with Kyoto's emission standards, while discounting the environmental benefits. By contrast, Bill Clinton, now out of office, believed that rather than undermine Kyoto, the United States should persuade India and China to participate. "Because even though Al Gore and I did help to develop the Kyoto Protocol, and I strongly supported it," he told *Meet the Press* in 2007. "I said at the time I thought India and China should be a part of it at a more graduated level." Failure for them to set limits on emissions was shortsighted because "there are enormous costs [from air pollution, water pollution, and so on]." Clinton thus concluded that "if we don't get the Chinese and the Indians in the system, we can't stop global warming."[13]

The administration also took steps to block the imposition of stricter emission standards for utilities. As part of the 1977 Clean Air Act Amendments, Congress established the New Source Review (NSR) permitting program. NSR guarantees that when permitting either new construction or the rebuilding of existing factories and utilities, new emissions must be as clean as possible. Vice President Dick Cheney was more concerned with adequate energy supplies than with environmental impacts. In the summer of 2001 he called EPA head Christine Todd Whitman to complain that the agency "hadn't moved fast enough" to ease pollution rules for aging power plants and oil refineries. He did not need to remind her that the industry had contributed generously to the Bush-Cheney campaign. Whitman warned him that without careful documentation the agency would find itself in court. Cheney wasn't buying it. He sympathized with industry officials who claimed that even when they performed routine maintenance, the Clinton administration charged them with violations and lawsuits. He wanted the rules revised quickly and "in a way that didn't hamper industry." Utilities should not face strict New Source regulations when they refurbished old plants, he insisted.[14]

When the EPA sent rule revisions to the White House, officials sent it back for "something that would be more pro-industry." In the end the White House ordered the rule rewritten and announced it in August 2003. This time the rule allowed some of the dirtiest plants to make major modifications without installing new pollution controls. By that time, Whitman was totally isolated within the administration and had announced her resignation. Publicly she explained that she wanted to spend more time with her family. But the real reason, she said, was the new rule and her conflict with Cheney. "I just couldn't sign it," she said. "The president has a right to have an administrator who could defend it, and I just couldn't." A federal appeals court later found that the rule the administration adopted violated the Clean Air Act and noted that the redefined rule would be valid "only in a Humpty-Dumpty world."[15]

That systematic resistance to climate change reform makes it all the more ironic that nothing did more to destroy Bush's reputation and undermine his popularity than Hurricane Katrina and its aftermath. This Category 5 storm slammed into the Gulf Coast between August 25 and August 30, 2005. Katrina crossed Florida, devastated the coasts of Alabama and Mississippi, before smashing into New Orleans and flooding the city. By the time it was over, Katrina affected much of the eastern United States and as far north as New York. It was one of the five deadliest hurricanes in American history, the worst since 1928, and did over $100 billion in damage.[16]

Most people called Katrina a natural disaster. It was nothing of the sort. While the hurricane was natural, the disaster was manmade. Over time more and more Americans have accepted the risk of living near the coasts and in other low-lying areas. New Orleans is largely under sea level, protected by a complex web of levees and dikes. Before the city became a major port for oil, gas, and petro chemicals, a complex of barrier islands and marshes protected it from all but the worst storm surges. To promote the energy industry, Louisiana allowed oil and gas companies to destroy most these natural barriers. The Army Corps of Engineers channeled the Mississippi from its meandering course to protect against flooding. Starved of silt, the delta began to shrink. When Katrina struck, the manmade defenses failed and the city was inundated. Most of the well to do escaped, but no one had made adequate provision to evacuate the elderly, disabled, and poor, the majority of whom were African American. For days, desperate survivors hung to rooftops. Thousands died, while tens of thousands huddled in the damaged Superdome sports arena.

Katrina forced Americans to consider a possible link between increasingly violent weather and global warming. Climate records made clear that temperatures were indeed rising as scientists had predicted. Warmer water creates more powerful storms. Was it a coincidence, as climate change deniers claimed, that nine of the ten most violent hurricanes on record occurred between 2004 (with three) and Hurricane Sandy in 2012? Scientists know that oceans today are on average one degree warmer than a century ago. The Gulf at the time Katrina became a Category 5 hurricane was two degrees warmer than normal. Further, *Nature* magazine published a study in 2005 that indicated that in the previous fifty years tropical storms around the world had intensified as temperatures rose. In 2011 the United States experienced fourteen separate weather events, ranging from Hurricane Irene to multiple tornado strikes, each causing more than $1 billion in damages. That set the record for costly disasters in a single year. If the weather was indeed getting more extreme, was it then not fiscally shortsighted to commit FEMA to the war on terror and cut its budget for storm relief?[17]

Barack Obama, much like Clinton, made a rhetorical commitment to deal with climate change, but environmental reform took a back seat to economy recovery. Early in Obama's first term the White House made clear that it planned to avoid discussing climate change and to focus instead on clean energy and jobs. The science on global warming, Obama's staff insisted, was too complex and contested to frame a coherent message. Republicans were busy turning the climate issue into a political football. Emboldened by the 2010 election, the Republican chair of the House Energy and Commerce Committee proposed legislation to strip the EPA of its power to regulate greenhouse gases under the Clean Air Act. "We firmly believe federal bureaucrats should not be unilaterally setting national climate change policy," he said.[18]

Despite his low profile on global warming, Obama chose to attend the 2009 Copenhagen conference, the first United Nations summit devoted exclusively to climate change. The administration called his participation "a sign of his continuing commitment and leadership to find a global solution to the global threat of climate change, and to lay the foundation for a new, sustainable and prosperous clean energy future." In the face of divisions among the participant nations and opposition at home, that commitment proved to be a shallow one.[19]

Eventually every member of the United Nations, 193 countries in all, sent delegates. When the delegates first met in Stockholm, atmospheric carbon dioxide had reached almost 330 ppm (parts per million); by the time the meeting at Copenhagen took place, the level had reached close to 390 ppm and was growing by several percent almost every year. The organizers hoped to frame a legally binding treaty that would commit the world community to reducing greenhouse gas emissions by 50 percent by 2050. Since the G-77 accounted for just 3 percent of greenhouse gases, any meaningful reduction depended on the actions of the G-20 (i.e., the world's top nineteen economies plus the European Union) that were responsible for 85 percent (China, Europe, and the United States alone equal around 50 percent).[20]

As protests clogged the streets, talks seemed on the verge of collapse. It was then that Obama and leaders from China, Brazil, and South Africa brokered a compromise. Two issues were at the core of the impasse: the old Stockholm rift between North and South and the rivalry between the United States and China. The two countries simply did not trust each other. China doubted the United States would carry out any pledge, while the Americans, bothered by the Chinese trade restrictions and bootlegging of intellectual property, did not believe much of anything the Chinese promised. Their resistance to any reasonable emissions verification further aggravated tensions.[21]

Underlying the disagreements at Copenhagen was once again the concern over sovereignty. The final treaty reflected the reluctance that many countries have of becoming answerable to an outside treaty authority. As one observer noted, "They will co-operate, but not under the threat of legal sanction." The Americans were, if anything, even greater sticklers on this point. Sovereignty issues plagued Wilson after Versailles and fed isolationist animosity to the United Nations. Even before Obama headed to Copenhagen, congressional Republicans had expressed their hostility to a binding agreement on climate change. Indeed, most Republicans continued to be climate change deniers. They sent a delegation to oppose the proceedings. Texan Joe Barton, the ranking Republican member of the House Committee on Energy and Commerce remarked, "I will not be one of the sycophants that say climate change is the biggest problem facing the world and we need to do all these draconian things that cost jobs."

Where Barton linked global warming restrictions to the economy and jobs, Senator James Inhofe from Oklahoma disparaged "the entire global warming, climate-change issue, which is an effort to dramatically and hugely increase regulation of each of our lives and business, and to raise our cost of living and taxes." In *The Greatest Hoax: How the Global Warming Conspiracy Threatens Your Future*, Inhofe set out to expose those "perpetuating the Hoax of global warming," and to explain why he believed their premises to be blatantly and categorically false. When a reporter in Copenhagen asked him about the origins of the hoax, Inhofe replied, "It started in the United Nations and the ones in the United States who really grab ahold of this is the Hollywood elite."[22]

By 2014 certain truths have become self-evident, despite continued vociferous opposition from climate change deniers. For one, the case for the human influence on global warming has become unassailable. Since its creation in 1988 the UN sponsored IPCC had in its first four reports never categorically made the case for the human role. Given that some that thousands of scientists contributed to the report and that some 120 governments review its content, the likelihood of politics entering into its formulation must be assumed. In 2014, however the IPCC stated the following:

"Human influence has been detected in warming of the atmosphere and the ocean, in changes in the global water cycle, in reductions in snow and ice, in global mean sea level rise, and in changes in some climate extremes. This evidence for human influence has grown since AR4. It is extremely likely that human influence has been the dominant cause of the observed warming since the mid-20th century."[23]

Surely, such certainty should have broken the logjam evident in Copenhagen and undermined the position of the Republican opposition in the US Congress. And surely anyone who anticipated a more enlightened policy process would be naïve or simply wrong.

One particular point of contention between Democrats and Republicans highlights their impasse. It involves the EPA's efforts to regulate utility emissions. The 1990 Clean Air Act, passed during the presidency of George H. W. Bush, required the EPA to formulate a rule on polluting gases. Opposition from special interests complicated its efforts to do so. The agency issued a rule in 2003, but the Bush administration exempted utilities from meeting the standards on mercury emissions, even though utilities were the primary source. As a results, many of the dirtiest plants remained in operation. A coalition of state governments and environmentalists sued, arguing the Bush rule violated the EPA's responsibility to reduce air pollution. A federal court in 2008 agreed that the rule evaded the Clean Air Act's requirement for mandatory cuts in toxic mercury pollution from power plants that burn coal and oil and ordered the EPA to rewrite it.

The battle over coal emissions, or as leaders of the GOP put it, the "War Against Coal," brought into focus the continued struggle over a progressive approach to both domestic and foreign environmental policy. Several times the Obama administration attempted to carry out court rulings to comply with requirements of the Clean Air Act, and repeatedly state and congressional conservatives fought back largely through the courts. In 2011 the EPA issued a new rule on utility emissions. At that time fossil fuels accounted for about 68 percent of all electricity generated in the United States and more than half of that came from coal. EPA director Lisa Jackson stressed the health and cost savings benefits of the new rule. It would, she asserted, save thousands of lives and offer economic and health benefits worth far more than the estimated $9.6 billion annual cost to utilities.[24]

For Republicans and the increasingly influential Tea Party insurgents, the public health and cost savings claims were deceptive. They charged that the rule would shut down scores of power plants, eliminate hundreds of thousands of jobs, and threaten electric supplies in some parts of the country. "The bottom line," said Scott H. Segal, who represented utilities, is that "this rule is the most expensive air rule that E.P.A. has ever proposed in terms of direct costs." Senator Inhofe vowed to block the new rule, calling it "a thinly veiled electricity tax that continues the Obama administration's war on affordable energy and is the latest in an unprecedented barrage of regulations that make up E.P.A.'s job-killing regulatory agenda."[25]

The Obama administration restoked those fires in June of 2014, when it issued new EPA rules on coal emissions. These were far stricter than earlier regulations designed to cut carbon emissions 30 percent by 2030. As before, issues of sovereignty, science, and sustainability underlay disagreements. Sustainability is obviously the long- term goal of reduced gas emissions as the symptoms of more violent weather, melting ice caps, and deteriorating water quality make painfully clear the consequences of further inaction. In that spirit the Obama administration in 2009 pledged that the United States would cut its greenhouse gases 17 percent from 2005 levels by 2020, and 83 percent by 2050. The 2014 IPCC report gave those pledges even greater impetus when it put the full weight of science behind the rising clamor for reducing global gas emissions.

Even as science and sustainability supported the case for coordinated national and international action on climate, sovereignty issues remained an impediment. At the state and federal levels, as well as among major world economies, special interests challenged the authority of those seeking new restraints. Domestically, coal-producing states such as West Virginia and Wyoming and upwind generating states, joined by traditional foes of enhanced federal regulation, led the outcry. The US Chamber of Commerce predicted that the rule might reduce GDP by $50 billion annually. The Obama administration had not been unmindful of those concerns. The new rules gave states a wide menu of policy options to comply with. They would be allowed to modify their electricity grids with renewables such as wind and solar, as well as introducing more efficient technologies and joining "cap and trade" programs.

Sovereignty, of course, also had international ramifications. China and India, both heavily reliant on dirty coal to power their electric grids, long resisted American proposals for more stringent standards. Why should they put their economies at risk if the United States did little to curb its own excess emissions? With the new EPA rules as a bargaining chip, US delegates at upcoming UN climate talks would hold a much stronger hand. "I fully expect action by the United States to spur others in taking concrete action," Christiana Figueres, executive secretary of the United Nations Framework on Climate Change, said. One positive step in that direction occurred in June when the Supreme Court ruled 6–2 that the EPA did indeed have the authority to protect downwind states from airborne pollutants.[26] This debate makes clear the need for solutions in which the authority of science trumps the parochialism of so many state actors.

For Progressives such as Theodore Roosevelt and Gifford Pinchot the need for balance between science and sovereignty would be self-evident. TR would flail the Joe Bartons and James Inhofes of his party, as he occasionally did such diehard reactionaries as Nelson Aldrich and Joe Cannon, for allowing narrow ideology and special interests to frustrate the public good. When Cannon resisted such reforms as meat inspection, TR used science to give added weight to Upton Sinclair's condemnations of the meatpackers. His global perspective, though containing elements of the jingoism and ethnocentrism of many contemporary conservatives, led him to negotiate an end to the Russo-Japanese War in 1906 and accept John Hay's "Open Door" principles. He was an imperialist, but also a realist. The battle against climate change reform thus highlights the ways in which current politics ignores the Progressive heritage. Reformers in that tradition conceive sovereignty and science as instruments to lead the world away from the precipice of global warming into a sustainable future.

Notes

1. John McNeill, *Something New Under the Sun* (New York: W.W. Norton, 2001), xxiv. For a brief explanation of water in the west see Fred Pearce, *When the Waters Run Dry: Water—The Defining Crisis of the Twenty-First Century* (Beacon Press: Boston, 2006), 9–18, 59–60.
2. Ian Tyrrel, *Crisis of This Wasteful Nation* (Chicago: University of Chicago Press, forthcoming), 12–20. Also see Douglas Brinkley, *The Wilderness Warrior, Theodore Roosevelt and the Crusade for America* (New York: Harper Perennial, 2010).
3. The classic statement on this concept is Sam Hayes, *Conservation and the Gospel of Efficiency* (Cambridge, MA: Harvard University Press, 1957).
4. The material on the seal hunting and bird treaty is in Kurk Dorsey, "The Potential and the Reality of Safeguarding the Environment Through American Diplomacy," in *Historians and Nature: A Comparative Approach*, eds. Ursula Lehmkuhl and Hermann Wellenruether (New York: Bloomsbury, 2007), 277–286. See also Kurk Dorsey, *The Dawn of Conservation Diplomacy* (Seattle: University of Washington Press, 1998).
5. "Welcome to the Anthropocene," *Economist*, May 28, 2011, 11. http://sandiegofreepress.org/2012/11/extreme-weather-watch-super-storm-sandy-the-new-normal.
6. http://www.aip.org/history/climate/public.htm.
7. Spencer Weart, *The Discovery of Global Warming* (Cambridge, MA: Harvard University Press, 2008), 67–68.
8. Ibid., 158–162.
9. Ibid., 164; http://www.ipcc.ch.
10. Weart, 166–167. http://unfccc.int/kyoto_protocol/items/2830.php.
11. Ibid., 167. On Bush's approach to environmental regulation see Jacob S. Hacker and Paul Pierson, *Off Center: The Republican Revolution and the Erosion of Democracy* (New Haven, CT: Yale University Press, 2005), 93–100.
12. http://www.presidency.ucsb.edu/ws/?pid=45811.
13. Ibid. Meet the Press: 2007 "Meet the Candidates" series, Sep 30, 2007.
14. Jo Becker and Barton Gellman, "Angler: The Cheney Vice Presidency: Leaving No Tracks," *Washington Post*, June 27, 2007. See also http://www.epa.gov/nsr/.
15. Ibid.
16. Richard D. Knabb, Jamie R. Rhome, Daniel P. Brown, National Hurricane Center (December 20, 2005) (PDF). Hurricane Katrina: August 23–30, 2005 (Tropical Cyclone Report). United States National Oceanic and Atmospheric Administration's National Weather Service.
17. Eric S. Blake, Christopher W. Landsea, National Hurricane Center (August 2011). "The Deadliest, Costliest, and Most Intense United States Tropical Cyclones from 1851 to 2010 (And Other Frequently Requested Hurricane Facts)," (NOAA Technical Memorandum NWS NHC-6). United States National Oceanic and Atmospheric Administration's

National Weather Service. November 27, 2012. http://www.c2es.org/science-impacts/extreme-weather/hurricane-katrina.

18. Darryl Fears, "House GOP Readies Bill to Prohibit EPA from Regulating Carbon Emissions," *Washington Post*, February 3, 2011.

19. Scott Horsley, "Obama To Attend Copenhagen Climate Summit," NPR, *All Things Considered*, November 25, 2009.

20. NOAA, Earth Monitoring Research Station, http://www.esrl.noaa.gov/gmd/ccgg/trends/.

21. John Broder, "Many Goals Remain Unmet in 5 Nations' Climate Deal," *New York Times*, December 18, 2009; Michael Levi, "The Party's Over: Why Copenhagen was the Climate Conference to End All Climate Conferences." *Slate*, Posted Monday, December 21, 2009, http://www.slate.com/articles/health_and_science/green_room/2009/12/the_partys_over.html.

22. http://crooksandliars.com/logan-murphy/republican-jim-inhofe-goes-copenhagen. See also Kurk Dorsey, *Whales and Nations: Diplomacy on the High Seas* (Seattle: University of Washington Press, 2013) who identifies sovereignty along with science and sustainability as the foundation of the Progressive conservation approach to environmental policy. From his perspective we can see how current Republicans have warped the Progressive worldview.

23. http://www.ipcc.ch/report/ar5/wg2/, 10.3–10.6, 10.9.

24. John Broder, E.P.A. "Issues Limits on Mercury Emissions," *New York Times* blog, December 21, 2011. http://www.eia.gov/tools/faqs/faq.cfm?id=427&t=3.

25. Ibid.

26. Robert Barnes, "Supreme Court: EPA Can Regulate Green House Gas Emissions with Some Limits," *Washington Post*, June 23, 2014. See also Coral Davenport, "Obama to Take Action to Slash Coal Pollution," *New York Times*, June 1, 2014.

12

Bringing Human Rights
and Women's Rights Home

From the Roosevelt Era to the Present

ELLEN CHESLER

The new Four Freedoms Park, Louis Kahn's stunning memorial to Franklin Delano Roosevelt, inhabits the southern tip of Roosevelt Island just east of midtown Manhattan with the austere yet powerful presence of ancient temple grounds. Two promenades lined by graceful linden trees—each representing a founding member state of the United Nations—face down the East River toward the broad expanse of the Atlantic Ocean and, far away, the European continent, whose freedom Americans under FDR's determined leadership helped secure. They converge at a simple structure of white granite with vistas open to the sky and sea. Etched in an interior wall are the famous Four Freedoms President Roosevelt proclaimed in January of 1941, to frame a moral argument for US military engagement in the Second World War months before Pearl Harbor. The words still resonate and inspire.[1]

Content at the start to view New Deal programs as the improvisations of a caring state in a time of crisis, Roosevelt, as many scholars now agree, came over the course of his presidency to a deeper understanding of social and economic well-being as necessary foundations of human security and therein of democracy. His landmark speech joined freedom of speech and freedom of worship, traditionally guaranteed in a US Constitution crafted out of the arguably simpler world of the eighteenth century, with new positive government obligations to secure "freedom from want" and "freedom from fear"—"everywhere in the world"—as he put it in characteristically simple but bold language appended to the typed draft of his remarks in his own handwriting.[2]

The park stands across the tidal waters of the East River from the imposing modernist structures of the United Nations. Designed in the early 1950s by a virtuoso partnership of American and Scandinavian architects, they are sleek, forward-looking, light-filled buildings of glass and stone, intended to reflect

Roosevelt's hope for a better world, secured by a strong American presence and by globally governed organizations that would protect human rights and marshal resources for human development.

Currently undergoing renovation, the UN buildings inspire faith in the possibility of dreaming big and of building bold partnerships to realize those dreams. But if the UN's architecture has more than withstood the test of time, what of the UN's animating principles?

While campaigning for president in 2008, Barack Obama lionized Roosevelt and his generation for creating the UN, the Bretton Woods institutions, and NATO—for recognizing that "instead of constraining our power, these institutions magnified it." Obama pledged to pursue essential reforms in these aging edifices of the postwar order—battered as they have been over so many years by the fissures of the Cold War and by continuous local and regional conflicts and realignments in the years since the Soviet demise. He challenged Americans "to keep pace with the fast-moving threats we face" not by retreating altogether from institutions of global governance, or by demanding perfection, but by retooling them to find better solutions to the problems that trouble our world and burden our conscience, problems the United States cannot solve on its own.[3]

Governing is never quite as straightforward as campaigning. Yet, in a stark repudiation of George W. Bush's confrontational course at the UN, President Obama has sent two of his most trusted foreign policy advisors there as ambassadors, Susan Rice and Samantha Power, both outspoken advocates of multilateralism and human rights. Former Clinton national security aide and senior Obama advisor Anthony Lake, took over at UNICEF. And former senior White House Counselor John Podesta, among others, has kept an eye on negotiations over the UN's Sustainable Development Goals, new targets to improve upon the much-heralded but only partial successes of the popular Millennium Development Goals adopted by the UN in 2000 to guide poverty alleviation efforts.

America also rejoined the newly reorganized and reformed UN Human Rights Council, a streamlined successor body to an unwieldy Human Rights Commission, and has engaged robustly with the bodies that oversee the few UN human rights treaties the United States has ratified—treaties to advance civil and political rights, to end racial discrimination, and to prohibit torture. We are there taking our punches even as revelation of questionable US military practices, the continuation of forced detention at Guantanamo Bay, and serious concerns about internet surveillance call into question our integrity on such matters.

Early on, President Obama publicly called for an end to the use of Bush-era enhanced interrogation techniques, since condemned by the US Senate Select Committee on Intelligence in a damning report on the Central Intelligence Agency, that contains detailed descriptions of antiterrorism practices commonly understood as torture, though the committee never actually uses that term.[4] And at the same time, in a show of support for policies advancing "freedom from want and fear," the

Obama administration filled leadership positions at the US Agency for International Development (USAID) and the World Bank, not with the high-profile financiers and businessmen typical of the past, but instead with Rajiv Shah and Jim Yong Kim, both physicians with proud commitments to public health as a basic human right.

Yet nowhere did President Obama's foreign policy realign more directly with Franklin Roosevelt's expansive vision for US global obligations than in the choice of Hillary Rodham Clinton as his first secretary of state. A consistent voice for a robust US military presence, Clinton is nonetheless widely respected for having crafted a foreign policy that artfully balanced "hard" and "soft" power.

Secretary Clinton is also well known for having integrated concern about human rights, and especially women's rights, into mainstream policy considerations by repeatedly invoking empirical data to demonstrate that women with greater political, economic, social, and cultural rights and opportunities help drive the prosperity and security of families, communities, and eventually nations.[5] In her framing, societies that routinely tolerate discrimination and fail to condemn violence against women and girls cannot hope to incubate the habits of respect and tolerance on which good citizenship and successful democratic practice depends. These behaviors, long hidden behind claims for pluralism in culture and religious belief, therefore demand universal legal remedy. Clinton positions the issue of women's rights as a moral imperative but also as a necessary condition of success in American defense, diplomacy, and development efforts—the right thing and also the smart thing to do. And through her efforts, large numbers of people who simply never thought this way before have come to agree. More than just rhetoric, she also left in place structural and policy changes at the US Department of State, which her successor, John Kerry, has earnestly advanced.[6]

Though trumpeted more energetically in recent years, none of these claims is entirely new and all have deep roots in the Roosevelt legacy and in the larger history of the UN's human rights and development efforts that ought to be more widely recognized. This brief essay looks back at the evolution of ideas about human rights over more than six decades and charts the development of a parallel language and institutional architecture of women's rights. It encourages progressives today to hold fast to the principles that underlie visionary Roosevelt-era rights and development constructs as our own intellectual and moral bedrock—as ideas and values that ought to remain the foundation for continued work on behalf of political, economic, and social justice, both in the larger world and right here at home.

THE ROOSEVELT VISION
FOR HUMAN RIGHTS

Franklin Roosevelt's "Four Freedoms" gained widespread attention around the world when he and Winston Churchill met secretly at sea in August of 1941 and

produced what came to be known as the Atlantic Charter, with its visionary proc-
lamation that people deserve the right to "live out their lives in freedom from fear
and want." Within a year twenty-four additional countries had joined in a formal
"Declaration of the United Nations" that pledged the allied nations to a war waged
in pursuit of basic human dignity. Growing recognition of Hitler's heinous crimes
against humanity then strengthened resolve for a new postwar order.[7]

The human rights regime inaugurated by the Atlantic Charter distinguished itself
by integrating traditional civil rights with a call for economic and social justice. It
also declared that the benefits of this vision would extend beyond nation-states to
grant protection to individual citizens within them and would be applied within, as
well as across, national borders. As the historian Elizabeth Borgwardt persuasively
argues, Roosevelt and Churchill may have approved language conferring rights
largely for inspirational or poetic effect and not fully contemplated the implications
for British colonialism and American segregation, but what began as merely a rhetorical flourish has had a profound impact.[8]

Indifferent to many skeptics, Roosevelt also held fast to his convictions. "True
individual freedom is not possible without economic security and independence,"
he proclaimed in his State of the Union Address of 1944, which outlined a second
US "bill of rights" that not only underscored the importance of established civil and
political freedoms but also the right to a useful job, a decent standard of living, adequate food, housing, health care, education, recreation, and a measure of economic
security during unemployment, disability and old age—rights not necessarily to be
secured by the Constitution but instead to be guaranteed through federal legislation
and enforced by the courts. Legal scholar Cass Sunstein takes the speech seriously
as a foundation for later advances in social welfare and heralds it as one of the most
important and underestimated of the twentieth century.[9]

In the final year before Roosevelt's untimely death in 1945, just as the war was
ending and weeks before the UN was chartered in San Francisco, a visibly weakened
and ailing president worked and traveled tirelessly as far as Yalta to secure the single
most important goal of his wartime presidency: the creation of the United Nations
and other multilateral institutions—including the World Bank, the International
Monetary Fund, a reinvigorated International Labor Organization, and the global
and regional human rights courts emanating from Nuremberg—all meant to assure
that if individual nations fail to protect basic human dignity, others, led by America's
example, would do so.[10]

In the formal practice of diplomacy, of course, Roosevelt's new way of thinking
required nothing short of an intellectual revolution. Immediate skepticism came
from professional diplomats, especially in the United States, where there was little
agreement on how to balance concern about human rights and global governance
with meaningful mechanisms of enforcement and concerns about the need to protect national sovereignty. In San Francisco, where the UN charter was finalized in
the spring of 1945, the will of the major powers prevailed—best exemplified by the

veto power of each of the five permanent members in the newly created Security Council. The General Assembly, meanwhile, was given responsibility to establish conditions for the respect of rights and the advancement of higher standards of living, but without much accountability. In London the following year, when the recently widowed Eleanor Roosevelt joined the five-member US delegation to the first meeting of the United Nations, she was shuffled off to the Social, Humanitarian, and Cultural Committee of the General Assembly, popularly known as "Committee III" and considered a relatively insignificant and safe berth.

Committee III, however, authorized a Commission on Human Rights that unanimously elected Mrs. Roosevelt as its chair and began drafting a human rights declaration. For three years she then presided patiently over contentious debate, earning widespread respect. The Universal Declaration of Human Rights (UDHR) begins with the bold conviction that "recognition of the inherent dignity and of the equal and inalienable rights of all members of the human family is the foundation of freedom, justice and peace in the world." It encourages all peoples and nations to adopt its specific provisions as "a common standard of achievement" and obliges citizens to accept ultimate responsibility as individuals for the enforcement of rights, even as it contains only the power to review—to name and shame—but not to sanction state violations.

Most significantly, the UDHR moves beyond traditional civil claims involving the personal liberties and political safeguards of individual freedom to an expanded definition of state obligation requiring investment in education, employment, health care, housing, safety, and social security as necessary foundations for productive citizenship. For Mrs. Roosevelt these commitments realized the firm conviction she shared with her husband that totalitarianism had taken root in the economic and social upheavals of the twentieth century.[11]

WOMEN'S RIGHTS AS HUMAN RIGHTS

The Atlantic Charter conferred rights on "all the men everywhere in the world," but women, whose lives were dramatically altered by the Second World War, also claimed its promise. The war ended with greater numbers of women than ever before educated, working for formal wages, and experiencing an unprecedented degree of freedom. Many entered civilian workforces to fill critical jobs, while others directly supported military operations as office personnel, nurses, and volunteers. Women in Europe joined movements of resistance, and in the colonial world they rose to positions of leadership in movements of national liberation and independence. Everywhere the rights of women were violated as they became civilian victims of conflict, enduring rape, prostitution, forced migration and other tragedies. These incontrovertible facts contradict common allegations in recent years that the modern women's rights agenda has largely been a product of Western feminism.

Eleanor Roosevelt was one of only seventeen female delegates from eleven countries at the UN's founding in London in 1946; however, supported by a robust nongovernmental community of activists, they immediately issued a statement calling
for women to engage in public affairs—to come forward and share in the work of
peace and reconstruction, as they had done in the war itself.[12] They also argued for
the creation of a Commission on the Status of Women (CSW), independent from
the Human Rights Commission, a move Mrs. Roosevelt at first opposed on the
grounds that a separate body was not likely to be equal in resources or influence.
With nearly unanimous sentiment for the opposite view that women would benefit
from focused attention, however, she changed her mind and had the US delegation
introduce the resolution to create the commission, which then played a major role
in drafting the Universal Declaration by insisting on gender-neutral language that
guaranteed rights to "all human beings" not just to men.

The UDHR thus stakes a landmark claim that discrimination against women
be viewed as a necessary and appropriate matter of international concern, not as
a category privileged and protected by local sovereignty or by local customary
or religious practices governing marriage and family relations. It also recognizes
that women oppressed in private places cannot realistically claim their legitimate
rights as human beings. The state must be obligated to extend rights to women and
eliminate everyday forms of discrimination. To these ends, the document goes on
to establish broad protections for women as citizens and workers and specifically
addresses long-contested matters of family law, including full consent to marriage
and divorce and the right to resources to care for children when divorced, widowed
or abandoned.[13]

Off the radar screen of US "Cold Warriors" skeptical of human rights, the women
of the CSW then managed to draft and negotiate the adoption of binding treaties governing women's political rights, nationality rights, consent and minimum
age of marriage, property rights, educational opportunities, and labor standards.
Landmark studies were also conducted documenting continued challenges and
leading to a new emphasis on the responsibility to provide women not just legal
protections but also greater benefits of development assistance.

In 1967 a formal Declaration on the Elimination of Discrimination Against
Women was written with the active participation of women from Afghanistan, who
in one of history's great ironies, introduced the concept that pervasive discrimination against women warrants the granting of special privileges since known as
"temporary special measures" at the UN, but an equivalent to the American legal
doctrine of affirmative action. The following year the UN marked the twentieth
anniversary of the UHDR with a special conference in Tehran, supported by the
ruling Pahlavi family under attack for violations of the rights of political dissidents,
where women's rights provided a rare arena of agreement including Russians eager
to call attention to the educational and employment opportunities their government had granted women, and Americans, for whom these issues were gaining

momentum as a result of an emerging second wave of feminism. The conference adopted resolutions encouraging support for a legal rights project to address gender discrimination and development assistance targeted to women, especially in agriculturally based economies based largely on women's labor. Most significantly, it identified family planning as a basic human right and paved the way for the establishment of a UN fund for population.[14]

Between 1975 and 1995, the UN sponsored four international conferences on women that produced wildly optimistic blueprints for the achievement of concrete gains. They have been dismissed by some as lacking both focus and practical strategies for implementation, while others insist that however often they may still be violated, these plans of action have raised awareness, shaped aspirations, and in countless significant and concrete ways helped change laws and reshape behaviors.

In 1979, following two decades of documentation and deliberation, the UN Declaration on Women was codified as the binding Convention on the Elimination of All Forms of Discrimination against Women, commonly known as CEDAW. This visionary international women's bill of rights cautiously acknowledges the importance of traditional obligations to the family but also establishes new norms for participation by women in all dimensions of life. It gives precise definition and actionable protection to a broad range of women's rights in marriage and family relations, including property and inheritance and access to health care, with an explicit mention of family planning. It establishes the principle of equal protection for women as citizens in their own right entitled to suffrage, political representation, and other legal benefits; to education, including elementary and secondary education that provides professional and vocational training free of gender stereotypes and segregation; and to formal employment, deserving of equal pay, Social Security benefits and protection from sexual harassment and workplace discrimination on the grounds of marriage or maternity. In 1992, CEDAW was expanded so that gender-based violence is also formally identified as a fundamental violation of human rights, and governments are encouraged to take action.

This breakthrough drew on claims by feminists of evidence of demonstrable abuses of women "including torture, starvation, terrorism, and even murder" that continue to be routinely accepted without legal recourse in many places. "Crimes such as these against any group other than women would be recognized as a civil and political emergency as well as a gross violation of the victim's humanity," Charlotte Bunch of the Center for Women's Global Leadership at Rutgers University wrote in a path-breaking 1990 article in *Human Rights Quarterly*. In 1993, at the Vienna Conference on Human Rights, drawing on a slogan that originated with a grassroots coalition of Philippine women, Bunch first made the claim that "women's rights are human rights," later trumpeted around the world and given resonance by Hillary Clinton at the UN Fourth World Conference on Women in Beijing.[15]

US ENGAGEMENT WITH HUMAN RIGHTS

From the start, Americans of all ideological stripes viewed human rights skeptically, insisting on the country's exceptional status with respect to rights protection, despite ample evidence to the contrary. Conservative Republicans saw Eleanor Roosevelt's commitment to social, economic, and cultural rights as a menacing back door to Communism and an affront to classic principles of liberal economics. Southern Democrats with senior positions as Senate committee chairs also feared the implications for Jim Crow–era racial practices. By 1951, the UN Human Rights Commission under her direction had drafted a Covenant on Human Rights, converting the declaration's general provisions into a binding treaty; however, it quickly fell victim to intensifying Cold War politics, with the Americans objecting to the inclusion of civil, political, social and economic rights under the same heading, and with the Soviets scuttling Mrs. Roosevelt's effort to broker a compromise by drafting two separate documents.

On taking office in 1953, President Dwight David Eisenhower announced to a shocked world that the United States would not be party to any human rights treaties and that Mrs. Roosevelt would not be reappointed when her term ended, despite an earlier commitment to non-partisanship at the UN. She then resigned immediately, traveling widely until her death nine years later, fervently promoting human rights against its many detractors and encouraging citizen education and involvement.[16]

All UN covenants on human rights remained locked in a stalemate until 1965, when global indignation over the apartheid policies in South Africa led to the adoption of the groundbreaking International Convention on the Elimination of all Forms of Racial Discrimination (ICERD). The United States, in the throes of its own civil rights revolution, then signed the treaty, although years would go by before the Senate assented to ratification. Within a year agreement was also reached on the terms of the two separate covenants Mrs. Roosevelt had long ago suggested: the International Covenant on Civil and Political Rights (ICCPR), which the Russians refused to ratify, and a second, the International Covenant on Social, Economic, and Cultural Rights (ICESR), which the Americans to this day have never signed. Nor did we ever bother to codify formal mechanisms for enforcing US obligations and cohering domestic law with human rights treaties. Still, an enduring system of international law was put in place, and the door was opened for human rights concepts and tools of enforcement to gain broader acceptance.

The administration of Jimmy Carter was the first to embrace human rights officially through the creation of a formal bureaucracy in the State Department, which focused on movements of liberation against oppressive regimes in Eastern Europe and in Latin and Central America. Carter signed the ICCPR and sent it to the Senate for ratification. At the same time, a robust nongovernmental human rights movement developed in the United States, its mission to protect citizens abroad from the unwarranted imposition of state power through suppression of assembly and expression, arbitrary arrest, imprisonment, and torture—the principal grounds on which human rights violations were long contested. To the extent this activity could be characterized as anti-Communist, it briefly gained bipartisan support, with President Ronald Reagan embracing human rights in defense of Soviet political dissidents, even as he provided cover for autocratic regimes elsewhere and undermined the activist social and economic legacy of the New Deal at home. Reagan signed the commonly known UN Convention against Torture in 1988, though it was not ratified until 1994, during Bill Clinton's presidency. Under George H. W. Bush, who had served as UN Ambassador under Richard Nixon, the Senate finally ratified the ICCPR in 1992.[17]

The fall of the Soviet Union had by then also presented an opportunity to reopen debate over human rights and broaden considerations in accord with more expansive original intentions. With the backing of well established US civil rights groups, and with the eyes of the world also focused on South Africa's transition to majority rule, President Clinton in 1994 also helped push ICERD through the Senate. While all three treaties remain burdened by reservations and understandings, which in the eyes of some critics significantly compromise their domestic value and impact, the plain truth is that the United States now regularly endures periodic UN reviews, standing before world bodies and laying bare its own often compromised record at home on such racially charged issues as discrimination in education, police brutality, incarceration, and capital punishment. These reviews also elicit hard-hitting shadow reports from US civil society organizations. For example, in the summer of 2014, a regular ICCPR review of US practices occasioned a damning analysis of segregation in US schools from the Leadership Conference on Civil and Human Rights, the nation's premier civil rights advocacy organization, with a membership of some 200 organizations.[18]

In the fractious political decades since, however, there have been no further UN treaty ratifications. Political scientist David Kaye recently observed in *Foreign Affairs* that the US Senate now routinely rejects treaties "as if it were sport."[19] Still eluding US endorsement are three important pillars of human rights enforcement: the International Covenant on Economic, Social and Cultural Rights (ICESCR), the Rome Statute authorizing the International Criminal Court (ICC), and the Convention on the Elimination of all Forms of Discrimination against Women (CEDAW). A treaty to expand the rights of the disabled is also still pending, despite a poignant (if shameful) recent floor debate featuring a wheelchair-bound former Republican Senator Robert Dole who urged passage on behalf of US veterans like himself who had given their limbs in service to their country.

A high procedural bar requiring a two-thirds majority, or sixty-seven Senate votes, hobbles the Senate, as does intensified conservative opposition to international entanglements generally and to the progressive social and economic norms that UN treaty bodies have had the courage to establish and defend, if not always to enforce, over many years. As a result, the United States, far from protecting its sovereignty, has gradually lost its leadership in shaping global practices on human rights and in other pressing global problem solving on such matters as monitoring of the seas, climate change, and nuclear deterrence, also addressed through treaty bodies.

As Kaye observes, Americans increasingly suffer the "self-inflicted wound of diminishing relevance." The rest of the world has moved on without us. With respect to human rights, this means that US judges and lawyers have much less influence on the development of legal standards around the world—a robust local and regional enterprise that now looks mainly to the European Court of Human Rights, which dates back to 1948, or to the Inter-American Court, in which we do not participate—or more recently to the African Court of Human and Peoples' Rights (ACHPR), established in 2004. This is a poignant irony given the increasing reach of Americans globally. By Kaye's account, the Obama administration has also constructed a patchwork of political and legal strategies to temporarily get around the Senate, lending US know-how and resources to institutions like the ICC or the UN's World Health Organization, without direct involvement in treaties. He calls this "stealth multilateralism." It represents a valiant effort but not one with the transparency or full legal force and effect of signing on to an international accord.[20]

Nowhere, perhaps, is the US impact more deeply compromised than in recent forums on women's rights. Today the rights of women are enshrined in international law and also in the constitutions and case law of more and more countries. Locally, lawyers all over the world regularly call on provisions of the CEDAW treaty when petitioning for further reforms. Meanwhile, a robust UN CEDAW committee meets regularly to review the progress of 188 UN member states that have ratified are making to address violations of its provisions. What is known in UN parlance as an "optional protocol" also permits petition to that committee by individual parties who have not been able to redress their grievances locally. And perhaps most significantly, the International Criminal Court recently agreed to try perpetrators of rape as war criminals, establishing the important precedent that criminal sanctions, not just moral ones, may attach to violations of women. Many CEDAW signatories originally exercised their UN-permitted right to reserve on aspects of the agreement not to their liking, especially Article 16 with its family law provisions. But the trend of recent years, even in historically conservative Muslim countries such as Morocco, Tunisia, and just recently, Yemen—though the matter, to be sure, is still contested and volatile—has been to remove these reservations altogether.

A recent report by the International Center for Research on Women highlights examples of how CEDAW has been translated into concrete legislation and also used by national and local courts, across a diverse range of countries: Mexico, in 2007, under major pressure from domestic women's groups and from the international community, drew on CEDAW's Article 19 to write a detailed General Law on Women's Access to a Life Free from Violence, since adopted by all thirty-two states and now fully enforceable as a matter of local criminal procedure. The highest court of Bangladesh in 2009 reached a landmark decision to prohibit sexual harassment in the workplace and then used CEDAW's Article 11 to issue guidelines for national legislation. The Philippines that same year passed what is known there as a "Magna Carta" for women, a comprehensive human rights instrument, relying on CEDAW for its definitions of what constitutes discrimination and in the drafting of specific provisions on equal representation and protection from violence. In Tajikistan, a land reform law was reformed to align with CEDAW Article 16, and in the immediate six years that followed, the proportion of women owning farmland rose to 14 percent, a gain considered significant. In Latin America, where increasing numbers of women are now serving as judges, a UN program provides training on state obligations under CEDAW, which now routinely inform court decisions. Kuwait, under pressure from the international community, finally extended suffrage to women in 2004 and within five years elected four women to its fifty-seat parliament. The Netherlands, a destination country for sex trafficking, responded to criticisms from the CEDAW committee with 2006 legislation increasing penalties for trafficker and protections for victims, among other reforms.[21]

These meaningful reforms and advances are occurring, however, without direct involvement by the American government. We are simply no longer at the table. Though CEDAW enjoys the active participation of more UN member states than any other treaty, the United States continues to reside in the unlikely company of Iran, Sudan, Somalia, and a few Pacific Island nations in having failed to ratify. President Jimmy Carter signed the treaty shortly before leaving office in 1979 and sent it to the Senate for ratification where it has remained in limbo ever since. For years the famously cantankerous Jesse Helms of North Carolina attacked the treaty as the work of "radical feminists" with "an anti-family" agenda. Hearings were held in 1994 and again in 2002, as George W. Bush's administration justified the war in Afghanistan at least in part as a response to the Taliban's gross violation of women's rights but then again prevented a floor vote.

It has long been difficult to generate grassroots energy in support of US ratification of CEDAW because of the widespread, if false, assumption that valuable as it may be to women elsewhere, American women don't really need CEDAW, since they are protected by a substantial body of US case law prohibiting sex discrimination in education and employment and protecting reproductive rights. Recent rulings by the US Supreme Court, however, challenge this complacency and call attention to the fact that the United States remains the only modern industrialized country in the world with no constitutional principle explicitly addressing sexual equality. American women's rights have, in effect, been cobbled together case by case by determined lawyers, arguing derivatively from the due process clause of the Fourteenth Amendment and from civil rights protections intended to cover race. Conservative decisions rendered over the past three years by a majority on the court undermining pay equity, class action law suits, the new contraceptive mandate in the Affordable Care Act, and abortion rights are examples of just how precarious

the situation of women actually remains. US Supreme Court Justices Stephen
Breyer and Ruth Bader Ginsburg have both written and spoken of the positive benefits of applying international standards in pursuing equality under U.S. law. They
cited ICERD in their concurring opinion in *Grutter v. Bollinger*, the University of
Michigan case that upheld the use of affirmative action, for example. Ginsburg also
points regularly to the value of CEDAW as a framework for increasing governmental obligation to promote women's full participation and to protect parenting by
addressing paid family leave, flexible work arrangements, and childcare.[22]

President Barack Obama and secretaries Clinton and Kerry have all publicly
endorsed CEDAW ratification but, seeing no immediate prospect of success, never
pushed the Senate Foreign Relations Committee to raise the matter. The Clinton
State Department's Global Ambassador for Women's Rights, Melanne Verveer,
acknowledged in Senate Judiciary Sub-Committee testimony that America's historic leadership on these issues is compromised by our failure to ratify, and that was
as far as it ever got. In a recent appearance, former Secretary Clinton when asked
about prospects for CEDAW ratification responded with a terse call to "change the
Senate."[23]

In the spirit of "stealth diplomacy," the Obama administration instead redoubled
its efforts to advance global women's rights by other means. To its credit, it put a
number of administrative reforms in place so that US investments in diplomacy and
development are for the first time held accountable to metrics of women's status
shown to impact the larger conditions of peace and prosperity our foreign policies
are meant to advance. Simply put, this means that officials high and low—including
ambassadors and foreign-service officers, many of them still skeptical—are now
instructed to take into consideration indicators long routinely ignored in assessing a country's well-being, such as the average age of women at marriage, female
birthrates, educational achievement, labor force participation, and political representation. Ironically, one of the most effective enforcers of this approach is the
Millennium Challenge Corporation, a bilateral development enterprise established
during the Bush presidency as an end-run around the UN, with authorizing legislation that under pressure from progressive women's rights advocates requires investments by partner governments in local women's organizations.

As Secretary of State, Clinton also released a US National Action Plan on Women,
Peace, and Security, bringing the country into compliance with UN Security Council
Resolution 1325, an agreement adopted to bring more attention and resources to
what is now widely recognized as an alarming incidence of violence against women
worldwide. Resolution 1325 and several subsequent Security Council actions also
link gender-based violence to larger conditions of insecurity and instability in countries and regions and mandate the integration of more women into UN-sponsored
conflict resolution and peace building. Having the powerful UN Security Council,
and not just the weaker General Assembly, take on women's rights itself represents
a step forward. US participation is also significant because the action plan extends

beyond diplomacy and foreign aid to incorporate Department of Defense operations and budgets with far greater reach and scale.

In signing on, senior Pentagon officials pointed to the Marine Corps' Female Engagement Teams and the Army's Cultural Support Teams—then supporting ongoing combat operations in Afghanistan by sending women soldiers to engage with local women's populations—as examples of American military strategies already in line with the new UN objectives. The National Action Plan also endorses increased US investment in programs for food security, public health, and small women-led business formation as effective conflict prevention tools. It advocates for strengthening protection for women and girls in conflict situations, with greater legal accountability for rape and services for female victims of violence. It encourages participation of women in peace processes as has been successful recently in small countries like Liberia, Darfur, and Kosovo. And, finally, it calls for greater support of women-led civil society organizations in post- conflict relief and reconstruction efforts and in refugee situations.[24] Recent headlines calling attention to the indifference of senior US military officials to accusations of sexual harassment and assault in their own ranks, however, underscores the need for greater accountability to the plan at home, as well as abroad.

Doggedly, the Clinton-led State Department also forged an "Equal Futures Partnership" among what now numbers twenty-seven major countries, along with representatives of the UN, the World Bank, leading corporations, and nongovernmental organizations, all committed to women's empowerment. The alliance, with continued high-profile support from the White House and Secretary of State John Kerry, acts as a clearinghouse, forging partnerships and jump-starting a host of worthy projects. Translating good intentions into concrete operational plans is always a worthy achievement, as are the efforts to build public-private partnerships to help women. But again they are nonbinding political agreements, lacking long-term enforceability or commitment.[25]

Also noteworthy was Secretary Clinton's strong support for new leadership at the World Bank, which has marshaled evidence to support the claim that the prosperity it seeks to advance in the world cannot be achieved without "engendering development." Major reports released in 2012 and 2014 argue forcefully that reforms in social and legal norms holding women and girls back are necessary drivers of stability and growth, a long-held principle of feminist economists and activists on the ground. The reports embrace a cross-cutting agenda linking shared prosperity to women's economic participation and corollary investments in women's education, reproductive and sexual health care, protection from violence, control over property and housing, support for the care of children and the elderly, and greater political representation. An institutional reorganization is currently underway to make the advancement of women's "voice and agency" a central dimension of future bank investments and programming. This is no small matter for an institution long criticized by progressives and others for top-down infrastructure projects that made no effort to advance human rights or protect workers of either sex and thus benefitted elites but did little to reduce poverty.[26]

CONCLUSION AND FUTURE PROSPECTS

Attention to human rights violations by major development institutions, and in recent years by several high-profile US-based global corporations, may well increase prospects for the advancement of human rights norms, despite the continued obstruction of conservatives in Congress. Credit is due to progressive leadership in Washington but also to the vitality of US-based nongovernmental organizations working in this field. In recent years an impressive array of them have vastly expanded programs to encompass a full range of human rights concerns: civil, political, economic, social, and cultural. None perhaps has greater impact than Human Rights Watch, now with programs in ninety countries. Human Rights Watch enjoys a well-earned reputation for exposing violations through carefully researched reports written with rigor and reliability and eliciting significant governmental response and reform. This venerable organization is forging local and regional collaborations to push the defense of human rights in new and innovative directions, especially with respect to women's rights, and has vastly expanded its reach and its impact. It now also supports a robust US domestic program, applying a human rights lens to violations of the US criminal justice and immigration systems, to discrimination based on race, gender, and sexual identity, and to rights of workers, in the face of the country's rising tide of inequality.[27]

The Center for Constitutional Rights has brought successful litigation on behalf of Guantanamo Bay detainees and other victims of the war on terror. So too Amnesty International is now building a "Bring Human Rights Home" campaign, focusing on US surveillance abuses but also on the rights of women and LGBT populations. The powerful Leadership Conference on Civil and Human Rights is not only engaging with UN human rights instruments and advocating US treaty ratifications including CEDAW but also taking on long-held notions of US exceptionalism by positioning socioeconomic justice in our country as a matter of fundamental human rights, just as they are seen elsewhere. Human Rights First, an association of lawyers who bring litigation on behalf of clients and also advocate with the US government, has likewise broadened its reach beyond traditional civil and political concerns. A new organization, the National Economic and Social Rights Initiative (NESRI), is also partnering with community-based organizations to build a broad grassroots movement for health, housing, education, and work with dignity, using the language of human rights. And, of course, protection and rights for gays and lesbians is advancing rapidly with a successful national lobbying effort organized under the banner of the Human Rights Campaign.[28]

To sustain this momentum may well require the congressional realignment Secretary Clinton endorses. It will also need continued executive vigilance and raises the stakes for maintaining progressive representation in the White House after 2016. Clinton recently announced a new program to gather data and document the progress women around the world have made in the two decades since Beijing, which she oversaw at the Clinton Foundation before launching her second bid for the presidency. As a woman who has by her own admission shattered a lot of glass, and may well break more, she called the program (with no apparent self-consciousness) "No Ceilings: The Full Participation Project."[29]

Continued support for an expansive human rights regime, however, will require an intellectual shift as well as a political one. Americans have in recent years too often come to associate the language of rights with identity-based claims pitting one group against another. This leaves us far behind other countries where human rights have taken root as an assertion of our common humanity and shared claims as individuals to basic necessities of life.

Bringing human rights home will also require conviction and courage in the face of inevitable naysayers. To that end, we might again take inspiration from Franklin Roosevelt and remember that the Four Freedoms—now so widely admired—inspired considerable derision in his own day. Many critics initially characterized the president's speech and its many promises as "unattainable nonsense." But Roosevelt, in response, simply leveled them as "literalists and skeptics" who, had they lived in a prior century or an earlier millennium "would have sneered and said that the Declaration of Independence was utter piffle . . . laughed uproariously at the Magna Charta . . . [or] derided Moses when he came from the Mountain with the Ten Commandments." If only we had leaders today who could talk that way.[30]

Notes

1. "About The Park," Franklin D. Roosevelt Four Freedoms Park. http://www.fdrfourfreedom-spark.org/pages/about-the-park.
2. Elizabeth Borgwardt, *A New Deal for the World: America's Vision for Human Rights* (Cambridge, MA: Belknap Press of Harvard University Press, 2005), 5.
3. Obama is quoted in Stewart Patrick, "The Case for Good Enough Global Governance," *Foreign Affairs* 93.1 (January/February 2014): 58.
4. http://www.intelligence.senate.gov/study2014.html.
5. Former Secretary Clinton made these points and underscored the importance of data in remarks announcing the release of "Voice and Agency: Empowering Women and Girls for Shared Prosperity," a report from World Bank Group (2014), http://live.worldbank.org/voice-and-agency-empowering-women-hillary-rodham-clinton.
6. Hillary Rodham Clinton, *Hard Choices* (New York: Simon and Schuster 2014).
7. See Avalon Project at Yale Law School "Atlantic Charter," Lillian Goldman Law Library, http://avalon.law.yale.edu/wwii/atlantic.asp; Avalon Project at Yale Law School "Declaration by the United Nations, January 1, 1942," Lillian Goldman Law Library, http://avalon.law.yale.edu/20th_century/decade03.asp; Borgwardt, 5.

8. Borgwardt, *A New Deal for the World*, 29.
9. Cass R. Sunstein,— *The Second Bill of Rights: FDR's Unfinished Revolution and Why We Need it More than Ever* (New York: Basic Books, 2004).
10. Stephen C. Schlesinger, *Act of Creation: The Founding of the United Nations: A Story of Superpowers, Secret Agents, Wartime Allies and Enemies, and Their Quest for a Peaceful World* (Boulder, CO: Westview, 2003).
11. "Universal Declaration of Human Rights," 10 December 1948, in *The International Human Rights of Women: Instruments of Change*, eds. Carol Elizabeth Lockwood, et al. (New York: American Bar Association, 1998), 138.
12. Ellen Chesler, "The Shoulders We Stand On: Eleanor Roosevelt and Roots of the Women's Rights Revolution," in *The Unfinished Revolution: Voices from the Global Struggle for Women's Human Rights*, ed. Minky Worden (New York: Seven Stories Press, 2012), 20–25, informs this first section on the evolution of "Women's Rights as Human Rights."
13. Eleanor Roosevelt, "Making Human Rights Come Alive," Speech to the Second National Conference on UNESCO, 1949, [http://www.udhr.org/history/114.htm]; Felice D. Gaer, "And Never the Twain Shall Meet? The Struggle to Establish Women's Rights as International Human Rights," in ed., Lockwood et al., *The International Human Rights of Women*, 8.
14. Arvonne S. Fraser, "Becoming Human: The Origins and Development of Women's Human Rights," *Human Rights Quarterly* 21. 4 (November 1999), 891.
15. "Convention on the Elimination of All Forms of Discrimination Against Women (CEDAW), 18 December 1979, in Lockwood et al., *The International Human Rights of Women*, 269–280. Charlotte Bunch, "Women's Rights as Human Rights: Towards a Re-Vision of Human Rights," *Human Rights Quarterly* Vol. 12, No. 4 (November 1990), 486.
16. Eleanor Roosevelt, "Eisenhower Administration Rejects Treaty," *My Day*, 8 April 1953, in Allida Black, *Courage in a Dangerous World: The Political Writings of Eleanor Roosevelt* (New York: Columbia University Press, 1999) 187–188. Also see: Carol Anderson, *Eyes Off the Prize: The United Nations and the African American Struggle for Human Rights, 1944–1955* (New York: Cambridge University Press, 2003).
17. Paul Gordon Lauren, *The Evolution of International Human Rights: Visions Seen* (Philadelphia: University of Pennsylvania Press, 2003).
18. Leadership Conference on Civil and Human Rights, Still Segregated: How Race and Poverty Stymie the Right to Education at http://www.civilrights.org/publications/reports/still-segregated/still-segregated-how-race.html.
19. David Kaye, "Stealth Multilateralism: U.S. Foreign Policy Without Treaties-or the Senate," *Foreign Affairs* 92.5 (September/October 2013): 113.
20. Kaye, 113–124.
21. Ann Warner, "Recognizing Rights Promoting Progress: The Global Impact of CEDAW" at http://www.icrw.org/publications/recognizing-rights-promoting-progress.
22. *Grutter v. Bollinger* 539 US 306 (2003) at https://supreme.justia.com/cases/federal/us/539/306/#annotation.
23. Clinton addressed a conference of the Roosevelt Institute at the Ford Foundation on September 12, 2014 at http://womenandgirlsrising.strikingly.com/.
24. United States National Plan of Action on Women, Peace and Security at http://www.whitehouse.gov/the-press-office/2011/12/19/united-states-national-action-plan-women-peace-and-security. Ellen Chesler, "A New Year's Resolution to Make Women Full Partners in Peace and Security" at https://rooseveltinstitute.org/new-roosevelt/new-year-s-resolution-make-women-full-partners-peace-and-security.
25. The Equal Futures Partnership to Expand Women's Political and Economic Participation, at http://www.whitehouse.gov/the-press-office/2012/09/24/fact-sheet-equal-futures-partnership-expand-women-s-political-and-econom.
26. World Bank Group, "Voice and Agency: Empowering Women and Girls for Shared Prosperity (2014).

27. Human Rights Watch, "World Report 2014" at http://www.hrw.org/world-report/2014.

28. For additional examples of grassroots work, see *Close to Home: Case Studies of Human Rights Work in the United States*, eds. Larry Cox and Dorothy Q. Thomas (New York: Ford Foundation, 2004).

29. No Ceilings: The Full Participation Project at https://www.clintonfoundation.org/our-work/no-ceilings-full-participation-project.

30. Quoted in Borgwardt, *A New Deal for the World*, 43, taken from Samuel I. Rosenman, *Working with Roosevelt* (New York: Harper and Bros., 1952), 387.

PART THREE

CRITIQUES

13

Barack Obama

Progressive?

JONATHAN ALTER

Any exploration of Barack Obama and progressivism must start with the understanding that the president is touchy on this question. In the summer of 2011, for instance, Obama made a speech at the National Urban League. Afterward he saw Professor Cornel West—recently of Princeton now of the Union Theological Seminary—sitting in the front row. The president is not known for his temper, but he charged down into the audience to confront West. I have a picture of this in my most recent book in which the president's face is twisted in anger, while West is smiling.

According to West, Obama said to him, apropos of nothing, "What is this 'I'm not progressive' shit you've been peddling all over? 'I'm not progressive?' What are you talking about?" A woman standing nearby said later that if it hadn't been the president of the United States, the person verbally thrashing Cornel West would have been hauled away by the Secret Service.[1]

So if Obama sees himself as a progressive, why is it that so many other people don't? I think the answer can be found, in all places, in a poem that I loved as a child. It's called "Miniver Cheevy" by Edward Arlington Robinson. It goes in part: "Miniver Cheevy, child of scorn, grew lean while he assailed the seasons. He wept that he was ever born, and he had reasons."

Miniver's reason for weeping was that he thought he had been born in the wrong time. He loved the Middle Ages. He loved knights in shining armor. He lived in his historical imagination and wanted to have been alive then instead of the nineteenth century. Obama doesn't weep that he was ever born; lack of faith in his purpose on earth has never exactly been one of his problems. But a part of him does wish he had been president in the 1960s or 1970s when it was possible to do big progressive things.

Obama's background, while slight in political terms (only four years in national politics before becoming president), is undeniably progressive. As a student he was involved in antiapartheid demonstrations and worked for the New York Public Interest Research Group, a pro-consumer group founded by Ralph Nader. When he graduated from Columbia University in 1983 he had his choice of high-paying jobs. At first he had a well-paid position in New York writing reports on international corporations in what he later described as "the belly of the beast." He quit the job, moved to Chicago, and found work as a community organizer with unemployed steel workers and other poor people.[2] There are few if any examples of such youthful dedication to progressive ideals among prior presidents, except perhaps LBJ working as a teacher in a Mexican American school in Texas in the 1920s.

Obama had more direct exposure to poverty and the need for progressive solutions than any president. But for reasons related to his race, he could never afford to be called a *fighting* progressive. This was a departure. Liberalism, in the words of historian Arthur Schlesinger Jr., has for nearly 200 years been a "fighting faith."[3] If he pressed too hard, Obama risked being seen as an angry progressive, which is a short step from being an angry black man. His ability to avoid that stigma has been a significant part of his political success. By staying calm, Obama may have denied his supporters the gratification of watching him land progressive punches, but he has also confounded conservatives, driving them into a kind of "Obama derangement syndrome" that prevents legislative compromise but that also helped reelect him in 2012.

Both Obama and Bill Clinton have been presidents in an era that won't allow them to be full-throated progressives. The contrast to earlier eras is stark. FDR and LBJ had huge Democratic majorities in the House and filibuster-proof super-majorities on all issues except civil rights in the Senate. Even so, FDR's power over Congress was gone by 1937 (four years into his presidency) and LBJ's by 1966 (three years into his). Obama got two years with a Democratic Congress and put a lot of legislative points on the board during that time.

Indeed, when Obama enjoyed strong Democratic majorities in his first two years, he had a progressive record that far exceeded anything enacted under John F. Kennedy, Jimmy Carter or Bill Clinton and approached the legislative success of Lyndon Johnson in 1964 and 1965.

Let's briefly review some of what Obama accomplished for progressivism in his first two years:

TARP. The $350 billion in Troubled Asset Relief Program (TARP) spending that Obama, as president-elect, lobbied through a skeptical Democratic Congress in late 2008 to early 2009 provided an important, quasi-socialist boost to the economy. This was the second "tranche" of a widely unpopular bank bailout that was nonetheless a huge Keynesian (read progressive) program. Without the distasteful bank bailouts, unemployment would, by the accounts of most economists, have quickly shot up to 20 percent. Instead it hit 10 percent and has slowly declined to under 7 percent. Obama made the same decision that Franklin Roosevelt did in 1933. New Dealers, almost unanimously, were contemptuous of FDR for missing a golden opportunity to take over the banks in 1933. Instead, Roosevelt decided to leave banking in private hands. So did Obama, and he was right. Following the advice of Krugman and Stiglitz to take over Citibank and perhaps others would have cost hundreds of billions in unnecessary bank bailouts when the banks taken over by the government experienced bank runs—a highly likely scenario.

It's true that besides health care, Obama had to set aside a progressive agenda in 2009 and 2010 to stop the bleeding. But even if some of the tourniquets he used were not the right progressive tourniquets, at least he was injecting money into the economy, while the Republican Party (not to mention Europe) preferred an austerity policy that harkened back to the disastrous conservative economic policies of the late 1920s that led to the Great Depression.

Auto bailouts. The government-backed rescue of the auto industry—a progressive policy by any standard—turned out to be a good move politically for Obama during his 2012 reelection campaign, but it was extremely unpopular when launched in 2009. The public reaction to the bailouts signaled to the White House that when the country had the choice to move left after an economic crisis, it declined to do so. The reaction to the auto bailout surprised Obama, who believed he had a chance to spearhead a New Deal–style response to the crisis. He knew that bailing out bankers would be unpopular but also thought that helping unemployed auto workers would be seen as appropriate. Even though the polling was awful on it, he went ahead and did it anyway.

The stimulus. The $787 billion stimulus enacted in 2009 was a huge progressive program. Readers conditioned by economists Paul Krugman and Joseph Stiglitz believed that this amount was inadequate, and as an economic matter, it was. But politically, there was no way, even among the Democrats, to have a stimulus that ended with a "T"—that went over a trillion dollars. Rahm Emanuel, Obama's first chief of staff, knew Capitol Hill from his time as a congressman and told the president the proposed stimulus could not exceed $1 trillion or it would not be approved by the Democratic Congress. He was never contradicted on this practical political point.

Spending $787 billion was an impressive amount of stimulus, especially considering that Congress only eighteen months earlier had rejected a $30 billion stimulus. It is important to remember that the month Obama took office the economy was losing 800,000 jobs a month. If the country stayed on that track, by the end of calendar year 2009, the United States would have been in the same position as it was in Roosevelt's first year as president: a full-scale Great Depression.[4]

But the programs worked. Instead of 25 percent unemployment, the US economy began adding about 150,000 jobs a month. That's anemic, but it's better than losing 800,000 a month. The American public, despite reelecting Obama, has pocketed that.

Dodd-Frank. In 2010, Congress approved the Dodd-Frank Wall Street Reform and Consumer Protection Act, a bill that sounded more progressive than it was.

But thanks largely to Elizabeth Warren, a Harvard law professor on leave to help the Obama administration, it contained a very progressive idea, the Consumer Financial Protection Bureau. When senators in both parties objected, Warren got critical backing from Obama himself, who overrode former Senator Chris Dodd and others who didn't want to include the pro-consumer bureau in the bill.

Iraq, Afghanistan, and Syria. Although foreign policy is beyond the purview of this chapter, ending two American wars begun under his predecessors must be chalked up as a progressive accomplishment. In the years since Vietnam, progressives tended to believe in restraint abroad. In 2013 Obama reversed years of increased presidential authority in warmaking by seeking approval from Congress before attacking Syria when it used chemical weapons against civilians. You can call this move a sloppy, busted, diplomatic play, but it reflected progressive ideals. And his decision not to intervene in Syria with US ground forces was in keeping with the country's desire not to embark on another major land war in the Middle East.

By the middle of 2014 Obama faced a stiff new foreign policy test in the form of ISIS's attempt to build a brutal new "Islamofascist" state (the late Christopher Hitchens's term for such evil extremists) inside Syria and Iraq. The president who was elected in part to end two wars was forced to launch a new one, at least from the air; and he was forced to confront the fact that with 20/20 hindsight he should have left a small residual force in Iraq to help keep the pressure on Iraqi President Nouri Maliki to make his government more inclusive of Sunnis; but this didn't happen and thus left Iraq susceptible to ISIS. Among those criticizing Obama's foreign policy in 2013 and 2014 was his former CIA director and defense secretary, Leon Panetta, who said the president had "lost his way" and had too often chosen professorial detachment over fighting for his policies. But contrary to GOP critics, Panetta concluded that "the jury is still out" on how Obama's presidency will stack up historically. I'm a bit more charitable. Because of Obamacare and the prevention of another Great Depression in 2009, Obama's legacy as a good president is secure. Whether he can be anything better remains to be seen.

Gay rights. Obama ended don't-ask-don't-tell in the military, came out in support of gay marriage, and mentioned gays and lesbians in an inaugural address for the first time in history. You can quibble with the way he got there, but that's true of Roosevelt and Social Security—FDR had to be shamed into it after trying to back away in 1935—and Kennedy on civil rights. JFK was slow but eventually stood strong for a major social change.

The environment. Upon taking office, President Obama pledged that by 2020 the United States' greenhouse gas emissions will be 17 percent below 2005 levels. He supported a cap-and-trade system to help achieve this carbon reduction goal, which was dead on arrival in the Senate thanks to Max Baucus, the chairman of the Senate Finance Committee. But in the face of congressional obstruction, he has issued a series of executive orders protecting the environment, with the most important being his recent establishment of new EPA standards to reduce greenhouse gas emissions from cars, trucks, and crucially, coal-fired power plants.[5] To date, US carbon emissions are down by roughly 10 percent, nearly two-thirds of the way to reaching the 2020 goal. Obama's stimulus bill also included roughly $90 billion in subsidies for America's burgeoning green energy sector, with the result that since 2009 wind power generation has doubled, and solar power has experienced a six-fold increase.[6] These moves make it clear that in spite of the difficulties in moving ahead legislation, and aside from a few exceptions, President Obama has been a progressive environmentalist president.

The affordable care act. Obamacare is an underappreciated achievement, not just for progressives but also for the United States. The best way to explain that is to look at the history of the idea of universal health insurance. It first appeared in the progressive ("Bull Moose") Party Platform of 1912. Theodore Roosevelt didn't win that election, and the idea didn't go anywhere. The idea came up again in the early 1930s when Franklin Roosevelt told Francis Perkins, his labor secretary, that he believed in cradle-to-grave coverage. But FDR decided not to include health security as part of Social Security for a few different reasons. Southerners, who controlled key congressional committees, didn't want blacks in their hospitals because it might hasten integration of hospitals. The American Medical Association, which did so much to stymie national health insurance under Harry Truman, was already against the idea of including health insurance, and had a very powerful and well-connected spokesman.

The well-respected physician, Dr. Harvey Cushing of Boston, happened to be the father-in-law of FDR's son Jimmy. After Cushing had breakfast with the president at the White House in 1935, there wasn't much further talk of health care being part of Social Security. This personal dimension to politics is something that Obama doesn't understand intuitively, and it has hurt him. But Obama actually moved faster than FDR on his signature progressive program. Where Obama introduced the Affordable Care Act shortly after taking office in 2009, Roosevelt did not introduce Social Security until the third year of his presidency. His liberal supporters were worried that he didn't really mean it. When the bill finally passed, it was a terribly racist piece of legislation. The Social Security Act of 1935 excluded every occupation held by African Americans, from farm workers to maids, because that was the only way to get it through the relevant congressional committees. It was a piecemeal piece of legislation.[7]

Senator Robert Wagner of New York and other New Deal liberals thought the bill was thin gruel. They were disappointed in the president. But Roosevelt understood that you have to start somewhere, then you can fix it in the years after initial passage. This is what Clinton in 1996 did with welfare reform, which originally was very harsh toward food stamp recipients and immigrants. Clinton went back and fixed it just as Roosevelt fixed Social Security, and subsequent presidents fixed it several times more. This is how major progressive legislation plays out, and the same will be the case for the Affordable Care Act.

After Roosevelt and Truman failed to enact national health insurance, John F. Kennedy and Lyndon Johnson picked up the idea. Johnson settled for Medicare and Medicaid, which were big achievements but still left large numbers of Americans uninsured. Richard Nixon tried it in 1971. The late Senator Ted Kennedy told me in an interview in 2002 that the biggest regret of his Senate career was that he didn't come to terms with Nixon on what today would be considered a progressive health-care plan. If Kennedy had lived, he would have been contemptuous of some of the liberal critiques of Obamacare. He learned a hard lesson about the regrettable progressive tendency to make the perfect the enemy of the good.

The efforts continued in the 1970s. Jimmy Carter tried hospital cost containment, which failed. Bill and Hillary Clinton introduced a plan in 1993 that flopped. Only Barack Obama has succeeded. He managed to achieve something that had eluded progressive presidents and not-so-progressive presidents for one hundred years. Now, you can say, "Well, it wasn't single-payer" or "There's no public option," and you would be right on the substance. I started writing in support of a single-payer plan almost twenty years ago in *Newsweek*. Clearly, as a policy matter, the single-payer system is the right approach.

But it continues to be a non-starter in American politics. Imagine if, theoretically, the Democrats had won approval of a single-payer system. Currently under Obamacare, about 2 percent of Americans now are going to lose their private insurance, and they're screaming like crazy. Imagine if more than 90 percent—millions and millions of people—were going to suddenly lose their private coverage and go into a government system. Bedlam.

Obama understood this, and instead of scoring points with progressives by fighting the good fight and raising the standard again for the right policy solution, he decided, "How about if we win for a change, and we get something important done." The result is that despite the disastrous rollout of the website and other problems with Obamacare, the United States has essentially ended the shameful era in American history where if you get sick, you may be so saddled with medical bills that you lose your house. For decades, more than half of personal bankruptcies were the result of medical expenses. No more.

That's a big progressive accomplishment, and it almost didn't happen. At the end of 2009 we saw the emergence (or reemergence) of a self-destructive progressivism with former Democratic National Committee chair Howard Dean and other liberal talking heads saying on MSNBC and other networks, "Kill the bill! Kill the bill!" Dozens of progressive Democrats on the House side felt the same way. For a couple of weeks in 2010 after Republican Scott Brown was elected to the Senate, it looked as if House Democrats would indeed bury Obamacare rather than vote for the Senate version, which was the necessary parliamentary tactic to assure passage.

Imagine if critics had indeed killed the bill. What would the chances be now of getting anything? Zero. Democrats would have lost the House anyway in 2010 (largely because of 10 percent unemployment) and had nothing to show for it.

When I was working on my first Obama book, Rahm Emanuel told me, "I begged the president not to do healthcare."[8] David Axelrod who has a disabled daughter and desperately wanted it, told the president, "Don't do it." Joe Biden said, "Look, the American people given the economic crisis will give you a pass if you don't do healthcare right now." They reminded him that he hadn't talked about it much during the 2008 campaign. When I asked the president, "Why did you do it?" He said, "Well Nancy Pelosi told me if we did this I'd probably go down ten points and we could lose the next election."[9] I repeated the question, "Why did you do it?" He said, "If we didn't do it now, it wouldn't have happened."[10] He was right. It was a courageous and historic political decision that he took over the objections of his staff. For all of its inadequacies, for all of the bumps in the road, it's "a big f-ing deal," as Joe Biden said on March 23, 2010, the day the bill was signed into law.[11]

So Obamacare and these other progressive achievements lie on one side of the ledger. But that leaves a number of policy areas where the president has not been so progressive: Targeted killings; NSA spying; failure to close Guantanamo (which he's now working on again); bollixing up housing programs meant to help those undergoing foreclosure (they are much improved of late); and failure to prosecute those in government who were guilty of torture and other offenses.

The biggest shortcoming has been on what should have been Job One. From the start of his administration, when he didn't even consider WPA-style government jobs programs, Obama has fallen short on job creation. He's right that economic growth and better education are the best ways to create jobs. And the president can be forgiven for using more of the stimulus to save existing jobs in state and local government than on infrastructure jobs that were not "shovel-ready" (a myth, as he discovered). But once the Affordable Care Act was signed, he needed to pivot immediately to a relentless campaign for more jobs.

Instead we got what I call, in homage to the Watergate tapes, the eighteen-and-a-half month gap. The period from the signing of the ACA in the winter of 2010, to the introduction of his jobs bill in the fall of 2011, is about eighteen months. This delay harmed the Obama presidency and certainly any interpretation of him as a vigorous progressive. The White House has offered a lot of excuses for why the president didn't pivot faster. There was no appetite for another jobs-based stimulus, even in the Democratic caucus. The 2009 stimulus was just kicking in. Everyone was distracted for months by the British Petroleum (BP) oil spill in the Gulf of Mexico. These may all be valid explanations, but they don't explain why Obama let the Republicans change the subject from job growth to deficit reduction, a significantly less progressive topic of national debate. It's true that the deficit was ballooning to more than $1 trillion, and the president needed to stand for fiscal responsibility. But he never explained in a clear, memorable way that lingered in the mind—with the sound-bites he disdains—why the United States could not simultaneously put its financial house in order and put Americans to work rebuilding the country.

Instead, as Obama later admitted, he took his eye off the ball. In August and September 2011, which he considers to be the low point of his presidency, he acknowledged that he had lost the thread of progressive ideas and needed to get back to the ideas that had brought him into politics in the first place. That's why he launched his reelection campaign in Osawatomie, Kansas, where Theodore Roosevelt had spoken more than 100 years earlier. By this time he was stumping hard for the American Jobs Act, a package of job creation ideas that was rejected by congressional Republicans even though many had voted for the same proposals in the past.

While Obama failed on a big infrastructure plan, he has succeeded in changing a tired narrative of American politics. The president has successfully interrupted the racial dynamic that conservatives have repeatedly exploited in recent decades. The normal story is that conservatives attack liberals, liberals get angry—and conservatives then say that blacks are "playing the race card." The incriminations and acrimony redound to the benefit of the attackers, the conservatives, and we get a poisonous climate unhelpful to the advancement of progressive ideas. Obama interrupted this pattern by signaling conservatives that he is not going to play their anger game. In his first term, he wanted Democrats to cut him some slack for not taking off the gloves. The question now is whether having been safely reelected, he will risk being more combative. He has come to understand that austerity was a detour for him and is now committed to a more explicit progressive agenda.

Looking ahead, what should Obama do to redeem his progressive potential? I'm reminded of a story involving Franklin Roosevelt and Sidney Hillman, who was a powerful labor leader and ally. Hillman complained about not enough prolabor action from the White House. FDR responded: Make me. Roosevelt was telling Hillman to build a progressive fire under him that might force him to do things he wanted to do anyway.[12]

Obama needs a thorough agenda of political reform, like the one of a century ago that was borrowed from the populists and implemented by the progressives. He has generally lacked the Rooseveltian spirit of experimentation and his White House has often suffered from a creativity gap in policy making.

But the Barack Obama story remains incomplete. It's much too early to render any verdict on this president. Obamacare cannot and will not be taken away from him. Conservatives, for all their noise, don't have the votes and they don't have the veto pen. Liberals, for all their quibbles about Obama, need to go to war over progressive ideas with the president they have, not the idealized one they still dream about.

Notes

1. Jonathan Alter, *The Center Holds: Obama and His Enemies* (New York: Simon and Schuster, 2013), 270–271.
2. Barack Obama, *Dreams from my Father* (New York: Random House, 1995), 138–143.

3. Arthur Schlesinger, Jr., *The Vital Center* (Boston: Houghton Mifflin, 1949), 256.

4. See Jonathan Alter, *The Defining Moment: FDR's 100 Days and the Triumph of Hope* (New York: Simon and Schuster, 2006).

5. "A Climate for Change: The EPA's Limits for Emissions are Important but not Enough," *Washington Post*, August 26, 2014.

6. Jonathan Chait, "Obama Might Actually be the Environmental President," *New York*, May 5, 2013.

7. Alter, *The Defining Moment*, 314–315.

8. Jonathan Alter, *The Promise: President Obama, Year One* (New York: Simon and Schuster, 2011), 397.

9. Alter, *The Promise,* 397

10. Alter, *The Promise,* 398.

11. "Vice President Caught on Mic; Calls Health Care a 'Big F-ing Deal'," *New York Daily News*, March 23, 2010, http://www.nydailynews.com/news/politics/vice-president-bi den-caught-mic-calls-health-care-bill-big-f-ing-deal-article-1.168126.

12. *Daily Kos*, May 14, 2009, http://www.dailykos.com/story/2009/05/15/731660/- Make-Me-Do-It.

14

Really Existing Progressivism

Its Strengths and Weaknesses in America

CHRISTOPHER CALDWELL

THE RESURGENCE OF PROGRESSIVISM

For a long time, the word "progressivism" was a way of hiding, not describing, what people on the left believed. In the 1980s and 1990s it was a skulking synonym for Michael Dukakis's liberalism. In the 1950s and 1960s, it was a way for red-diaper babies to describe what their families believed without horrifying schoolteachers who had voted for Adlai Stevenson and Hubert Humphrey. Like him or not, Barack Obama has presided over a restoration of the meaning "progressivism" had a century ago. We now understand progressivism much as Woodrow Wilson and the first muckrakers did: as the belief that politics must advance with science and accord with rationality.

Progressivism is the most powerful form of leftism and the least appealing, and for many of the same reasons. Its values—rationalization, modernization, efficiency, materialism—overlap with those of capitalism. It makes little contact with the age-old impulses that rightly provoke a suspicion of capitalism: R. H. Tawney's Christianity, for instance, or Éamon De Valera's nationalism. Progressives often think of themselves as the foes of the moneyed class, but they do not appear that way to non-progressives. They look like the self-righteous and self-deluded part of the moneyed class.

PROGRESSIVISM TODAY

If there is a day-to-day philosophy to progressivism, it involves making government more efficient and rational. Progressivism holds democracy to be the best system to the extent—and only to the extent—that it empowers expertise. It is not the best system when a Kansas school board orders the teaching of Creationism, or when

three-dozen states vote to block gay marriage. Kevin Mattson makes some interesting points about Democrats' relation to power over the past century. He mentions
Bill Clinton's "romantic view" of political power, and ties it to the way the left has,
since FDR, come to link charisma and power. But this comes with the territory.
There is a self-contradiction at the heart of Progressivism that is a standing invitation to hypocrisy: its claims to rule rest on cold rationality. But unless it can make
the public swoon (something politicians usually do through non-rational appeals),
it must rule undemocratically.

It is hardly a surprise, then, that almost every advance for Progressivism, even
if it begins through legislation, has involved aggrandizing the executive branch
through regulation. The 2010 Affordable Care Act is extreme in this regard. It
moves the actual process of *enactment* into the executive branch. We won't actually know—and we are not *supposed* to know—what kind of program Obamacare is
until the Department of Health and Human Services is finished writing the regulations for it.

In the United States, an additional factor tightens Progressivism's dependence
on executive power. Our 18th-century constitution, unlike the British constitution out of which it grew, hinders efficient and rational government by design. It
does not respect expertise. This is why the constitutional obsessions of the Tea
Party movement, which appear to most Americans as the enthusiasm of an isolated and disempowered minority, appear to Progressives as a mortal threat to the
Republic.

The revival of progressivism in the past two decades has owed much to government's increasing efficiency. When Bill Clinton said that "the era of big government is over," he was only coming to the same insight that, for instance, steel
magnates have. Technology now allows a steel mill to make more steel with a tenth
of the labor. Government can play that trick, too. Barack Obama did not need to
hire a million clerks to staff up for the Affordable Care Act. All he needed was
$4 billion to computerize medical records, which the 2009 stimulus had already
given him. The outsourcing of military tasks is evidence that this same process
is at work even in areas that are not Progressive priorities. Government can be
more effective and more intrusive with less manpower and a smaller budgetary
footprint.

But this efficiency comes at the price of blurring the line between government
and business. As a result, Progressivism, *when working as intended*, has regressive
consequences. Progressivism tends to be regulatory rather than legislative, because
regulation is designed to produce rational outcomes and legislation is "only"
designed to respect preferences. Regulation seemed an unqualified boon at the
dawn of the Progressive Era a century or so ago, when regulators could pursue their
work unmolested. But the situation is very different today, because powerful interests have simply shifted their attention from buying votes to capturing regulators.
Progressivism moves decisions from places where voting goes on to places where

lobbying goes on. Its victories have lately tended to come from rigging the judiciary and the bureaucracy against the popular will.

Moreover, Progressivism creates complexity, and complexity has a regressive quality all its own. Consider the Dodd-Frank financial regulatory legislation. Elsewhere in this book, Mike Konczal provides a fascinating account of how the old New Deal model of regulating banks and brokerages, built around the Securities and Exchange Commission, maps onto the model we use in the era of derivatives. Even if Dodd-Frank is analogous to earlier legislation, it stands apart in one significant respect: its length. An ordinary self-educated citizen of the 1930s could (albeit with a lot of effort) read the Glass-Steagall act and figure out what his local bank was doing wrong. Dodd-Frank is comprehensible only to a lobbyist.

A particular blind spot of Progressivism is the really existing class structure. Progressives are always hollering at conservatives that they should not mistake Barack Obama for a socialist. Well, Progressives should not mistake him for a social-ist, either. Progressivism empowers expertise, and expertise tends to be heavily con-centrated among society's winners. If you wanted to be polemical, you could say that Progressivism promotes people through the government in accordance with capitalism. Progressives tend to take for granted that they speak on behalf of the working class. This is baffling to non-Progressives. Academia, the crucible of tomor-row's ruling classes, is the great redoubt of Progressivism. Business has increasingly been taken over by the left, too.

Progressives very often talk about the Koch brothers and Sheldon Adelson and the unfair advantage Republicans get from such billionaires. Can you name any oth-ers? There's Paul Singer, who gives to conservative causes but is also now pouring money into the effort for gay marriage. (The Kochs have supported gay marriage, too, along with such Democratic politicians as David Pryor and Mary Landrieu, not that anyone has noticed.) But among Progressive billionaires you have Warren Buffett, who has made a full-throated defense of President Obama's tax policies, Bill Gates, Jeff Bezos, Ted Turner, Oprah Winfrey. It is a very long list, probably longer than the Republican list.

Lots of Progressives have become billionaires at Goldman Sachs, which is hardly a Republican firm. Hank Paulson went from being CEO of Goldman to running the Bush administration's treasury department, but this does not necessarily disprove our rule. Read his autobiography. When he told his mother that he was going to work for a Republican administration, she cried. When he told his daughter he was going to work for a Republican administration she stopped talking to him. Finally, look at the figures on giving that the Center for Responsive Politics compiles. In 2008, nineteen of the twenty ZIP codes that poured the most money into politics gave more of their money to Democrats than to Republicans. And they were almost twenty for twenty. In McLean, Virginia, Republicans got 52 percent of contribu-tions, versus 48 percent for Democrats.

This is not the only sense in which traditional stereotypes about the parties have reversed. Progressives often point to the rise of antigovernment impulses on the right. But in the old days—the original Progressive era, for instance—these were found mainly on the left. For decades, Progressives have scolded the right for the manner in which it has wrapped itself in patriotism. But today the left is more optimistic about America than the right. Jingoism and skepticism switched sides. Think of the various diplomatic efforts to advance "reproductive rights," starting with the Clinton administration's delegations to the Cairo conference on population in 1994 and the Beijing conference in 1995. There have been no countervailing initiatives of similar scope by Republicans. In a huge reversal, it is now Republicans (52 percent), more than Democrats (46 percent), who think the United States now does "too much" to tell the world how to live, according to a 2013 Pew poll.

CONCLUSION

In 2004 Howard Dean broke the Democratic Party of its yearning after consensus and freed it to follow a more independent and progressive direction. In 2006 and 2008 the party won smashing nationwide victories. The problem is, the ideological shift and the victories had nothing to do with one another. Democrats owed their success to a Republican president whom voters held responsible for losing two wars and destroying the world economy. Given a totally free hand, Progressives have been unable to broaden their coalition beyond those who are relieved that they are not George W. Bush. On the contrary! This past decade has been a glorious Indian summer for Progressives. But it occurred by accident, and it is drawing to a close. With their gains threatened in the coming years, Progressive leaders will likely rely more explicitly on their most natural allies: the winners of the global capitalist economy.

PART FOUR

THE FUTURE OF PROGRESSIVE POLITICS

A Progressive Agenda for the Twenty-First Century

JOSEPH E. STIGLITZ[1]

My intent in writing this chapter is to lay out what I see as a Progressive economic agenda for the twenty-first century. By its very definition, the Progressive agenda has to change, it has to *progress*—as our understandings of the economy and society change, and as technology, the economy, and society themselves change.

But before setting forth a Progressive agenda for the twenty-first century, I would like to explore the key beliefs and values of the Progressive movement. What is it that a Progressive economy should be striving for? Both the left and the right repeatedly pay homage to values, but too often, those values are either left unspecified, or are defined in ways that are so banal as to be uncontroversial: the value of the individual, the value of freedom, the value of the family.

As I see it, Progressives stand for a core set of values, which are far from banalities—values that many on the right would not subscribe to.[2] Too often, the progressive movement is implicitly defined by the conservatives and by what it opposes. Here, I want to deliniate the *positive* progressive agenda.

First on the agenda is the value of progress itself. Society can and should change to help us better achieve what we strive for. Thus the Progressive movement puts a high value on innovation—both technological innovation and social innovation. But in emphasizing change, Progressives do not ignore the legacy of the past, which is to say they value the ideas and understandings inherited from previous generations. This represents a fundamental difference between Progressives and conservatives, whose focus is on preserving the past and the attendant inequities and power structures that have often prevailed in earlier years.

The Progressive agenda is today's embodiment of the Enlightenment project: the belief that through rational and scientific enquiry we can learn, and what we learn can be used to improve well-being. Overall, the Enlightenment project has been enormously successful: for thousands of years, standards of living improved at a rate that was barely perceptible. Most individuals spent all of their energies simply to survive and to acquire the bare necessities of life such as food, clothing, and shelter. Today, because of the Enlightenment and the advances in science and technology that followed, those needs require but a few hours of work a week; the rest of our time can be devoted to the acquisition of goods beyond the bare necessities and to leisure activities, including the development of culture and science, the expanding of our horizons, and the raising of our living standards still further.[3]

We have come to understand too that there may be, at any point in time, limits to what we know or what can be known. Godel's theorem and the Heisenberg uncertainty principle represent the most forceful articulation of these limits to our knowledge. Progressives do not seek certainty where there is none; we have to live with uncertainty and ambiguity.[4]

This rational enquiry extends not only to the physical sciences but also to the social sciences, as well as to our understanding of man, his behavior, and his relationship with others.

Any research agenda attempting to improve the plight of the world's population must begin with an enquiry into the nature of man—what he cares about, what motivates him, how he thinks, and how he behaves. Modern economics is based on a certain conception of the individual. Individuals come into the world with well-formed preferences and beliefs. They are rational. But a rational enquiry into human behavior shows that these beliefs are not always well founded. Individuals' beliefs and preferences are at least partially culturally determined, and there are many ways and instances in which behavior is far from rational.[5] This helps explain why certain subcultures—those belonging to a particular political party, in particular locations, for example—embrace beliefs that seem so at odds with scientific evidence, such as the belief that climate change is a myth.[6]

The notion that individuals and their beliefs are malleable should fill us with hope: for it means that in principle, we might create a society in which more individuals conform to our ideals. We could create a society in which there is more trust, more charity, more cooperation, as well as less selfishness, less greed, and less corruption. We might create a society with less racism and prejudice.

But in another way, the changing nature of beliefs leaves us without an anchor. Standard welfare economics, for example, had a well-defined objective—increasing the well-being of individuals with well-formed preferences that specify the degree of happiness, satisfaction, or utility provided by any bundle of goods and activities. But if preferences themselves are malleable, what is it that we are supposed to maximize? By assuming preformed preferences and beliefs, economists had, however, taken the easy way out of some of the deepest and most important philosophical questions: What is a good society? What is a good individual?

Sketching what might be answers to these questions would take me beyond this short essay. But progressives share certain views on these matters. Individuals should, for instance, take into account how their actions affect others (or at least weigh the externalities[7] that they impose). Progressives also affirm the value of liberty, the right of others to do as they please, so long as their actions do not impose costs on others.

These views are also partially derived from rational analysis: we all live in a society that not only affects our preferences but also affects us in myriad other ways. Indeed, no individual is "self-created," although listening to commentary from the right (even from those who inherited their fortunes from their parents) one might have thought otherwise.[8] As Newton said, even the giants who have made the most profound contributions to our society stand on the shoulders of those who went before.[9] The individual and the collective are inextricably intertwined. And if that is so, we have to think hard not just about how what we do affects ourselves but also how it affects others.

There are many areas where the impacts on others can be quite significant. If I drive too fast, pollute the atmosphere or water, I can impose enormous costs on others, even death. My freedom is your unfreedom. No discussion of liberty can ignore this basic insight. Creating a good society entails imposing restrictions on what one individual does, when those actions might affect others.

There are some cases where, to use the economist's jargon, regulations, standards, restrictions can be Pareto improvements[10]: that is, everyone would be better off living with certain restrictions than with the absence of those restrictions. Without stoplights, no one could drive across Manhattan without fear of an accident or being caught in gridlock. Traffic regulations enhance the safety and speed for (almost) everyone. But often, some regulations provide more benefits to some at the expense of others.

The right has worked hard to give regulations a bad name. At the same time, they talk about the importance of the rule of law. But the law is nothing more than the basic rules and regulations that govern society. And it matters what rules and regulations are in place and whether they serve a few at the top or everyone in society. It matters too how they are enforced and implemented.

On the other hand, what individuals do privately—among consenting adults—should not be restricted. To be sure, someone else's well-being might be affected by the knowledge that something that he disapproves of is occurring. One could argue that there is, as a result, an externality, but Progressives believe that this is a category of externalities that shouldn't be regulated.

This is an arena in which progressives and the right couldn't be more different. Many on the right oppose gun control, arguing that it impinges on the freedom to carry guns. But there is a huge societal cost to that freedom: that cost being in the death of thousands of innocent victims. In balancing the right to live and the right to carry a machine gun, most progressives are solidly for the former.

The opposite is true when it comes to the issue of gay marriage and the extension of legal rights to same-sex couples. Here, Progressives argue that society is attempting to restrict actions that affect no one but the two consenting adults, and therefore there are no grounds for such restrictions. The right, often appealing to basic laws of nature, argues otherwise.

More generally, the right often makes appeals to long-standing institutions like marriage, as if they were God given and that history gives them sanctity. Progressives see institutions as something we create to serve our purposes, and as we come to understand better the purposes they serve, and the way they succeed or fail to fulfill those purposes (or how they might serve other ends), institutions get reformed, or even destroyed and replaced. Intellectual property law, for instance, is not part of natural law but is a human construct, designed to promote innovation. We need to understand the ways in which the latter accomplishes this and how it may actually impede innovation. So too for each of the institutions in our society.

This is not to say that progressives give short shrift to history. As I have said, institutions exist to serve certain needs. The fact that an institution has survived may indicate that it has served those needs well. But society and the economy change, and what served some needs well at one time may not serve them well at another. More importantly, the power structures—whose views are most reflected in existing arrangements—may change. An institutional arrangement that served yesterday's elites well may not be appropriate in a more democratic era.

Moreover, progressives recognize that one cannot create new institutions out of whole cloth. That is why evolutionary processes are often more successful than revolutionary processes. This is also why some of us were skeptical about the "shock therapy" approach to the transition from Communism to the market economy and preferred a more gradualist approach, where new democratic institutions and legal frameworks could be established as a market economy was being created. A market economy without an appropriate rule of law, we feared, would be a jungle. And so it turned out to be.[11]

Earlier in this paper, we explained how the actions of one individual affect others. We are interdependent. This makes it almost inevitable that society engages in collective action. By providing goods collectively,[12] and by providing rules and regulations, we all have a chance to be better off. But once one admits of the desirability of some collective action, one has to have some mechanism for collective decision making with rules and regulations that govern that process, including those that limit what can and cannot be subject to collective decision making. Here, too, progressives tend to share a firm belief in democratic, participatory processes. At the same time, they believe certain restraints on government are necessary. These views are reflected in the Bill of Rights guaranteeing freedoms of speech and religion. Today, we recognize other rights such as the right to privacy and the right to know (e.g., what the government is doing). But we also recognize that there are certain societal obligations, reflected in the Universal Declaration of Human Rights—including the right to health care and to certain other basic needs.

While both progressives and the right pay obeisance to democratic principles, there is often a difference in what is meant. Democracy means more than an election every four years. Modern Progressives put considerable weight on inclusive and participatory processes, aware that in the past certain views, and the views of certain groups, were not heard (or at least were not heard loudly) while other views, and the views of certain other groups, tended to dominate.[13] To be sure, progressives would like some views to be heard more loudly than others: for example, those views derived from evidence and sound reasoning. And they are wary of the power of money.

This is another arena where the progressives and the right couldn't disagree more. In the United States, the right has been actively engaged in a campaign of disenfranchisement of the poor, for which there is a long historical precedent.[14] At the same time, decisions like *Citizens United* and restrictions on campaign finance reform have enhanced the power of money to affect electoral outcomes. As I suggested in my book *The Price of Inequality*[15], America has become a country closer to "one dollar one vote" than to "one person one vote." A key challenge for the country is how to prevent America's outsized economic inequality from being *further* translated into political inequality. An active agenda of gerrymandering by the right has further reduced democratic representativeness and accountability.

The challenge of creating more effective, inclusive, participatory processes is one of the key issues facing the progressive movement. But while we may not know how to create an ideal system, we can identify changes that make the system worse. These are key battlegrounds for progressives today.

By the same token, we know how to increase accountability: "right to know" laws are essential.[16] But also essential is media diversity, to ensure that there is a free and fair marketplace of ideas. This will not be the case if media outlets are dominated only by the rich and powerful.

Antitrust laws were originally enacted more to prevent the concentration of political power than to ensure market efficiency. But in the more than one hundred years since these were first enacted during the administration of Theodore Roosevelt, we have narrowed our vision: we have forgotten the dangers that the concentration of economic power pose to our democratic political process—and nowhere is this more important than in the media. Equally significant, especially in the aftermath of the 2008 financial crisis, is the power of the big banks to stymie the wishes of most Americans to enact more effective regulations in the financial sector.[17]

I would also argue that there is one respect in which the Enlightenment project has failed: we must acknowledge that a significant portion of today's population, while benefiting from the advances of science, do not subscribe to its core tenets and deny one aspect of the findings of modern science or another. Many people do not believe in evolution, and many still do not believe in climate change.[18] But the analytic approach that underlies Progressivism has never come to terms with these seeming anomalies. As I noted earlier, one element of "rational enquiry" involves recognition of the limits of rationality. To make matters worse, it may be in the interests of some groups in society to encourage this kind of irrationality: oil companies stand to gain economically if more people believe that climate change is a hoax, and they are willing to use their money to persuade others that this is true. (In other contexts, the elites deliberately left large masses of the population undereducated.)

I have emphasized that the Progressive agenda is about change, but that raises questions: Change for what ends? What is it that we should be striving for? How do we know whether the change is making things better or worse? These are, of course, extremely complicated questions, encompassing all of the issues we have been discussing. But there is a short answer: change should enrich the lives of *all* citizens, to enable them to flourish and to live up to their potential.

In putting the matter this way, I emphasize one aspect of the Progressive agenda—that of social justice. Social justice and fairness have, of course, many dimensions—not just at a moment in time, but over generations. Part of social justice—and a key way in which its attainment is more likely to be assured—is ensuring *equality of voice*, especially in our political process. Part of social justice is equal access to justice—enshrined in the pledge of allegiance to the flag that school children recite every day. Justice is *for all*, not just for those who can afford it. There is the matter of justice across generations (what economists refer to as "intergenerational" justice). Despoiling the environment today puts those in future generations at risk.

Progressives believe that all individuals, regardless of their parentage, should have the right to live up to their potential and that there should equal opportunity for all. They also believe that *excessive* inequality is morally wrong; that it alters and effectively undermines the functioning of our society, our economy, and our democracy.[19]

There are some inequities that are so egregious that they call for special attention—for instance, inequalities in access to health care. Given all of this, the attainment of certain minimal standards (commensurate with a country's economic capacity), have come to be recognized as basic economic and social rights within the Universal Declaration of Human Rights.

Earlier I referred to the progressive commitment to equal access to justice. This is part of a broader commitment to the rule of law. But what progressives and conservatives mean by the rule of law can be markedly different. It is not *any* rule of law. After all, the feudal order was, in a sense, a rule of law, with well-defined obligations, constraints, and norms. In effect, it enshrined the principle that might makes right. It was a rule of law that served those at the top and acted to preserve a hierarchy. What Progressives mean by a rule of law is intricately related to precepts of social justice: a rule of law designed to protect the weak, not to preserve the entitlements of the strong; a rule of law which, both de jure and de facto, enshrines the principle of equality of all before the law.

In this brief discussion, I have had to elide several key issues. What do we mean by fairness? Many on the right believe that it is unfair to tax the rich whose wealth is their just desserts for what they have contributed to society. Progressives believe that no one is really self-made and that all of us are dependent on what we receive from others and from society more generally. Progressives also believe that there is more than a little bit of luck in determining certain personal economic outcomes.

What do we mean by *excessive* inequality? While that is an important question, for current policy discussions, we don't have to answer it: the level of inequality experienced in the United States and other countries is well beyond the level that should be viewed as acceptable. (Note that progressives do not call for complete equality. Even if that were attainable, there is a recognition that some inequality may be desirable to provide the incentives that are required in order for our economy to function.)

What does it mean to live up to one's potential? Although again I cannot give a full treatment here, let me say what it is not. It is not just maximizing one's income. Humans are more than goods-producing machines, which if fine tuned can do a better job in transforming inputs into outputs. Living up to one's potential means full use of one's mental and physical capabilities. It recognizes that we as individuals gain pleasure from using our minds and that when those talents are turned to problems of societal importance, society as a whole benefits. It recognizes too that we are social beings, and that, as such, social connections are important. Progressivism goes beyond materialism: man cannot live without bread, but man cannot live on bread alone.

Because this is so, progressives eschew GDP fetishism: the objective of our society is not to maximize GDP. As Robert Kennedy famously said, GDP "measures everything, in short, except that which makes life worthwhile."[20] Or, to quote FDR's first inaugural speech, "Happiness lies not in the mere possession of money; it lies in the joy of achievement, in the thrill of creative effort. The joy, the moral stimulation of work no longer must be forgotten in the mad chase of evanescent profits."[21]

THE PROGRESSIVE ECONOMIC AGENDA

Let us now turn our attention to the more narrow set of traditional economic issues: What should be or is the Progressive view of the role of the state in the economy? What should be the Progressive economic agenda? One cannot answer these questions without reference to the underlying foundations presented in the first part of this chapter: the nature of human choices, the relationship between the individual and society, our values and what we are striving for.

Given the high ground that the right has assumed in recent decades, perhaps it is best to begin with an explanation of the counter position and what is wrong with it. The right's economic worldview is predicated on the notion that markets, on their own, are efficient and stable and thus there is no need for government; and even if there were some minor problems, collective action (government) would at best be ineffective, and it would more likely make matters worse. It goes further: even when there is only one firm in a particular market, ever-present *potential* competition fully disciplines the monopolist; and even when there are externalities, Coasian bargaining can (given an assignment of secure property rights) lead to an efficient outcome.[22] There is no need for government intervention, say those on the right, although in some instances there is a need for *voluntary* collective action: for example, non-smokers might have to bribe smokers not to smoke, and so on.[23]

These views seemed to draw upon a long intellectual tradition dating back to Adam Smith, who explained how the pursuit of self-interest would lead, as if by an invisible hand, to the well-being of society. But Adam Smith was far more nuanced in his reasoning than his latter-day followers. He understood the proclivity of markets toward monopolization. He understood the role of government, for instance, in providing for education. Adam Smith was, in effect, describing one of the *attributes* of the market economy, one of the forces at play—countervailed by other forces going in other directions.

It would be nearly 175 years later before economists were able to show the sense in which competitive markets might lead to the well-being of society. This well-being is expressed as "Pareto efficiency," in which no one can be made better off without making someone worse off—a construct that pays no attention at all to distributive justice.[24] As research progressed, it became clear that contrary to the presumption of Smithians, the market was almost *never* efficient: the intellectual underpinnings of these doctrines (that I have referred elsewhere to as *market fundamentalism*) have been totally destroyed in the past thirty years. For instance, with imperfect and asymmetric information or with limited risk markets, markets are never Pareto efficient, even taking into account the costs of gathering information or creating markets.[25] Agency costs and externalities are rife. Markets on their own are not only inefficient, they may not be stable—witness the crises that have afflicted the global economy since the beginning of the era of deregulation.

Even a casual inspection of modern American capitalism has shown that this optimistic attitude regarding markets without government intervention has not worked well: cigarette companies were killing our citizens; chemical companies were polluting our rivers; energy companies are polluting our air; the financial sector neither allocated capital well nor managed risk—and polluted the global economy with toxic mortgages; monopoly power is a reality in large segments of the economy; and corporations often seem more interested in maximizing the well-being of their executives than in enhancing stock market value, let alone the well-being of society more generally.

It should also be clear that the market does not work in the way depicted by economic textbooks, where demand always equals supply. We have homeless people and empty homes. We have vast needs—investments required to retrofit the global economy to address the reality of global warming, and investment needs in infrastructure, technology, and education not only in developing countries but even in advanced countries—and yet we have vastly underutilized resources, large numbers of unemployed workers, and idle industrial plants and equipment. Some may claim there is a savings glut[26]; in truth, we have financial markets that seem unable to redeploy the world's scarce savings to where social returns are highest.

The progressive movement grew naturally from observing these repeated instances in which markets—in the nineteenth- and early-twentieth-century version of capitalism—seemed to be failing to serve the interests of society more broadly. Through the advances in economics over the past half-century, we have come to understand better these pervasive "market failures," and so we now know how to make markets better serve society.

This then is one of the responsibilities of government: *to make markets act like markets*[27], to act more like the textbook models in which what they do does serve societal interests. This entails passing and enforcing good laws on corporate governance, competition, bankruptcy, the environment, conflicts of interest, etc., and strong regulations that restrict the ability of anyone to impose large costs on others.

It is, perhaps, ironic that it has been left to Progressives, often seen as critics of markets, to make markets act like markets. It is not clear what the real problem of the right is: Do they really think that the pervasive market imperfections that have been noted do not exist? Or is it that corporate money sees that by rigging the rules in their favor, they can enhance their own short-sighted interests?

We should also recognize that markets don't exist in a vacuum. They function under a set of rules and regulations, and how they function depends on those rules and regulations. If those rules and regulations allow for greater scope for conflicts of interest, then there will be more "perverse" and inefficient behavior. There will be less trust—a subject to which I will return shortly.

Every rule (and more broadly every policy, every tax, every expenditure) affects not just the efficiency of the market but also the distribution. (This too was one of the main messages of *The Price of Inequality*.) When a bankruptcy law gives first priority to derivatives, it distorts the economy and enriches the bankers buying and selling these weapons of mass financial destruction.

Earlier, I described social justice as a basic Progressive value. But the Progressive equality agenda can be defended on more than just moral grounds: we pay a high price for our high level of inequality; we could have more growth and stability, greater efficiency, and higher standards of living and increased well-being.

This is a marked departure from how the right looks at matters. They see a trade-off between efficiency and equity, and they often argue that any attempt to achieve greater equality would be counterproductive—that it is those at the bottom who would most suffer. They seem to assert (without proving it) that we are in a Rawlsian equilibrium.[28]

Today, the vocabulary has shifted. Since as the rich have gotten richer, *most* of the economy has gotten poorer, it's hard to defend trickle-down economics.[29] Median household income adjusted for inflation is lower than it was a quarter century ago.[30] An economy that, over such a long period of time, fails to increase the living standards of a majority of its citizens is a failed economy.

Thus, rather than trickle-down economics, we need "trickle-up" economics: if those at the bottom and middle do well, so will those at the top. We need, in particular, to build out from the middle.

The argument of the right today is implicitly based on a counterfactual claim: were it not for all the money going to the top, the poor would be even poorer. For the rich are the job creators. Without them, the poor would not have even the meager incomes they have. But this contention flies in the face of both evidence and the right's own economic theories. When there is demand for goods, entrepreneurs will have an incentive to satisfy that demand. That is the nub of Smith's argument. But of course if there is no demand for goods, even the best of entrepreneurs will not make investments. Western economies have demonstrated no dearth of entrepreneurship: when demand was high (and even when tax rates were very, very high) jobs were created. When demand is weak, even if tax rates are low and firms are sitting on trillions of dollars of cash (so money is no constraint) jobs won't be created.

Even more corrosive for our economy, and for our sense of identity, is the lack of opportunity that has come to mark the United States and some other advanced countries. Some on the right claim that what matters is not equality of outcomes but equality of opportunity. But in saying that, they make two fundamental mistakes. The first is the assertion that the United States is in fact a land of opportunity. To the contrary: a young American's life prospects are more dependent on the income and education of his parents than in other advanced countries. And those countries that seek to emulate the US economic system are finding that opportunity is diminishing there as well.

The second mistake is to presume that one can separate inequality of outcomes from inequality of opportunity. Where economic inequality is great, so too is political inequality; and where inequality of outcomes is great, so too is inequality of opportunity.[31]

So far, I have described two of the central roles of government: promoting equality and social justice, and regulating the economy—establishing the rules of the game under which any system has to operate. There is a third role that most even on the right accede to: maintaining growth and stability. As the most recent economic crisis makes so apparent, markets are not self-regulating. They are prone to booms and busts. And when they go into recession, they are not quick to recover on their own. The government has an important role to play in modulating the excesses of markets and, when there is an economic downturn, in helping engineer a recovery.

But there are two more roles for government that are important parts of the progressive agenda: promoting growth, entrepreneurship, and development, and promoting social protection.

Government (collective action) can play a positive role in promoting growth, and—as evidenced by the chapters in this book—it has done so repeatedly. In fact, there are few successful countries in which government has not played that role.[32] Again, we now have a good understanding of why it is that markets are likely to underinvest, say, in basic research—and why it is that government made the critical investments that led to the transformation to modern agriculture and to the creation of modern telecommunications, from the first telegraph line to the modern Internet.[33]

We also have a better understanding of why government needs to play a central role in social protection—why markets have systematically failed in an efficient and fair manner to address widely recognized needs for social insurance, whether it be for retirement, unemployment, or health care.[34] Individuals value security, and yet markets do not seem adequately able to address these needs and desires; hence government has stepped in to fill the breach.[35]

We now recognize that different aspects of the economy are intertwined and that various sectors of the economy—and the policies that are supposed to govern them—have an impact on both economic efficiency and social equality. As economic policy is formulated, the fundamental progressive agenda laid forth in the first part of this chapter need to be borne in mind. Take, for instance, monetary policy, a subject which is usually thought of as technocratic. Conservatives have tried to use technocratic arguments as justification for the existence of an independent central bank that is largely focused on inflation. But an independent central bank, like that in the United States, can easily be captured by financial interests. When this occurs—as was the case in the lead-up to the 2008 financial crisis—little is done to ensure that the financial sector serves the rest of the economy and does not simply exploit it. In such a climate, the central bank may renege on its responsibility to ensure that the banks do not engage in predatory lending, abusive credit card practices, or exploit their market power to the detriment of the rest of the economy. In recent history the central bank's obsession with inflation led to greater financial instability—and almost surely higher levels of unemployment and inequality—than would have occurred if it had maintained a more balanced focus on inflation, growth, employment, and financial stability.[36]

We have also come to understand how inequality leads to macroeconomic instability and lower economic performance overall. The lower level of social cohesion, with the associated lower level of trust, has a direct impact on economic performance but an indirect effect as well, because of the lessened support for vital public investments in infrastructure, technology, and education. Because of these lower investments, larger portions of the population—especially those at the bottom of the economic pyramid—are not able to live up to their potential. Social inequities feed on themselves in a downward vicious circle. As a result we waste one of our most precious resources: human resources.[37]

CONCLUDING OBSERVATIONS

I have discussed at length the roles that successful governments can and have played in enhancing the well-being of society.

Some twenty-five years ago, I delivered a lecture in Amsterdam on the economic role of the state.[38] There, I explained at greater length how modern economic theory had shown why markets often fail to produce efficient or socially acceptable outcomes. These have been labeled "market failures," and I described the roles of the government in remedying these failures. The roles that I described roughly accord with those just illustrated.

I explained how the powers of government enabled it to potentially remedy these market failures but then went on to identify certain limitations of government (e.g., its limited abilities to make commitments, the fact that it had the power of compulsion made constraints on equity and due process more imperative but that these constraints were often costly).

Here, I want to comment briefly on how recent events and advances in economics over the past quarter century have modified and enriched our understandings of these issues—several of which I have already alluded to.

We have learned more about the strengths and limitations of government and learned more about how we can improve government performance. We have come to understand better the risks of capture of government (including cognitive capture)—the role of money and revolving doors—and how transparency can help. The reinventing government initiative during the Clinton administration also showed how we can improve both the efficiency and efficacy of government, making it more responsive to citizens. Some parts of the government have demonstrated remarkable competencies: for example, the transactions costs associated with Social Security are but a fraction of those associated with most private annuities. Looking around the world, the public health-care systems in Australia and many European countries manage to deliver better health outcomes at a fraction of the costs of America's largely private system. Citizens value and respect the teachers that teach their children, the firemen that protect their property, the policemen that ensure law and order. They even like their own Congressmen, overwhelmingly tending to reelect them. They tend to make denigrating remarks about *other* teachers, *other* Congressmen, and most importantly, about faceless gray bureaucrats. But the numbers of these bureaucrats, especially relative to the size of the population or the government's budget, has in fact been in marked decline, suggesting that government has become *more* efficient.

An understanding of the limitations of government has implications not so much for *what* the government does but *how* it does it. Even in countries with limited governmental capacities, it is still desirable, for instance, for the government to pursue industrial policies that promote faster growth, more equality, higher employment, and a better environment. But it may be desirable for such governments to utilize broader based instruments, like the management of the exchange rate.[39]

The financial crisis has, of course, made the reality of market failures all the more obvious, demonstrating that markets by themselves are neither efficient nor stable. It is not just that the market economy is not good at accommodating shocks; the market, in fact, amplifies them. It is also that the market economy is prone to create its own shocks, with credit cycles and asset bubbles.

Moreover, the recent crisis has heightened our sense that waste is not the monopoly of government: no government has probably resulted in a waste of economic resources on the scale of America's financial markets, with the cumulative loss from the gap between potential and actual output of the nation's overall economy now totaling trillions of dollars.

We have come to understand the importance of informational and related imperfections: agency costs are pervasive, in both the public and private sector. Deficiencies in corporate governance, no less than in public governance, are omnipresent. The economics profession has been slow to take on board Berle and Means[40] insights about the consequences of the separation of ownership and control, or Herbert Simon's observation that if there is a difference between public and private sector performance, it is *not* simply a matter of incentives: incentive problems are universal.[41]

By the same token, we have learned that privatization is no panacea. This is not just a theoretical observation. The only circumstances in which privatization would fully resolve the problems posed by government ownership are the highly restricted conditions under which markets are themselves Pareto efficient.[42] But real phenomena observed time and time again, from British railroads to Mexican roads, to American prisons to America's use of mercenary armed forces, shows us otherwise.[43]

We have seen that the imperfections of information are endogenous: banks and CEOs have the ability and incentives to distort the information that they reveal, to engage in nontransparent transactions.[44] And we have seen how they have fought for the right to maintain such lack of transparency, even within government-insured institutions.

We have come to understand that there are very important related macro-externalities. A crisis in one bank can lead to problems in other banks—and then to problems in the economy as a whole.

The most recent crisis has also heightened our understandings of the extent to which individuals can be exploited by others, as they were systematically, through insider trading, market manipulation (e.g., libor, foreign exchange), predatory lending, abusive credit card practices, etc. Most fundamentally, the notion that the economy can be well described by models based on rational well-informed individuals with rational expectations has been totally undermined.[45]

But what was perhaps most shocking about the crisis to people on both sides of the Atlantic, was the ample evidence of *moral turpitude,* especially in the financial sector. It was not that there was a disease that was particularly prevalent in the southern part of Manhattan, or that struck with a particular virulence in the early days of the twenty-first century, with a relapse a few years later. Rather, it was that the economic, political, and social system that had evolved over the preceding decades had given rise to an entire class of individuals without moral moorings. We had as such created a society in which many Americans found distasteful, all of which reinforces the observations I made at the beginning of this chapter: preferences and behavior are, in part, malleable and culturally determined, and the direction that the United States had taken since the beginning of the Reagan revolution was the wrong direction.

It is understandable that political disillusionment set in when those that had caused the crisis (i.e., the bankers) were bailed out, while innocent victims—those who lost their jobs and homes—were left largely to suffer on their own. The fact that in the aftermath of the crisis inequality worsened, with the top 1 percent getting 95 percent of the gains from 2009 through 2012[46] has led to further disillusionment with our political and economic system. For most Americans, the crisis is not over. We can trumpet having prevented another Great Depression; however, we cannot claim that we quickly restored America to prosperity. Indeed, as noted, the loss resulting from the Great Recession—measured by the gap between the trend line, where we would presumably have been had the crisis not occurred and the economy's actual output—amounts to trillions of dollars.

The crisis undermined our society's claim not just to fairness, but even to having a meaningful rule of law. We had rules governing what should happen when banks can't pay back what they owe: a seemingly well designed system of conservatorship. But we rode roughshod over these and basic principles of capitalism as we bailed out the bankers, their shareholders and bondholders, and we failed to hold accountable those who had caused the crisis. An even more egregious violation of the rule of law was manifested in the foreclosure crisis, where people who did not owe money were thrown out of their homes. A "good" rule of law is supposed to protect the vulnerable, not the rich and powerful. We did just the opposite.

President Clinton began his Administration with a manifesto called *Putting People First.* If one does put people first, it means a focus on the things they care about: jobs and wages, education, health and home, opportunity and security. The progressive economic agenda must concentrate on these. We know what to do to make significant progress on each of these fronts. We know what to do to increase equality and opportunity. The problem is the politics. And that is why a progressive economic agenda cannot be separated from a progressive political agenda.

Notes

1. The author is University Professor, Columbia University and chief economist, Roosevelt Institute. The author would like to acknowledge the helpful comments of David Woolner and of the other members of the November 2013 Roosevelt Institute conference in Dublin at which this was first presented ("Progressivism in America: Past, Present and Future"), and the assistance of Eamon Kircher-Allen.

2. There are, of course, large differences both within the Progressive movement and within the Conservative movement. Still, the values and economic agenda that I ascribe to Progressives would, I believe, garner widespread if not unanimous support; and my caricature of the Right (the Conservative movement) is, I believe, accurate in describing a set of beliefs adhered to by the vast majority of those of that persuasion.

3. This is a central theme of my 2014 book with Bruce Greenwald, *Creating a Learning Society: A New Approach to Growth, Development, and Social Progress* (New York: Columbia University Press, 2014).

4. That is, we cannot be sure either of the consequences of our actions, of the actions that others will take, or future states of the world.

5. This is a central message of the 2015 *World Development Report* of the World Bank, *Mind, Society, and Behavior.*

6. See "Climate Change in the American Mind," a 2013 report of the Yale Project on Climate Change Communication and the George Mason University Center for Climate Change Communication, available at <http://environment.yale.edu/climate-communication/files/Climate-Beliefs-November-2013.pdf>.

7. Externalities are simply the effects that individual actions have on others for which those are actions not compensated (in the case of positive externalities) or for which they do not provide compensation (in the case of negative externalities).

8. This point has important implications for taxation: Conservatives often argue *for* inequality on the grounds that the rich are simply receiving the *just deserts* from their contributions to society. Progressives note that each individual's productivity in fact is a consequence in large measure of what others have done, not only for him directly, but in creating the environment in which he can prosper. Thus, even if it were the case that compensation reflected individuals' (marginal) productivities, that productivity would not be what it is without the contributions of others. See the discussion below.

9. The precise quote is from a 1676 letter to Robert Hooke: "If I have seen further it is by standing on the shoulders of giants."

10. A Pareto improvement is simply change that makes one or more individuals better off without making anyone worse off.

11. There is a huge literature on this subject, with many warning that in the absence of the appropriate institutional framework, the transitions would fail to produce the desired benefits (see, e.g. J. E. Stiglitz, "Some Theoretical Aspects of the Privatization: Applications to Eastern Europe," *Revista di Politica Economica*, December 1991, 179–204. Also in M. Baldassarri, L. Paganetto and E.S. Phelps (eds.), *Privatization Processes in Eastern Europe* (St. Martin's Press: New York, 1993), 179–204. As the process unfolded, it became clear that these warnings were prescient. See, for instance, the keynote address I delivered as chief economist of the World Bank looking back at the first ten years of transition (J. E. Stiglitz, "Whither Reform? Ten Years of Transition," in *Annual World Bank Conference on Economic Development*, B. Pleskovic and J.E. Stiglitz (eds.), Washington: World Bank, 2000, 27–56). For a more extensive comparison of the gradualist Chinese approach and the shock therapy invoked in Russia, see Athar Hussain, Nicholas Stern, and J. E. Stiglitz "Chinese Reforms from a Comparative Perspective," in *Incentives, Organization, and Public Economics: Papers in Honour of Sir James Mirrlees*, Peter J. Hammond and Gareth D. Myles (eds.) (Oxford: Oxford University Press, 2000), 243–277. For a discussion of some of the theoretical explanations for the failure of shock therapy, see

K. Hoff and J. E. Stiglitz, "After the Big Bang? Obstacles to the Emergence of the Rule of Law in Post-Communist Societies," *American Economic Review*, 94(3), June 2004, 753–763 and K. Hoff and J. E. Stiglitz, "Exiting a Lawless State," *Economic Journal*, 118(531), 1474–1497. Some years later, as the process of transition continued, these perspectives were confirmed. See S. Godoy and J. E. Stiglitz "Growth, Initial Conditions, Law and Speed of Privatization in Transition Countries: 11 Years Later," *Transition and Beyond*, S. Estrin et al, eds. (Hampsire England: Palgrave Macmillian: Hampshire, England, 2007), 89–117.

12. The theory of public goods (P. Samuelson, 1954) explains why there are certain goods that can more efficiently be provided collectively. For a textbook treatment, see J. E. Stiglitz, *The Economics of the Public Sector* (New York: W.W. Norton, 5th edition, 2015).

13. When the US *Declaration of Independence* says that "All men are created equal," it did not mean, of course, that they were equal in all respects, but that there should be equality in their political voice. See Danielle Allen, *Our Declaration*, A Reading of the Declaration of Independence in Defense of Equality, Liveright Publishing. 2014. Recent decisions and actions (discussed below) often seem inconsistent with the values expressed in the Declaration of Independence.

14. See the papers prepared for the Roosevelt Institute's November 2013 conference in Dublin, "Progressivism in America: Past, Present and Future."

15. J. E. Stiglitz, *The Price of Inequality: How Today's Divided Society Endangers our Future* (New York: W.W. Norton, 20120).

16. See, for instance, A. Florini, ed *The Right to Know: Transparency for an Open World* (New York: Columbia University Press, 2007) and J. E. Stiglitz, "On Liberty, the Right to Know, and Public Discourse: The Role of Transparency in Public Life," in *Globalizing Rights*, Matthew Gibney ed. (Oxford: Oxford University Press, 2003), 115–156. (Originally presented as 1999 Oxford Amnesty Lecture, Oxford, January 1999.)

17. Though we saw their power even before the crisis, e.g. in the repeal of the Glass Steagall Act and the passage of legislation preventing the regulation of derivatives. See J. E. Stiglitz, *Freefall: America, Free Markets, and the Sinking of the World Economy* (New York: W.W. Norton, 2010).

18. According to "Climate Change in the American Mind" (Op. Cit.), nearly a quarter of Americans believe global warming is not really happening; according to a Pew study, a third of Americans reject the idea of evolution. See "Public's Views on Human Evolution," Pew Research Center, December 30, 2013, available at <http://www.pewforum.org/2013/12/30/publics-views-on-human-evolution/>.

19. This is a central theme of my book *The Price of Inequality, op cit*. The effects of excessive inequality on economic performance have now been well documented. See, for instance Andrew Berg and Jonathan D. Ostry, 2011, "Inequality and Unsustainable Growth: Two Sides of the Same 28 Coin?" *IMF Staff Discussion Note* 11/08.

20. Address at University of Kansas, Lawrence, Kansas, March 18, 1968. This view has been emphasized by the international Commission on the Measurement of Economic Performance and Social Progress, whose report is available as *Mismeasuring Our Lives: Why GDP Doesn't Add Up*, J. E. Stiglitz, J. Fitoussi and A. Sen (New York: The New Press, 2010).

21. There were many other remarks in FDR's First Inaugural that echo the themes stressed here: He spoke of "the falsity of material wealth as the standard of success," and that "we now realize as we have never realized before our interdependence on each other."

22. With well defined property rights, the "Coasian" view is that bargaining between affected parties would ensure efficiency. For instance, if the smokers in the room have been given the right to smoke, if the benefits of clean air to the non-smokers exceeds the benefits of smoking on the part of the smokers, they would "bribe" the smokers not to smoke. See Ronald Coase, "The Problem of Social Cost," *Journal of Law and Economics*, Vol. 3, 1960, 1–44. The result that such bargaining leads to efficiency only holds, however, if there are no transactions costs—and a number of other conditions are satisfied.

23. Thus, even the Coasian approach does not abnegate the need for collective action: Coase does not provide an alternative solution for the free rider problem in the context of public goods.

24. Arrow, K. J., 1951. "An Extension of the Basic Theorems of Classical Welfare Economics," *Proceedings of the Second Berkeley Symposium on Mathematical Statistics and Probability*, J. Neyman, ed. (Berkeley: University of California Press, 1951), 507–532; Debreu, G., 1954. "Valuation Equilibrium and Pareto Optimum," *Proceedings of the National Academy of Sciences*, 40(7), 588–592; and *The Theory of Value* (New Haven: Yale University Press, 1959).

25. B. Greenwald and J. E. Stiglitz, "Externalities in Economies with Imperfect Information and Incomplete Markets," *Quarterly Journal of Economics*, Vol. 101, No. 2, May 1986, 229–264

26. See for example Ben S. Bernanke's March 10, 2005 speech as Federal Reserve governor, "The Global Saving Glut and the U.S. Current Account Deficit," available at <http://www.federal-reserve.gov/boarddocs/speeches/2005/200503102/>.

27. This is the title of an important initiative of the Roosevelt Institute undertaken in the aftermath of the financial crisis.

28. John Rawls, in his classic 1971 book *A Theory of Justice* (Cambridge, MA: Harvard University Press), argued that society should maximize the well-being of the worst off individual.

29. Trickle down economics argued that money given to the rich would "trickle down" to the rest of society, and in so doing, everyone would benefit.

30. See U.S. Census Historical Income Table H-06.

31. This relationship has come to be called the Great Gatsby curve. There has been a wealth of research supporting the existence of this systematic relationship. See Alan Kruger, January 12, 2012, "The Rise and Consequences of Inequality in the United States," speech given as Chairman of the Council of Economic Advisors, available at <http://www.whitehouse.gov/sites/default/files/krueger_cap_speech_final_remarks.pdf>.

32. While a few years ago, this perspective would have seemed controversial, today it is much less so. One of the main items in the agenda of Justin Yifu Lin as Chief Economist of the World Bank from 2008 to 2012 was the promotion of industrial policies. See, e.g. J. Lin and J. E. Stiglitz, *The Industrial Policy Revoltuion I: The Role of Government Beyond Ideology* (New York and Houndmills, UK: Palgrave Macmillan, 2014). For a broader theoretical discussion, see J. E. Stiglitz and B. Greenwald, *Creating a Learning Societ: A New Approach to Growth, Development, and Social Progress*, New York: Columbia University Press, 2014.

33. See Maria Mazzucato, 2013, *The Entrepreneurial State: Debunking Public vs. Private Sector Myths*, London: Anthem Press.

34. These market failures are closely linked with problems of information asymmetries—moral hazard and adverse selection. Indeed, our understanding of these limitations largely grew out of the analysis of failures in the insurance market. See, e.g. Kenneth Arrow, "Uncertainty and the Welfare Economics of Medical Care," *American Economic Review*, 53(5), 1963, 941–97; Kenneth Arrow. *Aspects of the Theory of Risk-Bearing (Yrjo Jahnsson Lectures)*, Helsinki, Finland: Yrjo Jahnssonin Saatio, 1965; Richard Arnott and J. E. Stiglitz, "The Basic Analytics of Moral Hazard," *Scandinavian Journal of Economics*, 90 (3), 383–413, 1988; and Michael Rothschild and J. E. Stiglitz, "Equilibrium in Competitive Insurance Markets: An Essay on the Economics of Imperfect Information," *Quarterly Journal of Economics*, 90(4), 629–649, 1976. For further discussion, see J. E. Stiglitz, "Perspectives on the Role of Government Risk-Bearing within the Financial Sector," in *Government Risk-bearing*, M. Sniderman (ed.), Norwell, MA: Kluwer Academic Publishers, 1993, 109–130.

35. The failure to assess the value of security is one of the failings of GDP—and one of the reasons that reforms in social insurance, allegedly to improve economic performance may have had just the opposite effect (which would be apparent if economic performance were correctly measured). See Stiglitz, Sen, and Fitoussi, *op. cit.*

36. See J. E. Stiglitz, *Freefall, op cit;* J. E. Stiglitz, *The Price of Inequality, op cit.;* and J. E. Stiglitz, "Central Banking in a Democratic Society," *De Economist* (Netherlands), 146(2), 1998, 199–226. (Originally presented as 1997 Tinbergen Lecture, Amsterdam, October).

37. This is one of the central messages of my book *The Price of Inequality*.

38. *The Economic Role of the State*, A. Heertje ed. Oxford: Blackwells, 1989.

39. See B. Greenwald and J. E. Stiglitz, "Industrial Policies, the Creation of a Learning Society, and Economic Development," in *The Industrial Policy Revolution I: The Role of Government Beyond Ideology*, Joseph E. Stiglitz and Justin Yifu Lin (eds.), Houndmills, UK and New York: Palgrave Macmillan, 43–71.

40. *The Modern Corporation and Private Property*, (New York: Macmillan, 1932).

41. Simon H. A., 1991. "Organizations and Markets," *Journal of Economic Perspectives*, 5(2), 25–44

42. David Sappington and J. E. Stiglitz, "Privatization, Information and Incentives," *Journal of Policy Analysis and Management*, 6(4), 567–582, 1987.

43. By the same token, we have come to understand that ownership may not be the central issue: publicly owned enterprises may also not serve the public interest; they may exploit workers and abuse the environment. What is crucial is establishing control (regulatory) mechanisms; ownership may affect both access to information and the design of these mechanisms.

44. Edlin, A. and J.E. Stiglitz, 1995. "Discouraging Rivals: Managerial Rent-Seeking and Economic Inefficiencies," *American Economic Review*, 85(5), 1301–1312.

45. For a more extensive discussion of these failings, see J. E. Stiglitz, *Freefall, op. cit.* For a more technical discussion, see J. E. Stiglitz, "Rethinking Macroeconomics: What Failed and How to Repair It," *Journal of the European Economic Association*, 9(4), 591–645, 2011.

46. See updated tables to Thomas Piketty and Emmanuel Saez, 2003, "Income Inequality sin the United States, 1913–1998," *Quarterly Journal of Economics*, 118(1): 1–39. (Longer updated version published in A.B. Atkinson and T. Piketty eds. (Oxford: Oxford University Press, 2007); tables and figures updated through 2012 on the website of Emmanuel Saez, <http://eml.berkeley.edu/~saez/>.

16

The Way Forward

Progressive Problems, Progressive Hopes

E. J. DIONNE JR. AND ELIZABETH THOM

The election of Barack Obama in 2008 was widely taken as a sign that the United States was entering a period during which progressive ideas and policies would be ascendant.[1] As his presidency nears its conclusion, hope on the left has been replaced by uncertainty, despite the president's achievements.

Obama did preside over the passage of historic pieces of legislation, including the American Recovery and Reinvestment Act, the Affordable Care Act, and a reform of Wall Street. He took over at a moment when the economy was teetering on the edge of collapse and his policies (combined with those of the Federal Reserve) brought the country back to prosperity. Only a few presidencies witnessed (and contributed to) as profound and rapid a set of social changes as Obama's did in the areas of gay rights and gay marriage. And his executive actions, though controversial, led to the largest change in immigration law and practice in nearly thirty years.

Yet the other story of the Obama years is the rise of an increasingly extreme and militant conservative movement and the continuing shift of the Republican Party to the right. Rarely has a party been as disciplined in opposing and obstructing the agenda of a president. And rarely has the United States witnessed as sharp a shift from election to election as it did between 2008 and 2010 and again between 2012 and 2014. There was talk of a new American electoral system in which Democrats would enjoy a long term of success in presidential elections while Republicans would have a regular edge in midterm voting. The new progressive coalition's dependence on groups with histories of lower turnout in nonpresidential elections—particularly the young, but also Latinos and to some degree African Americans—created two very different electorates that rendered radically different judgments in two consecutive pairs of elections.

As noted at the outset of this book, there is intense debate over whether the United States should be seen as a conservative nation or a progressive nation. In one sense, the debate is misplaced, since the country has regularly displayed both conservative and liberal impulses and since individual voters themselves are often torn. One of the most widely quoted formulations about American public opinion is the 1967 observation of Lloyd Free and Hadley Cantril that Americans are ideological conservatives and operational liberals. As the political scientist Alan Abramowitz noted, their view comes down to the idea that "most Americans agree with broad statements of conservative principles" but that when it comes down to "specific programs addressing societal needs and problems" Americans "generally supported activist government." It is still broadly the case that on generalities ("small government," "deregulation," "decentralization," "entrepreneurship") Americans often like conservative ideas, but that on specific programs (Medicare, Medicaid, federal aid to education, consumer and environmental protection) Americans also want the government to act.

These tensions are reflected in the conflicting views of the American story on the left and the right. Broadly speaking, conservatives—and this view is articulated most strongly by Tea Party supporters—are convinced that the United States was conceived in laissez-faire, small government notions and that the country began going off the rails during the Progressive Era, animated by the use of "Hamiltonian means for Jeffersonian ends." Larger government supporting greater equality and democracy opened the way for all that followed: the Square Deal, the New Freedom, the New Deal, the Fair Deal, the New Frontier, the Great Society—and, as it would seem from some of the right-wing rhetoric, that greatest attack on freedom in human history, Obamacare. A great deal of the commotion in our politics today can be attributed to the deeply held beliefs of those who subscribe to this view and want to return America to the period before 1901: in other words, back to the Gilded Age.

The progressive view of American history rejects the notion that the United States was conceived in laissez-faire. Progressives argue that from the beginning Americans have always used government to advance the public interest and to promote economic development and prosperity.

Viewed from this perspective, the Gilded Age can be seen as an interruption in the normal course of American history, an aberration that led to the rise of both the populist and the progressive movements. Both sought to return the country to a tradition that saw democratic government as correcting for or enhancing the benefits of market outcomes.

It's always worth remembering that the first word of the constitution of the United States is, "we," found at the opening of the Preamble, which is the most underappreciated part of the document. It really is a kind of progressive manifesto. "We, the people of the United States, in order to form a more perfect union, establish justice, ensure domestic tranquility, provide for the common defense, promote the general welfare"—yes, welfare is right there in the first paragraph of the constitution of the United States.—"and to secure the blessings of liberty to ourselves and our posterity do ordain and establish this constitution." Again, it reads "ourselves," not "myself."

Those who defend "originalism," the notion that the Constitution's authors were in clear and unmistakable agreement about only one meaning of the document's words, overlook the battle between Alexander Hamilton—who in many ways was a conservative that my fellow contributor Chris Caldwell would deeply admire—and James Madison over establishing the Bank of the United States. Hamilton said the Constitution clearly authorized the government to create the bank, Madison stated that the Constitution flatly prohibited it. It was this fight that created the first two-party system. "Originalism" becomes difficult to defend if one considers that two of the principal drafters of the Constitution—and the original interpreters of it in the Federalist Papers—disagreed at the outset of our republic on such a central question.

Nor were Lyndon Johnson or Barack Obama the first presidents to support government intervention in the health-care system. That honor goes to another conservative in our history, President John Adams, who signed into law the first American version of socialized medicine in 1798. The measure created the Federal Marine Hospital Service, which funded hospitals across the country to treat sailors who were sick or got injured on the job. Perhaps there was a Big Sailors lobby back then, or perhaps the nation feared the illnesses brought back by sailors from overseas. Whatever the motivation, there is no record of a mass campaign against "Adamscare."[2]

Another conservative icon, Henry Clay, created what he called "the American system." Clay wanted to distinguish American economic activity from the "British system," which he said was based on laissez-faire. By contrast, we Americans believed in an active government that would promote economic development through protective tariffs and build up the country through "internal improvements." Today we describe these improvements of the roads and the canals with the rather less poetic word "infrastructure." Clay, like Hamilton, envisioned a role for government in creating a great industrial nation.

And Abraham Lincoln, the man who made Clay his personal hero, devoted his entire administration to preserving the Union and the power of the national government. During his time in office, Lincoln signed into law the Morrill Act that created the land grant colleges, favored railroad promotion (as did most politicians in his day), and through the Homestead Act used the federal government to encourage a nation of small farmers.

It was the Gilded Age that broke with this long tradition of government intervention. It's true, of course, that industry in that era was not as antigovernment as its rhetoric suggested. In that sense, it is not unlike industry now. Manufacturers continued to support the protective tariff, and business still sought government protection. But the Gilded Age also saw government blocked from taking measures to protect individuals in the new industrial era that was rising. A conservative Supreme Court was central to this new notion of severe limits on government's capacities. In its 1905 *Lochner v. New York* decision, the Court invalidated a New York law limiting the work day of bakers to ten hours on grounds that it interfered with the "liberty of contract" principle. And it was at the end of the Gilded Age, near the beginning of the Progressive Era, that the Court first declared that corporations were people in a footnote to the 1886 *Santa Clara v. Southern Pacific Railroad* decision. *Lochner* was eventually overturned in 1937, but the *Santa Clara* decision, and most recently, *Citizens United*, leave us wrestling with the strange doctrine of corporations as persons.

Comedian Stephen Colbert best captured the peculiarity of this notion when he asked former US Senator Russ Feingold, "Would you let your daughter date a corporation, sir?" during an appearance on his show in 2011.[3]

The decisions in *Lochner* and *Santa Clara* coupled with the politics of the Gilded Age called forth both the populist and the progressive revolt. Viewed in this light, the populists and the progressives can be seen not only as radical reformers but also as restorationists dedicated to returning our nation to its enduring traditions of an activist, democratic government.

A broad consensus emerged around these ideas that lasted for much of the twentieth century. But over the last three decades this consensus has fragmented, and today progressive values are being challenged in ways that we have not seen in more than a hundred years.

Evidence for this fragmentation can be seen in the conflicting views among the left over whether Bill Clinton and Barack Obama can be regarded as true progressives. Interestingly, both Bill Clinton and Barack Obama closely identify with Teddy Roosevelt. President Obama directly embraced TR's tradition by traveling to Osawatomie, Kansas, to lay out a more progressive agenda for his 2012 reelection campaign with a speech that closely echoed TR's 1910 "New Nationalism" address. Like TR, President Obama berated the power of wealthy interests and demanded a greater role for government in ensuring greater equality of economic and political opportunity.[4]

Many on the left, however, are not persuaded that either presidents Clinton or Obama are genuinely "progressive." Clinton had to govern in an era when conservatives were still seen as ascendant. Not for nothing did the progressive leader Robert Borasage once suggest that if Richard Nixon was the last president of the liberal era, Bill Clinton was the last president of the conservative era. Clinton's focus on ending deficits and his closeness to liberals with Wall Street backgrounds are often cited as signs of a less-than-progressive presidency. So, too, was his support for deregulating the finance industry. Clinton himself once complained in frustration to his aides: "I hope you're all aware we're Eisenhower Republicans here." With the Republican party moving rightward, it's true that Democrats began occupying ground once held by moderate and liberal Republicans.

As for President Obama, he supported the re-regulation of Wall Street but was reluctant to take on the financial system frontally, partly because he feared the American economy was close to collapse at the beginning of his administration and was reluctant to rattle a financial system at a time when it was so fragile. Moreover, he had to struggle with a Republican Party committed from the beginning of his administration to block his program. This meant that he had to compromise the size of his stimulus program to win a few necessary Republican votes (there were none to be had in the House) and to support a health-care plan closer in its design to the more market-oriented Mitt Romney plan in Massachusetts than to Clinton's plan in the 1990s—let alone a single-payer health system so prized on the left. In certain ways, both Clinton and Obama might be seen as defensive progressives, pushing the policy boundaries as far as they thought feasible.

Their defensiveness is not unique to the American center-left. Progressives in the other democracies face comparable challenges and find themselves on the defensive as well.

Foremost among these is the decline in well-paying blue-collar work and the concomitant decline in trade union membership. The rise of progressivism in the United States, particularly in the New Deal era, was supported by a mass industrial working class, the same base that supported the social democratic parties in Europe. The decline of the traditional working class has created large electoral and organization problems for social democrats in Europe no less than for progressives in the United States.

Globalization and the rise of transnational corporations has weakened the capacity of national governments to impose regulations and to tax and redistribute wealth. It is important not to exaggerate this decline in national power, and we should recognize that many of our European counterparts continue to use the tools of redistribution, regulation, and taxation more aggressively than Americans do. But the emergence of "too-big-to-fail" international financial and corporate entities has significantly disempowered national governments. This is a problem for progressives even though progressives often speak in international terms.

Closely related to impact of globalization is the challenge posed by the loss of prestige among governments. In the United States, much of this can be attributed to the anger caused by the Vietnam War and the Watergate scandal, both of which seriously weakened the standing of the federal government in the eyes of the public. It is an odd fact of American history that while Watergate was a scandal that scarred a Republican administration, its longer-term effect was to strengthen conservative forces in the Republican Party. By helping to discredit government, Watergate gave more credibility to conservative antigovernment themes. When Ronald Reagan declared that "government is not the solution to our problem, government is the problem," he was speaking to a mood that Watergate helped to create. Disillusionment with democratic government, again, is not a uniquely American problem. The rise of strong parties in Europe well to the right and to the left of the mainstream parties speaks to this sense of public impatience with traditional ruling groups and traditional government structures.

Another challenge is the growing dependence among the political parties on the left for electoral support from the educated middle and upper middle classes, rather than on working-class voters, the voters that traditionally represented social democratic points of view. There are still many working-class voters within progressive coalitions, but the overall effect of this change has been the supplanting of social democracy or New Deal progressivism with what we might refer to as "social liberalism" that stresses issues such as gay marriage and abortion rights.

The increasing diversity of the Western democracies poses another challenge. The divisions of race, ethnicity, and immigration status make it more difficult to develop a politics of the common good. Such an approach arises from the sense that "we are all in this together"—a phrase that progressives are rightly fond of. But this concept becomes problematic in the face of the question, "Who are 'we' anyway?" Progressives are indeed obligated to defend a capacious definition of "we," opposing discrimination and oppression against minorities and marginalized groups is a proud part of the progressive legacy. But this is not the same as resolving the challenges to social democracy and progressivism posed by diversity. The rise of far-right parties in Europe and the more nativist strains of the Tea Party movement in the United States require a clear response from the center-left.

Nonetheless, the political tides in the United States still run in a progressive direction. The demographic realities that helped elect and reelect Obama are not cure-alls for progressives, but they do point the way. The steadily rising share of the electorate made up of African Americans, Latinos, and Asians will make the political circumstances of conservatives increasingly difficult, particularly if their cause comes to be defined by phrases such as "take our country back." The "our" in that phrase is the flipside of the progressive challenge: If it is defined primarily in terms of an older and less diverse America, conservatives will have trouble moving forward. President George W. Bush realized this and issued a strong appeal to Latinos while supporting immigration reform. Mitt Romney's talk of "self-deportation" moved the party and the movement backward on this question, and it remains mired in difficulty.

Moreover, young Americans—the electorate of the future—are substantially more progressive than older Americans. The millennial generation is the only American generation in which self-identified liberals regularly equal or outnumber self-described conservatives in the polls. It is also the most diverse generation in our nation's history. And there is substantial evidence that the younger generation, while libertarian leaning on matters of personal freedom, is also more open to government intervention in the marketplace.

Environmentalism is very much part of the younger generation's progressivism. So is social openness, which leads to a historic shift in electoral tactics. Conservative wedge issues that were very effective against liberal candidates from the late 1960s into the mid-2000s have become reverse wedges and now threaten conservatives. The most notable of these is same-sex marriage, which is slowly but steadily becoming a majoritarian position in the United States and is gaining ground in Western Europe. Indeed, attitudes toward gay rights are almost entirely conditioned by age. Younger voters, even the more conservative among them, are overwhelmingly in favor of gay marriage. Opposition is concentrated among voters over the age of sixty-five—and even this group has shifted in a more liberal direction.

The drop in the crime rate in the United States is another reason why progressive politics seems to be resurgent. The rise of violent crime is always good for the party of order, which is usually the conservative party. The drop in the crime rate has had a number of direct political consequences. The election of Bill de Blasio, the strongly progressive mayor of New York City owed in part to his opposition to the police department's "stop and frisk" policy. The fall is the crime rate has also led to a drop in support for the death penalty. Gallup recently reported the lowest level of support for the death penalty in the United States in forty years.[5] It is down to 60 percent from 80 percent at its peak in 1994. The falling crime rate has also led to promising left-right coalitions on behalf of sentencing reform and in opposition to over-incarceration for nonviolent crime. It should be noted that these promising shifts also lay a burden on progressives at all levels of government: maintaining a low violent crime rate is essential to a healthier society but also to progressive politics.

Perhaps the most important change in the public dialogue is the rising awareness of the costs of economic inequality and the problem of wage stagnation. Occupy Wall Street may have passed on as a movement, but its effect on the public discussion—and in particular its popularization of the concept of a privileged "1 percent"—is unmistakable. Inequality played a large role in Obama's 2012 victory, and Mitt Romney aggravated his own problems—and his party's—with his comments about the "47 percent." The juxtaposition of the two percentages speaks to the reemergence of an older kind of class politics that gave rise to social democracy and New Dealism in the first place.

Even conservatives began calling out their party for putting such a heavy emphasis on the role of the business person and the entrepreneur—and offering so little to those who worked for them. Henry Olsen of the Ethics and Public Policy Center was devastating in his description of the 2012 Republican campaign. "Obama effectively asked: Which do you like better? Would you prefer the Republican alternative as exemplified by the candidacy of Mitt Romney and the policies he and his party have proposed in Congress and on the stump?" Olsen wrote in *National Affairs*. "One would have thought that Romney would actively join the debate. In a way he did, for he often emphasized that America was a land where anyone could start from scratch and build a business." But there was a problem here, Olsen noted, in "the subtle implication . . . that people who did so were the best Americans and everyone else was just along for the ride. It is in that sense that the phrase 'you built that' and laments about 'makers' versus 'takers' were the essence of Romney's America."

Olsen argued that conservatives had forgotten "a core constant in American politics," which involved "the willingness to use government power to help individuals advance in life." He concluded: "If American principles simply require hands-off government, then American principles have not been part of our politics for a very long time. A hands-off approach is not what American politics and principles require; it is a parody of what America and American conservatism mean."[6]

Olsen has been particularly brave among conservatives in calling his own side to account for ignoring the working class. But he is not alone. And note his declaration that using government to help Americans advance is a "core constant in American politics." This is a direct challenge to the Tea Party and libertarian view of history that denies the very past that Olsen insists should be celebrated. The future of American politics thus hangs not only on what progressives do, but also on whether conservatives begin to revise their own radically antistatist orientation of recent years.

The desire of progressives for a less defensive, more assertive declaration of their own commitments helps account for the rise of Senator Elizabeth Warren as a major spokesperson for her party. She has been unapologetic in defending the view that government plays a central role in ensuring shared growth and containing abuses of economic power. She shares Ronald Reagan's skill as an explainer who uses storytelling, simple clarity, and sustained argument. And she has helped refocus her party on "bread and butter" concerns, notably with her emphasis on student loan debt, medical bankruptcy, and consumer protection in the financial sphere.

But how does the progressive and Democratic setback of 2014 fit into this narrative? There can be no denying the sweep of the Republican triumph. In certain ways the 2014 results were even worse than those of 2010. Four years earlier the economy was still ailing, and a new wave of conservative activism in the form of the Tea Party was roiling politics. In 2014 the economy was better, ideological energies on the right had abated to some degree—yet Democrats suffered an even more stinging defeat. They lost Senate seats in the presidential swing states such as Iowa, Colorado, and North Carolina and lost governorships in their most loyal bastions, from Massachusetts to Maryland to Illinois.

Perhaps the most significant message from 2014 may have come not from those who voted but from those who didn't. The United States Election Project estimated voter turnout at 36.2 percent, the lowest since 1942. In his post-election press conference, President Obama addressed the nearly two-thirds of Americans who did not vote by saying, "I hear you too."

He may well have had those voters in mind when he issued his executive order to stop the breakup of the families of undocumented immigrants. A large share of the potential voters who stayed home were Latinos, many of them dispirited over congressional failure to act on immigration.

According to the Public Religion Research Institute's 2014 Post-Election American Values Survey, which re-interviewed 1,399 respondents who had been contacted in a preelection poll, Latinos comprised just 8 percent of all voters—but 22 percent of nonvoters. African Americans were roughly equally represented among nonvoters (12 percent) and voters (11 percent). Whites made up a larger share of voters (73 percent) than nonvoters (56 percent.)

The nonvoter pool was also overwhelmingly young: millennials, those aged eighteen to thirty-four, made up 47 percent of the nonvoters and just 17 percent of voters. On the other hand, 54 percent of those who reported voting were over the age of fifty. The electorate was also skewed by education and class: those with more schooling were much more likely to vote. The survey found that 53 percent of nonvoters did not attend college, compared with 38 percent of those who said they voted. Among nonvoters, 44 percent made less than $30,000 a year; among voters, only 26 percent were in that lower income group. At the other end of the socioeconomic scale, 23 percent of nonvoters but 33 percent of voters had college degrees or advanced degrees; respondents earning $100,000 or more annually accounted for 7 percent of nonvoters, but 17 percent of voters.

Not surprisingly, partisans were more likely to cast ballots in the midterms than Americans without partisan leanings. But Republican partisans turned out at a higher rate than Democrats. The survey found that Republicans made up 21 percent of the nonvoter pool but 28 percent of those who said they voted. Democrats accounted for 31 percent of nonvoters and 34 percent of voters. Independents accounted for 42 percent of nonvoters but only 33 percent of voters. There was an even stronger skew ideologically in favor of conservatives. Liberals accounted for 26 percent of nonvoters compared with 25 percent of voters. Conservatives, on the other hand, made up 34 percent of nonvoters but 42 percent of voters. Moderates, like independents, were the most likely to stay home. Among nonvoters, 38 percent called themselves moderate; among voters, only 31 percent did.

The nonvoters in this election cycle issued a warning to both parties. In 2010 Democrats lost in a landslide because of a significant demobilization of key parts of their 2008 electorate. They were determined to avoid the same fate in 2014 and invested heavily in voter turnout efforts. These had an effect in some states, particularly with African American voters. But on the whole, as these figures and the exit polls suggest, many of the Democrats' core constituents again avoided voting in the midterms. The party will face a long-term problem if it has the capacity to win presidential elections but then faces sharp losses in the House, the Senate, and in state governments in the off years.

Republicans had one repetitive but effective theme in 2014: they cast the election as a referendum on the president and turned out his opponents. The Democrats lacked a unifying theme, and in its absence, all their organizing efforts proved insufficient. As a Republican operative told the *National Journal*'s Amy Walter, "You can't win on turnout if you are losing on message."

The Democrats were tongue-tied on the issue that mattered most: the economy. And the nonvoters, if anything, cared even more about economics than the voters did. The survey found that while 36 percent of voters listed the economy as the issue most important to their choice, 41 percent of nonvoters did—not surprising in light of their economic circumstances. Democrats were reluctant to tout Obama's significant economic achievements—the broad recovery from collapse, the drop in the unemployment rate to below 6 percent, high stock prices and low gas prices. They feared that doing so would make them seem out of touch with the many Americans whose wages are stagnating. But neither did they present a broad program for lifting incomes and living standards. Solving their economic dilemma is the Democrats' key task between now and 2016.

But Republicans have no reason to rest easy. The party failed to take any Senate seats in Democratic states; all but two of its gains came in states that had supported Romney in 2012. And the 2016 electorate will in no way resemble the conservative-tilting voter pool of 2014. The participation of the young will increase, as it did between 2010 and 2012. Latino voters will almost certainly be back in large numbers, motivated, perhaps, by the battle for immigration reform that Obama initiated. And the presidential electorate will be less affluent. Republicans, too, need a rendez-vous with voters disappointed by their economic circumstances.

For Republicans, there is no greater imperative than to respond to friendly crit-ics such as Olsen and begin to think seriously about policies aimed at lifting up the nonwealthy. This is a central challenge to the new policy entrepreneurs on the right who call themselves "reform conservatives." Yet the evidence so far is that while the party may adjust its rhetoric, it is still unprepared for the major policy renovations a new approach would require.

It thus falls to progressives both to defend the real achievements of the Obama years—among them the Affordable Care Act, various redistributive initiatives around the Earned Income and Child Tax Credits, and the restoration of economic growth through mildly but unmistakably Keynesian policies—and become far more creative and aggressive about the urgent need to restore middle- and working-class wage growth. Such an approach is central to re-mobilizing the progressive base and winning over working- class white voters who, for all the talk of a "rising American electorate," are still important to progressive victories.

This is a policy challenge that progressives are finally beginning to meet.[7] It is vital that they do so—not primarily for electoral reasons but because creating a good society requires widely shared economic growth and a renewed recognition that that self-improvement and social improvement are allies.

Acknowledgment

The authors would like to thank the Roosevelt Institute and the Clinton Institute for their fine work in organizing the conference that led to this book and also extend a special thank you to David Woolner for his exceptional work, help, and guidance on this essay.

Notes

1. Peter Beinart, "What Barack Obama Can Learn from FDR—and What the Democrats Need to Do," *Time*, November 24, 2008, 30–32.
2. *The Daily Show*, July 19, 2012. http://thedailyshow.cc.com/videos/ogqchb/e-j--dionne This is one of my favorite tidbits from American history, a tidbit I once made reference to on Jon Stewart's show, except that I made the mistake of referring to sick and injured seamen. You can only imagine what Jon Stewart did with that, so it's been sailors ever since!
3. *The Colbert Report*, April 28, 2011. http://thecolbertreport.cc.com/video-playlists/2wuars/colbert-report-07056/8ureil.
4. David B. Woolner, "For Men and Not for Property: Lessons for the President from Theodore and Franklin Roosevelt," January 5, 2015, Next New Deal, http://www.nextnewdeal.net/men-and-not-property-lessons-president-theodore-and-franklin-roosevelt.
5. http://www.gallup.com/poll/178790/americans-support-death-penalty-stable.aspx.
6. Henry Olsen, "Conservatism for the People," *National Affairs*, No. 18, Winter 2014, 95–106.
7. Two important and detailed contributions to a new progressive economics are Lawrence Summers, Ed Balls et al., *Report of the Commission on Inclusive Prosperity*, Center for American Progress (January 2015); and Joseph E. Stiglitz et al., *Rewriting the Rules of the American Economy*, the Roosevelt Institute (May 2015). The authors should note that E.J. Dionne was a member of the Inclusive Prosperity Commission. See: CAP: https://cdn.americanprogress.org/wp-content/uploads/2015/01/IPC-PDF-full.pdf; and Roosevelt: http://www.rewritetherules.org/report/

INDEX

Page numbers followed by *f* and *t* indicate figures and tables, respectively.

Ackerman, B., 106
ActBlue, 106
Adams, John, 235
Affordable Care Act
    cost efficiency mechanisms, 118
    executive branch enactment of, 210
    individual mandate, 58
    legislative history of, xix, 203–5
    as political legacy, 42, 66, 124, 242
    Republican opposition to, 53, 56, 61n47
Afghanistan, 156–57, 184, 189, 202
African Americans
    civil rights movement, 11–12, 21, 96
    human rights, 11–12
    incarceration rate, 131–32
    political party affiliations, 21
    poverty, 129
    unemployment rate, 130
    union premium, 133
    voter turnout 2014, 240
    voting rights, 96
African Court of Human and Peoples' Rights
    (ACHPR), 188
Agricultural Adjustment Act of 1933, 22
Ailes, Roger, 52
Alter, J., xxi
Alterman, E., xviii
American Dream Initiative, 68
American Finance for the 21st Century (Litan/
    Rauch), 82
"American Foreign Policy: a Progressive View," 23
American Liberty League, 55
American Medical Association, 33, 203
American Recovery and Reinvestment Act
    (ARRA), 23, 42, 70, 77, 201, 233, 237
Americans for Tax Reform, 50, 54
Apartheid, 11–12, 187

Armey, Dick, 47
Army Cultural Support Teams, 191
Atlantic Charter, 181–83
Axelrod, David, 205

Bailouts, 83–84, 201, 228
Bakiya, J., 71
Balogh, B., 7
Banking system regulation. *see also* Dodd-Frank
        Financial Reform Act
    antitrust laws, 219
    currency, gold standard, 8–10
    Democratic support of, 12
    federal deregulation of, 68–69
    Glass-Stegall Act of 1933, 69, 82, 92,
        92n2, 230n17
    Great Recession (*see* Great Recession)
    origins, 5
    shadow banks, 89, 92
    TARP, 42, 92n5, 200–201
Barro, B., 71
Barton, Joe, 174
Baucus, Max, 202
Bernstein, J., 53
Bethune, M. M., 21
Biden, Joe, 205
Bipartisan Policy Center, 100
Boehner, John, 51
Bollinger, Grutter v., 190
Borgwardt, E., 182
Bork, Robert, 50, 51
Bosnian war, 41, 45n56
Bowles, Erskine, 70
Brandeis, L., 85
Breyer, Stephen, 192
Bring Human Rights Home campaign, 192

Brinkley, A., xx
Brooks, R., xxi
Bryan, William Jennings, 3, 6, 8
Buchanan, Pat, 51
Buckley, William F., 48, 49
Buckley vs. Valeo, 103
Buffett, Warren, 211
Bunch, C., 185
Burger King, 134, 136
Bush, George H. W., 50, 51, 147, 169–70, 175, 187
Bush, George W.
    climate change policy, 171–72
    compassionate conservatism, 51
    domestic policy, 51–52, 66, 171
    federal deregulation under, 68–69
    foreign policy, 51, 148
    media, Internet strategy, 52
    moral imperative *vs.* military might, 26–27
    public perception of, 52, 238
    UN policy, 180
    women's rights, 189
Bush, Jeb, 57

Caldwell, C., xxi, 235
Calhoun, John, 74
Campaign finance, 99, 101–8
Cannon, Joe, 176–77
Cantril, H., 234
Cap-and-trade system, 202
Capital in the 21st Century (Piketty), 99, 137
Capitalism and Freedom (Friedman), 9–10, 73
Carter, Jimmy
    characteristics as leader, 39–40
    deregulation under, 69, 82
    health care reform, 204
    human rights, 186–87, 189
    policy achievements, 200
    Reagan debate, 73
Carville, J., 55
Center for American Progress, 141
Center for Constitutional Rights, 192
Center for Women's Global Leadership, 185
Chait, J., 57
Cheney, Dick, 171–72
Chesler, E., xxi
Child Tax Credit, 242
China, 170, 171, 174, 176
Chinese Exclusion Acts, 11
Christian Coalition, 50
Churchill, Winston, 181–82
Citizens United, 99, 101–4, 219, 236
Civil rights
    FDR, 21, 96, 202
    movement, 11–12, 21, 96
    Truman, 34–35, 96

Civil Rights Act of 1964, 38, 49, 131
Clay, Henry, 74, 235
Clean Air Act of 1990, 171, 172, 175
Climate change. *see also specific Presidents*
    coal emissions regulation, 175–76, 202–3
    conservation policy, 166–68
    epistemic closure, 54–55
    international conferences, 169–70, 173–74, 176
    Kyoto Protoco, 170–71
    opposition to perception of, 169–76, 219–20
    overview, xxi
    regulations, standards, 168–72
    resource crisis, 165–66
    scientific findings, 169, 174–75
    sovereignty issues, 167–68, 174, 176
    utility emissions regulation, 175–76, 202–3
    weather, violent, 172–73
Clinton, Bill
    characteristics as leader, 40–41, 45n56, 51
    climate change policy, 170, 171
    domestic policy, 66, 69–71, 100
    federal deregulation under, 68–69, 82
    human rights, 187
    legacy, xvii–xviii
    political environment, 200, 228
    as progressive, 236–37
    welfare reform, 203
Clinton, Hillary, xvii–xviii, 40–41, 181,
        185, 190–93
Club for Growth, 54
Coal emissions regulation, 175–76, 202–3
Colbert, Stephen, 236
Collective responsibility, 75–76, 216, 218,
        220–21, 230n21, 234–35
Commission on the Status of Women
        (CSW), 184
Commodity Futures Trading Commission
        (CFTC), 91
Communism, 35, 48
Community Action Programs (CAP), 38
The Conscience of a Conservative (Goldwater), 49
Conservatism. *see also* Republican Party;
        Tea Party
    anti-government ethos, 48–49, 77
    economic policy fallacies, 221–25
    freedom of contract policy, 8, 10–11, 235–36
    hard money doctrine, 8
    ideological basis of, 7–10, 13n11, 48–52,
        229n2, 234
    laissez-faire policy, 7–8, 234, 235
    legacy, xviii–xx
    media, Internet strategy, 52
    origins, 48
    resistance to Progressivism by, 7–8
    Southern Strategy, 49–50
    stereotypes, 212

Consumer Financial Protection Bureau (CFPB), 91
Convention on the Elimination of All Forms of Discrimination against Women (CEDAW), 185, 187–92
Corollary to the Monroe Doctrine, 141, 158n1
Corporate regulation, 5, 7, 8. *see also* Dodd-Frank Financial Reform Act
Corruption in America (Teachout), 102
Cox, O., 134
Cushing, Harvey, 203

Dahl, R., 99
Daschle, Tom, 42
Dawley, A., 11
Dean, Howard, 212
De Blasio, Bill, 239
Debs, Eugene V., 3
Declaration of Independence, 67
Declaration of the United Nations, 182
Declaration on the Elimination of Discrimination Against Women, 184
Delay, Tom, 170
DeMint, Jim, 54
Democratic Leadership Council (DLC), 40, 68
Democratic Party. *see also* Progressivism
  climate change policy, 170
  conservatives in, 48–49
  demographics, 12–13
  electoral support, 237–38
  human rights, 186
  ideological basis of, 10–11
  labor organization alliance, 20–21
  New Deal coalition, 20
  partisanship in, 97
  political environment, xix, 210
  political strategy, 53–54, 57–58
  reform wings of, 3–6
  voter turnout 2014, 240–42
Derivatives, 87–88, 91, 223
Dewey, John, 43
Dingell, John, 109
Dionne, E. J., xxi, 57
Direct democracy reforms, 4–5, 10–12
Dodd-Frank Financial Reform Act
  bailout, panic prevention, 83–84
  capital allocation efficiency, 86–87
  capital requirements, 89–90
  competition, prices, 87–88
  consumer, investor protection, 85–86
  derivatives, 87–88, 91, 223
  disclosure, 84–86
  goals of, xx, 83–87, 201–2
  history, 82–83, 92nn1–2
  lender of last resort, 89, 93n9
  limitations, 88–89

  liquidation, 90–91
  political basis, xix, 81–82, 211
  private-label securitization, 82, 92n1
  public utility approach, 88
  resolution authority, 90–91
  Securities Act, 91
  Securities Exchange Act, 91
  shadow banks, 89, 92
  shareholder revolution, 87, 92n8
  transparency, 84–85
Dole, Robert, 187
Dollar Diplomacy, 141
Douthat, Ross, 57
Drudge Report, 52

Earned Income Tax Credit, 66, 71–72, 242
Economic Bill of Rights, 34
Economic insecurity, xx–xxi, 111–15, 112*f*, 114*f*, 119–20. *see also* inequality
Economic Opportunity Act of 1964, 38
Education funding, 74, 76
Eighteenth Amendment, 5
Eisenhower, Dwight, 36, 48, 49, 76–77, 186
Emanuel, Rahm, 201, 205
EMILY's List, 106
Employment Act of 1946, 35
Enhanced interrogation, 26, 180–81
Enlightenment project, 215–16, 219
Environmental Protection Agency (EPA), 50, 171–76, 202–3
Epistemic closure, 54–55
Equal Futures Partnership, 191
European Court of Human Rights, 188

Fair Election Campaign Act of 1974, 103
Fair Labor Standards Act, 20
Farmers' Alliance, 4, 5, 7, 12, 13
FDIC, 90–91
FEC, McCutcheon vs., 99, 101–4, 219, 236
Federalist Society, 50
Federal Marine Hospital Service, 235
Federal Migratory Bird Bill of 1913, 167
Federal Pure Food Law, 85–86
Federal Reserve, 5, 89
Federal Reserve Act of 1913, 5
Federal Trade Commission Act of 1914, 5
Feingold, Russ, 236
Feldstein, M., 71
FEPC (Fair Employment Practices Committee), 34
Fields, Stephen, 4
Fifteenth Amendment, 75
Figueres, C., 176
Financial reform. *see* Dodd-Frank Financial Reform Act

Foner, E., 75
Food stamps, 38
Foreign policy. *see also specific Presidents*
    consumption, 144
    global complexity, interconnectedness,
        142–45, 158n1
    global threats, 144–45
    human rights, 151, 153–54
    international law, 143–44, 151, 153–54, 159n11
    progressive, xxi, 141–42, 150–55
    social safety net, 152–54
    uncertainty, unpredictability, 145–47, 151–53
    United States role, 147–49, 152–55
    wealth inequalities, 144, 148, 151
Four Freedoms, 24–25, 34, 179, 181–82
Four Freedoms Park, 179–80
401(k)s, 65, 113–14, 121–23, 126n10
Fourteenth Amendment, 75, 189
Fox News, 52
Free, L., 234
FreedomWorks, 47
Friedman, Milton, 9–10, 73
Frost, Karl, 33

G. I. Bill of Rights of 1944, 76
Galbraith, John Kenneth, 34, 36, 45n42
Gay rights, 192, 202, 211, 217–19, 233, 238–39
Geithner, Timothy, 70
Gelpern, A., 83
General Law on Women's Access to a Life Free
        from Violence, 188–89
Gerken, H., 107
Gilded Age, 8–10, 166, 234–36
Gingrich, Newt, 51, 170
Ginsburg, Ruth Bader, 192
Glass-Stegall Act of 1933, 69, 82, 92,
        92n2, 230n17
Global Climate Coalition (GCC), 169–71
Globalization, 6, 26, 142, 147–48, 237
Global warming. *see* climate change
Goldman Sachs, 211
Goldwater, Barry, 49–50
Gorbachev, Mikhail, 50
Gore, Al, 170
Government (federal)
    as agent of change, 72, 234–42
    campaign finance, 99, 101–8
    citizens' rights expansion, 75–76
    corruption in, 99, 101–4
    filibusters, 101
    as growth enhancer, 65–78, 79n29, 224–28,
        230n22, 231nn32–35
    growth-enhancing tasks of, 71
    income tax role, 7–8
    inequality influences, 99–104

institutional failure in, 98
    mortgage guarantees, 76
    New Deal role (*see* New Deal)
    participation limitation efforts, 98–99
    partisanship in, 97
    polarization in, 97–98, 101
    political dysfunction of, 96–100
    political equality, 103–4
    political opportunity, 104–8
    public education funding, 74, 76
    Reconstruction era legislation, 75
    redistricting, 101
    reform, structural solutions to, 100–101
    role of generally, xx, xxiin6
    subsidies, 83–84
    transportation network construction by, 74
    voting rights, 98–99
"Government by the People" legislation, 106
Graham-Leach Act of 1999, 69
Grangers, 4, 12
Great Depression, 23–24, 33, 76
Great Recession
    deregulation as cause of, 69, 82, 87
    economic stagnation since, 71, 99
    moral turpitude as cause of, 227–28
    overview, vii–viii, xx
    political legacy, 72, 77
    poverty during, 129–30
    unemployment during, 130
Great Risk Shift, 111–15, 112f, 114f
Greenbackers, 4, 5
Greenberg, S., 55
Grossman, M., 53
Group of 77, 169, 173–74
Grumet, J., 100
Grutter v. Bollinger, 190

Hacker, J., xx–xxi, 97, 100, 132, 136
Hamilton, Alexander, xviii–xix, 235
Hayek, Friedrich, 48
Head Start, 38
Health-care reform, 40–41. *see also* Affordable
        Care Act
Health spending, 115–18, 116f, 124–25
Hedge funds, 88
Helms, Jesse, 189
Heritage Foundation, 54, 58, 71
Hofstadter, Richard, 18, 20, 49
Homestead Act, 235
Hopkins, D., 53
Huckabee, Mike, 73
Human rights. *see also* women's rights
    African Americans (see African Americans)
    disability, 187
    enhanced interrogation, 26, 180–81

FDR, 181–83
  foreign policy, 151, 153–54
  gay rights, 192, 202, 211, 217–19, 233, 238–39
  international committees, declarations, 183–87
  overview, xxi, 179–81, 192–93
  United States role, 186–92
  women's rights as, 183–85
Human Rights Watch, 192
Humphrey, Hubert, 38, 45n42
Hurricane Katrina, 52, 69, 172–73
Hurricane Sandy, 168, 173
Income tax. *see* taxation
India, 170, 171, 176
Inequality. *see also* human rights; poverty;
    unionization; women's rights
  budget deficit, 70, 72–73
  communal responsibility, 75–76, 216, 218,
    220–21, 230n21, 234–35
  economic insecurity, xx–xxi, 111–15, 112f,
    114f, 119–20
  equal opportunity for all, 66
  federal deregulation, 68–69
  full lives, 66–67, 221
  government as growth enhancer, 65–78, 79n29,
    224–28, 230n22, 231nn32–35
  government influences on, 99–104
  government revenue *vs.* GDP growth,
    70–71, 77–78
  government's role, 66
  industrialization, 74, 75
  inflation, 1970s, 73
  life, liberty, pursuit of happiness, 67, 71, 220–21
  market failure economics, 66, 239
  market incentives, 69–72
  political, 219, 230n13
  political opportunity, 104–8
  poverty, 132–33, 137
  social justice, 220–21, 223–24, 230n22
  taxation in (*see* taxation)
  tax credits, 69
  wealth, 144, 148, 151

Inhofe, James, 174–76
Insurance (health), 115–18, 116f, 124
Inter-American Court, 188
Intergovernmental Panel on Climate Change
    (IPCC), 169, 174–75
Intermediate-Range Nuclear Forces Treaty, 50
International Convention on the Elimination of all
    Forms of Racial Discrimination (ICERD),
    186, 187, 190
International Covenant on Civil and Political
    Rights (ICCPR), 186, 187
International Covenant on Social, Economic, and
    Cultural Rights (ICESR), 186

International Criminal Court (ICC), 187
Iraq War, 42, 156–57, 202
ISIS, 202

Jackson, Lisa, 175
Jacobs, M., 34
Jefferson, Thomas, xviii–xix, 74
Jim Crow laws, 11, 12
Job Corps, 38
Job creation, 206
John Birch Society, 48, 49
Johnson, Hiram, 6
Johnson, Lyndon B.
  campaign strategy, 49–50
  characteristics as leader, 37–39, 45n42
  health care reform, 204, 235
  legacy, xviii–xix
  political environment, 96, 200
  war on poverty, 129

Karpf, D., 107
Kaye, D., 187, 188
Kazin, M., xviii
Kelley, Florence, 11
Kennedy, John F., 36–38, 96, 200, 202, 204
Kennedy, Robert, 221
Kenworthy, L., 66, 70–71
Kerry, John, 181, 190, 191
Keynesian economics, 22–23, 77
Kibbe, Matt, 47
Kim, Jim Yong, 181
Knights of Labor, 4, 5, 12
Koch brothers, 211
Konczal, M., xx, 211
Korean War, 35, 36
Kuwait, 189
Kyoto Protoco, 170–71

La Follette, Robert, 7, 49
Land grant colleges, 74
Landrieu, Mary, 211
Latin America, 186, 189
Latinos, 129–31, 133, 233, 238, 240, 242
The Law of Peoples (Rawls), 153
Leadership Conference on Civil and Human
    Rights, 187
Legal Services Corporation, 38
Lessig, L., 102
Levin, Yuval, 57
Lew, J., 92
Lewis, David, 109
Lewis, Fulton Jr., 33
Libya, 157

Lincoln, Abraham, 21, 74, 235
Lindert, P., 71
Lipitor, 117
Litan, R., 82
Lochner v. New York, 8, 235–36
Long, Huey, 18
Lovett, R. M., 23
Luxembourg Income Study, 65–66
Lytle, M., xxi

MacArthur, Douglas, 35
Macune, Charles, 7
Madison, James, xviii–xix, 235
Madrick, J., xx
Mahon, J., 71
al-Maliki, Nouri, 202
Mann, T., 51, 97, 98
Marine Corps' Female Engagement Teams, 191
Mason, J. W., 87
Mattson, K., xviii, xx
McCain, John, 52
McCarthy, Joseph, 33, 35
McCarthyism, 36, 96
McConnell, Mitch, 54
McCutcheon vs. FEC, 99, 101–4, 219, 236
McDonalds, 134, 136
McMillan, Jimmy, 115
McNeill, J., 165
Medicare/Medicaid, 6n47, 38, 53, 117–18, 152
Mettler, S., 125
Migratory Bird Treaty of 1916, 167
Mill, J. S., 66
Millennials, 238–39, 241
Millennium Challenge Corporation, 190
Millennium Development Goals, 180
Milosevic, Slobodan, 41
Moley, Raymond, 20
Monroe Doctrine, 141, 158n1
Moral Equivalent of War (MEOW), 40
Morrill Act of 1857, 74, 235
Morris, Dick, 41
Moyers, Bill, 38
Murdoch, Rupert, 52
Mykleby, M., 154

Nasonex, 117
National Action Plan on Women, Peace, and
    Security, 190–91
National Association of Manufacturers (NAM), 33
National Commission on Fiscal Responsibility
    and Reform, 70
National Economic and Social Initiative
    (NESRI), 192
National Energy Policy (NEP), 40

National Industrial Recovery Act of 1933, 22
National Labor Relations Act of 1935, 20–22,
    135, 136
National Review, 48, 57
NationBuilder, 106–7
Netherlands, 189
New Deal. *see also* poverty; social contract
    civil rights movement, 21
    economic policy, 22–24
    ideological basis, 19–20, 33
    legacy, 20–21, 27–28, 28n8, 32, 95–96
    overview, 17–18
    public works construction, 21
    social safety nets, 21–22, 109–10
    welfare state creation, 21–22
New Source Review (NSR) permitting
    program, 171–72
New York, Lochner v., 8, 235–36
New York Times, 52
Nineteenth Amendment, 5, 76, 79n29
Nixon, Richard
    background, 34
    campaign strategy, 33, 36, 49
    domestic policies, 50
    federal deregulation under, 69
    legacy, xix
    Watergate scandal, 39, 237
Noah, T., 132
No Ceilings: The Full Participation Project, 193
Norquist, Grover, 50, 54
Norway, 71

Obama, Barack
    background, 199–200
    characteristics as leader, 41–42
    climate change, 173–76, 202–3
    domestic policy, 23, 42, 70–72, 77, 200–205
    foreign policy, 42, 148, 156–58, 202
    health care reform, 42, 235
    human rights policy, 180–81, 188
    job creation, 205–6
    opposition to, 54, 98
    policy achievements, 200–205, 233
    political environment, 200, 233, 236–37
    political strategy, 10, 41–42, 56, 239
    as progressive, xvii–xviii, xxi, 199–206,
        211, 236
    public perception of, 55, 200
    racism, 206
    stealth multilateralism, 188
    stimulus package, 23, 42, 70, 77, 201, 233
    women's rights, 190, 191
Obamacare. *see* Affordable Care Act
Occupy Wall Street, 137, 239
O'Connor, Sandra Day, 50

Office of Price Administration (OPA), 34–35
Olsen, H., 239–40
On Liberty (Mill), 66
Opportunity
    economic, 111, 120
    equal for all, 66
    political, 104–8
    in Progressive agenda, 224
Ornstein, N., 51, 97, 98
Overton, S., 106

Packer, G., 125
PACs, small donor, 106
Pager, D., 132
Pakistan, 157
Panetta, Leon, 202
Pareto efficiency, 222
Paulson, Hank, 211
Pegler, Westbrook, 33
Pelagic hunting, 167–68
Pelosi, Nancy, 205
Penn, Mark, 41
Perkins, Frances, 109
Perlstein, R., 55
Philippines, 189
Pierson, P., 97, 100, 132
Piketty, T., 99, 137
Pinchot, Gifford, 166, 176
Podesta, John, 180
Ponnuru, R., 57
Populist Party, 4–6, 11
Porter, W., 154
Postel, C., xx
Poverty. *see also* inequality; New Deal;
    unionization
    causes of, 56
    concentrated, 129–30
    Earned Income Tax Credit, 66,
        71–72, 242
    elderly, 129
    employment trends, 130–32
    incarceration rate, 131–32, 148
    inequality, 132–33, 137
    involuntary part-time work, 131
    low-wage workers, 130–31, 136–37
    mobility, 132, 134, 135*f*
    occupational segregation, 131–32
    policy drift, 132, 133
    predistribution *vs.* redistribution, 136
    trends, 72, 129–30, 134–37, 135*f*
    union declines, 132–34
    union premium, 133
    wage theft, 131
The Price of Inequality (Stiglitz), 219,
    223, 230n19

Private-label securitization, 82, 92n1
Progressive agenda
    accountability, 219
    beliefs, changing, 216, 219–20
    collective responsibility, 75–76, 216, 218,
        220–21, 230n21, 234–35
    democracy, 218–19
    economic, 221–25, 231nn32–35, 232n43
    Enlightenment project, 215–16, 219
    goals of, 236
    government as growth enhancer, 65–78, 79n29,
        224–28, 230n22, 231nn32–35
    institutions, 218
    market fundamentalism, 221–23,
        231nn32–35
    monetary policy, 225
    opportunity, 224
    privatization, 227
    rational enquiry, 216, 219–20
    rules, regulations, 217–19, 220, 223, 230n22
    social justice, 220–21, 223–24, 230n22
    voting rights, 218–19
Progressivism. *see also* Democratic Party
    challenges to, xix–xxi, 9–13, 43,
        212–13, 237–42
    class structure, 211
    concepts of, 45n45, 65–67, 209, xxiin5
    elitism within, 6
    executive power dependency, 210
    ideological basis of, 6–10, 13n11, 215–21,
        229n2, 229n7, 234–35
    legacy, xviii–xix, 4–5
    origins, 3–6
    political environment, xix–xx
    regulatory nature of, 210–11, 220
    resurgence of, 209
    socialism, 4–6, 11, 211
    stereotypes, 212
Prohibition, 5
Proposition 30, 10
Pryor, David, 211
Public education funding, 74, 76

Rand, Ayn, 48
Rauch, J., 82
Rawls, J., 152, 153
Reagan, Ronald
    campaign strategy, 49, 50, 73, 237
    characteristics as leader, 50–51
    domestic policy, 57, 66, 96
    federal deregulation under, 82
    human rights, 187
    legacy, xviii–xix
RedState, 52
Rehnquist, William, 50

Republican Party. *see also* Conservatism
   challenges to, 57–58
   climate change opposition, 169–76
   Evangelical Christians influence, 50
   human rights, 186–88
   ideological basis of, 10–11
   moderates, liberals in, 48–49, 51
   opposition to Truman by, 32–33
   partisanship in, 97
   polarization in, 97–98, 101
   political environment, xix–xx, 54–55
   political strategy, 6n47, 51–57, 201
   reform wings of, 3–6, 9, 57
   Social Security, Medicare privatization,
     6n47, 53
   voter turnout 2014, 240–42
Republican Revolution, 51
Retirement benefits, 113–14, 120–23, 126n10
Richardson, H. C., xxiin6
Roberts, John, 103
Robertson, Pat, 50
Rodgers, D., 6–7
Rome Statute, 187
Romney, Mitt, 56, 238, 239
*Room to Grow: Conservative Reforms for a Limited
   Government and a Thriving Middle Class*, 57
Roosevelt, Eleanor, 21, 183, 184, 186
Roosevelt, Franklin D.
   characteristics as leader, 18–20, 32
   civil rights, 21, 96, 202
   Economic Bill of Rights speech, 27
   economic policy, 22–24
   foreign policy, 23–27
   Four Freedoms, 24–25, 34, 179, 181–82
   health issues, 18
   human rights, 181–83
   legacy, xviii–xx, 17, 20–21, 27–28, 28n8,
     32, 179
   moral imperative *vs.* military might, 26–27
   motivations, 19, 24, 31–32, 35
   New Deal (*see* New Deal)
   political environment, 200
   universal health insurance, 203
Roosevelt, Theodore
   African American rights, 11–12
   Bull Moose campaign, 3, 5, 203
   conservation policy, 166–67, 176–77
   election 1912, 3, 6, 9
   foreign policy, 141, 158n1
   influences on, xx
   legacy, xviii–xix, 49, 236
   motivations, 5, 7–9, 11
   "New Nationalism" speech, 10
   universal health insurance, 203
Rove, Karl, 51–52, 171
Rubio, Marco, 57

Run for America, 107
Russian Federation, 151, 158, 167
Ryan, Alan, 67
Ryan, Paul, 6n47, 53, 110

Sanders, E., 4
Sanford, Mark, 51
Santa Clara v. Southern Pacific Railroad, 9, 236
Santelli, Rick, 47
Santorum, Rick, 51
Sarbanes, J., 106
Scalia, Antonin, 50
Schlafly, Phyllis, 48
Schlesinger, A. Jr., 36, 38, 45n42, 45n45, 200
Schlesinger, James, 40
Schmitt, M., xx
SCOTUS. *see* U. S. Supreme Court rulings
Seal hunting, 167–68
Securities Act, 91
Securities Exchange Act, 91
Segal, S. H., 175
Seifert, E., 55
Seventeenth Amendment, 4–5, 76, 79n29
Shah, Rajiv, 181
Shareholder revolution, 87, 92n8
Simon, H., 227
Simpson, Alan, 70
Sinclair, Upton, 11
Singer, Paul, 211
Sixteenth Amendment, 4, 12
Slemrod, J., 71
Smith, Adam, 222, 224
Social contract. *see also* New Deal
   discourse, 109–11, 109f
   economic insecurity, xx–xxi, 111–15, 112f,
     114f, 119–20
   economic opportunity, 111, 120
   401(k)s, 65, 113–14, 121–23, 126n10
   government-managed retirement
     accounts, 122–23
   health spending, 115–18, 116f, 124–25
   insurance (health), 115–18, 116f, 124
   insurance, portable, 120
   reform goals, 118–20
   reform mechanisms, 123–25
   retirement benefits, 113–14, 120–23, 126n10
   risk shifting, 112–13
   Social Security, 121–22, 152
Social Darwinism, 13n11, 75–76
Socialism, 4–6, 11, 211
Social justice, 220–21, 223–24, 230n22
Social safety nets, 21–22, 109–10
Social Security, 121–22, 152
Social Security Act of 1935, 21–22, 109, 203
Somalia, 157

Sorensen, Ted, 36
Southern Pacific Railroad, Santa Clara v., 9, 236
Southern Strategy, 49–50
Soviet Union, 21, 26, 35, 40, 50, 146, 184,
    186, 187
State Children's Health Insurance Program, 100
Stevenson, Adlai, 36
Stiglitz, J., xxi, 219, 229n1
Stimson, Henry, 18
Summers, Larry, 70
Sumner, William Graham, 7, 8
Sunstein, C., 54, 71, 182
Survey of Economic Risk Perceptions and
    Insecurity (SERPI), 112f
Sweden, 71
Syria, 42, 157–58, 202

Taft, Robert A., 33
Taft, William H., 141
Taft-Hartley Act, 35
Tajikistan, 189
Tarbell, Ida, 7
Taxation
    Conservative resistance to, 7, 53, 55–57, 174
    economic expansion via, 65, 67–68, 71,
        72, 77–78
    economic insecurity, xx–xxi, 111–15, 112f,
        114f, 119–20
    government as growth enhancer, 65–78, 79n29,
        224–28, 230n22, 231nn32–35
    in inequality, 67–68, 70–72, 76–78, 229n8
    Jim Crow laws, 11, 12
    origins, 4, 7–8
    Proposition 30, 10
    public education funding, 74, 76
    race, caste enforcement via, 12
    Reagan, 96
    social justice, 220–21
    Social Security, 122
    tax credits, 69
Taylor, B., 144
Teachout, Z., 102
Tea Party. *see also* Conservatism; Republican Party
    climate change policy, 169–71
    ideological basis of, 9–10, 47–48, 55–56, 60n28
    legacy, xx
    political strategy, 55–56
Television, 107
Tenth Amendment, 48
Tesler, T., 55
A Theory of Justice (Rawls), 152
Thompson, Fred, 68
Thompson, J. M., xx
Tilford, D., 144
Tonkin Gulf Resolution, 39

Troubled Asset Relief Program (TARP), 42, 92n5,
    200–201
Truman, Harry S.
    characteristics as leader, 32, 35
    civil rights, 34–35, 96
    Economic Bill of Rights, 34
    foreign policy, 35
    opposition to, 32–35
    policy agenda, 33–34
    successor, 36
    universal health insurance, 203
Truman Doctrine, 35
Tugwell, R., 32
Turner, F. J., 166

U. S. Supreme Court rulings
    campaign finance, 99, 101–4
    citizen's rights, 75, 96
    conservatives nominated to, 50
    corporate personhood, 9
    equality, 189–90
    freedom of contract, 235–36
    income tax, 4
    sovereignty issues, 167–68
    voting rights, 98
UN Convention against Torture, 187
UN Human Rights Commission, 180, 186
Unionization. *see also* inequality; poverty
    employer retaliation, 136
    fusion agreements, 12
    impacts, 136–37
    iron-clad contracts, 8
    National Labor Relations Act, 20–22, 135, 136
    opposition to, 8, 12
    political system influences of, 99–100
    union declines, 132–34
    union premium, 133
United Nations, UN Charter
    CEDAW committee, 188
    climate change, 169, 174
    Committee III, 183
    Fourth World Conference on Women, 185
    human rights, 180, 182–83
    US foreign policy, 143–44, 151, 157, 159n11
    women's rights, 183–85, 188
United Nations Conference on the Human
    Environment, 169
"United Nations Framework Convention on
    Climate Change," 170
United States
    air power impacts, 25, 45n56
    budget deficits causes, 68
    as center-right country, xvii–xviii, xxi, 233–35
    consumption in, 144
    crime rate drop in, 239

United States (*Cont.*)
  diversity, demographics in, 238
  drone strikes, 157
  economic insecurity, xx–xxi, 111–15, 112*f*,
      114*f*, 119–20
  employment trends, 130–32
  foreign policy role, 147–49, 152–55
  Great Depression, 23–24, 33, 76
  Great Power cooperation, 25–26
  Great Recession (*see* Great Recession)
  human rights role, 186–92
  isolationism *vs.* engagement, 24–26, 35
  moral imperative *vs.* military might, 26–27
  pelagic hunting, 167–68
  pre-K education in, 72
  segregation in, 11–12, 187
  voter turnout 2014, 240–42
  women's rights, 188–92
United States Election Project, 240
Universal Declaration of Human Rights, 183, 184,
      218, 220
UN Security Council Resolution 1325, 190–91
Utility emissions regulation, 175–76, 202–3

Valeo, Buckley vs., 103
Vermeule, A., 54
Verveer, Melanne, 192
Vienna Conference on Human Rights, 185
Vietnam War, 35, 39, 45n42, 237
Volcker Rule initiative, 88
Volunteers in Service to America (VISTA), 38
Voter turnout 2014, 240–42
Voting rights
  African Americans, 96
  government role in, 98–99
  Progressive agenda, 218–19
  U. S. Supreme Court rulings, 98

  voter-ID requirements, 99
  women, 5
Voting Rights Act of 1965, 38

Wagner, Robert, 203
Wallace, George, 49
Wall Street Journal, 33, 52
Walmart, 134, 136
Warren, D., xxi
Warren, Elizabeth, 202, 240
Watergate scandal, 39, 237
Welch, Robert, 49
Welfare reform, 41
West, Cornel, 199
Whitman, Christine T., 171–72
Wilson, Woodrow
  foreign policy, 141
  influences on, xx, 6
  legacy, xviii–xix
  political shift, 3
  segregation policies, 12
Winthrop, John, 148–49
Women's rights. *see also* human rights
  international committees,
      declarations, 183–87
  as moral imperative, 181
  overview, xxi
  reproductive, 50
  United States role, 188–92
  voting, 5
Woolner, D., xx
World Bank, 191–92
World War II, 24–26
Wright, Zephyr, 38

Yemen, 157